Congregational chapel (URC), Longham, Dorset.   (38)

ROYAL COMMISSION ON THE HISTORICAL MONUMENTS
OF ENGLAND

An Inventory of

Nonconformist
CHAPELS
and
MEETING-HOUSES
in South-West England

Christopher Stell

London·HMSO

©Crown copyright 1991
First published 1991

ISBN 0 11 300036 7

British Library Cataloguing in Publication Data
A CIP catalogue record for this book is
available from the British Library

Printed in the United Kingdom for HMSO Dd 292012 C8 10/91

TABLE OF CONTENTS

LIST OF ILLUSTRATIONS

(illustrations are exterior photographs unless otherwise stated)

CHAIRMAN'S FOREWORD

Lord Ferrers, my predecessor as Chairman of the Royal Commission, outlined the history of the RCHME's involvement with the recording of nonconformist buildings in his foreword to Mr C. F. Stell's volume on Central England. When this was published, in 1986, further volumes were not envisaged. However, the success of this earlier publication, and the very positive comments of its reviewers, have encouraged Commissioners to proceed with this second volume on the chapels and meeting-houses of south and south-west England.

Commissioners are again indebted to Mr Stell for his endeavours in recording the great wealth of surviving buildings in an area notable for the strength of early nonconformity. To him also must be credited not only the text of this volume but also the measured drawings and sketches which illustrate it.

Mr Stell retired from full-time service with the Royal Commission in 1989, but he has continued on a consultancy basis with the completion of this volume. The Commissioners are indebted to him for the work which he has done with care and scholarship over many years. It is thanks largely to Mr Stell that there is now a much wider and more informed awareness of the architectural and historical importance of nonconformist buildings. Commissioners hope that the publication of this second volume will stimulate interest still further, and will better inform all those concerned with the future of a class of building which continues to be subject to threat, by both demolition and ill-advised alteration.

The detailed archive upon which this published account is based will be available for public consultation at the National Monuments Record, RCHME, 23 Savile Row, London W1X 2JQ.

PARK OF MONMOUTH

COMMISSIONERS

The Rt Hon. The Baroness Park of Monmouth, C.M.G., O.B.E.
Maurice Warwick Beresford, Esq.
Martin Biddle, Esq.
Richard Bradley, Esq.
Robert Angus Buchanan, Esq.
Mrs Bridget Katherine Cherry
John Kerry Downes, Esq.
John Davies Evans, Esq.
Richard David Harvey Gem, Esq.
Derek John Keene, Esq.
Peter Erik Lasko, Esq., C.B.E.
Trevor Reginald Mortensen Longman, Esq.
Geoffrey Haward Martin, Esq., C.B.E.
Gwyn Idris Meirion-Jones, Esq.
Antony Charles Thomas, Esq., C.B.E., D.L.
Malcolm Todd, Esq.

Secretary
Tom Grafton Hassall, Esq.

PRINCIPAL MONUMENTS

List of monuments described in this Inventory that are recommended by the Commissioners as being 'most worthy of preservation'. (For the complete list for England see the Forty-second Interim Report of this Commission, Command No. 9442, 1985.)

Monument numbers, in brackets, are followed by page references.

Berkshire

Abingdon. Baptist chapel, Ock Street. (1) 1.

Aston Tirrold. Presbyterian chapel. (5) 3.

Newbury. Wesleyan chapel, Northbrook Street. (43) 10.

Reading. St Mary's Chapel. (49) 14.

Wallingford. Friends' meeting-house, Castle Street. (66) 17.

Woodley and Sandford. Former Congregational chapel, Loddonbridge Road. (74) 20.

Cornwall

Camborne-Redruth. Gwennap Pit. (16) 23.

Gwinear-Gwithian. Wesleyan chapel, Gwithian. (69) 30.

Kea. Friends' meeting-house, 'Come-to-Good'. (76) 32.

Penzance. Wesleyan chapel, Chapel Street. (117) 38.

Penzance. Wesleyan chapel, Newlyn. (120) 40.

Penzance. Bible Christian chapel, Tredavoe. (123) 41.

St Gluvias. Wesleyan chapel, Ponsanooth. (165) 47.

St Ives. Former Wesleyan chapel, Lelant. (177) 48.

St Just. Wesleyan chapel, Chapel Road. (180) 48.

Truro. Wesleyan chapel, Union Place. (213) 54.

Devonshire

Bideford. Great Meeting-house, Bridgeland Street. (10) 61.

Chulmleigh. Independent chapel, East Street. (46) 65.

Culmstock. Friends' meeting-house, Spiceland. (64) 72.

Dalwood. Baptist meeting-house, Loughwood. (65) 76.

East Budleigh. 'Salem Chapel'. (72) 78.

Exeter. George's Meeting-house. (75) 79.

Exmouth. Congregational chapel and almshouses, Point-in-View. (84) 83.

Ottery St Mary. Jesu Street Chapel. (141) 91.

Pancrasweek. Wesleyan chapel, Lana. (144) 93.

Dorset

Bridport. Old Meeting-house, East Street. (11) 107.

Hampreston. Congregational chapel, Longham. (38) 117.

Lyme Regis. Coombe Street Chapel. (46) 118.

Poole. Congregational chapel, Skinner Street. (69) 124.

Hampshire

Havant. Former Presbyterian meeting-house, The Pallant. (28) 140.

Lymington. Congregational chapel, High Street. (39) 142.

Mortimer West End. The Countess of Huntingdon's Chapel. (42) 143.

Ringwood. Old Meeting-house, Meeting-house Lane. (50) 146.

Tadley. Old Meeting-house. (62) 151.

Winchester. Congregational chapel, Jewry Street. (70) 152.

Somerset

Bath. The Countess of Huntingdon's Chapel, The Vineyards. (13) 162.

Bath. Walcot Chapel. (17) 164.

Bridgwater. Christ Church Chapel, Dampiet Street. (30) 167.

Frome. Rook Lane Chapel. (74) 175.

Ilminster. Old Meeting-house, East Street. (87) 179.

Kingsbury Episcopi. Middle Lambrook Meeting-house. (92) 181.

Long Sutton. Friends' meeting-house. (99) 183.

Shepton Mallet. Cowl Street Chapel. (136) 188.

Shepton Mallet. Wesleyan chapel, Paul Street. (138) 191.

Street. Friends' meeting-house. (152) 193.

ACKNOWLEDGEMENTS

During the compilation and writing of this volume, the author has incurred many debts to friends, colleagues and acquaintances.

Especial thanks are due to Mr David Butler for his generous and unstinted advice on Friends' meeting-houses and for kindly reading the relevant entries. Of those who have expended much time and energy to ensure a high degree of accuracy in the Inventory, particular acknowledgement is made to Mr Roger Thorne whose painstaking reappraisal of the entries for Devonshire in particular has been invaluable. Grateful thanks are also due to the Rev. Thomas Shaw and Mr John Probert for their assistance with the investigation and in correcting the text for Cornwall; to Mr H. Godwin Arnold for advice on portions of the Berkshire text and other matters; to the Rev. Malcolm Adams for his hospitality while recording the chapels on the Isles of Scilly; to the former Royal Commissioner, Dr Ralegh Radford, for his early encouragement and hospitality, and to the former Secretary and Royal Commissioner, Mr Richard Dufty, for his continued support.

The help and encouragement already recorded in the previous volume from members of the various nonconformist historical societies is again gratefully acknowledged; to these must now be added the members of the Chapels Society, formed in 1988 to further the study and preservation of this class of building.

To all ministers, church officers and others who, when called upon often without warning to permit an inspection of their premises, responded with almost uniform kindness, further thanks must be extended; without such co-operation the task would have been impossible. The staff of Dr Williams's Library, whose courteous assistance has placed many writers in their debt, have again provided an invaluable service.

Of the staff of the Royal Commission, particular thanks are again due to Dr Bridgett Jones for her researches in the files of numerous record offices and to the staff of the photographic section for their assistance throughout the work.

C.F.S.

EDITORIAL NOTES

Denominational names used are generally those in use when the buildings were erected. Methodist chapels appear under the name of the original society where this could be ascertained. Presbyterian and Congregational chapels now used by the United Reformed Church (URC) are so indicated in the text. No general attempt is made to distinguish the present grouping of continuing Congregational or Baptist congregations not involving a change in their principal designation; most of the latter, where not otherwise stated, will be found to be of Particular Baptist origin. Unitarian and Free Christian congregations appear under their proper historical appellations.

The name 'meeting-house' or 'chapel' although not generally given should be assumed to be included as appropriate in the heading of each entry. The designation 'church', as increasingly applied indiscriminately to ecclesiastical structures, is avoided as incorrect and tending to ambiguity in the present context. 'Former' indicates that the building is now used by another stated denomination or for other purposes. Closure or demolition is noted where this could reliably be determined but in view of the time which has continued to elapse since many of the records were made, further changes will inevitably be found to have taken place.

The measured drawings are reproduced to uniform scales of 12 and 24 feet to the inch (1:144 and 1:288). Sequence hatching has been adopted throughout: the original or principal work is indicated in solid black, secondary work by cross-hatching and later minor additions by single-line hatching; where necessary this is more fully explained in the accompanying text. Dimensions are quoted in the text for monuments built prior to 1800; these are internal unless otherwise stated, the length of the principal axis of the original pulpit or rostrum being given first.

Historical information concerning the origins and development of individual congregations necessarily derives in the main from published sources. The accuracy of these varies considerably and although they have been used with caution some errors may remain. Corrections or comments on any statement in this Inventory will be gratefully acknowledged.

Boundary Changes. The arrangement of the Inventory follows that of the previous volume, being by historical county and civil parish, the names and boundaries being taken as those obtaining immediately prior to local government reorganization in 1974. The changes affecting the volume area are indicated on the map (p. xviii); these comprise the transfer of Bath and much of north Somerset to form part of a new administrative county of Avon, and of the Vale of the White Horse with much of north-west Berkshire which were added to Oxfordshire; from Hampshire several parishes around Bournemouth have been transferred to Dorset and the Isle of Wight has been constituted a separate county. The entries for the Isle of Wight and the Isles of Scilly will be found at the end of the Inventories for Hampshire and Cornwall respectively. County changes within the area of the present Inventory are indicated in italics beside individual parish names.

Conversion Table

1 inch = 25.4 mm

1 foot (12 inches) = 304.8 mm

1 yard (3 feet) = 914.4 mm

1 mile (1760 yards) = 1.6 km

PREFACE

In this, the second volume of the Inventory of Nonconformist Chapels and Meeting-houses in England, covering seven counties in the south and south west of the country, the limitations of date and denomination which applied to the first necessarily continue, the major part of the fieldwork for the whole of the country having been undertaken as a single exercise. These limitations, which are detailed in the Preface to the previous volume, are briefly that the buildings of all denominations commonly regarded as comprising Protestant nonconformity are included; particular attention has been paid to buildings erected before 1800 but many of later date will also be found and no major chapel or meeting-house dating from before 1850 has been knowingly omitted. Selected later buildings of up to 1914 have been noted and the need for further research in that quarter is acknowledged, but in the counties of the south west the strength of early nonconformity and the wealth of buildings already available considerably reduced the need for much later rebuilding as compared with the industrial areas of the north. That is not to decry some of the later achievements in chapel building which include an early example of reinforced concrete construction at Sidwell Street, Exeter, Devon (81), an elaborately Gothic village chapel at Churchill, Somerset (53), by Foster and Wood, paid for by a private benefactor, Tarring's audacious Congregational spire in Salisbury, Wilts (111), and the twin-spired Great Meeting-house in Bideford, Devon (10), beside the more numerous but pedestrian essays in the Gothic revival by W. J. Stent of Warminster, the ubiquitous and generally recognizable designs of W. F. Poulton of Reading, or the less numerous but equally notable chapels by another architect from the south west, R. C. Bennett of Weymouth.

It is hoped that the publication of this volume will stimulate public interest and research in this still neglected class of building. The inexorable progress of time since much of this survey was completed has seen a continued depletion in support for many of the places described, with neglect, despair, closure and conversion or demolition seen, not infrequently, as a fore-ordained sequence from which it is impossible to escape. The loss by structural failure of the very disparate cob chapels at Crediton, Devon (56), and Cripplestyle, Dorset (3), may have been in part unavoidable; the demolition of Manvers Street Chapel, Trowbridge, Wilts (148), was inexcusable, while the conversion of Halfway House Chapel, Nether Compton, Dorset (61), to a private house, a form of 'preservation' often regarded as acceptable, illustrates the potentially destructive nature of this remedy in which little of consequence beyond the structure of the front wall has remained. The unfortunate effect of attempts to 'modernize' a simple chapel which is still in use is seen at Winterborne Dauntsey, Wilts (161), while the changes wrought upon Coombe Street Chapel, Lyme Regis, Dorset (46), by a moribund church and its eventual conversion to a private museum are unsurpassed in the sorry history of the maintenance of our most important nonconformist monuments. The equally regrettable closure of George's Meeting-house, Exeter, Devon (75), in circumstances which do little credit to anyone concerned, the retreat of Unitarian congregations from Ringwood, Hants (50), and Ilminster, Somerset (87), the years of dereliction and uncertainty bestowed upon Rook Lane Chapel, Frome, Somerset (74), by the departure of its congregation and the even longer period of neglect suffered by the Countess of Huntingdon's Chapel at Mortimer West End, Hants (42), are matters on which it is impossible to remain silent.

The distressing attrition in the number of relatively unspoilt chapels and meeting-houses by past denominational indifference, by ill-advised alteration, by unsympathetic conversion, from which charge not even the heritage industry is exempt, is unevenly balanced by such a successful restoration as that of Loughwood Chapel, Devon (65), by the National Trust, or the retention in use of the chapel at Grittleton, Wilts (70), by private purchase, a mode of transfer currently forced upon potential benefactors by the inflexible nature of charitable trusts. More hopeful for the future is the increasing number of chapels receiving grants for repairs from English Heritage, several of which appear in this volume area; but until there is a much wider awareness of the interest, the historical and architectural importance and the visual quality of many of these buildings, further grievous and quite avoidable losses are likely to ensue.

CHRISTOPHER STELL

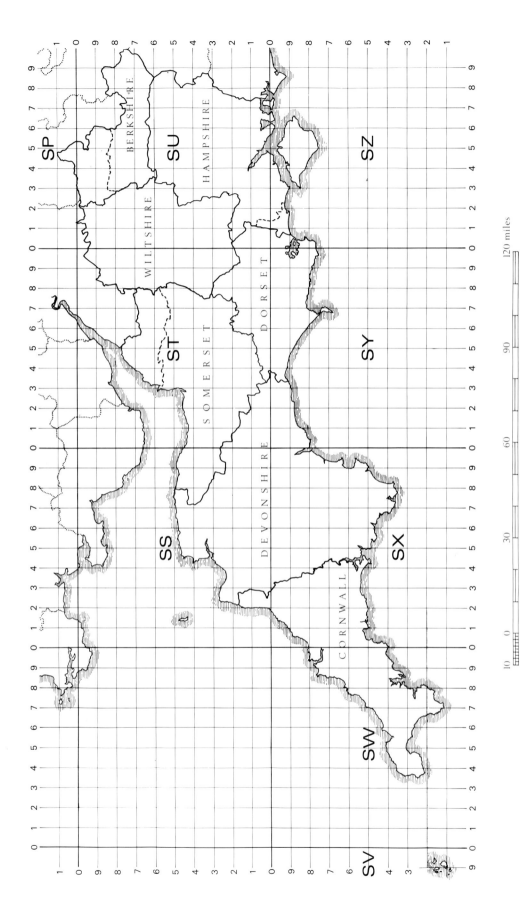

COUNTY BOUNDARIES. The boundaries of county areas within the present volume are indicated by continuous lines. Alterations resulting from the formation of the county of Avon and the enlargement of Oxfordshire and Dorset are shown by broken lines. County boundaries outside the volume area are in dotted lines.
© Crown Copyright.

AN INVENTORY OF

NONCONFORMIST CHAPELS AND MEETING-HOUSES

IN SOUTH-WEST ENGLAND

BERKSHIRE

Some of the earliest traces of organized dissent in the county are to be found amongst the congregations of Baptists which gathered into regular churches in the mid 17th century. Of these, the Longworth church was particularly notable; although in the early 18th century this removed to a new meeting-house at Cote, north of the Thames (*see* Oxfordshire (6)), its influence continued to be felt in the former locality and the meeting established in Buckland in the late 18th century (11) may have been a revival of the earlier interest. At Abingdon (1) the Baptist church is of equally ancient origin, lending its name to one of the first associations of churches of this denomination. Several Quaker meetings were also established by the late 17th century, but none was of any size. Congregations of Presbyterians and Independents appeared in all the major towns in the years following 1662 and in 1672 dissenters in Newbury even succeeded in licensing the Town Hall as a place of worship.

The remaining portion of the Presbyterian meeting-house at Abingdon (3), of 1700, is one of the few tangible reminders of a substantial early nonconformist congregation to survive in Berkshire. Waterside Chapel at Newbury (41) of 1697 was, at least until the removal of its fittings, a monument of exceptional architectural importance, as is the chapel of 1728 at Aston Tirrold (5), one of the few early buildings to pass into the hands of the Presbyterian Church of England. The Friends' meeting-houses at Great Faringdon (26) of 1672, Wallingford (66) of 1724 and Uffington (63) of 1730, are all tiny single-cell buildings, a characteristic again found at Maidenhead (39) in the early 19th century; the more sophisticated Reading meeting-house (52) of 1835 was divided by shutters which rose into the roof space. Several fragments of late 18th-century chapels remain, the only substantially complete example being St Mary's Chapel, Reading (49). Although

refronted, St Mary's is exceptional in originating in a direct secession from the established church to which it was eventually transferred.

Several 19th-century chapels are noteworthy; the miniature Gothic chapels with dwarf steeples built during Rev. James Sherman's ministry at Reading – Caversham Hill (51), Wargrave (68), and Woodley (74) – together with Binfield Heath (*see* Oxfordshire (46)), form a distinct group. The typically plain, pedimented brick Georgian chapel was seen at its best in Windsor (72), while the fully developed temple front at Abingdon (1), of 1841, is a striking example of Baptist preference for the classical style, a predilection also exercised at Wokingham (73) in 1860 by the prolific Reading architects, Poulton and Woodman. The use of the Gothic style in the Baptist chapel at Bourton (7) of 1851 may be traced to the influence of a local patron. Methodist architecture, although not plentiful, includes an important Gothic chapel of 1837–8 for Wesleyans in Newbury (43), which has one of the last surviving examples in England of a communion recess behind the central pulpit. The use of the Gothic style by Calvinistic Methodists is seen at Maidenhead (38) in 1841, while it appears in a fully developed and grandiose form in the Wesleyan chapel at Abingdon (4) in 1873–5.

The principal building material in the county is brick, with some use of dark-glazed facing bricks as at Thatcham (60) and Bucklebury (13); stone is also much in evidence but, apart from a late example of *c*.1800 at Grove (28), the only timber-framed meeting-house is the fragment at Abingdon (3) of 1700. Slate predominates as a roofing material, but tiled roofs are not uncommon and several buildings still have a covering of small stone slates; the only remaining example of thatch was on a small Wesleyan chapel at Boxford (8), now altered following closure and conversion to a house.

ABINGDON   *Oxfordshire*
(1) BAPTIST, Ock Street (SU 494971). The church, which originated in the mid 17th century, was one of the original members of the 'Abingdon Association', formed in 1652. A

meeting-house built on the present site *c*.1700 was rebuilt in 1841 and refitted in 1882. The chapel, designed by John Davies of London and opened 21 October 1841, is of brick with a stucco front and slated roof. The S front, which closely resembles that of

Baptist chapel, Ock Street, Abingdon. (1)

the Baptist chapel at Hitchin, Hertfordshire, of 1844, is of three bays with tall Roman Doric columns supporting an entablature and pediment and narrow flanking wings with pilasters; the three principal bays have each a round-arch doorway and window above. The side walls are of five bays with two stages of windows. The interior has a gallery around three sides supported by cast-iron columns; at the N end is an original decorative wall arch with supporting pilasters.

Fittings – *Chairs*: six, two with open-balustered backs, shaped tops and arms, *c*.1841. *Communion Table*: with turned legs, 18th-century. *Monuments*: in chapel – on N wall (1) Daniel Turner A.M., 1798 (*see DNB*); (2) Rev. John Evans, pastor, 1813; (3) John Kershaw A.M., pastor, 1842; below E gallery (4) Richard Blackwell Kendall, 1828, and Mary his widow, 1852; (5) Thomas Kendall, 1797, and Frances his widow, 1824; (6) William Ballard, 1844, and Elizabeth his widow, 1854; below W gallery (7) Esther, wife of John Harris, 1831, Charles Dundas, her brother-in-law, 1824, and her daughters Hannah, 1814, and Jane, wife of William Copeland, 1838; (8) John Tomkins, 39 years deacon, 1846, tablet in marble surround with Roman Doric pilasters, entablature, and pediment; (9) John, son of John and Esther Harris, 1841, William Alder, his brother, 1850, his sisters

Frances Strange, 1843, Esther, 1844, Elizabeth, 1848, and William Badcock, husband of the last, 1853; in gallery (10) Benjamin, son of Joseph and Sarah Tomkins, 1752, white marble tablet on mottled marbled backing, broken pediment with shield-of-arms, and apron with consoles; (11) Joseph Tyrrell, 1820, Sarah his widow, 1836, and their children Elizabeth Avery and Joseph Tyrrell; (12) Avery Tyrrell, 1837, and two children; in burial-ground – S of chapel (13) Sarah, wife of John Hall, 1712, loose headstone with scrolled border and death's head; (14) headstone with laudatory inscription in scrolled border, early 18th-century; E of chapel (15) John Kay, 'who gave up his livelihood as a Minister of the Established Church through conscientious objections to the Prayer Book' *c*.1841, 1860; (16) John Tomkins, 1708, modern memorial; other Tomkins monuments adjacent include Hannah, 1761, with shield-of-arms, and William, 1808. *Plate*: includes a pair of two-handled cups of 1719, given by Benjamin Tomkins, and four pewter plates dated 1749.

BM (1841) 642. Ivimey II (1814) 61–6; IV (1830) 420–2.

(2) STRICT BAPTIST, Checker Walk (SU 499970). 'Abbey Chapel' was built in 1831–2 for William Tiptaft, former vicar of

Sutton Courtenay. Small chapel of brick and slate, much altered and enlarged in 1961 and 1975.

Paul VI (1969) 289–324. Philpot, J.C., *Memoir of the Late William Tiptaft* (1867).

(3) Former CONGREGATIONAL, The Square (SU 496971). The congregation originated in the late 17th century, when Dr Henry Langley, formerly Master of Pembroke College, Oxford, and other ejected ministers, conducted services in the district. A meeting-house was built in 1700 and registered for Presbyterians on 12 October. The church became Congregational in the late 18th century after a period of heterodoxy. In 1862 a new chapel was built against the S front of the meeting-house and the earlier building was converted for Sunday-school use, re-roofed and a floor inserted.

The former meeting-house at the rear of the chapel has rendered timber-framed walls with altered windows. The front formerly had two entrances and three cross-framed windows at gallery level. The building was shortened by about 10 ft at the S end when the new chapel was built. A sketch plan of 1799 gives

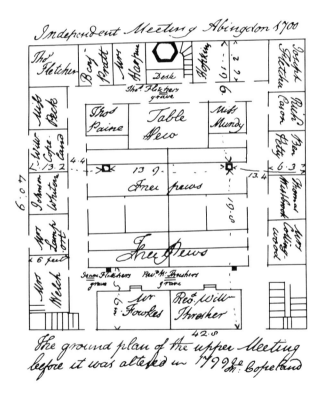

Independent Meeting Abingdon 1700

The ground plan of the upper Meeting before it was altered in 1799 Jn.º Copeland

the overall dimensions as 40 ft 9 in. by 42 ft 8 in. Two tall posts of pine, of circular section with moulded caps and bases, support the valley beam of the former roof structure; these have curved braces above the capitals and one post is carved with the initials and date 'WB/CH/1700'. The date 1774 on a panel on the E wall may refer to a renewal of the rendering. The chapel of 1862 by J.S. Dodd has an ashlar S front of four bays with Corinthian pilasters and a pediment. The interior has a gallery around three sides with open cast-iron front. (Closed 1968, converted to offices 1989; URC congregation united with Methodists at (4))

Fittings – *Monuments*: in chapel (1) Rev. William Francis Sharp, 1844; (2) Rev. William Thresher, 1806; externally against E wall (3) William Copeland, 1817, Elizabeth his first wife, 1790, Mary his second wife, 1826, *et al.*; (4) 'family vault of Ebenezer Copeland', Frances Strange Copeland, 1829, Fletcher Copeland, 1836, and Mary Ann Copeland, 1837. *Plate*: includes three mugs, 1761, 1764, 1768 (stolen 1974).

Stevens, J., *Two Centuries Young, Abingdon Congregational Church, 1700–1900* [c.1900]. Summers (1905) 214–24.

(4) WESLEYAN, Conduit Road (SU 493972). The first Wesleyan chapel in Abingdon, opened in Stert Street in 1823, was succeeded by another in Ock Street in 1847. The present building, 'Trinity', erected in 1873–5 to the designs of W.H. Woodman of Reading and largely financed by John Creemer Clarke MP, a wealthy manufacturer, is a large structure of polygonal masonry with ashlar dressings in the Decorated style. It comprises a nave, chancel, transepts and NW tower and spire; ancillary buildings are grouped around an open courtyard.

Tranter, D.B., *A History of Trinity (Wesleyan) Methodist Church, Abingdon* [c.1975].

ASTON TIRROLD   *Oxfordshire*

(5) PRESBYTERIAN (SU 554860). The congregation originated in the late 17th century following the preaching of Richard Comyns and Thomas Cheesman, ministers ejected in 1662 from Cholsey and East Garston. Meetings were held for some time in converted barns and the present meeting-house was erected in 1728 by Joseph and Richard Fuller, two of the principal members of the

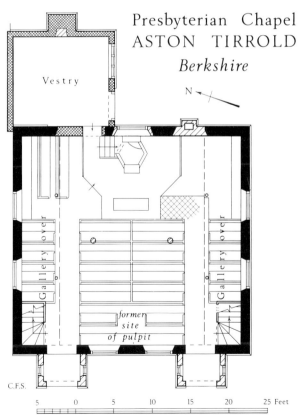

Presbyterian Chapel
ASTON TIRROLD
Berkshire

Presbyterian chapel (URC), Aston Tirrold. (5)

society. By the late 18th century the church, formerly Presbyterian, had come to be regarded as Congregational, although it was served for some time by ministers in the Countess of Huntingdon's Connexion; in 1873 it joined the Presbyterian Church in England (now URC).

The chapel has brick walls and a hipped tiled roof with central valley. The W front has two segmental-arched doorways, now covered by porches added in 1864–5, and two round-arched windows which formerly flanked the pulpit; two similar windows occupy the N and S walls, but on the E side are traces of two smaller upper windows and two below, partly blocked in the late 18th century when a vestry was added against this side; a circular window was inserted in the E wall when the internal orientation was reversed.

The interior (26¼ ft by 28½ ft) was turned about and considerably refitted in 1864–5: two posts supporting the roof structure were replaced by cast-iron pillars, an E gallery was probably removed, N and S galleries were refronted, the pulpit re-sited and the lower seating renewed.

Fittings – *Books*: P. Doddridge, *The Family Expositor* . . . , two volumes only, II (1740), VI (1756), the last inscribed 'These Books belong to Aston Meeting They were bought by Messrs. Joseph and Benjamin Fuller of Mrs Holdsworth for the use of the Minister of Aston Meeting'; Jer. Taylor and William Cave, *Antiquitates Christianae* . . . (9th edn 1703); Matthew Henry, *An Exposition of the Old and New Testament*, volumes II to IV only (1793–4). *Clock*: case of Parliament clock, shaped top and cheeks to pendulum case, chinoiserie decoration, signed 'James Chater, Lond.', 18th-century, hands and mechanism renewed.

Inscriptions: on bricks at SW corner of W wall, 'IC+', 'WC 1728', 'TIR'. *Monuments*: in chapel (1) John Fuller, deacon, 1834, Jane his wife, 1804, and three children; (2) Eliza, wife of Joseph Humfrey Fuller, 1832, and Eliza Jane their daughter, 1833, marble tablet with pediment and dove with olive branch in low relief, signed 'Godfrey, Abingdon'; (3) Mercy Bullard Harriss, 1839, similar to previous monument; externally, in W wall (4) Rev. Joseph Griffith, 1818; (5) Rev. Josiah Holdsworth, 1763, and Mary his widow, 1780; in S wall of vestry (6) Eliza Merch[ant], headstone, 18th-century. *Pulpit*: hexagonal with fielded-panelled sides, early 18th-century, altered.

McDonald, F., *Monument to Faith* (1978). *PHSJ* IV (1928–31) 71–5. Summers (1905) 277–80.

BEECH HILL

(6) BEECH HILL CHAPEL (SU 700643), registered as a Baptist meeting-house in September 1794 and supported by a benefaction from Abraham Atkins of Clapham, is a small building of brick with a half-hipped tiled roof. The longer N and S walls have each two altered or inserted windows and the upper courses of the S and W walls have been rebuilt. An E porch was built *c*.1890 and a vestry subsequently added at the opposite end. The interior (23¾ ft by 18 ft) has been refitted but parts of the former pulpit are incorporated in a later rostrum.

Baptistery: centrally in floor, on main axis. *Inscriptions*: on bricks in N wall '. . . B 1794', 'W.W. I.B. 1794'. *Monument*: in chapel on W wall, Rev. James Rodway, 33 years pastor, previously missionary to West Africa for Baptist Missionary

Society from 1795, 1843, also Mary his wife, 1836, marble tablet signed Savage, Reading.

Payne (1951) 92. Rippon, J., *The Baptist Annual Register* III (1798) 4. Summers (1905) 295–6.

BOURTON   *Oxfordshire*

(7) Former BAPTIST (SU 231871). Now Village Hall. Gothic chapel built by Henry Tucker of Bourton House to designs by W. F. Ordish and opened 19 October 1851 by the Hon. and Rev. Baptist W. Noel. S front with pointed-arched doorway, wheel window and bell-cote with one bell on apex of gable, four-bay sides, four-light window at N end with Decorated tracery.

Former Baptist chapel, Bourton.   (7)

Former Wesleyan chapel, Boxford.   (8)

BOXFORD

(8) Former WESLEYAN (SU 426716). Brick with half-hipped thatched roof, built c.1810 but refenestrated in the mid 19th century; trace of former tall window between lancets at W end. (Sold c.1980, thatch replaced)

BRIMPTON

(9) BAPTIST (SU 557655). Ashlar walls, three-bay gabled front with pointed-arched openings under thin moulded labels. Built c.1843 for a church formed in that year. Contemporary manse attached.

   Monument: in chapel, Rev. Charles Rixson, 1851.

BUCKLAND   *Oxfordshire*

(10) Former PRESBYTERIAN (SU 342977). House, 'Pound Corner', on W side of Buckland Road, was built c.1700 for a congregation which in the early 18th century shared a minister with the church in Faringdon; it was converted into cottages and refenestrated in the late 18th century. The walls are of rubble and the roof is hipped and covered with old stone slates partly replaced by tiles. The front E wall has near the N end a flat arch

Former Presbyterian chapel, Buckland.   (10)

above a former wide doorway. Tall openings or recesses centrally in the N and S walls have been blocked. In the W wall at mid height was a series of four windows with flat-arched heads. The interior (20 ft by 40 ft) has been entirely altered and a floor inserted; the roof is supported by three trusses with tie-beams, collars and raking braces.

   Stanley (c.1935) 140–1.

(11) Former BAPTIST, Summerside Road (SU 343977). A substantial 'capital messuage' formerly designated 'Somerset House' and believed to have been the principal building of the Manor of St John is referred to in a lease of 1562; it appears to have been built in the late 15th or early 16th century. About 1710 the property was divided into two separate dwelling-houses and in or about 1783 the SW part was converted for use as a meeting-house in connection with the Baptist congregation at Cote (*see* Oxfordshire (6)).

   The building has rubble walls and stone slated roofs. The SE front, probably rebuilt in the late 18th century, has two round-arched windows and a late 19th-century gabled porch; a doorway

to the right with four-centred arched timber lintel leads to a through-passage. The rear wall, partly covered by a two-storeyed late 18th-century former cottage, has two windows of this period with plain wood frames and leaded glazing. At the SW end is a large late-mediaeval chimney-breast and, to its left, a narrow gabled wing of two storeys. The interior ($24\frac{1}{4}$ ft by $18\frac{3}{4}$ ft), rising through two former storeys, has a gallery at the NE end partly above the through-passage. The fittings were largely renewed in the late 19th century but the pulpit against the SW wall incorporates some late 18th-century bolection-moulded fielded panelling. (Chapel closed c.1976 and converted to a house)

   Wright, A. S. N., *The History of Buckland in the County of Berkshire* (1966) *passim*.

(12) THE DIPPING-HOUSE, Buckland Road (SU 343978). A building on the E side of the road of which only the lower parts of the walls remain has been claimed to be a former baptistery. The walls are of rubble and the roof was gabled and covered with stone slates; in the W wall were two windows with stone mullions, a wider mullioned window at the N end and entrance opposite. Inside is a tank 15 ft by 8 ft fed by a spring, and at the S end a platform about 8 ft square. Probably 18th-century, perhaps built as an open baptistery and subsequently roofed over.

   Stanley (c.1935) 138–9, pl. fcg 150.

BUCKLEBURY

(13) CONGREGATIONAL, Turner's Green (SU 539691). Gabled front of dark-glazed headers and red brick dressings; date 1840 on small tablet above central window. Many initials on bricks in front wall.

   Summers (1905) 103–7.

CHILDREY   *Oxfordshire*

(14) WESLEYAN (SU 361876). At N end of the green, opened 1849. Gabled front, in glazed header-bond brickwork, three graduated lancets above a central pointed-arched entrance.

   Railings: in front of chapel, cast-iron, signed 'C. Hart, maker, Wantage'. (Front wall collapsed 1986)

CHOLSEY   *Oxfordshire*

(15) BAPTIST (SU 588863). Brick with later rendering, half-hipped tiled roof. Built 1823, much altered c.1900. Inscribed bricks in front wall.

COOKHAM

(16) Former WESLEYAN (SU 897853). Built 1846, superseded 1903–4 by chapel at Cookham Dean; reopened 1911 as parish hall after alterations by Col F. C. Ricardo, whose arms it bears. Now the 'Stanley Spencer Gallery'.

(17) Former PRIMITIVE METHODIST, Cookham Dean (SU 871855). Brick and flint, now rendered; gabled front with tablet dated '1842, rebuilt 1858'. Converted to house in 1977; monuments grouped in separate enclosure include cast-iron head and foot markers with pierced ornament, signed 'Coles, Warfield', c.1900.

DRAYCOTT MOOR   *Oxfordshire*

(18) WESLEYAN, Southmoor (SU 399981). Rubble with brick and ashlar dressings. Gabled front dated 1841.

DRAYTON *Oxfordshire*

(19) BAPTIST (SU 476941). Brick with gabled front, wide pointed-arched windows and doorway, blind window over entrance and small roundel inscribed 'ISAAC WINTER BUILDER 1834'.

FERNHAM *Oxfordshire*

(20) Former CONGREGATIONAL (SU 293920). 'Zion Chapel', built in 1830, was closed by 1960 and is now in secular use. The walls are of rubble with brick quoins. Gabled front with central entrance between two tiers of windows, manse adjacent to rear.
  Summers (1905) 236-7.

'ZION CHAPEL', FERNHAM

FINCHAMPSTEAD

(21) BAPTIST (SU 794631). Early 19th-century. Red brick with low-pitched slate roof, three-bay front and pedimented gable; later porch.

Baptist chapel, Finchampstead.   (21)

FRILFORD *Oxfordshire*

(22) CONGREGATIONAL (SU 441972). Brick with slate roof half-hipped to rear; three-bay gabled front with pointed-arched openings and Y-tracery; dated 1841. (URC)
  Summers (1905) 238-9.

FYFIELD AND TUBNEY *Oxfordshire*

(23) BAPTIST, Fyfield (SU 422984). Brick and tile, with broad three-bay W front and four-centred arched windows with wooden Y-tracery; built *c*.1840 and enlarged to N by one bay in later 19th century.

GREAT FARINGDON *Oxfordshire*

(24) BAPTIST, Christopher Square, Faringdon (SU 287953). A Baptist church formed in the mid 17th century died out *c*.1761; services were later resumed and at the end of the 18th century the meeting-house was rebuilt. The present chapel, rebuilt or altered in the mid 19th century, has walls of rubble with ashlar dressings and the roof is covered with stone slates partly replaced by tiles. Three-bay W front with lancet windows.
  Monuments: S of chapel (1) Rev. George Capes, minister, 1835, and Jane his wife, 1834, table-tomb; (2) Richard Steed, 1721, with laudatory verse.
  Payne (1951) 68, 86.

(25) Former CONGREGATIONAL, Faringdon (SU 288955). The chapel, built in 1840, replaced one of 1799-1800 erected by John Fidel, a builder, with whom the cause commenced. The walls are of stone, rendered at the front, with rusticated ashlar dressings.

Former Congregational chapel, Faringdon.   (25)

Three-bay front with pointed-arched windows and a battlemented pediment. A gallery next to the entrance supported by cast-iron columns retains its original seating and traces of a singers' pew.
  Monument: in chapel, Rev. Daniel Holmes, 27 years pastor, 1836. (Chapel sold to Roman Catholics *c*.1975 following local union with Methodists)
  Summers (1905) 229-34.

(26) FRIENDS, Lechlade Road, Faringdon (SU 285956). The meeting-house, built in 1672, was only in intermittent use during the 19th century. In 1891 it was being used 'by a devoted lady for

Friends' meeting-house, Faringdon. (26)

Evangelical services' and more recently as a Scout hall; it was reopened for meetings in 1980. The building, concealed behind a high boundary wall, has rubble walls with some brick and ashlar dressings and a steeply pitched hipped roof covered with stone slates. An ashlar porch at the SW end was added in the early 19th century. One original window in the NW wall, now blocked, has a flat-arched brick head with keystone; other windows have been altered. The interior (33½ ft by 16½ ft) has a dado of 19th-century panelling rising behind the site of the stand.

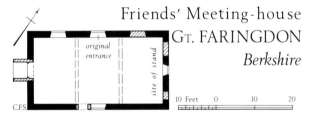

Friends' Meeting-house
Gt. FARINGDON
Berkshire

original entrance

site of stand

10 Feet 0 10 20

C.F.S.

The burial-ground to NE has no monuments, but stones reset in a side path include one to Marian Lockey, 1734. *Royal Arms*: on outer face of entrance door, 20th-century.

(27) Former WESLEYAN, Gloucester Street, Faringdon (SU 286955). Built c.1837, converted to Masonic Hall 1921. Stone and slate, three-bay front with stone-columned porch and two tall round-arched windows, now blocked.

GROVE   *Oxfordshire*

(28) STRICT BAPTIST (SU 401897). Seceders who left the Baptist church in Wantage in 1805 built themselves a new meeting-house at Grove, opened 1821. This has brick walls to the lower part; the upper stage is timber-framed and rendered but was probably originally weatherboarded. The roof is tiled, hipped to the S and half-hipped to the N. There is a deep gallery at the N end. Extensive repairs were made in 1884.

Paul VI (1969) 325–39.

Strict Baptist chapel, Grove. (28)

HAMPSTEAD NORRIS

(29) Former WESLEYAN (SU 530763). Rebuilt 1854.

HUNGERFORD

(30) CONGREGATIONAL, High Street (SU 337684). An existing building, fitted up as a meeting-house in 1801 for a congregation (now URC) formed in the previous year, was largely rebuilt in 1817; after the erection of the present chapel in 1840, it was converted to a schoolroom.

The former meeting-house standing behind the chapel has brick walls and a tiled roof hipped to the W and half-hipped to the east. The rear W wall has two altered round-arched windows and two stones inscribed with the date 1817 and initials JF, SVF; there are three similar windows in the S wall. A small window near the W end of the N wall, now blocked, has a flat-arched head of glazed headers. There is an external door in the E wall and a gallery at that end.

The present chapel, adjacent to the E, is of brick with a hipped slate roof. The front is of three bays divided by pilasters. A stone below the SE corner was laid 28 May 1840, 'the chapel erected A.D. 1817 having become inadequate . . . '.

Monuments: in burial-ground; include a table-tomb to Jane, daughter of [Rev.] Richard and Jane Frost, 18[4]7, and seven headstones of mid 19th century and later.

Summers (1905) 125–33.

(31) Former WESLEYAN, Church Street (SU 336685). Tall early 19th-century building of brick and slate, rendered on S side and extended to E in mid 19th century and later to the west. It was superseded in 1869 by a Gothic chapel in Charnham Street (demolished since 1970) and is now in commercial use. The N and S walls have each two tall sash windows, the E extension which incorporates a gallery has round-arched upper windows and a pedimented S entrance.

A small burial-ground to the S has two table-tombs, one to John Hogsflesh, 1842, *et al.*, and several headstones, including one to James, eldest son of Rev. James Allen, Wesleyan minister, 1846.

KINGSTON LISLE   *Oxfordshire*

(32) Former BAPTIST (SU 327878). 'The Chapel House', built

and supported by Abraham Atkins of Clapham, was registered as a meeting-house in October 1779. A Baptist church was formed in 1790. Meetings ceased before 1930 and the building is now occupied as a house. The walls are of chalk rubble with brick dressings and the roof is tiled. The S front is of five bays with two doorways and two tiers of segmental-arched windows, some with original iron casements.

Gates: double iron gates and standards, late 18th-century.

Payne (1951) 82.

LAMBOURN

(33) WESLEYAN, Chapel Lane (SU 327790). Brick with three-bay gabled front and two tiers of round-arched windows. Dated 1835.

LONGCOT   *Oxfordshire*

(34) WESLEYAN (SU 274908). Small brick chapel, c.1842–5.

LONGWORTH   *Oxfordshire*

(35) CONGREGATIONAL (SU 390993). Rubble and slate with brick dressings. Three-bay gabled front with pointed-arched windows, keystones and imposts; dated 1848. Sunday-school at rear, of stone, added 1853 and later. (URC)

Summers (1905) 238–9.

MAIDENHEAD

(36) BAPTIST, Marlow Road (SU 884814). Three-bay front in polychrome brickwork, 1872.

(37) CONGREGATIONAL, West Street (SU 888813). A Presbyterian congregation formed in the late 17th century owed its origins to the work of William Brice, ejected minister of Henley-on-Thames, for whose house a meeting-house licence was issued in 1672. After a period of decline in the 18th century the cause was revived by Rev. John Cooke (minister 1784–1826) and became Congregational (now URC). The present site was bought and a new meeting-house erected in 1785; the building was greatly altered and enlarged c.1860–70.

Congregational chapel (URC), Maidenhead.   (37)

The original meeting-house, of which the side and rear walls remain, was of brick and had a pedimented S front of three bays with two tiers of round-arched windows. The side walls had each a single pilaster buttress with moulded capping, and two round-arched windows, now divided and altered. The late 19th-century alterations, probably by Poulton and Woodman of Reading and closely resembling their work at Lozells Chapel, Birmingham (*CYB* (1862) 294), included an enlargement to the S with a wide arched recess containing the principal entrances and wings enclosing gallery staircases. The interior (originally about 45 ft by 34½ ft) has a gallery around three sides supported by fluted Roman Doric columns of cast iron. The ceiling has a segmental plaster vault formerly with roof lights and five partly exposed trusses with king and queen-posts.

Fittings – *Bureau*: in vestry, with brass plate 'originally the property of the Revd. John Cooke', 18th-century. *Monuments*: on N wall (1) Rev. J. B. Pearce, 11 years pastor, 1838, white marble tablet surmounted by draped urn; (2) Rev. John Cooke, 45 years minister, 1826, white marble sarcophagus-shaped tablet signed 'Clark & Son, Reading'. *Plate*: includes four two-handled cups of 1771, 1804 and 1838; an inscribed pewter cup dated 1784 is in the Richardson collection at Truro Museum, Cornwall.

Summers (1905) 45–53.

(38) Former COUNTESS OF HUNTINGDON'S CHAPEL, High Street (SU 886811). A Society of Calvinistic Methodists, formed in 1828 by separation from the Congregational Church, erected the present chapel in 1841. In 1858 this was sold to the Wesleyans whose society, founded in 1829, had previously occupied a chapel of 1833 in Bridge Street. It remains in Methodist use.

The chapel, of yellow stock brick with stone dressings, was originally of four bays to which E and W galleried transepts were added in 1877–8. The N front is gabled and has angle buttresses formerly rising to crocketted pinnacles and an open stone parapet with ogee-arched bell-cote at the apex, also lacking its pinnacles. Above a later porch is a three-light window with perpendicular tracery between two cusped lancets.

Bell: in bell-cote, said to have been brought from Bray church in 1841 together with the clock (since replaced) and to be inscribed SAMVELL KNIGHT MADE MEE 1703.

Hardiment, P., *Methodism in Maidenhead, 1829–1979* (1979).

(39) FRIENDS, West Street (SU 887813). Small building (20 ft by 12 ft) of brick with later rendering and hipped tiled roof; built 1803 to replace a meeting-house of 1742, much altered and extended to the front.

MARCHAM   *Oxfordshire*

(40) Former BAPTIST, Cothill (SU 464995). Brick and slate with pointed-arched windows. A small roundel in the front gable is inscribed 'ISAAC WINTER BUILDER 1830'. Chapel closed by 1977.

NEWBURY

(41) WATERSIDE CHAPEL, Toomer's Court (SU 472672). A substantial Presbyterian congregation developed in Newbury in the late 17th century. Several ejected ministers found refuge in the town and in 1672 the former rector Benjamin Woodbridge took out a licence here as a Presbyterian teacher. From 1686 a barn was used jointly by Presbyterians and Independents but in 1697 the societies separated, the Presbyterians, later to become Unitarian, building a new meeting-house for the 'Upper Meeting' which remained with little alteration until 1947 when

Waterside Chapel, Newbury. (41)

most of the fittings were removed; it was demolished c.1961 and the site is now occupied by 'The Waterside Centre'.

The meeting-house was a square building of brick with a triple roof hipped and tiled; the walls had a brick platband at midheight, a moulded eaves cornice and two tiers of windows. In the S front were two wide doorways between four windows, the end two blocked, and four original windows above with two narrower ones added; at the centre of the front was a stone tablet dated 1697. The side walls had each five bays of windows, the lower with wooden cross-frames, some altered or enlarged. In the N wall were two tall round-arched windows flanking the site of the pulpit and to each side two tiers of windows, the upper pair blocked. At the N end of the E wall was a small vestry added in the early 18th century.

The interior (50½ ft square) had a flat plaster ceiling and was divided by two rows of four tall timber columns supporting the valley beams. Along the S end was a gallery, probably an early addition, with staircase in the SW corner having moulded balusters and handrail, and newels with ball finials.

Fittings – Prior to 1947 the building is said to have had a three-decker pulpit and central communion table. *Monuments*: N of chapel, a few broken fragments remained in 1977, including John Clark, 1830. *Plate*: included a mug of 1705 with shield-of-arms of

Waterside Chapel, NEWBURY, *Berkshire*

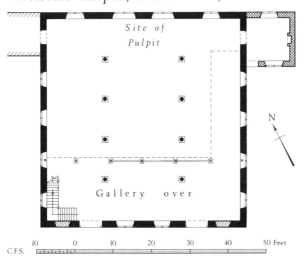

Site of Pulpit

N

Gallery over

10 0 10 20 30 40 50 Feet
C.F.S.

Howard (stolen 1971).

Evans (1897) 180–1. Summers (1905) 136–41.

(42) CONGREGATIONAL, Cromwell Place (SU 470673). The dissenters' meeting, which from 1686 occupied a converted barn on the present site, contained an Independent element which retained the use of this building after the removal of the Presbyterians in 1697. The meeting-house was rebuilt in 1716 and again in 1822. The latter building, of brick with a pedimented front of three bays was replaced c.1965. The 'Congregational School Rooms' alongside the entrance to the chapel yard, built in 1856–7, of red brick with blue brick pilasters, have two central entrances and arched side entrances with carved corbels representing Milton, Whitefield, Watts and Raikes.

Monuments: reset headstones include (1) Thomas Knight, 1787, Hester his mother, 1761, eleven of his children who died in infancy and Henry Biggs his grandson; (2) Rev. William Sedgley, 1754; (3) Rev. John Winter, 38 years pastor, 1823, and Martha his widow, 1839; (4) Rev. William Dryland, 31 years pastor, 1853; (5) James Purdue, 'an eminent clothier of this town', 1789. *Plate*: includes a two-handled cup of 1777; two other cups of 1671 and 1681 were sold c.1970. (URC)

Summers (1905) 136–48.

(43) WESLEYAN, Northbrook Street (SU 470675). The Methodist society in Newbury dates from 1770 when John Wesley, excluded from the dissenters' meeting-house and denied the use of the old playhouse because 'the good mayor would not suffer it to be so profaned', preached in a large workshop. This was replaced in 1804 by the first regular chapel and followed in a few years by the present building opened in 1838.

The chapel is designed in the Gothic style with ashlar facing to the walls and tall lancet windows between stepped buttresses. The E front is divided by two tall octagonal buttresses rising to open turrets and has a central entrance with open stone-vaulted porch. The interior, reseated in the late 19th century, has a continuous gallery supported by cast-iron columns. At the W end, behind a centrally sited pulpit, is a recessed communion area with an organ loft above.

Communion Table and *Chairs*: c.1837. *Font*: octagonal stone shaft supporting pottery fontlet, c.1860. *Organ*: Gothic case, mid 19th-century, extended at sides c.1930. *Pulpit*: stone, octagonal, with cusped panelled sides supported by central octagonal stem with moulded base, stone stair with iron balustrade, 1837. *Tables of Lord's Prayer, Creed and Decalogue*: on wall behind communion table, repainted in late 19th century.

READING

(44) BAPTIST, King's Road (SU 719734). The congregation originated in the mid 17th century as two separate General and Particular Baptist churches which united c.1700. The chapel, built in 1834 to a design by John James Cooper, has stone walls and a slate roof. The front of five bays with tall pilasters carrying a cornice and three-bay pediment was added in the late 19th century. A smaller meeting-house was built at the rear in 1975 prior to redevelopment of the chapel. (Demolished since 1985)

Council for British Archaeology, *Hallelujah!* (1985) 25. White, B. R., 'The Baptists of Reading 1652–1715', *BQ* XXII (1967–8) 249–70.

Wesleyan chapel, Northbrook Street, Newbury. E front.   (43)

Wesleyan chapel, Northbrook Street, Newbury. (43)

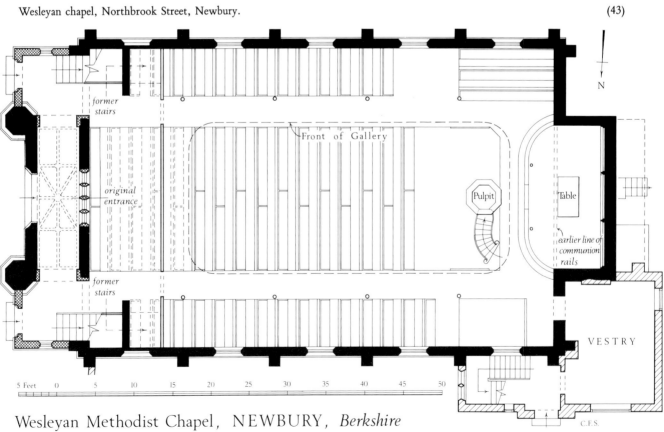

Wesleyan Methodist Chapel, NEWBURY, *Berkshire*

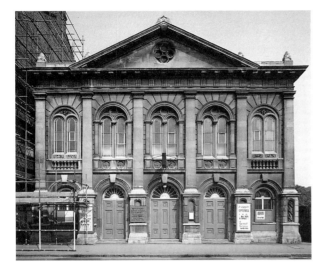

Baptist chapel, King's Road, Reading.   (44)

(45) STRICT BAPTIST, South Street (SU 720731). 'Zoar Chapel', 1869.

'ZOAR' STRICT BAPTIST CHAPEL, READING   CFS 1976

(46) BAPTIST, South Street, Caversham (SU 715748). Brown brick with white brick banding, corner tower enclosing staircase

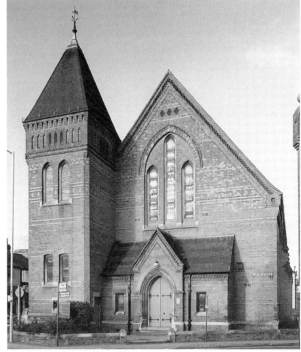

Baptist chapel, Caversham.   (46)

to former gallery; interior refitted. Built 1875-7 superseding a chapel of 1865-6 in Gosbrook Road which became the 'West Memorial Hall'. Both buildings by Alfred Waterhouse.

Arnold (1976) 7. Payne (1951) 113. Sawyer, E. and Shield, A., *Caversham Baptist Free Church 1872-1972* (1972).

(47) CONGREGATIONAL, Broad Street (SU 714734). A congregation of Presbyterians and Independents formed in the late 17th century, of which Rev. Thomas Juice, ejected from St Nicholas's church, Worcester, was first pastor, divided in 1717. The Independents retained the use of the meeting-house on the present site, rebuilding it in 1800. Many alterations were made during the 19th century, the most extensive being in 1892 when a row of shops and offices was built in front of the chapel, entirely concealing it from view, and the interior almost completely refitted.

The chapel has brick walls and a slated pyramidal roof. The front wall, now largely internal, is of five bays with two tiers of round-arched windows; the entrances, formerly in the penultimate bays, have been re-sited. The interior ($45\frac{1}{2}$ ft by $46\frac{3}{4}$ ft) has rebuilt galleries and a domed plaster ceiling rising into the roof space. (Proposed conversion to retail use *c*.1988)

Fittings – *Monuments*: reset in passage W of chapel (1) Mary Eliza, wife of Rev. Thomas Chivers Everett, 1828; (2) Cornelius Poulton, 1856, Mary his widow, 1869, and three children, signed 'Wheeler Bros.'; (3) Mary Anne Lamb, grand-daughter of Rev. T. Noon, 1856, and Caroline, her sister, wife of Rev. James Dean, 1858; (4) Margaret (Fenton) wife of William Winkworth, 1816, and Mary Ann their daughter, 1816; (5) Mary, wife of Rev. Thomas Arnold, 1812; (6) Rev. T. Noon, 1795, Mrs. A. Noon, 1775, Mrs. P. Noon, 1780, *et al.*, signed 'Wheeler'; (7) John

Coster Elkens, 1824, *et al.*; (8) David Fenton, 20 years deacon, 1831, Mary his wife, 1827, and David their son, 1826; (9) Emily Southgate, 1834, *et al.*; (10) Margaret, wife of Rev. William Legg, 1847, and two children; (11) Edward Talfourd, deacon, 1833, and Anne his widow, 1838; (12) Eliza, wife of Robert Davidson, 1801, and James their son, 1801.

Plate: includes two pairs of plain cups, 1805 and 1810. *Pulpit*: with inlaid and mahogany-veneered front, *c*.1800, altered. *Radiators*: in back gallery, two, of eight fluted columns joined at top and inscribed 'T. G. Williams & Sons Ventilating Radiator', mid 19th-century.

Brain, W. J., *Broad Street Chapel, Reading, 1662 to 1912* [*c*.1930]. Legg, W., *Historical Memorials of Broad Street Chapel, Reading* (1851). Summers (1905) 156–75.

(48) CONGREGATIONAL, Queen's Road (SU 720732). 'Trinity Chapel', built in 1848–9 for a congregation formed by secession from Broad Street Chapel, was designed by W. F. Poulton; it was greatly enlarged in the later 19th century by the addition of aisles and transepts. The walls are of rubble and the roof tiled. The original N wall has octagonal corner buttresses formerly rising to tall pinnacles, and three graduated lancets. On the NE buttress is a scroll with the date of erection. (Chapel demolished since 1976)

CYB (1858) 245. Summers (1905) 194–7.

(49) ST MARY'S CHAPEL, Castle Street (SU 713733). An evangelical ministry at the parish church of St Giles under Rev.

William Talbot led at his death in 1774 to the temporary formation of an Independent congregation. On the death of his successor, the Hon. and Rev. W. B. Cadogan, in 1797, a separate congregation was formed for the maintenance of Calvinistic liturgical worship and a chapel, built on the site of Reading Gaol, was opened 16 December 1798. After the departure in 1836 of the last and most notable Independent minister, Rev. James Sherman, to become minister of the Surrey Chapel, London, the trustees licensed the building as an Episcopal Chapel, causing a major secession of Independents (*see* (50)).

The chapel, built in 1798 to designs by Richard Billing, is of brick with a slate roof. In 1838–40 Henry and Nathaniel Briant added a S portico with six Corinthian columns supporting a pediment behind which rose a narrow tower with pedimented sides (upper part removed 1964); a chancel was also added at the N end. The original S front, partly visible inside the added vestibule, is of three bays with slightly projecting centre with quoins, central and side entrances and a round-arched former window above. The side walls have each five tall round-arched windows. The interior (66 ft by 52¾ ft) is little altered, with galleries around three sides supported E and W by four Roman Doric columns above which tall Ionic columns carry cornices and a segmental plaster barrel vault over the central space. The gallery staircases have been re-sited in the front vestibule.

Floorslab: below SE staircase, to [   ] Grant M.D., 1832. *Light Fittings*: two pendant gas 'star lights', each of 36 burners,

St Mary's Chapel, Reading.   (49)

St Mary's Chapel, Reading. Exterior before alteration.   (49)
Photograph by H. Felton.

Caversham Hill Chapel, Reading.   (51)

mid 19th-century. *Seating*: box-pews with fielded-panelled sides, scratchings on rear gallery pews include date 1799.

EM (1836) 563. Leaver, R. A., *A Short History of Saint Mary's Chapel, Castle Street, Reading* (1973). Summers (1905) 166, 178–87.

(50) Former CONGREGATIONAL, Castle Street (SU 713732). Those members of the Independent congregation in Castle Street (*see* (49)) who objected to the action of the trustees in transferring the building to the established church separated in 1836 and in the following year opened a new chapel on the opposite side of the road. This continued in use until *c.*1955 but is now in commercial occupation. The chapel, designed by J.J. Cooper, has a front of five bays rendered in stucco with an altered three-bay entrance formerly with fluted Doric columns, round-arched upper windows and a pedimental parapet; the side bays are rusticated to the lower stage and have plain pilasters above with incised ornament.

Summers (1905) 184–7.

(51) CAVERSHAM HILL CHAPEL (SU 720759) was built in 1827 for an Independent congregation during Rev. J. Sherman's ministry in Reading. The walls are of Bath stone in five bays with pilaster buttresses and triangular-headed windows. Narrow tower at SW end with battlemented parapet and three stages of windows with two pointed-arched lights and moulded labels. Interior refitted.

Summers (1905) 187–9.

(52) FRIENDS, Church Street (SU 717730). A Quaker meeting established in 1655 met from 1671 in a building in Sun Lane, now part of Broad Street. In the later years of the 17th century, following procedural disputes, the meeting divided, part occupying the former meeting-house whilst the remainder met on hired premises in Sims Court, London Street. By 1716 the two factions had reunited, building a new meeting-house on the N side of Church Street. This was superseded by the present building on the same site, opened in 1835.

The meeting-house has walls of red brick and a slate roof. The broad S front, partly covered by an extensive annexe built in 1964 to replace a contemporary porch and retiring rooms, has four upper windows with hung sashes, those at each end set lower than the centre pair. The N wall has four tall windows uniform in size. The gabled W end is treated as a formal composition with a central doorway with double doors, stone surround and consoles below a moulded cornice, flanked by a pair of blind window recesses filled with glazed brickwork in header bond. In both E and W gables is a circular ventilator.

The interior ($55\frac{1}{4}$ ft by $34\frac{3}{4}$ ft) is divided into two compartments by a three-centred arch formerly closed by counter-weighted sliding shutters, now removed. A similar arch at the E end rises above the front of the stand. The stand has an open-balustraded front and a single wall-bench rounded at N and S ends. Two raised seating platforms flank the W entrance. Some contemporary open-backed benches remain. On the S side of the E room is an arched recess for a cast-iron heating stove.

The roof, approached by a vertical ladder concealed in the NE corner, is supported by eight trusses, the centre pair set close together flanking the site of the upper half of the shutters, some of the mechanism for which remains in position. The trusses, of light scantling, have pairs of diagonal braces each side of a king-strut assisted by five pairs of iron straps.

The burial-ground N of the meeting-house has many small flat marker-stones of the early 19th century and numerous uniform round-topped headstones, including Alfred Waterhouse, 1873.

Penney (1907) 8–9. Smith, H. R., 'The Wilkinson-Story Controversy in Reading', *FHSJ* I (1903–4) 57–61.

(53) Former PRIMITIVE METHODIST, London Street (SU 718732). Tall three-bay front with giant Ionic columns *in antis*, by William Brown, built 1842 for a Literary, Scientific and

Mechanical Institute. Inscription on frieze 'Primitive Methodist Chapel 1866', now obliterated.

SANDHURST

(54) BAPTIST (SU 840613). Red brick, black and yellow dressings and slate roof, pointed-arched windows; by W. Ranger, 1880. *See* advertisement for 'Ranger's Model Chapels', *CYB* (1892) advt p 26.

Baptist chapel, Sandhurst. (54)

SOUTH MORETON   *Oxfordshire*

(55) STRICT BAPTIST (SU 560883). Rendered walls, with two-storeyed cottage at S end. Built *c*.1834.

STANFORD IN THE VALE   *Oxfordshire*

(56) CONGREGATIONAL (SU 343938), rubble with brick dressings and slate roof, built 1831 refronted in brickwork 1922, original date-tablet reset. Lean-to schoolroom at side dated 1864.
   Summers (1905) 234–5.

(57) Former PRIMITIVE METHODIST, High Street (SU 343932). Red brick with yellow and blue dressings. Circular window with obliterated inscription dated 1888. Converted to house 1981.

FORMER PRIMITIVE METHODIST CHAPEL, STANFORD IN THE VALE   C·F·S·1981

SUNNINGDALE

(58) BAPTIST (SU 953677). Dated 1828, enlarged to front late 19th century.

Monument: SE of chapel, to Frederick William Victtuler, 1843, and Henry John Hooper, 1848, flat slab.

(59) CONGREGATIONAL (SU 952677). Brick with Bath stone dressings and slate roof, traceried windows, single-stage buttresses, and corner turret formerly with tall wooden flèche; polygonal preaching apse. By W.F. Poulton, 1865. (Disused 1977)
  CYB (1866) 330.

THATCHAM

(60) CONGREGATIONAL, Church Lane (SU 516673). The chapel, built in 1804 for a new congregation (now URC) on land given by John Barfield, has brick walls and a slated roof hipped to the rear. The gabled W front of dark-glazed bricks, reused from the demolished Dunston House of 1725, has three round-arched windows; the centre one above a columned porch is set in a thickened wall panel with separate dentil cornice. The windows in side and back walls have been altered. The interior is square and has a W gallery.

Congregational chapel (URC), Thatcham. (60)

Monuments: in chapel (1) John Barfield, 1851, white marble tablet with female weeper on dark marble backing, signed 'R. Brown, 58 Gt. Russell St., London'; (2) Rev. Ebenezer White, ten years pastor, 1859, white marble tablet surmounted by urn on grey marble backing, signed 'E. Pearce, 163 & 165 Euston Rd., London'; (3) Elizabeth, wife of John Barfield, 1819, and Mary his second wife, 1820; W of chapel (4) Samuel, son of William and Ann Hemming, 1821; (5) Ralph, infant son of Rev. Ralph and Hannah Wardle, 1818, and their daughters Elizabeth and Isabella, 1832.
  The former British School N of chapel is dated 1846.
  Summers (1905) 204–8.

(61) WESLEYAN (SU 518675). Opened 1834. Gabled front with recent porch. Enlargement to rear in progress 1988.

UFFINGTON   *Oxfordshire*

(62) STRICT BAPTIST (SU 305892). Wide brick frontage with glazed headers; two sash windows with external shutters secured internally by cross-headed bolts, later porch to right and date-stone '1831' between windows. Internal baptistery constructed 1859.

Paul VI (1969) 340–55.

Strict Baptist chapel, Uffington.   (62)

(63) Former FRIENDS (SU 305890). Small single-cell meeting-house originally about 22 ft by 19½ ft externally, with walls of squared stone with brick dressings and a hipped roof covered with small stone slates. Built in 1730 for a meeting settled *c*.1712; fell to disuse *c*.1762, sold 1821, converted to cottage and S wall rebuilt. Entrance in E wall between two former windows, two small windows opposite.

Former Friends' meeting-house, Uffington.   (63)

WALLINGFORD   *Oxfordshire*

(64) BAPTIST, Thames Street (SU 609894). A meeting-house built in 1794 by Robert Lovegrove, who formed the church and acted as first pastor, was enlarged *c*.1819. The present building with rendered walls and hipped slate roof dates principally from *c*.1819 although it may incorporate earlier work. It was given a pedimented stucco front in the late 19th century.

Ivimey IV (1830) 432.

(65) Former CONGREGATIONAL (SU 608894). A Calvinistic secession from St Mary's parish church in 1785 led to the establishment of a separate congregation supported by ministers of the Countess of Huntingdon's Connexion. The present chapel, opened in 1799, was closed by 1905 and subsequently used for storage; since 1928 it has served as St John's Roman Catholic Church. The front wall set back between adjacent houses is of glazed brickwork in header bond with red brick dressings.

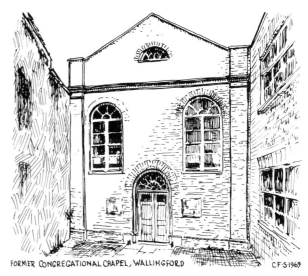

FORMER CONGREGATIONAL CHAPEL, WALLINGFORD   C.F.S.1969

Terminal pilasters and a moulded brick dentil cornice frame a wide round-arched doorway and two similarly arched upper windows; in a low gable above the cornice is a small lunette with intersecting glazing bars. The interior was entirely reconstructed in 1958 and since 1969 a porch has been built in front.

Monument: in front yard, to John Chapple, 1835, and Mary his widow, 1840.

Summers (1905) 300–6.

(66) FRIENDS, Castle Street (SU 607896). The meeting-house, built in 1724 and closed from 1854 to 1926, stands behind houses on the W side of the street. The walls are of brick, formerly

Friends' Meeting-house, WALLINGFORD, *Berkshire*

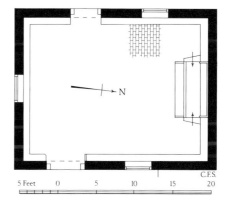

5 Feet   0   5   10   15   20

C.F.S.

Friends' meeting-house, Wallingford.   (66)

glazed, with a low plinth, platband and dentil cornice; the roof is hipped and tiled. In the E wall is a wide doorway with moulded architrave and double doors; in the opposite wall a similar but narrower entrance opens from the former burial-ground. Windows in E, W and S walls have hung sashes. The interior (24 ft by 18 ft) has a brick floor and a dado of plain horizontal boarding behind wall-benches. An original *stand* at the N end has turned supports to an upper front rail. Other seating includes eight plain open-backed benches with arm-rests.

WANTAGE   *Oxfordshire*

(67) WESLEYAN, Newbury Street (SU 398878). Built *c*.1845, by R. W. Ordish. Gabled front of rubble with stepped string-course above two-centred arched doorway. Schools behind, brick and slate, by Poulton and Woodman, *c*.1856.

WARGRAVE

(68) WARGRAVE CHAPEL, High Street (SU 786787). The last of the Independent village chapels around Reading to be built during the ministry of Rev. J. Sherman was erected in 1835. It has rendered walls and a slate roof, and comprises an E vestry, a

Wargrave Chapel.   (68)

WARGRAVE CHAPEL, *Berkshire*

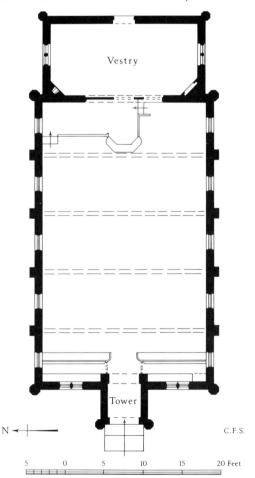

rectangular meeting-room of five bays and a W tower of three stages above the front entrance; octagonal corner buttresses at the front rise to small battlemented finials. The principal windows have two-centred arched heads with cast-iron frames. The interior has cusped scissor trusses to the roof; a four-centred arch behind the pulpit is filled with panelling and has doorways opening to the vestry. The seating has been mostly replaced but two original box-pews remain at the W end and the pulpit with panelled front is also of 1835. (Converted to house 1988, all interior fittings removed. *Inscription*: stone tablet from S boundary wall reset over inserted fireplace 'OW and LWW 1856'.)

Summers (1905) 192–3.

WELFORD

(69) Former PRIMITIVE METHODIST, Weston (SU 401738). Modest brick chapel dated 1864, on N bank of River Lambourn.

WHITE WALTHAM

(70) WALTHAM CHAPEL, Paley Street (SU 871763). Built 1837 for Independents. Brick with gabled front and porch with pointed-arched entrance.

Summers (1905) 52.

WINDSOR

(71) BAPTIST, Victoria Street (SU 965766). Pedimented stuccoed front of three bays, dated 1839. Two Ionic pilasters, between *antae*, entablature with frieze ornamented with roundels and palm swags, central entrance and two tall round-arched windows with foundation tablets below. Common-brick sides of five bays. Gallery at entrance, later schoolrooms at rear.

Glass: in front windows with coloured sunbursts at head.

Monuments: reset headstones at rear include John Jackson Wilmshurst, 1841, cast-iron.

Neal, B., and Smith, Ruth, *A Royal Heritage: History of the Baptist Church Victoria Street, Windsor, 1838–1982* [1982].

Baptist chapel, Victoria Street, Windsor. (71)

(72) CONGREGATIONAL, William Street (SU 966767). A church formed after 1781 met in various premises, including two cottages in Beer Lane (now River Street) which were converted to a meeting-house in 1788; a chapel was built on the site of a theatre in High Street in 1814. A new chapel on the E side of William Street was built and possibly designed by Jesse Hollis in 1832–3. The walls are of yellowish stock brick and the roofs slated. The W front with brick corner pilasters and pediment dated 1832 is of three bays with two tiers of windows, the upper ones with round-arched heads of two orders; the central entrance has a porch with Greek Doric columns and entablature and iron railings at the sides incorporating bootscrapers. The interior has a gallery around three sides supported by cast-iron columns. The seating was renewed in the late 19th century but the pulpit, rebuilt as a rostrum in 1912 with brass lamp standards of that period, incorporates the original square desk with panelled front and acanthus scrolled corners. The windows have iron frames and original double-glazed panes.

Monuments: in chapel (1) Joseph Chariott, 1848; (2) Rev. Alexander Redford, 36 years pastor, 1840, and Rebecca his widow, 1852; in front of chapel, two monuments to the foregoing, also (3) John Hillman Hetherington, 1843, *et al.* (Chapel rebuilt by URC, 1979)

Lee, A., *The Centenary Story of the Congregational Church, Windsor, 1832–1932* (1932). Summers (1905) 72–81.

Congregational chapel, William Street, Windsor. (72)

WOKINGHAM WITHIN

(73) BAPTIST, Milton Road, Wokingham (SU 810689). The congregation, originally connected with the church in Reading, was formed into a separate society in 1778. A meeting-house reputedly built in 1773 and enlarged in 1810 and 1827 was replaced by the present building in 1861. The chapel, designed by Poulton and Woodman, has walls of red and yellow brick with stone dressings. The SW front has a pedimented centre with three round-arched doorways and a row of five windows above. The pulpit is set in an apsidal recess facing the entrances.

Inscription: at foot of NW staircase, on square stone in floor, date 1773 with initials RW or AW, believed to be from former meeting-house.

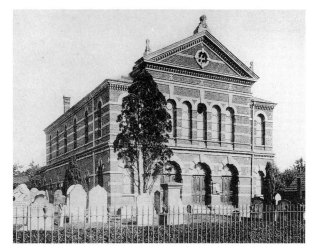

Baptist chapel, Wokingham. (73)

British School, W of chapel, 1841, low brick front with arcade of three blind arches and doorway in fourth bay; platband inscribed 'Baptist Sunday School 1808' (its date of formation).

Ivimey IV (1830) 430–1. Sale, P., *The Story of the Baptist Church, Wokingham, 1774–1924* (1924).

WOODLEY AND SANDFORD

(74) Former CONGREGATIONAL, Loddonbridge Road, Woodley (SU 767729). The first of Rev. J. Sherman's village chapels built *c.*1825 is a small building of Bath stone with a slate roof. The sides are of five bays with lancet windows and cast-iron frames; at the E end is a large vestry and at the opposite end a porch with belfry over forms a small tower of two stages with battlemented parapet and dwarf stone spire. The interior (28¾ ft by 18¾ ft) has a low-pitched roof with scissor trusses; at the E end are two arches opening to the vestry. *Bell:* one, in tower.

Summers (1905) 191–2.

WOOLHAMPTON

(75) CONGREGATIONAL (SU 574668). Built *c.*1811; church formed 1842. S wall of blue-glazed bricks has two original windows with segmental pointed-arched heads flanking the former entrance; new doorway made in W wall *c.*1890.

Former Congregational chapel, Woodley. (74)

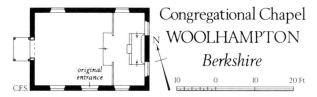

Congregational Chapel
WOOLHAMPTON
Berkshire

Segmental plaster ceiling, altered rostrum pulpit with original shaped back-board. (Demolished *c.*1975)

Summers (1905) 213.

WOOTTON   *Oxfordshire*

(76) Former CONGREGATIONAL (SP 476017). Built 1850, transferred to Wesleyans 1887. Brick with stone dressings, gabled front with pointed-arched openings, later porch.

Summers (1905) 238–9.

The Old Dissent in Cornwall is principally marked by the activities of the Quakers whose earliest dated monument, a rough granite table-tomb of 1677 in their burial-ground at Brea, near Lands End (179), recalls one of the many families of Friends who suffered the sequestration of goods or loss of liberty in defence of their religious scruples. The oldest Friends' meeting-house still remaining in the county, at Marazion (100), was built in 1688, but the most outstanding in situation, design and fittings is 'Come-to-Good' at Kea (76), built early in the following century and retaining all the essentially simple characteristics associated with this denomination.

Presbyterian congregations, commonly developing from the work of ministers ejected in 1662, have left little mark on the county. Although eleven such societies existed in the early 18th century, none now survives in unbroken succession; some were re-founded by Independents in the late 18th century; others failed, perhaps after a period of heterodoxy but without further progressing into the Unitarianism common in other parts of the country. The only early 18th-century Presbyterian meeting-house recorded, at Launceston (53), has been altered almost beyond recognition.

Cornwall is *par excellence* a Methodist county in which the number and prominence of their chapels forms an essential feature of the landscape. The early introduction of Methodism to St Ives, by 1743, its rapid spread and the growth of innumerable societies has been the subject of much local research and publication. Many chapels were rebuilt or enlarged after 1800 and the few remaining 18th-century preaching-houses are generally small, as at Morvah (104) of 1744 or Cubert (48) of 1765, or are fragments incorporated into later buildings as at St Ives (171) of 1784; by contrast, the former chapel in Coinage Hall Street, Helston (75), of 1797 illustrates the needs of a large town congregation by the end of the century. The preaching-pit at Gwennap (16), in use from 1762, is a tangible reminder of the system of open-air preaching adopted by Methodists especially in the earlier years of the movement, although adapted, as were the pits at Newlyn (108) and Indian Queens (154), to a more regular and genteel pattern in the early 19th century.

The continued expansion of Wesleyan Methodism throughout the 19th century and the emergence of new or separatist groups, of which the Bible Christians were the most prominent in Cornwall, led to greatly increased chapel building. The three successive chapels at Illogan Highway (24) typify the growing demands of an expanding population, but smaller buildings, many of which are listed here, proved adequate for country congregations. In most of the major towns large Wesleyan chapels were built in the early 19th century which, although variously transformed later in the century, were seldom replaced; amongst the most notable of these are Truro (213) and St Austell (144).

Although the great differences in size produced equally varied designs, one feature common to many Cornish chapels is the wide-arched entrance with double doors and a fanlight. Examples vary from the plain and almost prison-like front of Goldsithney (124), now demolished, to the comparatively elaborate elevation of Ponsanooth (165). Internal arrangements were more uniform but in many of the larger chapels a communion area was provided behind the pulpit, usually in an apse, in accordance with the precedent set by Wesley's Chapel in City Road, London. No example of this now survives unaltered but many traces remain, and the communion apses in the 1797 chapel at Helston (75) and the 1815 chapel of Carharrack (21), for example, are prominent external features. In the smaller chapels the pulpit is more usually set at the back of a large 'leaders' pew' intended for the use of the Class Leaders, flanked by fixed seating, as at Treen (193), and formerly at St Anthony-in-Meneage (140). Of particular note were the fittings at Mingoose Chapel, St Agnes (136). The use of Gothic details is rare except for the occasional use of lancets or intersecting glazing bars, the Congregational chapel at Tregony (208) and the Wesleyan at Porthkea (82) being examples from the first and second halves of the 19th century. The Romanesque style is seen in Baptist chapels at Helston (74) and Penzance (115), but the pedimented temple front at Truro (211) was more in keeping with Baptist preferences.

Unless otherwise stated, buildings are of local stone, generally granite rubble, and the roofs are covered with slates. Cob is used for walling at 'Come-to-Good' meeting-house (76) and at the Wesleyan chapels at Gwithian (69) and Roseworthy (70), all of which have thatched roofs, and in a few other small early 19th-century chapels. Brick appears in the early 19th century for some window arches, and later in the century for polychrome decoration, but is otherwise noticeably absent from the county.

ALTARNUN

(1) Former METHODIST (SX 224812). A chapel was built in 1795 for a society which had met from *c*.1748 in a cottage at Trewint (SX 221805), known as 'Digory Isbell's cottage', now housing a small collection of Wesleyan memorabilia. The chapel, enlarged or rebuilt in 1836, has a hipped roof. The principal room is raised above storage cellars and approached by an external flight of stone steps. Above the central entrance is a sculptured head of John Wesley in low relief bearing the date 1836, the work of the local

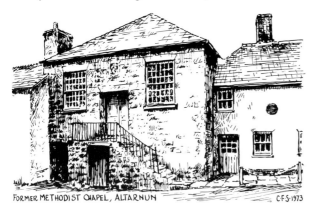

FORMER METHODIST CHAPEL, ALTARNUN   C·F·S·1973

sculptor Nevil Northey Burnard whose birth is commemorated by a plaque on the adjacent cottage. A new Wesleyan chapel was erected nearby in 1859.

Shaw, T., *Trewint, the Story of the Isbell Cottage, Trewint, Altarnun* [*c*.1967].

BLISLAND

(2) Former WESLEYAN (SX 100732), at W end of green, now hotel annexe. Plain rectangle with two altered windows at E end, opposite the entrance. Built 1812 superseding a preaching-house of 1798.

Bible Christian chapel, Blisland.   (3)

(3) BIBLE CHRISTIAN (SX 112736). 'Ebenezer Chapel', dated 1879; gabled front, lancet windows, and pointed-arched doorway with nook shafts. (Derelict 1969)

(4) BIBLE CHRISTIAN, Temple (SX 147734). Polychrome brick arches to openings. Dated 1875. (Disused 1969)

BODMIN BOROUGH

(5) WESLEYAN, Fore Street, Bodmin (SX 069670). Large chapel of stone with rendered dressings, three bays with two tiers of round-arched openings between gabled front wings. Built 1840, drastically altered and enlarged 1885. Interior now floored at gallery level.

BOTUSFLEMING

(6) WESLEYAN (SX 408612). Rendered three-bay front; opened 1854.

BREAGE

(7) FREE METHODIST, Ashton (SW 604287). Half-hipped roof, narrow round-arched windows, end entrance in later porch; dated 1842.

(8) WESLEYAN, Breage (SW 616281). High walls and hipped roof. Wide central doorway with lintel and two windows above with round-arched brick heads and intersecting glazing bars.

Wesleyan chapel, Breage.   (8)

Gwennap Pit, Busveal.   (16)

Gallery around four sides supported by marbled columns, original box-pews in centre. Opened 1833, rostrum pulpit and organ chamber added late 19th century.

(9) WESLEYAN, Carleen (SW 616301). Rendered walls and half-hipped roof, pair of plain doorways and two small pointed-arched windows above; dated 1833.

(10) WESLEYAN, Kenneggy Downs (SW 571292). Date-stone of 1841 reset in front wall of later chapel.

BUDOCK

(11) WESLEYAN, Budock Water (SW 784322). Date-stone of 1843 reset in front wall of 1897 chapel.

CALLINGTON

(12) WESLEYAN, Haye Road (SX 357697). Rendered pedimented front with round-arched upper windows. Built 1845, enlarged and refitted 1868, further accommodation 1872.

CALSTOCK

(13) Former FREE METHODIST, Gunnislake (SX 433716). Hipped roof, brick window arches, mid 19th-century. Now Salvation Army.

(14) BIBLE CHRISTIAN, Harrowbarrow (SX 399701). Rendered walls and hipped roof, three-bay front with tall round-arched windows and circular tablet dated 1842.

CAMBORNE-REDRUTH

(15) Former WESLEYAN, Adjewhella, near Barripper (SW 636387). Three-bay gabled front with round-arched windows; mid 19th-century.

(16) GWENNAP PIT, Busveal (SW 717418). The best preserved of the three Methodist preaching-pits in Cornwall originated as a former mineworking which John Wesley adopted in 1762 as a suitable auditorium. The pit took its present form in 1806 when

Wesleyan chapel, Busveal. (16)

it was reconstructed and surrounded by a stone wall. It is a circular amphitheatre approximately 100 ft in diameter with twelve concentric grass-covered steps for seating and two plain stone pillars marking the preaching place.

The Wesleyan *Busveal Chapel* built in 1836, adjacent to the pit, has a hipped roof and end entrance.

Shaw (1967) 20, 47–8.

(17) WESLEYAN, Chapel Street, Camborne (SW 647400). 'Wesley Chapel', a large building of granite ashlar with rendered sides and roof half-hipped at the front, was built in 1828 and altered in 1911. The front wall of five bays with a three-bay pediment has two tiers of round-arched windows; a central porch with two pairs of Doric columns was extended across the frontage in 1911 to form a loggia of three bays with end vestibules. The interior has a former communion apse behind the pulpit and a gallery around three sides. (Interior reported reseated and altered since 1973)

Wesleyan chapel, Chapel Street, Camborne. (17)

Fittings – *Love-feast cups*: three, white pottery with two handles, one decorated in black and purple with scenes of eastern chariotry, signed 'W. & L. Fenton', two with equestrian scenes. *Monument*: George Smith, author of *History of Wesleyan Methodism* (1857–61), 1868, marble tablet surmounted by obelisk with portrait roundel carved in relief, by Nevil Northey Burnard.

(18) WESLEYAN, Centenary Street, Camborne (SW 652402). 'Centenary Chapel', built in 1839 to supplement the foregoing,

has an elaborately rendered two-stage front of five bays with Corinthian pilasters, pediment and segmental sub-pediment. Prior to 1887 the front was an austere composition with giant pilasters supporting a Doric entablature and pediment and had entrances only in two short flanking wings. The interior has a former communion apse behind the pulpit, altered 1939.

Probert (1966) 8, fig. 13.

Wesleyan Centenary Chapel, Camborne. (18)

(19) Former FREE METHODIST, North Parade, Camborne (SW 651403). Rendered two-stage front with pediment and wide-arched entrance; opened 1860. Alongside to rear, former chapel of the Teetotal Wesleyan Methodist connexion built 1842.

Shaw (1967) 80.

(20) PRIMITIVE METHODIST, Trevenson Street, Camborne (SW 651399). Mid 19th-century, later chapel alongside. (Demolished since 1973)

(21) WESLEYAN, Carharrack (SW 731414). The present building dated 1815 replaces an octagonal chapel of 1768. It has a rendered three-bay front with a pediment and later embellishments. Behind the late 19th-century pulpit is a former shallow communion apse with two tall round-arched windows now cut

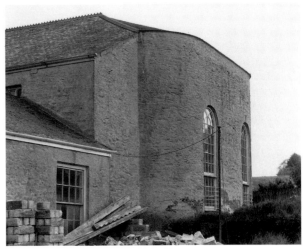

Wesleyan chapel, Carharrack. Apse. (21)

Wesleyan chapel, Carharrack.   (21)

across internally by an organ gallery. Some original seating remains in the galleries.

(22) BIBLE CHRISTIAN, Carharrack (SW 732415). Gabled front with round-arched openings outlined in red and yellow brick. Circular tablet dated July 1883, with altered denominational name, to memory of Billy Bray whose 'Great Deliverance' chapel built 1840 on a more remote site (now farm shed, SW 739417) was the forerunner of the present building. (Later chapel demolished 1988)

   CMHAJ VII pt 4 (1988) 130–2.

(23) WESLEYAN, Forest (SW 684378). Gothic, 1882; Sunday-school to N on site of 1829 chapel.

(24) WESLEYAN, Illogan Highway (SW 679416). Three successive chapels in close proximity: the first of 1809 is a low building concealed behind its larger successor; the second of 1839 has a gabled front with projecting centrepiece; the present chapel alongside was built in 1908.

   Shaw, T., *Methodism in Illogan 1743–1958* (1958).

(25) FREE METHODIST, Chili Road, Illogan Highway (SW 679417). Elaborate three-bay front with Italianate details; dated

Wesleyan chapels, Illogan Highway. From rear.   (24)

Wesleyan chapel, Pool. (30)

Wesleyan chapel, Redruth. (32)

1850 but foundation stones of 1888 indicate a refronting. (Demolished since 1973)

(26) WESLEYAN, Kehelland (SW 622411). Dated 1891; Sunday-school behind with plain gabled front is probably the former chapel of c.1800.

(27) WESLEYAN, Lanner (SW 716399). Built 1828, rebuilt 1844, refronted 1903.

(28) Former BIBLE CHRISTIAN, Lanner (SW 716401). Dated 1866, now village hall.

(29) BIBLE CHRISTIAN, Penponds (SW 635393). Gabled front, two tall round-arched windows with brick heads, entrance at side; dated 1844.

(30) WESLEYAN, Pool (SW 672415). Three-bay front, round-arched windows and three-centred arched doorway; dated 1862. Side walls of three bays, extended to rear.

(31) Former FRIENDS, Church Lane, Redruth (SW 696418). The meeting-house, built c.1814 and now used by The Apostolic Church, has a hipped roof; the N elevation is symmetrical with a central doorway, now blocked, between pairs of large sash windows, all with stone lintels. Uniform round-topped headstones in burial-ground with dates from 1820.

FORMER FRIENDS' MEETING-HOUSE, REDRUTH   CFS 1973

(32) WESLEYAN, Wesley Street, Redruth (SW 701421). 'Wesley Chapel' is a large building of 1826, extended to rear 1867, with a pedimented ashlar front of six bays, round-arched upper windows and a colonnaded porch of four bays with end bays added in the late 19th century.

Dolbey (1964) 145–6, pl.17.

(33) FREE METHODIST, Fore Street, Redruth (SW 700421). A society of the Wesleyan Methodist Association formed in 1838 built a chapel in Fore Street in the following year. This was replaced by a new chapel on the opposite side of the street opened in 1865. The second chapel is a very large Italianate building by T. Simpson of Nottingham with a rendered front of five bays having a giant order of Corinthian columns and pilasters and a balustraded parapet surmounted by urns. (Demolished 1973)

Probert, J. C. C., Fore Street Methodist Church, Redruth (1965).

(34) Former PRIMITIVE METHODIST, Plain-an-Gwarry, Redruth (SW 696425). The elaborate Italianate chapel of 1882 (closed c.1975) stands opposite its early 19th-century predecessor. The latter is a plain building with two tiers of windows and arched former entrance. A gallery with coved front remains around three sides; on the fourth wall are three slate tablets with the Lord's Prayer, creed and decalogue, cut by Amos Nicholls, 1827 (since removed to Memorial Building of 'Wesley Chapel', Redruth).

(35) WESLEYAN, Tuckingmill (SW 661411). Pedimented front of squared stone with rusticated quoins, two tiers of round-arched windows and wide-arched entrance; dated 1843. (Demolished since 1973)

(36) WESLEYAN, Voguebeloth (SW 677434). Pedimented three-bay front with tall round-arched windows and wide doorway with fanlight, dated 1866. Patterned cobbled front path. Seating includes central 'leaders' pew'.

CAMELFORD

(37) Former WESLEYAN, Chapel Street (SX 105837). Rendered gabled front, round-arched doorway and three upper windows; dated 1810. Burial-ground to W with slate headstones and table-tombs. (Converted to secular use since 1973)

(38) FREE METHODIST, Fore Street (SX 106837). Gabled centre and later wings, two-centred arched entrance raised above street level between flanking lancets. Storage cellars below chapel. Opened 1837, enlarged and refitted late 19th century.

(39) BIBLE CHRISTIAN, Victoria Road (SX 109839). Hipped roof, three-bay front with tall rectangular windows, all openings with stone lintels cut with false voussoir joints; opened 1841. 'Bethel' Sunday-school attached, dated 1885.

Free Methodist chapel, Fore Street, Redruth.   (33)

(40) Former WESLEYAN, Helstone (SX 089814). Small chapel, subsequently Bible Christian, with hipped roof and end entrance with lunette tablet above dated 1826. Two pointed-arched windows in each side wall with keystones and intersecting glazing bars; similar pair in end wall flanking the pulpit. Pitchpine pews and late 19th-century rostrum replace original fittings.

Former Wesleyan chapel, Helstone.   (40)

(41) WESLEYAN, Trewalder (SX 074821). The original building of c.1803 at SE end has walls of slatey rubble and a hipped roof. Widened and extended to NW in later 19th century.

CHACEWATER

(42) WESLEYAN, Station Road (SW 750445). Three-bay front, 'Erected 1832, Renovated 1905'.

(43) Former PRIMITIVE METHODIST, East End (SW 751445). Three-bay front with simple pediment and wide round-arched entrance, dated 1830. Brick heads to side windows. (Closed before 1980 and converted to house)

CROWAN

(44) WESLEYAN, Leedstown (SW 605342). Ashlar front of three bays with simple pediment, rusticated quoins, round-arched doorways and windows. Dated 1862.

(45) Former BIBLE CHRISTIAN, Leedstown (SW 607345). Rendered walls, three-bay gabled front with altered entrance. Date-stone 1837 defaced.

(46) WESLEYAN, Praze-an-Beeble (SW 637358). Rendered front with low parapet, bracketed cornice, round-arched upper

WESLEYAN CHAPEL, PRAZE-AN-BEEBLE   CFS 1973

windows and central doorway. Opened 1828, front embellished in late 19th century.

(47) WESLEYAN, Townshend (SW 592330). Gabled front with brick dentil cornice and round-arched brick heads to doorway and two upper windows. Tablet in gable dated 1871. Contemporary round-ended gallery and rostrum painted white and gold. Former chapel opposite, long and low with pointed-arched windows; early 19th-century.

CUBERT

(48) Former METHODIST (SW 787579). The former preaching-house, now a café, was built in 1765 by Joseph Hosken of Carines. The walls are of rubble surmounted by cob and the hipped roof is now covered with asbestos sheeting. A brick porch has been added at the E end. The interior, a plain rectangle (24½ ft by 20½ ft) rounded at one corner, has no early fittings; the original floor is said to have been of lime ash and the pulpit was described as 'about the size of a currant box'.

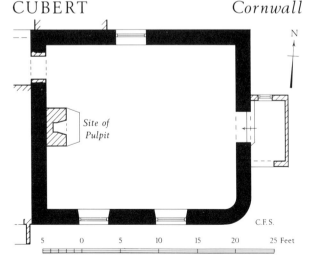

Former Methodist Preaching-house
CUBERT   *Cornwall*

Site of Pulpit

C.F.S.

(49) WESLEYAN (SW 785579). Three-bay gabled front with round-arched windows; built 1848 to replace the foregoing.

CURY

(50) WESLEYAN (SW 682214). Early 19th-century, with gabled three-bay front, three-centred arched doorway and two round-arched upper windows. Present chapel of 1890 adjacent.

DAVIDSTOW

(51) FREE METHODIST, Tremail (SX 163865). Gabled front with large two-centred arch enclosing pointed-arched doorway with rusticated surround and intersecting glazing bars in fanlight; three side windows with similar glazing. Opened 1838.

DULOE

(52) WESLEYAN METHODIST ASSOCIATION (SX 237578). Small chapel built *c*.1840 with slate-hung side wall and plain rendered front. Enlarged by one bay and porch added 1865. Sunday-school adjacent built *c*.1856 on site of a former road.
  Bolitho (1967) 19–20.

DUNHEVED OTHERWISE LAUNCESTON

(53) CASTLE STREET CHAPEL, Launceston (SX 330847). A licence was issued under the 1672 Indulgence to a Presbyterian teacher at Dutson (1 mile NE). A regular congregation was in existence in Launceston by 1694 but this appears to have died out by the late 18th century. A new Congregational cause (latterly 'Independent Evangelical') was commenced following a series of meetings in 1777, and in the following year John Salter or Saltren was licensed to preach in a newly erected house in the suburb of Newport. In 1788 this congregation bought the old Presbyterian meeting-house in Castle Street and altered it for their own use.

CASTLE STREET CHAPEL, LAUNCESTON   CFS 1973

  The meeting-house with rendered rubble walls and a hipped slate roof was built in 1712, but alterations, and particularly external embellishments of the late 19th century, have obscured all earlier details. The front half of the building may date from the early 18th century; it is approximately square and has an E front of three bays with two tiers of round-arched windows and a gable above the middle bay.
  Hyde, K. E., 'The Union Church at Launceston, Cornwall', *BQ* XIV (1951–2) 117–24, 153–60, 203–12, 257–64.

(54) WESLEYAN, Castle Street, Launceston (SX 331847). A Methodist society formed in the mid 18th century opened a preaching-house in Back Lane, now Tower Street, in 1764,

which was rebuilt in 1789 and enlarged in 1796; it was demolished in 1865. The first chapel on the present site was built in 1810, largely rebuilt in 1862 and replaced by the existing building in 1869–70. The latter, in the Gothic style by James Hine and Alfred Norman of Plymouth, has a tower and spire at one corner. (Spire demolished 1984)

Toy, H. S., *The Methodist Church at Launceston* (1964).

(55) BIBLE CHRISTIAN, Tower Street, Launceston (SX 331848). The first chapel, of 1851, with a plain gabled front of rubble with brick dressings, stands alongside its more elaborate Gothic successor of 1897. (Later chapel closed 1975 and demolished; former converted to house)

EGLOSKERRY

(56) WESLEYAN, Tregeare (SX 244867). Opened 1844. Lancet Gothic with two battlemented porches, graduated lancets behind pulpit. No gallery, interior refitted.

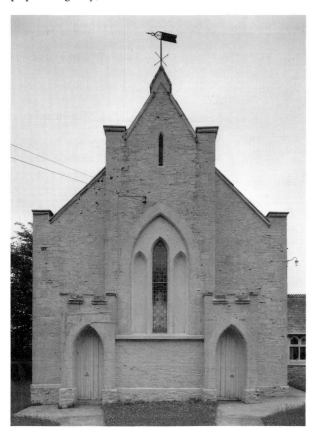

Wesleyan chapel, Tregeare.   (56)

FALMOUTH

(57) Former BAPTIST, Webber Street (SW 807330). Baptist activity in the neighbourhood of Falmouth has been traced to the late 17th century and meeting-houses are known to have existed at Treliever and subsequently at Penryn. Meetings ceased *c.*1741 and were only recommenced in 1769 when the first Baptist meeting-house in Falmouth was opened; a church was formed in 1772 by dismission from Chacewater. After a further closure

*c.*1790–1803, services were resumed and the first chapel on the Webber Street site erected. The chapel was rebuilt *c.*1814–19 after structural failure and continued in use until 1877 when a new chapel was opened in Market Street, itself superseded in 1939 by one at Western Terrace. The Webber Street chapel, which became a Salvation Army hall, was derelict by 1973.

The chapel stands in Saffron Court behind houses on the N side of Webber Street through which it is approached by an arched passage. The walls are rendered. Windows have round-arched heads with intersecting glazing bars. A wide segmental apse at the E end resembles the communion apse of Methodist chapels and may have been designed for a similar purpose. An oval gallery is supported by two fluted Doric columns and by smaller late 19th-century cast-iron columns.

Fereday, L. A., *The Story of the Falmouth Baptists* (1950).

(58) Former FRIENDS, Gylling Street (SW 810325). Meetings commenced in the mid 17th century. The present meeting-house, built in 1873 replacing one of 1803 in New Street, has a steeply pitched slated roof and stone walls with buttresses and lancet windows.

Penney (1907) 24–9.

(59) Former BIBLE CHRISTIAN, Berkeley Vale (SW 806328). The chapel was built in 1867–8 for a society which previously occupied a chapel in Smithick Hill built *c.*1830. In 1956 the combined Methodist societies removed to the reconstructed Wesleyan chapel of 1874–6 standing on the site of a chapel of 1791 in Killigrew Street. The Bible Christian chapel has since been used by a formerly Congregational church (now URC) which previously met in High Street; this church commenced as a Presbyterian society in the late 17th century which was re-formed *c.*1769 following the failure of the original cause. The chapel has a pedimented front with paired entrances and a row of three arched windows above.

Anon., *The People Called Methodists in Falmouth* (1956). Ball (1955) 11.

FEOCK

(60) WESLEYAN, Carnon Downs (SW 800404). Rendered pedimented front of three bays with two tiers of round-arched windows: dated 1825.

FORRABURY AND MINSTER

(61) Former WESLEYAN, Boscastle (SX 100907). The chapel built for Wesleyans by John Rosevear in 1807 was largely rebuilt by Thomas Pope Rosevear *c.*1825 and later transferred to the Wesleyan Methodist Association. In the gabled end wall is a former arched entrance and two upper windows with intersecting glazing bars. In front are two tall round-arched windows; a gablet and corner staircase and entrance-tower were added *c.*1904. Early 19th-century end gallery and rostrum pulpit.

Inscriptions: reset externally, tablets from former chapels: from 'Ebenezer' Wesleyan chapel, 1837; from 'Siloam' Bible Christian chapel, Boscastle, 1859; from Bible Christian chapel at Treworld, 1¼ miles E, 1838.

(62) Former WESLEYAN, Boscastle (SX 099908). Rendered gabled front, much altered; now Post Office. (For date-tablet 1837 *see* (61))

FOWEY

(63) WESLEYAN, Polkerris (SX 093522). Gabled front with lunette, porch later; opened 1850.

GERMOE

(64) WESLEYAN, Balwest (SW 596300). Front to N with simple pediment, round-arched doorway and two upper windows; opened 1829.

GWENNAP

(For Gwennap Pit *see* CAMBORNE-REDRUTH (16))

(65) WESLEYAN, Crofthandy (SW 740424). Dated 1844.

(66) WESLEYAN, Frogpool (SW 760400). Rendered gabled front with arched entrance and two upper windows; dated 1843.

(67) BIBLE CHRISTIAN, Hicks Mill (SW 767411). The chapel, opened in 1821, enlarged in 1824 and later, has a rendered front wall with two tiers of windows and a central entrance not evident in early engravings. The roof is hipped and the plan is nearly square with a polygonal organ-apse added at the rear. Galleries around three sides were inserted in 1861 and a Sunday-school was built alongside at the same date.

Ephemera: in lobby, printed notice dated 1891 warning against annoyance of the congregation.

GWINEAR-GWITHIAN

(68) Former METHODIST, Deveral (SW 592352). The chapel, reputedly opened *c*.1793–4 and claimed (prior to closure *c*.1980) to be the oldest Methodist chapel still in use in Cornwall, is a small low building with rendered walls perhaps partly of cob, originally about 37 ft by 20 ft externally, with a later S porch and a vestry added at the N since 1885. The seating comprises box-pews stepped up slightly to the S in front of which is a space formerly occupied by benches.

CMHAJ IV (1972–5) 151–2.

(69) WESLEYAN, Gwithian (SW 587412). Small chapel (29¾ ft by 20 ft) of rubble topped with cob and a hipped roof covered with straw thatch, built in 1810. Gallery at W end with wide cove below panelled front; seating renewed late 19th century.

Dolbey (1964) 96–7.

Wesleyan chapel, Gwithian.   (69)

(70) Former WESLEYAN, Roseworthy (SW 617397). Small chapel of similar materials to the foregoing, built in 1825. The windows all have semicircular-arched heads; the entrance, originally at the E end, was moved to the S side in the later 19th century and the interior was refitted with stepped seating facing a rostrum. (Rebuilt in facsimile for domestic use 1980)

Shaw (1967) 41.

Wesleyan Chapel at Roseworthy
GWINEAR-GWITHIAN   *Cornwall*

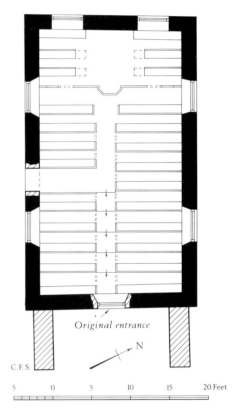

Original entrance

N

C.F.S.

5   0   5   10   15   20 Feet

(71) WESLEYAN, Wall (SW 608368). Three-bay gabled front of squared stone with quoins and two tiers of windows separated by a platband; wide round-arched doorway; circular tablet dated 1829.

HAYLE

(72) WESLEYAN, Chapel Lane, Copperhouse (SW 568378). The first Methodist chapel at Copperhouse was built in 1784. In 1785 John Wesley wrote (Journal, 27 August) 'It is round, and all the walls are brass; that is brazen slags. It seems nothing can destroy this, till heaven and earth pass away.' Its successor of 1815–16 has a rendered front of three bays, much altered in the late 19th century. The interior with a gallery around four sides has a three-centred arch opposite the entrance in front of a shallow apse enclosing the organ at gallery level; the lower part of the apse may have served as a communion area. (Demolished 1973)

(73) Former WESLEYAN, Foundry (SW 559372). Dated 1845. Now in commercial use.

Former Wesleyan chapel, Roseworthy. (70)

HELSTON

(74) Former BAPTIST, Wendron Street (SW 661275). A small chapel built in 1802 for a newly formed congregation was superseded by the present building opened 8 November 1837. The chapel, in the Romanesque style by Philip Sambell, has a gabled front with a central doorway, five-bay arcade above and a small wheel window in the gable. Converted to cinema before 1939.

BM XXX (1838) 29. Ivimey IV (1830) 306.

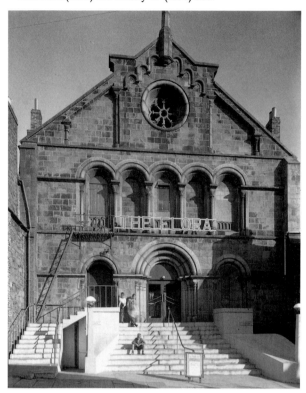

Former Baptist chapel, Wendron Street, Helston.   (74)
Photograph, 1949, by H. Felton.

(75) WESLEYAN, Coinage Hall Street (SW 658274). The present chapel of 1888 stands in front of its predecessor, now converted

Former Wesleyan chapel, Coinage Hall Street,
Helston. From rear.   (75)

for Sunday-school use. The former chapel, registered in December 1797, has two tiers of round-arched windows. The N front of squared stone in five bays is largely concealed by the later building. The S wall has a wide segmental communion apse at the centre. The interior ($52\frac{1}{4}$ ft by $38\frac{3}{4}$ ft) had a gallery around three sides, now floored over.

Probert (1966) 10–11.

KEA

(76) FRIENDS, 'Come-to-Good' (SW 813403). Several Quaker meetings resulted from the visit of George Fox and others to Cornwall in 1656. Friends from the parishes of Kea and Feock met for some years in the house of Walter Stephens in Feock and in the last decade of the 17th century the meeting occupied a rented building. In 1707 a subscription was commenced for building a new meeting-house at Kea and this was completed in 1710 at a cost of £53 8s. 3d. A gallery was added in 1716. In 1967 a wooden porch at the W end was replaced by a larger vestibule.

The meeting-house, opened 13 August 1710, has walls of cob on a stone base and a hipped thatched roof. The original entrance was at the centre of the S side between buttresses forming a rudimentary porch; each side of this are original wooden framed windows of three lights with external shutters. An entrance was made at the W end in the early 19th century and the former doorway altered to a window. At the E end an open thatched linney of the 18th century provided shelter for the horses of members and attenders.

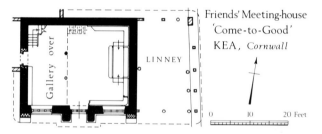

The interior (26 ft by $20\frac{1}{4}$ ft) has an open trussed-rafter roof and simple pine fittings. The W gallery, formerly approached by a staircase against the N wall, now re-sited in the NW corner, has a boarded front with open-balustraded top; it is lit by a window in the W wall. A similar window in the E wall is blocked and covered by the linney. The stand at the E end is short and has a plain boarded front and back, shaped ends and altered arm-rests. Seating in the body of the building comprises tall and slender open-backed benches; backless forms in the gallery include one of the 18th century with moulded edges and shaped supports.

Arnold (1960) 97–9. MS records in County Record Office, Truro. Pallett, H., *et al.*, *Come-to-Good and the Early Quakers in Cornwall* (1968).

(77) Former BIBLE CHRISTIAN, Baldhu (SW 764423). 'Bethel Chapel' built in 1842, now used as a studio, is the successor to a small chapel near Cross Lanes, built by Billy Bray largely through his own efforts. It is square with a three-bay gabled front and round-arched windows.

Bourne (1877) chapter 4.

Friends' meeting-house, 'Come-to-Good'.   (76)

Friends' meeting-house, 'Come-to-Good'. (76)

(78) WESLEYAN, Baldhu (SW 778426). Adjacent to the chapel of 1889 is a low square Sunday-school building with a hipped double roof supported internally by two timber columns; early 19th-century, possibly the former chapel.

(79) Former WESLEYAN, Hugus (SW 774439). Hipped roof, entrance in later porch, two windows at side with altered heads, rear gallery. Opened 1830, refitted late 19th century.

(80) BILLY BRAY'S CHAPEL, Kerley Downs (SW 765437). After completing his chapel near Cross Lanes (77), Billy Bray commenced another for the Bible Christians at Kerley Downs, the trust deed of which is dated 4 July 1835. It was originally a small building with 'three windows, one on one side, and two on the other' which was nicknamed 'three-eyes'. The present chapel, an enlargement or rebuilding of the mid 19th century, is covered with a later rendering and has a rebuilt brick porch at one end. There are three windows in each side wall.

'Billy Bray's Chapel', Kerley Downs.   (80)

The fittings mostly date from the late 19th century but include a *chair* with flat wooden seat inscribed 'BILLY BRAY BALDHU 1839'.

Bourne (1877) chapter 4.

(81) Former WESLEYAN, Penweathers (SW 804438). Hipped roof, end entrance and two round-arched windows in side wall; opened 1842. (Converted to house since 1973)

(82) WESLEYAN, Porthkea (SW 830421). Three-bay gabled front with pointed-arched windows, later porch, and trefoiled tablet dated 1869. Minor rooms below chapel.

KENWYN

(83) WESLEYAN, Shortlanesend (SW 809476). Small three-bay chapel opened 1840. Sunday-school added and entrance altered 1904.

KILKHAMPTON

(84) Former WESLEYAN, Thurdon (SS 287108). Rendered walls and hipped roof, central entrance with two small pointed-arched gallery windows above and tablet dated 1840. Larger similarly arched windows to side walls, all with borders of blue glass in marginal glazing. Original rostrum pulpit with round shafts and trefoiled arches. School-room built 1863. (Closed *c.*1982 and converted to house)

Traditional Homes (April 1988) 28–34.

LADOCK

(85) WESLEYAN (SW 892509). Dated 1816 but altered and refitted in late 19th century.

LANDEWEDNACK

(86) WESLEYAN, Lizard (SW 706125). Three-bay front with pedimented gable and round-arched openings with brick dressings. Two tiers of windows in side walls. Interior with continuous round-ended gallery. Built mid 19th century, possibly enlarged to rear and partly refitted later.

Wesleyan chapel, Lizard.   (86)

LANIVET

(87) Former WESLEYAN (SX 038642). Now shop. Three-bay gabled front with altered entrance and tablet dated 1842. Two windows in each side wall, all with stone lintels.

LAUNCESTON (*see* DUNHEVED OTHERWISE LAUNCESTON)

LEWANNICK

(88) WESLEYAN, Trevadlock Cross (SX 267796). The chapel, dated 1849 on a tablet on the W wall, replaces a building of 1810, the date of which appears on a stone reset above the N porch. Windows have pointed-arched heads and a circular window at the E end has a simple pattern of coloured glass. The pews have dwarf doors.

Monument: in chapel on W wall, John Nanscawen Dawl, 1840, and Grace his wife, 1830, 'two of the founders of this church', *et al.*, late 19th-century. Wesleyan School, 1846, adjacent.

LINKINHORNE

(89) WESLEYAN, Rilla Mill (SX 297734). The chapel, opened 1846, has N and S entrances and lancet windows; the E end, altered by the addition of a chancel, is gabled and has angle buttresses with pinnacles. Transeptal Sunday-school wing at W end added in late 19th century.

LISKEARD

(90) WESLEYAN, Dobwalls (SX 216651). Opened 1859, extended 1889.

(91) BIBLE CHRISTIAN, Trewidland (SX 256599). Gabled front with segmental-arched entrance; built 1835, restored 1880.

LISKEARD BOROUGH

(92) WESLEYAN METHODIST ASSOCIATION, Greenbank (SX 252647). The chapel, built in 1838 on the proceeds of the sale of £1 shares, has a rendered pedimented front of three bays. It was considerably altered internally in 1875 and the front partly obscured by a porch and flanking wings added in 1925.

Bolitho (1967) 16–19, 49, 51. Shaw (1967) 39.

(93) WESLEYAN, Barn Street (SX 251643). The chapel built in 1846 replaced one of 1841 which had been destroyed by fire. It was enlarged in 1862 and further altered and refitted in 1907.

Bolitho (1967) 22–3, 44.

LUDGVAN

(94) WESLEYAN, Crowlas (SW 516333). Three-bay front with two tiers of round-arched windows, later rendering; hipped roof. Opened 1834.

(95) Former PRIMITIVE METHODIST, Nancledra Hill (SW 495353). Long, low front with porch and three windows; dated 1855.

(96) PRIMITIVE METHODIST, Ninnes Bridge (SW 514359). Small three-bay chapel with round-arched openings; dated 1873.

Slater, P. E., *History of the St Ives Fore Street Methodist Church* (1962) 38–40.

LUXULYAN

(97) BIBLE CHRISTIAN, Innis (SX 026622). The small and remote chapel stands on the site of a *Friends' burial-ground* which was given to William O'Bryan in 1819. The chapel, rebuilt in 1846, has rendered walls and a gabled front with later E porch; there are two sash windows in the S wall and one smaller window opposite. Original fittings include large pulpit at W end with leaders' seats in front and open-backed benches.

Monuments: in burial-ground S of chapel, slate headstones (1) George Romery, 1843, and Mary his wife, 1840; (2) William Allen of Little Torrington, Devon, itinerant Class and Prayer Leader, 1845; (3) Thomasine, mother of William O'Bryan, 1821, signed 'Edgcombe, Truro'.

Bourne (1905) 70–1.

MADRON

(98) WESLEYAN, Little Bosullow (SW 417340). Front with dressed quoins, three-centred arched doorway with blind fanlight, two round-arched upper windows with intersecting glazing bars, and tablet dated 1845. Two sash windows with lintels in each side wall. Original gallery at entrance supported by two Roman Doric columns; lower seating includes plain benches with added backs, box-pews in gallery.

MAKER-WITH-RAME

(99) CONGREGATIONAL, Garrett Street, Cawsand (SX 435504). The chapel, built for a church formed in 1793, was much altered in the later 19th century and any early work is concealed. It stands on a sloping site and has Sunday-school rooms beneath.

Monuments: in chapel, on E wall (1) William Rowe, 1848, 'founder of the first Sabbath-day School in this place'; (2) Rev. George Moase, pastor, 1856.

MARAZION

(100) FRIENDS (SW 518307). George Fox passed through Market Jew (Marazion) in 1655 prior to his imprisonment in Launceston Gaol. Support for his views increased in the late 17th century and from 1679 a regular meeting was held at the house of John Taylor. In 1687 Taylor gave the site of the present meeting-house which was opened in 1688. Repairs carried out in 1742 appear to have involved the partial rebuilding of the gable wall and one of the sides. Meetings ceased in 1842 and in 1879 the meeting-house was in a serious state of decay; a proposal to demolish the building resulted in an offer to repair it at private expense and this work, including a new roof, was commenced in 1880. Meetings resumed in 1918.

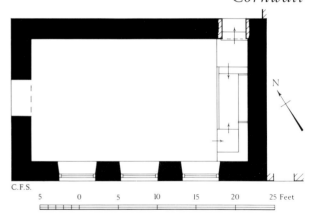

Friends' Meeting-house, MARAZION
Cornwall

The meeting-house has coarsely pointed rubble walls; the roof is gabled at the NW end but the SE end is hipped. The entrance has an 18th-century door-frame with later door, and a flat canopy supported by shaped brackets. Three windows low in the SW wall have external shutters and hung sashes; the woodwork of the centre window has been renewed. The interior (27¾ ft by 15¼ ft) has an original stand at the SE end with shaped flat balusters and square newels with knob finials.

MAWGAN-IN-MENEAGE

(101) WESLEYAN, Garras (SW 703239). Early 19th-century chapel with unusual bowed front with four-centred arched doorway and window above; galleried interior with some original seating and railed 'leaders' pew' in front of late 19th-century pulpit. Former

Friends' meeting-house, Marazion.   (100)

Wesleyan chapel, Garras, Mawgan-in-Meneage.   (101)

chapel 50 yards N with low rubble walls and altered roof, late 18th-century.

MAWNAN

(102) WESLEYAN, Carwinion Road, Mawnan Smith (SW 779287). Front of squared rubble with pedimented centre and three round-arched upper windows. Opened 1848.

MICHAELSTOW

(103) BIBLE CHRISTIAN, Treveighan (SX 075795). Low walls and hipped roof, end wall with tablet dated 1828 and later porch; windows with later brick surrounds.

MORVAH

(104) Former METHODIST (SW 402354). The original preaching-house built in 1744 is a small building (24 ft by 33 ft externally) with low rubble walls and a roof formerly half-hipped and thatched; the entrance and two principal windows face south west. A later Wesleyan chapel, also disused, which superseded it in 1866 adjoins at the S corner.

Communion Cup: (in private possession, 1969) small lustreware cup, early 19th-century.

(105) Former BIBLE CHRISTIAN (SW 403354). Altered gabled front of three bays with round-arched windows; early 19th-century with date-tablet replaced 1882 on conversion to Board School. Now used for storage.

MORWENSTOW

(106) Former WESLEYAN, Woolley (SS 253167). Broad three-bay front with pointed-arched windows and gabled porch; opened *c.*1822. Sunday-school later. (Closed 1971 and converted to house)

MYLOR

(107) WESLEYAN, Kersey Road, Flushing (SW 809340).

Rendered gabled front of three bays with round-arched windows, date 1816 painted in roundel above entrance.

NEWLYN

(108) METHODIST PREACHING-PIT, Newlyn East (SW 824563). Circular auditorium with stepped earth sides and preaching platform to E, early 19th-century. A small building close to the N entrance has a stone tablet dated 1852 set in the adjacent ground.

(109) WESLEYAN, Newlyn East (SW 827563). The chapel, superseded in 1883 but reopened since 1973, was built in 1832. Originally of three bays, with a central entrance on the S side and windows with round-arched brick heads, it was subsequently enlarged to the W and two new entrances, since replaced by a porch, made at the E end.

NEWQUAY

(110) Former FREE METHODIST, St Columb Minor (SW 837620). Small chapel with two round-arched windows to road, mid 19th-century. (Converted to house since 1973)

(111) Former WESLEYAN, St Columb Minor (SW 838622). Gabled three-bay front with central rectangular recess enclosing round-arched doorway with fanlight and upper window. Date-tablet 'WMC 1850' in gable. Segmental boundary wall at front with stone gate piers and original cast-iron railings.

NORTH HILL

(112) WESLEYAN, Coad's Green (SX 295768). The chapel, opened in 1849, is of three bays with lancet windows; it was extended to W and refitted in late 19th century.

Monuments: in chapel (1) William Stevens Keast, 1850; in burial-ground (2) Richard and Isaac Bowden, 1833; (3) Joseph Jenkin, 1834, slate headstone, signed 'E. Wadge'; also many other later headstones of slate, some with traces of gilding and colour.

(113) WESLEYAN, North Hill (SX 271765). Three-bay front with round-arched windows and later porch; hipped roof. Tablet above porch dated 1810.

PADSTOW URBAN

(114) WESLEYAN, Church Lane, Padstow (SW 916754). Large chapel with altered gabled front and two tiers of round-arched windows; built 1827, enlarged 1906. (Demolished since 1973)

PENZANCE

(115) BAPTIST, Clarence Street (SW 471303). The church formed in 1802 first met in the 'Octagon Tabernacle' in South Parade which had been built *c*.1778 or 1788 by seceders from the Old Meeting (*see* (116)). The present chapel of 1836, by P. Sambell of Truro, has a gabled front rendered in stucco with Romanesque chevron and zig-zag enrichment to round-arched openings and a blind wheel window below the apex of the gable.

(116) Former CONGREGATIONAL, Market Jew Street (SW 475305). The Old Meeting, originally Presbyterian, traced its origins to Joseph Sherwood who was ejected from the vicarage of St Hilary in 1662. A meeting-house built on the present site in 1707 was rebuilt in 1807–8 and again renewed in 1870–1. This last had a gabled front of three bays with rusticated quoins and

dressings to two tiers of round-arched windows and was surmounted by a small bell-cote. The front wall was demolished *c*.1970 on conversion to a supermarket but the side and rear walls remain.

Ball (1955) 8. Sime, A. H. M., *Penzance Congregational Church, 1662–1936* (1936).

(117) WESLEYAN, Chapel Street (SW 474301). The chapel, built in 1814, was refronted and refitted in 1864. The front wall of squared granite has a columned loggia between pavilions, two wide round-arched doorways with fanlights, seven round-arched upper windows with Venetian-traceried frames, and a panelled parapet. The back wall has wide rounded corners enclosing a communion area in which the communion table flanked by tables of creed, decalogue and Lord's Prayer was, prior to 1964, fronted by a central pulpit and reading desk. A continuous gallery is supported by wooden columns with moulded capitals.

Baptist chapel, Clarence Street, Penzance. (115)

Inscription: reset above rear doorway to adjacent hall, granite tablet with initials and date 'R D 1602'. *Monuments*: in chapel (1) William Carne, 1836, with later inscription to Joseph Carne, 1865; (2) Rev. Richard Treffry, jun., 1838; (3) Rev. Samuel Symons, Wesleyan missionary, 1844; (4) Rev. John Reynolds, 1854.

Probert (1966) 8–9. Shaw (1967) 68.

(118) WESLEYAN, Chapel Street, Mousehole (SW 468262). The first chapel, built 1783–4 and enlarged 1813–14, was replaced by the present building in 1833. It was drastically altered 1898–1905 and the exterior rendered, but the three-bay entrance front with wide central doorway and two tiers of round-arched windows retains the principal elements of the early 19th-century design.

Beckerlegge, J. J., *Two Hundred Years of Methodism in Mousehole* (1954).

Wesleyan chapel, Chapel Street, Penzance.   (117)

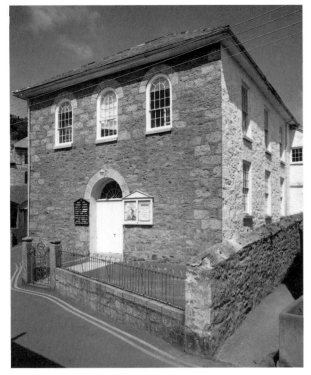

Free Methodist chapel, 'Mount Zion', Mousehole. (119)

(119) FREE METHODIST, Mousehole (SW 469266). The chapel, built in 1844 and subsequently named 'Mount Zion', has a hipped roof, walls of three bays with two tiers of sash windows in each side and a wide round-arched central entrance.

    Beckerlegge, op. cit. 5, 16.

(120) WESLEYAN, Newlyn (SW 462288). Large chapel of 1834, enlarged 1866, with hipped roof and front of three bays with

Wesleyan chapel, Newlyn. (120)

Wesleyan chapel, Newlyn. Interior before 1950. (120)

round-arched upper windows, wide central entrance with fanlight and columned porch and two smaller doorways perhaps originally windows. Interior with continuous round-ended gallery and original seating has remains of former communion area behind late 19th-century pulpit. Communion rails re-sited in front of pulpit c.1950.

    Communion Table: behind pulpit, early 19th-century.

    Probert (1966) 11–12.

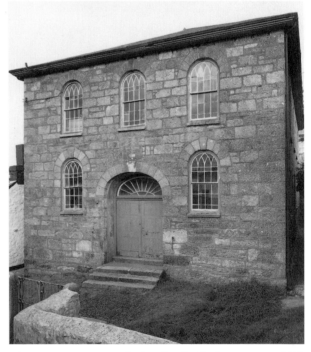

'Ebenezer' Primitive Methodist chapel, Newlyn. (121)

(121) PRIMITIVE METHODIST, Boase Street, Newlyn (SW 463285). 'Ebenezer Chapel', built 1835 and partly superseded in 1927 by 'Centenary Chapel', Gwavas Road, has a hipped roof and three-bay front with wide three-centred arched entrance and two tiers of round-arched windows. (Reported sold 1984)

Bible Christian chapel, Tredavoe.   (123)

(122) Former TEETOTAL METHODIST, Sheffield (SW 458268). The former chapel built *c.*1845 was transferred to the Methodist New Connexion in 1860, and later to the Wesleyans for whom it eventually served as a school; it adjoins the disused Wesleyan chapel of 1908. The walls are of large blocks of granite rubble with two windows at the front and a later tablet above the doorway inscribed 'WESLEYAN SCHOOL...'.

(123) BIBLE CHRISTIAN, Tredavoe (SW 453285). Small remotely sited chapel with gabled front, rustic quoins and blind upper window; pedimented porch with two-centred arched entrance. Dated 1844, and named 'Jehovah-Jireh' in a Hebrew inscription on upper window cill. Interior with box-pews, railed rostrum pulpit and 'leaders' pew'. Small communion table with turned legs, *c.*1844.

PERRANUTHNOE

(124) WESLEYAN, Goldsithney (SW 546307). Plain rectangular front of squared stone and hipped slate roof, opened 1841. Central round-arched entrance with double doors and fanlight, and three round-arched upper windows. Side walls of three bays with two windows; extended to rear. (Demolished May 1984 and a new chapel erected on site)

(125) Former BIBLE CHRISTIAN, Rosudgeon Common (SW 556295). Broad three-bay front with round-arched entrance and sash windows; half-hipped roof. Dated 1858, superseded by new chapel 1904 and later used as Sunday-school. (Derelict 1985)

Wesleyan chapel, Goldsithney.   (124)

PERRANZABULOE

(126) Former WESLEYAN, Perranwell (SW 777527). Double-gabled front dated 1867; cobbled entrance-court with pattern of hearts. (Closed 1987)

(127) WESLEYAN, Rose (SW 777549). Three-bay front with simple pediment and round-arched openings; dated 1865 but perhaps incorporating part of the structure of a chapel of 1839. Refitted late 19th century.

POUNDSTOCK

(128) Former WESLEYAN METHODIST ASSOCIATION, Bangors (SX 208995). Rendered walls and hipped slate roof; tablet in E wall inscribed 'Methodist Free Church 1840'. Two pointed-arched windows in longer N and S sides with wooden Y-tracery and coloured glass in marginal lights. (Converted to house 1987)

PROBUS

(129) Former WESLEYAN (SW 899479). The chapel dated 1825 was converted in that year from a malthouse, replacing a preaching-house of 1788 elsewhere in the village. It was further altered and refitted in the late 19th century and a gable added to the front wall in 1889. The walls are rendered; the W front is of three bays with two tiers of pointed-arched windows and doorway off-centre in the middle bay. (Converted to sale room *c*.1975 and adjacent schoolroom of 1866 fitted as chapel)

Shaw, T., *Methodism in Probus, 1781–1961* (1961).

(130) Former BIBLE CHRISTIAN (SW 900478). Small chapel on E side of High Street, formerly Back Lane, built 1822; walls of rubble and cob with plain gabled front and altered entrance. Now a workshop.

Shaw, op. cit. 22–5, 39–41.

(131) WESLEYAN, Tresillian (SW 869466). Gabled front with four-centred arched entrance; two pointed-arched windows in each side wall with brick arched heads. Opened 1831.

QUETHIOCK

(132) BIBLE CHRISTIAN, Blunts (SX 344629). 'Salem Chapel', dated 1843, was transferred to the Wesleyans *c*.1888. Central doorway replaced by window and date-stone reset below in late 19th century.

(133) WESLEYAN, Quethiock (SX 314648). Rendered walls and half-hipped roof. Opened 1839, two-storeyed porch added and chapel refitted in late 19th century.

ROCHE

(134) WESLEYAN, Chapel Road (SW 989603). Three-bay gabled front with two tiers of round-arched windows; built 1835 but renovated and date-tablet renewed 1877.

ST AGNES

(135) Former WESLEYAN, Blackwater (SW 736462). The chapel, built gradually 1820–4, has a hipped roof and brick arches to the central doorway and to two round-arched upper windows. The date 1822 appears on a tablet of the late 19th century, at which period the interior was partly refitted.

Gallery: from former preaching-house, Kenwyn Street, Truro, early 19th-century. *Paving*: in front of chapel, cobbled path widening to a patterned semicircle. *Plate*: includes a pair of lustreware communion cups with simple leaf engraving. (Chapel sold for commercial use *c*.1984)

Shaw (1967) 40.

(136) Former WESLEYAN, Mingoose (SW 710488). Prior to its conversion to a cottage *c*.1970, this was an exceptionally fine example of a country chapel retaining an almost complete set of original fittings. The chapel, which may have superseded an earlier building nearby, was erected in 1851. The exterior is plain

Former Wesleyan chapel, Blackwater. (135)

Former Wesleyan chapel, Mingoose, St Agnes. (136)

with a hipped roof, round-arched windows with intersecting glazing bars and a wide central entrance with semicircular fanlight. The interior has a flat plaster ceiling with ornamental ceiling rose.

Fittings – *Clock*: above internal lobby, signed 'Walter Letcher, St Agness'. *Hat Rails*: with wooden pegs, carried across side

Former Wesleyan chapel, Mingoose, St Agnes.   (136)

Mingoose Chapel, ST AGNES, *Cornwall*

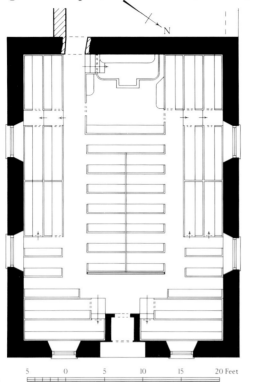

C.F.S.

5   0   5   10   15   20 Feet

windows. *Pulpit*: rostrum with panelled centre and balustraded sides, supported on four dwarf marbled columns. *Seating*: 'Leaders' pew' in front of pulpit, box-pews at sides and rear, and in the central area open-backed benches with shaped ends divided by a rail along the main axis of the building.

(137) WESLEYAN, Mithian (SW 746503). Square, with half-hipped tiled roof and round-arched windows with brick heads. Opened 1800 but entirely refitted in late 19th century. The front originally had a central entrance and two upper windows.

(138) WESLEYAN, Mount Hawke (SW 715475). Opened 1820, altered 1906.

(139) WESLEYAN, Porthtowan (SW 693470). A society formed in the late 18th century, and which numbered amongst its members the eccentric itinerant preacher 'Foolish Dick' (Richard Hampton), built a small chapel in 1820, superseded by a larger building in 1841. The former, which became the Sunday-school, is a low building with half-hipped roof; its successor which stands alongside has a gabled front with central doorway and window over, with three-centred arched heads. (Second chapel demolished 1978, replaced 1980 by new chapel N of the first)

Methodist Recorder (29 May 1980). Shaw (1967) 37, 56–8.

ST ANTHONY-IN-MENEAGE

(140) BIBLE CHRISTIAN (SW 780247). Small chapel with half-hipped roof, built 1829, has one round-arched window with brick dressings facing the road, two windows opposite in the N wall and two flanking the pulpit. The fittings are typical of this

Bible Christian chapel, St Anthony-in-Meneage.   (140)

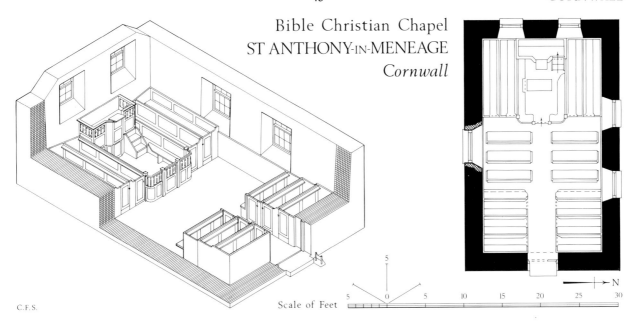

Bible Christian Chapel
ST ANTHONY-IN-MENEAGE
Cornwall

C.F.S.   Scale of Feet

period with box-pews alongside the entrance, open-backed benches in the space in front, and a 'leaders' pew' with further box-pews flanking it. The rostrum pulpit is of slightly later date. (Chapel closed and sold for conversion to cottage 1973)

ST AUSTELL URBAN

(141) BAPTIST, West Hill (SX 012524). The chapel by F. C. Jury of St Austell, dated 1899, stands alongside its *c*.1833 predecessor, a small gabled building with rendered walls and round-arched front windows, now in commercial use.

    B. Hbk (1903) 391.

(142) CONGREGATIONAL, Victoria Place (SX 014524). Rendered front of three bays, the upper part (altered 1969–73) previously had vermiculated quoins, gabled centre with date 1850 in plaster cartouche, cross finial and moulded parapets to side openings.

    Ball (1955) 27.

(143) FRIENDS, High Cross Street (SX 015525). The meeting-house dated 1829 replaced buildings of 1788 and *c*.1690 on other sites. The roof is hipped and the long front wall of ashlar has four plain sash windows; entrance at one end directly into the smaller of two meeting-rooms which are separated by a passage with screen walls of vertically sliding shutters.

Friends' meeting-house, St Austell.   (143)

Monuments: small headstones reset from burial-ground at Tregongeeves (about 1½ miles SSW) include Daniell Eliot, 1711, and many of 19th-century date.

    Hodgkin, L. V. (Mrs Holdsworth), *A Quaker Saint in Cornwall* (1927) 172–8.

(144) WESLEYAN, Bodmin Road (SX 012526). Large chapel, now 'St John's', with five-bay front, prominent end bays, and two tiers of windows, was built in 1828 and altered mainly internally in 1892. The porch, surround to central upper window and small raised pediment to the centre bay appear to be additions.

Wesleyan chapel, Bodmin Road, St Austell.   (144)

(145) BIBLE CHRISTIAN, Bethel (SX 035530). Services commenced in 1819 and were held for a time in 'Will Allen's Barn', a small building described as 'tied to the hedge with straw ropes to keep it from being blown away by the wind'. The first chapel, built in 1822, 50 yards W of its successor and now converted to two cottages, has low walls and a hipped roof. The second

chapel, built 1836 and enlarged to W 1862, has a gabled front of three bays with two tiers of round-arched windows.

Uren, C., *The Bethel Methodists (St Austell) 1819–1969* (1969).

(146) WESLEYAN, Charlestown (SX 038518). Pedimented W front of ashlar in three bays with two tiers of round-arched windows and open porch with Roman Doric columns. Dated 1827.

(147) WESLEYAN, St Blazey Gate (SX 061537). 'Leek Seed Chapel' built 1824, altered 1903, has a hipped roof partly concealed at the front by an added parapet and small gable. The W front is of three bays with two tiers of windows, the upper windows round-arched, and a central entrance with open porch. The name derives from William Stephens's action in preserving the building fund from thieves by threatening to ignite a heap of leek seed under pretence of its being gunpowder.

Monument: NW of chapel, to William Stephens, 1822, and Mary his wife, 1816, granite and slate table-tomb, signed 'Isbell, Truro'.

Shaw (1967) 19.

(148) Former BIBLE CHRISTIAN, St Blazey Gate (SX 059536). Inscribed 'Ebenezer Bible Christian Chapel Built by R. Tyzzer 1842'; three round-arched windows in front wall with intersecting glazing bars. Near W corner a rectangular plaster panel forms a simple noticeboard.

ST BURYAN

(149) WESLEYAN (SW 410258). Three-bay gabled front with round-arched windows; front rendered and upper windows altered in late 19th century. Opened 1833. (Rebuilt 1980–1)

ST CLEER

(150) BIBLE CHRISTIAN, Hocking's House (SX 243682). Chapel of almost square plan with hipped roof, front and rear walls respectively rendered and slate hung. Three-bay front with rusticated granite quoins to round-arched openings and shaped tablet above entrance dated 1846. Gallery around three sides; box-pews against side walls face inwards, large 'leaders' pew' in front of later pulpit. In front of chapel is a small burial-ground and a detached Sunday-school with stable below dated 1870.

Miscellaneous: in NE boundary wall, granite block dated 1812 from a former, possible Bryanite, chapel at Redgate (SX 2268).

Bolitho (1967) 13.

Bible Christian chapel, Hocking's House.   (150)

(151) WESLEYAN REFORM, Tremar Coombe (SX 254688). Three-bay front with rusticated granite quoins and brick dressings; hipped roof. Dated 1863.

ST COLUMB MAJOR

(152) Former CONGREGATIONAL, Fore Street (SW 913635). The chapel, originally built about 1795 for a church formed in that year, was subsequently enlarged and appears to date principally from the early 19th century. It was closed in 1939 and has since been used as a workshop. The building, set back behind others on the E side of the street, has a hipped roof, the front wall has dressed stone quoins, a central entrance and three upper windows all round-arched, and three windows in each side wall. An E gallery has been removed.

Ball (1955) 18–19.

(153) Former BIBLE CHRISTIAN, Fore Street (SW 912635). Behind other buildings on W side of street, rendered front and hipped roof, pointed-arched entrance and paired lancets above, with tablet N of doorway dated 1812.

(154) METHODIST PREACHING-PIT, Indian Queens (SW 918587). Large circular auditorium with stepped earth sides and platform of rubble and turf to SW, known from 1850 as 'Queens Sunday-school Amphitheatre'.

(155) FREE METHODIST, Indian Queens (SW 917587). Alongside 'Immanuel Chapel' of 1876 is a former early 19th-century chapel with hipped roof and narrow round-arched entrance.

(156) BIBLE CHRISTIAN, Talskiddy (SW 913654). Small chapel with rendered walls and half-hipped roof; opened 23 November 1834.

ST ENDELLION

(157) WESLEYAN METHODIST ASSOCIATION, Port Isaac (SW 996807). The former chapel at Roscarrock Hill, built 1837, is of three bays and has a hipped roof with small bell-cote at the front. The principal entrance is raised above a basement doorway and flanked by two tiers of round-arched windows with intersecting glazing bars. Larger chapel built alongside in 1869.

Probert (1966) 16, 25. Shaw (1967) 41, 83.

ST ENODER

(158) Former BIBLE CHRISTIAN, Summercourt (SW 890560). Low building with walls of cob on granite rubble, built *c*.1800 and enlarged to E in early 19th century.

ST ERME

(159) WESLEYAN, Trispen (SW 843503). Hipped roof; three-bay front with central round-arched doorway with fanlight and two upper windows, all with brick arched heads. Opened 1846.

ST ERTH

(160) WESLEYAN (SW 550352). Rendered walls, three-bay gabled front; built 1826–7, much altered *c*.1900.

Probert (1966) 13.

ST ERVAN

(161) BIBLE CHRISTIAN, Penrose (SW 876707). Small three-bay chapel dated 1861.

(162) Former WESLEYAN, Rumford (SW 897702). Small early

19th-century chapel with hipped roof; slight front extension, slate-hung with pointed-arched openings; now Women's Institute Hall. Present chapel to N, 1907.

ST EVAL

(163) FREE METHODIST, Tregona (SW 859699). Small chapel with cob walls on a rubble plinth, later slate hanging, and hipped roof; opened 1838. Narrow entrance to W and two windows on N and S sides. Original seating with shaped ends, and 'leaders' pew' in front of later rostrum.

ST GENNYS

(164) FREE METHODIST, Brockhill (SX 151960). Built 1842, enlarged to E and porch added late 19th century. Cobbled forecourt with linear pattern in white pebbles.

ST GLUVIAS

(165) WESLEYAN, Chapel Hill, Ponsanooth (SW 757377). Large chapel of squared granite, built 1843; truncated pediment with shaped apex, prominent centre bay with rusticated surround to arched entrance. Prior to late 19th-century alterations there was a tall box-pulpit and a communion apse behind it with a small circular window above the communion table.

Probert (1966) 10. Shaw (1967) 72.

Wesleyan chapel, Ponsanooth.   (165)

ST GORAN

(166) CONGREGATIONAL, Gorran Haven (SX 013417). Small chapel converted from former fish store 1812, rebuilt or refurbished 1864.

Ball (1955) 28. CYB (1865) 312. Roberts, J. K., The Mevagissey Independents, 1625–1946 (1946) 23.

(167) WESLEYAN, Gorran Haven (SX 011415). Small chapel with half-hipped roof, pointed-arched windows and end entrance. Opened 1830, refitted.

(168) Former WESLEYAN, High Lanes (SW 988431). Gabled front, round-arched windows. Opened 1817, enlarged and refitted c.1879.

ST HILARY

(169) WESLEYAN, Halamanning (SW 560309). Plain rendered walls and half-hipped roof, opened 1854. Contemporary fittings of box-pews, open-backed benches and 'leaders' pew' in front of balustraded rostrum pulpit.

ST IVES

(170) COUNTESS OF HUNTINGDON'S CHAPEL, Fore Street (SW 517407). A Presbyterian congregation which met in St Ives until c.1770 originated in the preaching of Joseph Sherwood who had been ejected in 1662 from the vicarage of St Hilary. The present congregation, claiming the same descent, was formed in 1804 by Robert McAll, formerly a student from Trevecka College. The chapel, reported in the 1851 census as erected in 1824, has a gabled front with three-centred arched entrance and fanlight and two round-arched upper windows. The rebuilt apex of the gable and shaped barge-boards indicate a late 19th-century renovation.

Ball (1955) 9–10.

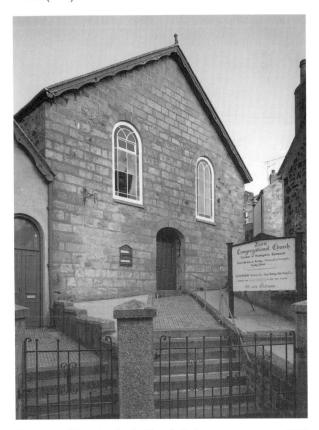

Countess of Huntingdon's Chapel, St Ives.   (170)

(171) METHODIST, Street-an-Garrow (SW 516404). The first Methodist society in Cornwall was in existence by 1743; the present chapel of 1784 faces the site of the house of John Nance where John Wesley stayed during his earliest visits. The chapel was much enlarged in the early 19th century and only parts of the front wall remain visible of the original structure. The N front is of rubble, coursed to the E but random to the W, each half having a three-centred arched entrance with fanlight, a simple

Methodist chapel, Street-an-Garrow, St Ives. (171)

Venetian window above and a third round-arched window between. The S wall facing Chapel Street is rendered and divided into three parts by plain pilasters with the name 'Wesleyan Chapel' on a central pedimented panel in the parapet. The S and W sides have two tiers of windows, the upper ranges of four and five respectively have semicircular-arched heads.

The 'Wesleyan Schools' E of the chapel, dated 1845, have a S front of squared granite in five bays with a three-bay pediment.

(172) BIBLE CHRISTIAN, St Peter Street (SW 519409). Built 1824, greatly enlarged and dated 1858; hipped roof, three-bay front with round-arched doorway and windows with keystones.

(173) PRIMITIVE METHODIST, Fore Street (SW 518408). 'Ebenezer' chapel was built in 1831 for a society which originated in 1829. It has a hipped roof; the front wall, now rendered, is of three bays with a central three-centred arched entrance and three round-arched upper windows. Galleried interior with some original fittings.

Drawings: charcoal sketches by W. H. Y. Titcomb for paintings, including 'Primitive Methodists at prayer' which illustrates the chapel interior, late-19th century. *Love-feast cups*: set of four, one now in Digory Isbell's cottage, Trewint, with two handles, of white glazed pottery inscribed in black with chapel name and 'Missioned June 15th 1829'.

Slater, P. E., *History of the St Ives Fore Street Methodist Church* (1962).

(174) WESLEYAN, Halse Town (SW 508387). The front, dated 1833, is partly concealed by later vestry wings. Central entrance with lintel and two brick-arched upper windows. (Closed *c*.1975)

WESLEYAN CHAPEL, HALSE TOWN CFS 1973

(175) Former METHODIST NEW CONNEXION, Halse Town (SW 504388). Three-bay front with later brick bell-cote, gabled ends with ball finials, mid 19th-century.

(176) WESLEYAN, Hellesveor (SW 503398). The former chapel has low walls of coursed granite, half-hipped roof and end entrance; large painted inscription 'Hellesveor 1844'. The present chapel of 1937 adjacent to it formerly stood at Trezelah, Madron (SW 477339).

(177) Former WESLEYAN, Lelant (SW 543368). Three-bay front of squared granite with two tiers of round-arched openings, panelled parapet and truncated pediment with tablet dated 1834. Above the pediment is a later square clock chamber and octagonal wooden bell-cote. A circular blocking in the parapet indicates the former position of a clockface. (Converted to secular use, interior gutted and bell-cote removed)

Probert (1966) 18, 25.

(178) Former PRIMITIVE METHODIST, Lelant (SW 545371). Built 1859, closed 1909. Now Village Hall.

ST JUST

(179) FRIENDS' BURIAL-GROUND, Brea (SW 376273). Rectangular enclosure surrounded by a low rubble wall; blocked gateway on SW side with chamfered jambs. A modern tablet records that the ground was used for 36 interments between 1659 and 1789.

Monument: in N corner, granite slab 2 ft 2 in. by 5 ft 7 in. and about 1 ft 2 in. deep supported at ends by roughly shaped granite blocks; upper surface inscribed in large capitals 'HEARE·IS· BVRIED·THAT·VIRTIOVS·WOMAN·PHILLIP·THE· WIFE·OF·JOHN·ELLIS·WHO·DEPARTED·THIS·LIFE· THE·XX·DAY·OF·THE·X·MONTH·*1677*' – John Ellis and his family were notable Quaker sufferers during the Commonwealth and Restoration.

Penney (1928) *passim*.

(180) WESLEYAN, Chapel Road (SW 369316). The large chapel (78 ft by 56 ft) facing one end of Chapel Street was built in 1833, enlarged and reseated in 1860, and further altered in 1893. The E front of granite ashlar, perhaps altered in 1860, has a wide columned porch enclosing two round-arched doorways; the original date-stone is reset in the pavement of the porch. The interior has a continuous round-ended gallery with box-pews and later seating below. At the W end behind the rostrum pulpit is a rectangular former communion area (7¾ ft by 22½ ft) with a circular window behind the site of the communion table and

Former Wesleyan chapel, Lelant, St Ives.　　　　　　　　　　　　　　　　　　(177)

Wesleyan chapel, Chapel Road, St Just. (180)

wooden panels with the decalogue, Lord's Prayer and Apostles' Creed.

Probert (1966) 9.

(181) Former BIBLE CHRISTIAN, Queen Street (SW 367314). Opened 1842 and subsequently enlarged. Rendered three-bay front with small raised pediment. (Derelict 1969, since demolished)

(182) WESLEYAN REFORM UNION, Bosorne Terrace (SW 367313). Rendered three-bay front with tall round-arched windows. Dated 1860.

(183) Former WESLEYAN, Bojewyan (SW 391347). Broad three-bay front with porch between plain sash windows. Opened 1841.

(184) WESLEYAN, Trewellard (SW 376337). Coursed granite front with simple pediment, round-arched doorway and two upper windows, dated 1833. Possible former communion area behind rostrum.

Probert (1966) 12.

ST JUST-IN-ROSELAND

(185) WESLEYAN, St Just (SW 853358). Pointed-arched windows with brick arches; later porch. Opened 1812.

(186) WESLEYAN, Chapel Terrace, St Mawes (SW 847332). Rendered front to road of three bays with quoins and platband; entrance in gabled end to right. Opened 1816, much altered.

(187) Former BIBLE CHRISTIAN, Trethewell (SW 856360). Hipped roof, three-bay front with pointed-arched windows and intersecting glazing bars. Built 1836, converted to house 1973.

ST KEVERNE

(188) BIBLE CHRISTIAN (SW 762198). 'Zoar Chapel' dated 1877. Small three-bay chapel with round-arched windows, on isolated site.

'Zoar' Bible Christian chapel, St Keverne. (188)

(189) BIBLE CHRISTIAN, Ponsongarth (SW 755180). Small chapel with half-hipped roof, end entrance with four-centred arched head; pointed-arched window opposite with intersecting glazing bars. Opened 1833.

ST KEW

(190) Former WESLEYAN, Chapel Amble (SW 997755). Built 1828, briefly occupied by Wesleyan Methodist Association who later bought it for use as a schoolroom. Low building of cob on a rubble plinth with half-hipped roof.

Bible Christian chapel, Ponsongarth. (189)

(191) WESLEYAN METHODIST ASSOCIATION, Chapel Amble (SW 997755). Close S of (190); built c.1839, with three-bay gabled front and pointed-arched windows.

(192) Former WESLEYAN, Trelill (SX 044781). S front with round-arched doorway and two upper windows, circular panel with painted date 1812. Later occupied by Wesleyan Methodist Association.

ST LEVAN

(193) WESLEYAN, Treen (SW 394230). Small chapel built 1834 with entrance in gabled end and two windows in each side wall.

Wesleyan chapel, Treen. (193)

Original pulpit with panelled sides and semi-octagonal centrepiece, 'leaders' pew' in front and box-pews each side; other seating replaced.

(194) WESLEYAN, Trethewey (SW 380238). Rendered walls with pediment and round-arched windows. Box-pews to lower floor, galleries at N and S ends. Opened 1868.

ST MICHAEL PENKEVIL

(195) WESLEYAN, Mertherlane (SW 860433). Broad three-bay front with segmental-arched brick heads to windows, entrance in later porch. Segmental recess behind altered rostrum for former preacher's seat, flanked by tables of the decalogue painted on metal panels. Opened 1842, refitted.

ST PINNOCK

(196) BIBLE CHRISTIAN (SX 192631). 'Bethel Chapel' dated 1843 is a low building with half-hipped roof; Sunday-school added at right-angles to front.
   Bolitho (1967) 31–3.

(197) BIBLE CHRISTIAN REFORMERS, Connon (SX 196628). The chapel was built in 1865 by supporters of Samuel Catts, a preacher expelled from the Bible Christian ministry, after the refusal of the trustees of Bethel Chapel (196) to allow him to preach there.
   The society joined the Wesleyan Reform Union which here united with the Methodist church in 1959.
   Bolitho (1967) 31–3.

SANCREED

(198) BIBLE CHRISTIAN, Tregerest (SW 410318). Dated 1862, porch added 1896.

SITHNEY

(199) WESLEYAN (SW 636289). Plain doorway in E wall with two sash windows above; galleried interior. Opened 1859. (Proposed conversion to house 1979)

STITHIANS

(200) Former WESLEYAN, Hendra (SW 725371). The chapel, dated 1814 but partly refitted c.1860–70, is a large building with rendered front having two arched doorways with fanlights and an open-columned porch. There is a continuous round-ended gallery. The rostrum pulpit has a bowed centre, balustraded sides

Former Wesleyan chapel, Hendra. (200)

and terminal pedestals supporting twin brackets with oil lamps. Seating in the gallery and in the centre below is in box-pews.
   Font: stone painted to resemble marble, with fluted circular bowl on square fluted and tapered stem and moulded base, inscribed 'J.M. 1843'.

(201) FREE METHODIST, Penmennor (SW 724370). Dated 1866.

STOKE CLIMSLAND

(202) BIBLE CHRISTIAN, Downgate (SX 367728). Three-bay front, opened 1854. Later commemorative tablet 1898.

(203) BRETHREN, Hampt (SX 389743). 'Jehovah Jireh' chapel, dated 1835, has a rendered front of three bays with a segmental-

Former Wesleyan chapel, Hendra. (200)

'Jehovah Jireh' Chapel, Hampt. (203)

arched entrance in a small granite porch, and a wide round-arched window above. The burial-ground contains many monuments of the later 19th century. (Chapel disused 1973)

(204) WESLEYAN METHODIST ASSOCIATION, Upcott (SX 380760). The former 'Downhouse' chapel on the N side of the road has an end-gable entrance and small tablet above with the denominational name and date 1850. Its successor of 1885 in a simple Gothic style stands opposite. (Former chapel converted to house since 1973)

TORPOINT

(205) WESLEYAN, Quarry Street (SX 439551). Rendered walls with pedimented gable at SE end, paired doorways and two tiers of windows. Dated 1795 but greatly altered and enlarged in 1908. (Demolition proposed c.1986)

TOWEDNACK

(206) WESLEYAN, Coldharbour (SW 491378). Three-centred arched entrance with round-arched window over and two similar windows in each side wall; rear gallery. Opened 1845.

(207) WESLEYAN, Nancledra (SW 496361). Dated 1844. Three-centred arched entrance and two round-arched upper windows; columned porch added 1904. Sunday-school of 1910 to N in similar style.

TREGONEY

(208) CONGREGATIONAL, Fore Street, Tregony (SW 925449). A meeting-house built in 1776 was replaced by the present building on the SE side of the street in 1824. It has a gabled front of three bays with pointed-arched openings and three dwarf obelisk finials on the gable. An oval tablet is inscribed '1824/IC/1876'. There is a gallery around three sides.

Ball (1955) 11–12.

Congregational chapel, Tregony. (208)

(209) WESLEYAN, Fore Street, Tregony (SW 926450). Front with two round-arched windows and date 1824 between.

TREMAINE

(210) Former WESLEYAN (SX 237889). Small chapel with gable entrance and two sash windows in side wall facing road; opened 1847.

TRURO

(211) Former BAPTIST, River Street (SW 824449). A Presbyterian society in existence from the early 18th century had ceased to meet by 1789 and their meeting-house in Kenwyn Street, built 1708, was then let to Baptists. This newly formed congregation, which until 1807 was part of the Chacewater Church, enlarged the meeting-house in 1791, later added a gallery and finally, in 1850, removed to the present site on the N side of River Street.

Former Baptist chapel, Truro. (211)

The chapel, designed by Philip Sambell, has a front of granite ashlar in three bays with giant pilasters and a pediment with arched cornice above the centre bay. (Used from c.1986 by the Royal Institution of Cornwall)

Ivimey IV (1830) 304–5.

(212) FRIENDS, Pauls Terrace (SW 827452). A building was acquired in 1704 for use as a meeting-house and a request was made in that year to Falmouth Monthly Meeting for provision of a 'quarter hundred of deals' for seating. It is not clear whether the meeting survived to the end of the 18th century and the issue of a licence in 1817 for Quakers to use a room in the house of James Bawden in St Mary's parish may indicate a fresh start. The present meeting-house at Truro Vean, built in 1825, has walls of squared stone and a hipped roof. The front wall facing SW has four windows with flat-arched heads and a low central porch; a second entrance is at the SE end. The interior is divided by a passage with vertically sliding shutters at each side. The larger room at the NE end has a stand with end entrances and two rows

of seating. The smaller room at the opposite end has a corresponding stand divided centrally by the SE entrance.

The burial-ground to the NW has uniform round-topped headstones with dates from 1826. *Noticeboard*: small wood panel, black lettering and decoration on white background with pointing hand and 'This WAY IN', 19th-century. (Interior altered *c.*1980)

(213) WESLEYAN, Union Place, Pydar Street (SW 825450). 'St Mary's Chapel', built 1829–30 to replace an earlier preaching-house in Kenwyn Street, was enlarged in 1868 and 1884. The front wall of granite ashlar in three bays has giant pilasters doubled to the centre bay, and a pediment with ornamental circular ventilating panel; the central doorway is flanked by fluted Greek Doric columns and the side entrances have eared architraves. Upper windows to front and side walls are round arched, with rectangular windows below in the side walls.

The interior (77½ ft by 53¾ ft), formerly seating over 1,500 persons, has a continuous round-ended gallery with late 19th-century panelled front supported by cast-iron columns. Behind the later large mahogany rostrum is a shallow apse for the original communion area.

Dolbey (1964) 146–7.

(214) BIBLE CHRISTIAN, St Clement Street (SW 828449). A society formed *c.*1814 by John Boyle united with the Bible Christians in 1817. The chapel, opened 8 August 1834, stood behind other buildings until 1875–6 when it was enlarged to the front and a Sunday-school added at the rear. The latter was enlarged in 1885 and again in 1901–2. The present chapel, which incorporates that of 1834, has been much altered. The gabled front of three bays has a late 19th-century foundation stone with the date 1835. (Sold for commercial use *c.*1975)

Bourne (1905) 453. Tonkin, R. E., *A St Clement Street Journal* (1968).

(215) Former METHODIST NEW CONNEXION, Castle Street (SW 823449). The chapel, built in 1834, now an auction room, has a rendered front of three bays with paired pilasters and a pediment. Traces of a former communion area remain behind the rostrum. Former Sunday-school adjacent. (Demolished 1988)

Wesleyan chapel, Union Place, Truro. (213)

TYWARDREATH

(216) WESLEYAN, Well Street (SX 086542). Hipped roof and three-bay front with two tiers of windows; opened 1828, front altered late 19th century.

(217) Former BIBLE CHRISTIAN, Glenview (SX 086545). Rendered three-bay front with tall round-arched windows, hipped roof. Built 1858, now Women's Institute Hall.

VERYAN

(218) BIBLE CHRISTIAN, Portloe (SW 939395). Rendered walls and hipped roof, chapel at upper level with pointed-arched windows, schoolroom below; opened 1843.

(219) WESLEYAN, Trewartha (SW 924397). Opened 1826; half-hipped roof, front rendered and wide gabled porch added late 19th century.

WADEBRIDGE

(220) CONGREGATIONAL (SW 988724). Gabled front with lancets; 1874 by Austin Stripp.
     CYB (1875) 438.

(221) WESLEYAN METHODIST ASSOCIATION (SW 994724). The chapel in Egloshayle Road, built in 1838 with the proceeds of the sale of £1 shares, was reputedly designed for possible conversion to houses; it was nicknamed 'forty windows chapel'. The walls are rendered and the windows have four-centred arched heads. Much altered 1892. (Derelict 1973, since demolished)
     Shaw (1967) 18, 39.

WARLEGGAN

(222) WESLEYAN (SX 154690). Altered front, two segmental-arched windows with keystones in S wall; built 1821, altered 1881.

WEEK ST MARY

(223) BIBLE CHRISTIAN (SX 237975). Loose in front of 1888 chapel, stone tablet from predecessor inscribed 'ZION CHAPEL 1843'. (Part of former chapel reported to remain at rear of Sunday-school)

ZENNOR

(224) Former WESLEYAN, Porthmeor (SW 432371). Low walls and half-hipped roof, two sash windows in S wall; early 19th-century. Now a cottage.

(225) Former WESLEYAN, Trendrine (SW 476395). Low walls and half-hipped roof, round-arched entrance at NE end; early 19th-century. Now a cottage.

FORMER WESLEYAN CHAPEL, TRENDRINE   C·F·S·1973

ISLES OF SCILLY

Apart from a brief visit to Scilly by John Wesley in 1743, during the course of his first mission to Cornwall, no further Methodist activity is recorded until the end of the 18th century. In June 1799 a 'late erected house' on St Mary's was licensed, although the denomination is not stated; a separate Wesleyan circuit was established in 1812, and several chapels built, of which that in Garrison Lane (229) is of comparatively high quality. The most lasting Methodist influence was exercised by the Bible Christians who, with the aid of female itinerant preachers, arrived in 1821 and soon gathered a strong congregation on St Martin's, followed c.1830 by work on St Agnes and, probably shortly after, on St Mary's. Baptist missionaries also visited the islands in the early 19th century, but the later and more successful Baptist cause on Bryher is of interest as being of native origin.

BRYHER

(226) Former BAPTIST (SV 879150). The chapel, built by a congregation formerly meeting in a cottage, was opened 24 June 1877; a church was formed in 1914. The building is a simple rectangle with gabled ends, two windows with granite lintels in N and S walls and a single doorway near the W end of the S wall. Converted to a cottage, attic storey added and windows lowered c.1971.
     Shaw, R.N., *The Story of the Baptist Church on the Island of Bryher, Isles of Scilly* (1937).

FORMER BAPTIST CHAPEL, BRYHER   C·F·S·1973

ST AGNES

(227) Former BIBLE CHRISTIAN (SV 878084). Small mid 19th-century chapel with gabled end walls, later rendering on three sides and added porch to south. Tall round-arched windows with

Former Bible Christian chapel, St Agnes.   (227)

Former Bible Christian Chapel, ST AGNES

5 Feet 0 5 10

Cornwall (Isles of Scilly)

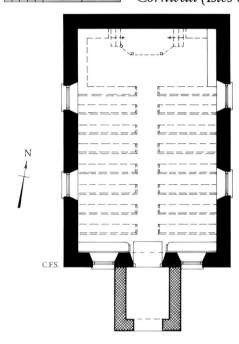

N

C.F.S.

keystones and similarly arched entrance inside porch. The interior, lined with a dado of vertical boarding, retains traces of a rostrum pulpit at the N end and fragments of seating. Now used as a public hall.

ST MARTIN'S

(228) BIBLE CHRISTIAN (SV 929155). The chapel, built in 1822, has rendered walls and a hipped roof. A Sunday-school of similar materials and with a half-hipped roof was added at the S end and the chapel refitted *c*.1900. The chapel has two small windows at the N end flanking the pulpit, two windows in the side walls possibly enlarged, and two at the back of the S gallery. The rostrum pulpit incorporates some early 19th-century panelling. The S gallery is original and has a panelled front supported by two turned wood columns and a staircase in the SE corner.

Bourne (1905) 104, 228.

ST MARY'S

(229) Former WESLEYAN, Garrison Lane (SV 902105). Substantial building of granite ashlar and rubble and a hipped roof, built *c*.1830, now used for leisure activities and principal fittings removed. The E front of three bays has two tiers of round-arched

FORMER WESLEYAN CHAPEL, GARRISON LANE, ST MARY'S   C·F·S·1973

Bible Christian chapel, St Martin's.

(228)

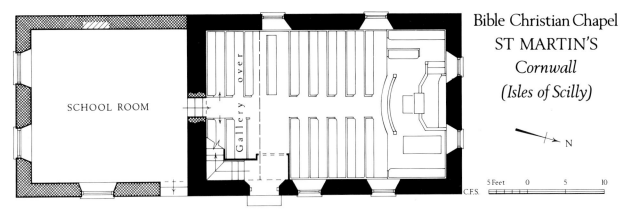

Bible Christian Chapel
ST MARTIN'S
Cornwall
(Isles of Scilly)

SCHOOL ROOM

Gallery over

C.F.S.

5 Feet   0   5   10

windows and a similarly arched central entrance with keystone. The sides are of two bays and in the rear wall are two windows, now blocked, which flanked the pulpit. The interior has an original gallery around three sides rounded to the E with a panelled front supported by four turned wood columns; a panelled screen remains inside the front entrance. The blockings of the W windows retain traces of painted tables of the decalogue and on a panel below are the remains of a black-letter text. (Proposed conversion to visitor centre 1986)

(230) Former BIBLE CHRISTIAN, Church Street (SV 904105). Principal walls of squared granite with hipped roof, built *c*.1830–40 and a lower wing added at the E end in 1854 for a day-school. The original E entrance is now internal and there appear to have been two small windows in the wall above. The S wall has two upper windows with hung sashes, one lower window

has been altered and a second replaced by a round-arched doorway. Two tall windows at the W end, now blocked, flanked the pulpit. The interior has a gallery around three sides supported by turned wood columns. The building was superseded in 1899–1900 by a new chapel 100 yards further east. A floor has been inserted to the central area and the upper part converted to a Masonic Hall; the lower floor is used as a Church Room.

(231) Former WESLEYAN, Holy Vale (SV 920116). Low walls of large granite blocks; broad S front with two windows and narrow doorway. Built in mid 19th century, closed before 1940, and now in commercial use.

(232) Former WESLEYAN, Old Town (SV 915104). Built *c*.1860, formerly with tall windows in W front, entrance to right and steeply pitched roof; closed *c*.1930 and converted to house with altered roof-line and fenestration.

The county, which ranks by area as the third largest in the country and has long occupied a position of strategic and mercantile importance, is equally prominent in its contribution to religious dissent. Ministers were ejected from over one hundred places in 1662 or before, and the subsequent emergence of dissenting congregations, mostly of the Presbyterian order, left a legacy of meeting-houses which few other counties can rival. The Exeter controversy, which preceded the removal of Rev. James Peirce from James's Meeting and was the cause of the celebrated conference at Salter's Hall in 1719, is of outstanding significance in the history of dissent; it marked the point from which the terms Presbyterian and Independent came to take on a doctrinal rather than an organizational meaning. The broad foundations of the older dissent within the county discouraged an early spread of Methodism, presenting a striking contrast with the adjacent county of Cornwall, but in the years following the death of John Wesley many small societies were formed, the origin and spread of the Bible Christians being of particular importance especially in the north west of the county. Devonshire also figures in the early history of the Brethren, both in Plymouth, which lent its name to one section of the movement, and at Teignmouth where Ebenezer Chapel (173) is associated with the first ministry of George Müller.

Conversion of existing buildings for use as meeting-houses is exemplified in the former Abbot's Hall at Tavistock (166) and in the occupation of a mediaeval Priory at Bovey Tracey (14), subsequently rebuilt. The loss of Bowden Hill Chapel at Crediton (56) of c.1729, a building notable for its size and construction, is greatly to be regretted, but the chapels at Chulmleigh (46), East Budleigh (72) and Jesu Street, Ottery St Mary (141), all retain features of interest, while the Baptist meeting-house at Loughwood (65) is of particular note for its early date and eloquently remote situation. The principal building of the later 18th century is George's Meeting-house, Exeter (75), of 1760, but the Baptist chapel at Prescott (63) of 1785 is also remarkable for the quality of its fittings, and the former Unitarian chapel in Devonport (151) of 1790 is an early example of building by liberal dissenters not directly connected with any established Presbyterian congregation. Outstanding amongst the many early 19th-century buildings is the Friends' Meeting-house at Spiceland (64) of 1815, while the Wesleyan chapels at Marwood (116) of 1829 and Lana (144) of 1838 are representative of some of the best country craftsmanship in their denomination. The almshouse chapel at Point-in-View (84), near Exmouth, the Bible Christian at Ebberly Lodge, Roborough (153), and the former Wesleyan at Starcross (104) are all notable as buildings of unusual character.

Rubble walls and slate roofs predominate amongst the numerous small chapels with which the county abounds but although the major example of cob construction, at Crediton (56), has been lost a few smaller instances of this material remain, particularly in the south east. The earliest brickwork also occurs in that region at Ottery St Mary (141), but its use, even in the 19th century, was on a very limited scale. Few buildings outside the towns exhibit any elaboration of style, but the Ionic fronts to the Wesleyan chapel at Ashburton (2) and the Congregational chapel at Crediton (57) are notable essays in the Classical style, while Gothic elements occur in an early form at Teignmouth (173), in a more elaborate but still immature manner at Bideford (10) and in such typical examples of the later years of the Gothic Revival as Southernhay, Exeter (see note under 77), Sherwell Chapel, Plymouth (148), and the Wesleyan chapel at South Molton (163).

ASHBURTON

(1) GREAT MEETING-HOUSE, North Street (SX 755700). The Presbyterian meeting, latterly Congregational, originated in the late 17th century with the preaching of John Nosworthy and William Pearse, ministers ejected in 1662 from Ipplepen and Dunsford. The meeting-house, dating from the 18th century, was first placed in trust in 1739, it was heightened, re-roofed and remodelled internally in 1791, and further altered and enlarged to the E in 1818. Prior to 1791 the roof was supported by two posts, and until 1818 the pulpit remained against the N wall flanked by a pair of windows. A horseshoe-shaped gallery facing the former pulpit was introduced in 1791 but replaced by the present galleries in 1818.

The meeting-house has walls of rubble and a slated roof. The W front of 1818 has a wide round-arched central doorway and two tiers of windows. Some windows in the S wall have wooden frames of the early 18th century; the former pulpit windows in the N wall have been altered. The E wall, partly built into rising ground, has three windows, the middle one formerly a doorway giving access to the 1791 gallery. The interior (originally $32\frac{3}{4}$ ft by 40 ft, lengthened to 57 ft), which has been much altered, has a rostrum pulpit at the E end and galleries along the N and S walls supported by cast-iron columns; a W gallery has been removed. (Closed *c*.1985)

Fittings – *Candle Sconces*: on pulpit, pair, each of two branches. *Chandelier*: eight branches, brass. *Clock*: at W end, circular face and Chinoiserie panel on case, 'Martin Dunsford, Ashburton'. All the above are of late 18th-century date, given by Sir Robert Palk. *Glass*: in middle window of E wall, representation of Presentation in the Temple, Flemish, 16th-century, formerly in chapel of Royal Female Orphanage, Westminster Bridge Road, London, reset here 1934. *Monuments*: in chapel, on S wall (1) Rupertia Hill, wife of Henry Gervis, surgeon, 1835; (2) Mary Eales, 1820; (3) Solomon Tozer, 1844; (4) Rev. John Nosworthy, 1677, and Rev. William Pearse, 1690, erected late 19th century; (5) Peter Fabyan Sparke, 1843, Sarah his sister, 1839, and Hester Margery Amery, 1839; W of chapel (6) John Colton, 1794, and Agnes his wife, 1794; (7) William Jerman, 'Clerk of this Meeting House 27 years', 1809, and Mary his widow, 1810; (8) Grace Fabyan, 1796. *Plate*: includes a pair of Sheffield plate cups, one inscribed 'Walk Esq Donum', early 19th-century. *Seating*: in galleries, early 19th-century.

CHST XII (1933–6) 186–92, 236–8.

(2) WESLEYAN, West Street (SX 756698). The chapel, built in 1835, has rendered walls and a hipped slate roof. Side walls of five bays with two tiers of small windows. Two-storeyed classroom extension erected at front 1908 and original portico of four giant Ionic columns and pediment rebuilt on new frontage. Galleried interior with late 19th-century fittings.

AXMINSTER

(3) CONGREGATIONAL, Chard Street (SY 299986). An Independent church (now URC) formed in 1660 under Bartholomew Ashwood, Rector of Axminster, continued in existence after his ejection and met until 1698 in a hired house at Weycroft within

Wesleyan chapel, Ashburton. (2)

the parish. A meeting-house erected in Axminster in that year, and opened on '14th of 6th month' (August), appears to have continued in use until *c*.1827 when the present chapel was built on an adjacent site.

The chapel has stone walls and a slate roof. Three-bay two-stage front of ashlar with four-centred arched openings and a central doorway with window above set in a tall arched recess. Stone Y-tracery inserted into windows and interior refitted *c*.1875. Sunday-school E of chapel with rubble walls partly rendered occupies the site of the former meeting-house of 1698 and may incorporate part of its structure, but was largely rebuilt in 1875.

Monuments: in chapel (1) Rev. James Small, 48 years pastor and 31 years tutor of the Western Academy, 1834; in burial-ground (2) Thomas Marshall, 1817, and Anna his sister, 1831, table-

Congregational chapel (URC), Axminster. (3)

tomb; (3) Rev. Francis Grub Stevens, 1813, and Elizabeth his widow, 1831, table-tomb.

CHST IV (1909–10) 2, 107–12. Howard, K. W. H. (ed), *The Axminster Ecclesiastica 1660–1698* (1976).

(4) Former WESLEYAN, Castle Street (SY 297986). The chapel, built in 1796 and in Methodist use until 1894, is a tall rectangular building (27¼ ft by 38¾ ft externally) of brick above a rubble base and has a hipped slate roof. The NW front has a wide round-arched upper window between two formerly square windows

Former Wesleyan chapel, Axminster. (4)

and irregularly spaced openings below. The upper windows on the SE side are similar to those in the front wall. The NE end has two blocked windows with a stone tablet between, inscribed 'JM 1796'; a wide doorway has been pierced in this wall.

AXMINSTER HAMLETS

(5) WESLEYAN, Smallridge (ST 302010). The chapel, opened 1813, has rendered walls on a rubble plinth and a hipped roof

Wesleyan chapel, Smallridge. (5)

formerly thatched but now covered with corrugated iron. The plan is unique with convex front and rear walls.

Temple (1974) [23–4].

BARNSTAPLE

(6) BRETHREN, Grosvenor Street (SS 562334). 'Grosvenor Street Chapel', or 'The Room', was built *c*.1840 for supporters of

Robert Chapman, formerly Baptist minister of Ebenezer Chapel, Barnstaple. Rendered gabled front of three bays with wide porch added. Plain hall with segmental-vaulted ceiling and rear gallery with shuttered front; original open-backed benches. *Floorslabs*: in passage behind chapel, include Eliza wife of John Bryant, 1846, and (their children) Anne, 1841, Eliza, 1846, Jane, 1846.

Rowdon (1967) 142–5. Thompson (1885) 20–4.

(7) BIBLE CHRISTIAN, Bear Street (SS 560334). 'Thorne Memorial', 1876 by W. C. Oliver, enlarged and tower added 1891. Stone with gabled front between wings, Gothic details, galleried interior with liberal use of cast-iron. Tablet on front wall to James Thorne of Shebbear (1795–1872).

Bourne (1905) 539–40. Hayman (1885) 173–4.

BEER

(8) CONGREGATIONAL, Fore Street (SY 229893). The church, founded in 1700, was formerly regarded as Presbyterian. The present chapel, occupying an irregular site on the W side of the street, was built in 1855 and enlarged at the back in 1880. The interior was refitted in 1926 and a hall was added at the rear, the E end partly rebuilt and the galleries replaced in 1933. The gabled front wall of flint with stone dressings has two doorways and windows with cusped tracery.

Congregational chapel, Beer. (8)

BERE FERRERS

(9) WESLEYAN, Bere Alston (SX 448669). 'Mount Zion' chapel, opened 1841; rendered front of three bays with pointed windows.

BIDEFORD

(10) GREAT MEETING-HOUSE, Bridgeland Street (SS 454268). An Independent church gathered in Bideford prior to 1658 by the Rector, Rev. William Bartlett, continued under his ministry after his ejection in 1662. A secession which occurred *c*.1694 led to the formation of the 'Little Meeting' which became heterodox and disbanded by 1760. The Great Meeting (now URC) built their first permanent meeting-house on the present site in 1696 and that was succeeded by the existing building, opened 26 October 1859. Illustrations of the former meeting-house show a double-gabled front to the street with two entrances, and the central valley of the roof supported internally by an arcade of four bays with substantial piers and two-centred arches. The pulpit was at the W end and there was a gallery along the N side.

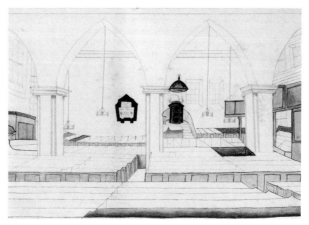

Great Meeting-house, Bideford. Before 1859. (10)

The Great Meeting-house, or 'Lavington Chapel' (named after Samuel Lavington, minister 1753–1807), has a gabled S front of stone with two thin towers and tall spires ornamented with plain octagonal pinnacles, cornices decorated with carved heads, and windows with cusped stone tracery. The architect's initials E.M.W[hite]. appear at the base of the SW tower. The interior has E and W side galleries only.

Fittings – *Clock*: Parliament clock with octagonal face, signed 'Ephraim Dyer, Bideford', early 18th-century. *Monuments*: in chapel (1) Rev. Samuel Lavington, 1807, and Mary (Shepherd) his wife, 1790; (2) Rev. Samuel Rooker, 1832. *Paintings*: small watercolour sketch of interior of former meeting-house; also portraits of Rev. and Mrs Samuel Lavington. *Plate*: includes four standing cups of 1634, 1637, 1656 and 1679, two with donatory inscriptions of 1737 and 1747.

James, T. H., *The Great Meeting (Now Lavington Congregational Church) Bideford 1648–1948* (1948).

(11) WESLEYAN, Landcross (SS 461243). Dated 1854, rebuilt 1880–1. (Closed 1988)

BISHOP'S NYMPTON

(12) WESLEYAN, Newtown (SS 765252). Snecked rubble walls with pointed-arched windows; three-bay gabled front with tablet dated 1849.

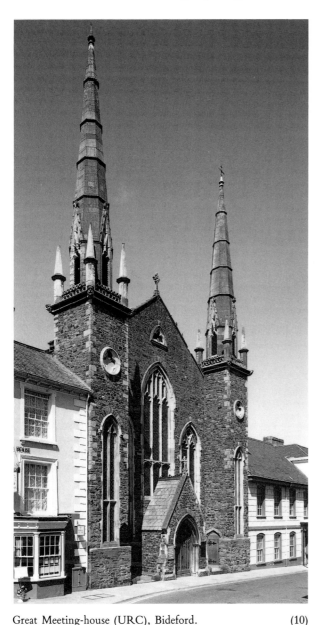

Great Meeting-house (URC), Bideford. (10)

BLACKAWTON

(13) WESLEYAN (SX 808509). Rendered front with pointed-arched upper window. Tablet in front gable 'EBENEZER 1823'. (Closed since 1973)

BOVEY TRACEY

(14) BAPTIST, Hind Street (SX 815785). A Presbyterian meeting which existed in the early 18th century is believed to have occupied the mediaeval Priory chapel. The chapel subsequently passed into the possession of a Baptist congregation formed in 1773 which enlarged the building in 1805–7. On 10 June 1821 the church wrote to the local Baptist Association '... the state of our very ancient place of worship gives us much concern. It is a building of Popish origin and still bears some vestiges of the superstition of those remote ages. It is supposed to have stood several hundred years, but having undergone frequent repairs is at length so completely decayed that it is thought absolutely necessary to rebuild it...'.

The present chapel, on the site of its predecessor, was opened 16 September 1824. It has rendered rubble walls and a slate roof. The E front is gabled and has a wide porch. The S wall of four bays with two tiers of windows, the upper ones with round-arched heads, has a doorway with flat hood supported by shaped brackets. Lofty interior with gallery around three sides retaining original seating; Sunday-school added against W wall.

Gateway: S of chapel, stone with moulded jambs and two-centred arched head, mediaeval, with later inscription 'IS 1823'.
Monuments: in chapel (1) Thomas Luscumbe, 1798; (2) Moses Savery, sergemaker, nearly 30 years deacon, 1817, Mary his wife, 1803, and their daughters Ann, 1808, and Elizabeth Foster, 1806, marble tablet surmounted by urn; in burial-ground S of chapel, headstones of early 19th century and later reset against boundary walls.
BM XVI (1824) 532.

BRADNINCH

(15) BAPTIST, Millway (ST 000039). Rendered front of three bays with triangular-headed recesses between pilasters and similarly shaped upper windows; dated 1832. 'Much enlarged and improved' after 1846.
B.Hbk (1875) 272–4.

BRADWORTHY

(16) WESLEYAN, Bradworthy Cross (SS 313124). Low-built rendered walls, three round-arched windows and later porch to S, large box-pulpit at W end. Opened 1842. (Entirely refitted 1985)

BRANSCOMBE

(17) Former WESLEYAN (SY 189888). Random rubble with larger quoins and slate roof formerly thatched. Gabled to front and rear with shouldered eaves and ball finials. Built 1831, superseded 1900 and converted to a pair of cottages.
Temple (1974) [18].

BRATTON FLEMING

(18) BAPTIST (SS 645378). Rubble and slate. Narrow pointed-arched windows. Built 1850 for church formed c.1799.
Thompson (1885) [18].

(19) BIBLE CHRISTIAN (SS 646378). Rubble and slate, three-bay gabled front with round-arched openings and circular tablet dated 1854.

BRAUNTON

(20) WESLEYAN (SS 490366). Rendered walls with round-arched windows, much altered. Opened 1833.
Monuments: in burial-ground, reset slate headstones, (1) Ann Mock, 1848; (2) Catherine, wife of John Waring, 1844; (3) Richard Lavercombe, 1842, Sarah his widow, 1862, and Mary their daughter, 1844; also (4) William Dyer, 1839, brick table-tomb with slate capping. (New chapel built and former converted to secular use since 1980)

BRENTOR

(21) BIBLE CHRISTIAN, North Brentor (SX 481814). 'Providence Chapel', rendered rubble and slate, with gabled entrance and round-arched side windows, was built c.1847. Interior refitted.

BRIDESTOWE

(22) Former BIBLE CHRISTIAN (SX 513892). Rubble walls partly rendered and hipped slate roof, pointed-arched windows in side walls with intersecting glazing bars; built 1844. Superseded by present chapel nearby and converted for Sunday-school use in 1907.
Parsons (1972) 173–81.

BRIXHAM

(23) CONGREGATIONAL, Bolton Street (SX 924558). The chapel on the E side of the street was built in 1842–3 for a newly formed congregation. Rendered front with canted angles, slightly projecting centre bay with cusped traceried window above pointed-arched entrance; wide bracketed eaves probably replace a parapet. (URC)

Congregational chapel (URC), Brixham. (23)

(24) WESLEYAN, Fore Street (SX 924560). The chapel, built in 1816, enlarged to the rear in 1871 and refitted, has a rendered front of five bays with an open porch supported by two columns.

Wesleyan chapel, Brixham.   (24)

BROADHEMBURY

(25) CONGREGATIONAL, Kerswell (ST 079060). Rendered walls, possibly cob, on rubble plinth. Three small windows facing street with traces of former entrance to right. Built c.1815 for church founded in that year. Refitted late 19th century.

BROADHEMPSTON

(26) BAPTIST (SX 805662). 'Salem Chapel' erected 1844 has rubble walls and a tall hipped slate roof. Central entrance in N wall with Tuscan-columned porch and single sash window above. Small raised gateway in N boundary perhaps for mounting. *Monument*: in front of chapel, to Edward Palk 'whom divine grace constrained to erect and give the chapel in this place for the worship of God . . . ', 1857, and Elizabeth his wife, 1823, buried at Wolborough. (Subsequently used by Brethren, now closed)

(27) Former WESLEYAN (SX 800663). Rendered walls, roof half-hipped to front, round-arched windows. Built 1822, altered. (Converted to house since 1973)

BUCKLAND BREWER

(28) BIBLE CHRISTIAN, Thornehillhead (SS 414165). 'Salem Chapel', opened 28 February 1830 and enlarged and refitted 1863, has rendered walls and round-arched windows formerly with external shutters. *Monuments*: in burial-ground, many 19th-century slate headstones.

   Bourne (1905) 197.

BUCKLAND MONACHORUM

(29) Former BAPTIST (SX 489684). Rubble walls and lancet windows with cast-iron frames, dated 1850. (Converted to residential hostel 1981)

   Baptist Times (20 August 1981).

BUDLEIGH SALTERTON

(30) BAPTIST, Little Knowle (SY 058821). 'Ebenezer Chapel', dated 1844, altered 1887, has a rendered pedimented front with terminal pilasters and two rusticated round-arched doorways; gallery with coved front supported by two cast-iron columns. Some original box-pews remain to the lower floor, and open-backed seating with central dividing rail in the gallery.

BULKWORTHY

(31) Former BIBLE CHRISTIAN, Haytown (SS 383144). 'Bethel Chapel', dated 1841, now a workshop, has rubble walls and a slate roof. Rendered front with two small upper windows and tablet with name, date and text from Haggai 2:9.

   Monuments: in front yard (1) Susanna, widow of William Woolridge, 1879; (2) Elizabeth Walter, daughter of William and Mary Ann Ching, 1847.

BURLESCOMBE

(32) MISSION ROOM, Appledore (ST 070145). Behind The Lamb p.h., built 1820, reputedly by a Quaker family, and in use by Brethren as the Blackdown Hills Mission from c.1900; enlarged 1914. Small rendered building with round-arched windows and end gallery.

   White, R. H., *Strength of the Hills: The Story of the Blackdown Hills Mission* (1964) 113.

BURRINGTON

(33) Former BAPTIST (SS 633171). 'Gospel Hall', now Brethren, has small slate tablet in front gable dated 1846, signed 'Howell'. Two segmental-arched windows in S wall.

(34) BIBLE CHRISTIAN (SS 639168). 'Bethesda Chapel', dated 1829 but much enlarged, has rendered walls, slate roof hipped at one end and pointed-arched windows.

CADELEIGH

(35) Former BIBLE CHRISTIAN, Little Silver (SS 917093). Rubble walls, gabled entrance front and pointed-arched windows. Built 1843, refitted 1889. Earlier cottages adjoin at rear.

CHAGFORD

(36) Former BAPTIST, Southcombe Street (SX 701876). Built as 'Zion Chapel' 1823, sold to Bible Christians 1842, closed 1934, now used by Brethren as 'Ebenezer Gospel Hall'. Granite rubble with rendered front and round-arched windows.

CHARDSTOCK

(37) Former BIBLE CHRISTIAN, Churchill (ST 299023). 'Ebenezer Chapel', built 1840. Gabled ends with ball finials; two round-arched windows in one side wall only.

   Temple (1974) [23].

CHARLES

(38) BAPTIST, Brayford (SS 687347). Baptists, whose principal supporters were Joseph and Mary Gould, baptized 1792, met jointly with the Wesleyans until 1815 when they formed a separate congregation. The chapel erected in 1820 has rendered walls and a slate roof. The N wall facing the road is blank but a date-tablet probably removed from the W wall has been reset here. There are two round-arched windows in the S wall. A

Former Bible Christian chapel, Haytown.   (31)

Sunday-school was built at the W end in 1924. The interior has been refitted and contains a wall monument to Joseph and Mary Gould and Rev. W. Cutcliff, 44 years pastor, erected 1901.

Monuments: in burial-ground S of chapel, slate headstones (1) Joseph Gould, 1817, stone reputedly ejected from parish churchyard at Charles and remains reburied here; (2) Rev. Edward Widlake, 1829; (3) Jane Cutcliffe, 1836, and William Knibb Cutcliffe, 1847, signed 'Philip Pile, Bratton', (4) Mary, wife of Joseph Gould, 1826.

Newnam, S., *John Winzer or The Parish Apprentice* (1901). Thompson (1885) 13–18, 120.

(39) Former WESLEYAN, Brayford (SS 687347), 50 yards E of the Baptist chapel, built 1813 on land given by Joseph Gould (*see* (38)). A small plain building with a segmental-arched entrance in the N gable wall. A new chapel was built nearby in 1927.

Monuments: in burial-ground to S and W several slate headstones of the later 19th century.

CHERITON BISHOP

(40) WESLEYAN, Cheriton Cross (SX 774930). Rendered walls and pointed-arched windows. Opened 1842, rebuilt 1874, entrance re-sited 1894.

CHITTLEHAMHOLT

(41) BRETHREN (SS 650209). Rubble with pointed-arched windows; built 1838 for a congregation gathered by Robert Gribble. Burial-ground with slate headstones.

Rowdon (1967) 147–51.

CHIVELSTONE

(42) Former CONGREGATIONAL, Ford (SX 789408). The church formerly meeting here claimed to have originated in 1662. The chapel, built in the late 18th century but now derelict, stands in an extensive burial-ground. It has walls of thin coursed rubble and a hipped roof latterly covered with slates. The E front has a central doorway with wooden pedimented hood and shaped brackets between two wide segmental-arched windows with keystones. The walling above the window heads appears to be a heightening and incorporates a small window, now blocked, above the entrance. There are three similarly arched windows in the S wall and two in the N, with a later vestry against the E end of the N wall. The interior ($48\frac{1}{2}$ ft by 30 ft) had a flat plaster ceiling; the pulpit was at the W end. The roof is supported by king-post trusses. (Door-hood removed and other features lost or re-sited since 1973)

Former Congregational chapel, Ford. (42)

FORMER BAPTIST CHAPEL, CHUDLEIGH   C·F·S·1973

Monuments: in chapel, on W wall (1) Rev. William Miles, 25 years pastor, 1855; on N wall (2) Rev. William Evans, 40 years pastor, 1810, and Margaret his widow, 1822; in burial-ground, many slate headstones – N of chapel (3) Mary, wife of Philip Edmonds, 1815, *et al.*; (4) Mary, wife of George Gillard, 1814; E of chapel (5) John Barry, 1806. S of chapel (6) Sarah, wife of William Ford, 1854, *et al.*; (7) Robert Bucknell, minister of Torcross, 1849; (8) Mary, wife of Rev. Thomas Mountford, 1825; (9) Richard Heath, 1795, Mary his wife, 1795, William their son, 1795, and [   ] their daughter.

(43) BIBLE CHRISTIAN, East Prawle (SX 781365). Low rubble walls rounded at one corner, hipped slate roof; opened 1848.

CHUDLEIGH

(44) Former BAPTIST (SX 873799). The chapel stands N of the village adjacent to a stream. It was built *c*.1848 for a church formed in that year. The building is large, with rendered rubble walls and a slate roof. The pedimented S front has a central entrance with crudely detailed porch and three tall upper windows. At the N end is a blocked Venetian window. (Closed and converted to house since 1973)

(45) CONGREGATIONAL, Woodway Street (SX 868797). The chapel, built in 1830 for a formerly Presbyterian church (now URC) which claims to have originated in 1662, replaced a meeting-house reputedly built in 1710. The gabled front wall is rendered with two tiers of round-arched windows in three bays, a central pedimented doorcase and blind window above. Interior with rear gallery refitted late 19th century.

Monuments: in chapel (1) John Petherick, 1836, and Elizabeth his widow, 1856; (2) Rev. John Allen, 40 years minister (*c*.1822–62), 1884, and Eliza his widow, 1885; (3) James Davison, minister, 1841, and Elizabeth his widow, 1847.

CHULMLEIGH

(46) INDEPENDENT, East Street (SS 689143). Puritan influences in Chulmleigh can be traced to 1633 when John Shaw, a licensed preacher, was invited to the town as a lecturer where he remained for three years. The houses of John Bowring and Digory Cocks were licensed in 1672 for Presbyterians or Independents and a small congregation was in existence by 1694 in which year John Cudmore succeeded Thomas Hart as pastor. The present building was erected in 1710, John Moore of Tiverton recording in his diary under 17 August 'Gave Mr Dig. Lock [*sic*] towards ye meeting-place for ye building of it at Chimleigh, 10s' (*CHST* IX (1924–26) 186). Meetings ceased about 1776 and the building

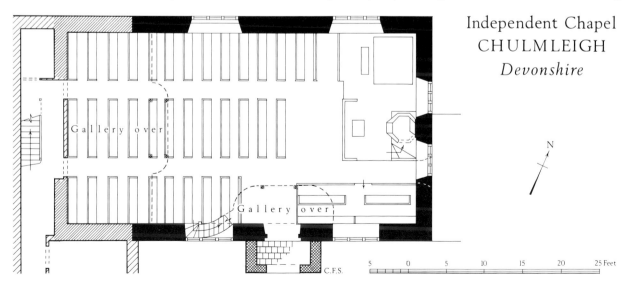

Independent Chapel
CHULMLEIGH
Devonshire

N

Gallery over

Gallery over

C.F.S.

5 0 5 10 15 20 25 Feet

Independent chapel, Chulmleigh.

(46)

'was neglected and almost reduced to a heap of ruins' but repairs were effected in 1793 and again c.1803–4 and the church was re-formed in 1809. The chapel was enlarged to the W and a school-room built at the SW corner in 1836; in 1882 the interior was partly refitted.

The chapel has walls of rubble and a hipped slated roof. The S front has a gabled porch with semicircular outer arch and a date-tablet of 1710; in the wall above is a small window and below it a later tablet bearing the spurious date 1633. Two wide windows with pointed-arched heads flank the porch. There are two similar windows in the N wall and two windows with renewed lintels at the E end flanking the pulpit. The W end has been altered. The interior (originally 34½ ft by 24 ft) has a flat plaster ceiling to the original area and a raised ceiling above the W gallery. There is a smaller gallery on the S side above the entrance. The seating was replaced in 1882. The original roof structure remains with two king-post trusses with braced principals, the braces to the E truss strongly curved, supporting double purlins and a square-set ridge-piece.

Fittings – *Bell*: in bell-cote at SW corner, c.1836. *Chair*: incorporating carved 17th-century back panel. *Chandeliers*: two, brass, of 6 and 8 branches, early 19th-century. *Clock*: on front of W gallery, in wooden case with Gothic tracery, c.1836. *Communion Table*: small oak table with four baluster legs, early 18th-century, top and drawer later. *Galleries*: two – against S entrance, small singers' gallery with rounded panelled front supported by two turned-wood columns, with some original seating and staircase to W with vase finial to lower newel, c.1800; at W end, on four columns with panelled front and rounded projecting centre, early 19th-century but with earlier balusters reused in staircase and landing to west. *Inscription*: on wall of lobby at W end, square iron tablet recording 1836 enlargement, signed 'Howell'. *Monuments*: in chapel – on N wall (1) John Cudmore, 12 years pastor in succession to Thomas Hart, 1706, painted octagonal wooden tablet surmounted by urn, early 19th-century; (2) Richard Darracott, pastor, 1727; (3) William Skinner, 1826, *et al.*; (4) Roger Howell, 1839, *et al.*; on E wall (5) Rev. Thomas Sharp, 32 years pastor, 1858; on S wall (6) Rev. Joseph Hooker, pastor, descendant of the historian John Hooker of Exeter, and great-grandfather of the botanist Sir William Hooker, 1748, erected 1882; externally, on S wall (7) children of Richard and Mary-Ann Howell, 1822–44, slate, signed 'Howell'; (8) Mary Turner, 1818; (9) Rev. Thomas Sharp, 1858, Frances his wife, 1843, and Sarah Clark his sister, 1814, slate signed 'Howell'. *Pulpit*: octagonal with three tiers of bolection-moulded panels, similarly panelled back-board, and octagonal canopy with shaped top supported by wrought-iron pendant and dove finial, early 18th-century incorporating some earlier material in canopy. *Shields-of-arms*: on N wall, on two diamond-shaped wooden panels, arms of Bowring and Stuckley, inscribed 'Arms of John Bowring who gave this ground' and 'Arms of Lewis Stuckley who built this chapel 1633', late 19th-century.

Cording, J. G., *A Short History of the Congregational Church, Chulmleigh, Devon, Established 1633* (1933).

(47) Former WESLEYAN, New Street (SS 686142). Two round-arched windows in rendered front, now workshop, Early 19th-century.

(48) BIBLE CHRISTIAN (SS 687144). Rendered gabled front partly concealed by 1883 Sunday-school. Slate tablet inscribed 'BETHLEHEM CHAPEL 1836', signed 'Howell'.

CHURCHSTOW

(49) BAPTIST BURIAL-GROUND, Venn (SX 699467). Square enclosure with high rubble boundary walls and gateway on W side; the land was given in 1673 by Arthur Langworthy of Hatch to the Baptist church meeting in and around Loddiswell, but now at Kingsbridge (106). About fifty monuments remain of the 18th and 19th centuries, many slate headstones and remains of three table-tombs; the earliest monument is a headstone to Joseph Hingson, 1711/12. Also, loose and broken, slate tablet from a former chapel inscribed 'PROVIDENCE MEETING/DEDICATED/In the Reign of King James the Second 1687/REBUILT/In the Reign of King George the Third 1787/by ye LOVERS of ye GOSPEL of JESUS CHRIST/...Nicholas Beer, Thomas Phillips, Deacons...'.

Adey, W. T., *An Historical Account of the Baptist Church, Kingsbridge, 1640–1899* (revised 1940) 12–13.

COLYTON

(50) GEORGE'S MEETING-HOUSE, Church Street (SY 245940). The Presbyterian congregation formerly meeting here claimed to have originated with the ejection in 1662 of the vicar, Rev. John Wilkins, who continued to preach privately until his death in

George's Meeting-house, Colyton. *Sketches by A. Weight Matthews, 1903, from scrapbook of George Eyre Evans.*   (50)

1667. Two houses were licensed for meetings in 1672 and a meeting-house was in existence by 1693. The society divided c.1711 over a disputed appointment. Ministers of heterodox views occupied the pulpit from the 18th century. Services ceased in 1939 and the meeting-house was subsequently converted and much altered for use by a Youth Club.

The present building, standing on the site of its predecessor, was erected in 1746. It has walls of flint, formerly rendered, with brick dressings, and a slate roof previously thatched. The entrance was at the SW end with a columned porch, removed c.1970; there are two wide round-arched windows with key-stones in the side walls and similar windows at a higher level at the gabled ends. The interior (48¼ ft by 25¼ ft), now divided into two storeys, has a segmental plaster vault. A schoolroom added at the S corner in 1844 has a dated tablet on its outer NW wall with the names of the minister and chapel wardens. Some fragments of 19th-century wall monuments remain; all are trans-cribed in Evans (1898), as are the inscriptions from the now destroyed burial-ground to the north west.

Evans, G. E., *Colytonia: A Chapter in the History of Devon* (1898). Murch (1835) 332–42. *UHST* v (1931–4) 417–20.

(51) Former CONGREGATIONAL, King Street (SY 245941). The chapel built in 1814 and enlarged in 1831 was transferred to Methodist use in 1964. Rendered gabled front with porch and large round-arched windows.

Temple (1974) [26–7].

Former Congregational chapel, Colyton.   (51)

(52) Former WESLEYAN, Rosemary Lane (SY 247942). Rendered gabled front of three bays with round-arched openings, built 1838.

Temple (1974) [26–7].

(53) Former WESLEYAN, Colyford (SY 251926). Rubble walls, partly rendered, and slate roof. Built 1833, refitted 1873. Thatched roof replaced 1898. (Converted to house since 1973)

Temple (1974) [27–8].

COOKBURY

(54) BIBLE CHRISTIAN (SS 409060). Rendered walls and half-hipped slate roof, opened 1840.

CREDITON HAMLETS

(55) Former BIBLE CHRISTIAN, Copplestone (SS 770027). Built 1831, superseded 1888 by new chapel across road (Down St Mary parish). Long rendered front partly refenestrated since 1980, formerly with two chapel windows at mid height facing road, cottage to left and small extension to right.

Thorne, R. F. S., *Methodism in Three Parishes: The Story of Copplestone Methodist Chapel 1831–1981* (1981).

CREDITON TOWN

(56) BOWDEN HILL CHAPEL, Crediton (SS 834002). Crediton provided a refuge for several of the ejected ministers who in 1672 took out licences in the town as Presbyterian teachers. A society of that denomination developed in the later years of the century and erected the meeting-house on Bowden Hill about 1729. By the mid 18th century, when a separate Independent congregation was established, the Presbyterians had begun to tolerate hetero-dox opinions and the pulpit came eventually to be supplied solely by Unitarian ministers. A serious landslip in 1963 rendered the building unsafe and the congregation disbanded prior to the collapse of the structure c.1971; the site has since been cleared. The chapel was a building of major importance as an example of a large and early meeting-house of considerable quality and as an outstanding example of cob construction of which it was claimed to be the largest in Great Britain. The following description refers to its condition in 1967.

The chapel has walls of red cob on a sandstone plinth, formerly rendered in plaster but later covered on three sides by a hard concrete coating. The roof is half-hipped and covered with slates. The front wall facing NE is of five bays with a coved plaster cornice; the centre bay projects slightly and has a steeply pitched pediment enclosing an oval window. The central doorway has a round-arched head and a wooden canopy with open pediment and barrel-vaulted soffit with foliage decoration supported by shaped brackets; above the doorway is a circular window and to right and left are two pairs of tall round-arched windows with original mullioned and transomed wood frames with leaded glazing. The SW wall has four windows matching those in the front wall and in the narrower end walls are square cross-framed windows behind and below the galleries. The SE wall has been strengthened by three tall external buttresses and has a blocked outer doorway near the NE end. A vestry was added at the W corner in 1740.

The interior (42¾ ft by 55½ ft) has a tall barrel-vaulted plaster ceiling rising from moulded cornices along the front and back

Bowden Hill Chapel, Crediton.   (56)

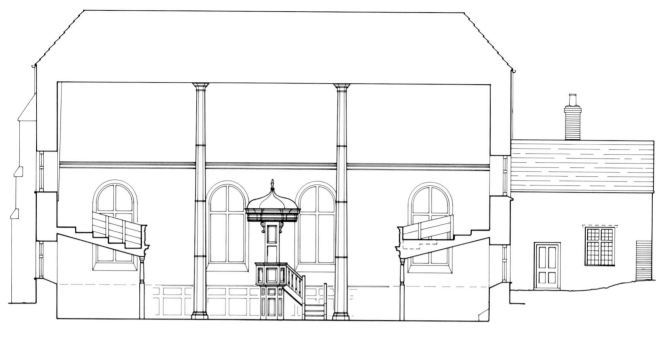

Section facing South , with elevation of Vestry

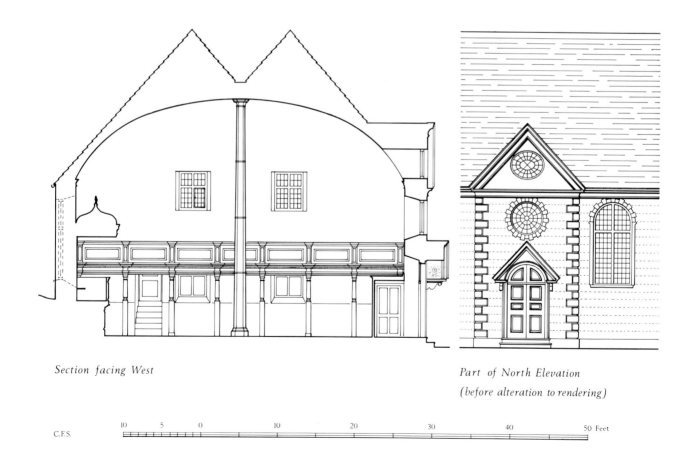

Section facing West

Part of North Elevation
(before alteration to rendering)

C.F.S.   10   5   0   10   20   30   40   50 Feet

Bowden Hill Chapel, CREDITON TOWN, *Devonshire*

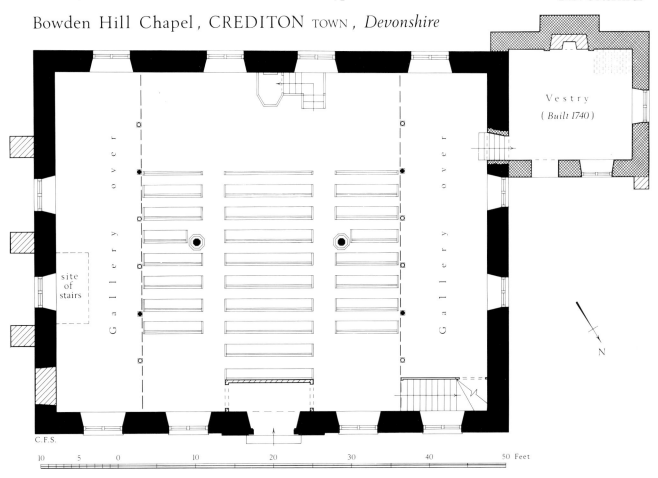

Vestry (Built 1740)

Gallery over

Gallery over

Gallery

Gallery

site of stairs

C.F.S.

N

10   5   0   10   20   30   40   50 Feet

walls. The roof is supported by two tall octagonal oak posts covered by later boxing. There are separate galleries at each end, that to the SE no longer accessible; the fronts are supported by rows of turned columns of which two each side are original, the others replace inserted screen walls removed *c*.1930. The vestry, raised 4 ft above the level of the chapel, has a plaster ceiling with central decorated boss and the date 1740 in raised numerals around it.

Fittings – *Clock*: on SW wall, but prior to late 19th-century refitting above entrance facing pulpit, Parliament clock with octagonal face and decorated case, signed 'John Tickell, Crediton', height 9 ft, mid 18th-century (now at Moretonhampstead, *see* (127)). *Monument*: against NW wall, to Emma, daughter of William and Mary Burdge, 1844. *Plate*: includes a cup of 1840 (this, together with some late 19th-century seating, is now at the General Baptist Chapel, Horsham, Sussex). *Pulpit*: hexagonal, with panelled back-board and hexagonal domed canopy with flaming urn finial and marquetry soffit, *c*.1729.

Evans (1897) 60–1. Murch (1835) 454–60. *UHST* VI (1935–8) 53–4; XIII (1963–6) 22–3, 80–4.

(57) CONGREGATIONAL, High Street (SS 830004). Built 1865 for church formed 1757, probably by separation from Bowden Hill Chapel. Pedimented front with giant order of Ionic pilasters carrying entablature arched over centre bay; by Thomas Oliver.

Former *burial-ground*, 50 yards E behind 107 High Street, occupies site of mid 18th-century meeting-house.

CYB (1864) 293.

Congregational chapel, Crediton.   (57)

CRUWYS MORCHARD

(58) CONGREGATIONAL, Way Village (SS 885103). Rubble and slate, gabled front with lancet windows, built 1847, porch added 1883.

CULLOMPTON

(59) BAPTIST, High Street (ST 021075). The chapel, built 1743 and registered July 1744, has walls of cob refronted in brickwork and a slate-covered roof. The building originally had a central entrance on the W side and the pulpit was probably against the opposite wall. Major alterations in the late 19th century involved heightening the walls, re-siting the entrance at the N end, re-fenestration of the W wall, the addition of a gallery adjacent to the new entrance and an organ chamber at the opposite end, followed in 1882 by the erection of a Sunday-school at the rear. In 1964 the front wall was refaced but retained the 19th-century openings. An original segmental-arched window remains in the back wall covered by a later vestry, and a repainted tablet above it is inscribed 'BUILT 1743'. The interior (26 ft by 47 ft) has been refitted but a former baptistery, now superseded, remains at the E side.

Monuments: in chapel (1) William Stark, 1829, and Elizabeth his widow, 1838; (2) Samuel Rumson, pastor, 1805.

(60) Former CONGREGATIONAL, Tiverton Road (ST 018074). Rendered three-bay front with pointed-arched windows. Built 1830–1, closed late 19th century.

Inscription: on front wall, recording gift of building by Frederic Burrow to parishioners of Cullompton in commemoration of Queen Victoria's Diamond Jubilee, 1897. Now in commercial use.

FORMER CONGREGATIONAL CHAPEL, CULLOMPTON

(61) POUND SQUARE CHAPEL (ST 021070). The Presbyterian congregation (now Unitarian) claims descent from Rev. W. Crompton, ejected from the living of Cullompton in 1662, who 'continued with his people after his ejectment, and spent many years among them without that encouragement he deserved'. The first meeting-house on the present site was opened *c*.1698. In 1814 this was 'so much decayed as to render further assembling in it dangerous' and it was replaced by a smaller building which had rendered walls and pointed windows with intersecting tracery. The present chapel, by R. M. Challice of Exeter, which succeeded it in 1912, is a modest Gothic building of red brick.

Fittings – Monuments: in chapel (1) Rev. Samuel Morgan, 1794, and Elizabeth (Stevenson) his wife, 1783, tablet erected 1827; in front yard (2) Rev. Richard Evans, 1743; (3) Rev. Matthew Lee Yates, 1847; (4) Rev. John Davis, 1824. *Plate*: includes a mug of 1693 and a pewter plate dated 1686.

Evans (1897) 63–4. Murch (1835) 302–12. Palmer II (1802) 13. *UHST* VI (1935–8) 55–6.

(62) WESLEYAN, The New Cut (ST 020073). The Methodist society in Cullompton flourished in the late 18th century, having 101 members in 1778 and in 1792 becoming the head of the circuit. The present chapel, erected in 1806 on the site of a smaller building of 1764 at the upper end of Dunkley's Court, W of the main street, was largely rebuilt after a fire in 1872. It has rubble walls rendered to E and S and a hipped slate roof. The E front has a wide round-arched doorway and one small oval window only, at the rear of the gallery.

Chick (1907) 47–8.

CULMSTOCK

(63) BAPTIST, Prescott (ST 091144). Baptists have met here since the beginning of the 18th century, first as members of the church at Newhouse, Upottery, but becoming autonomous in 1745. The first meeting-house on this site was built *c*.1715–18 and replaced by the present chapel in 1785. In spite of 'renovation' in 1892, in which the pulpit and lower pews were renewed and the window-frames altered, the interior remains a notable example of unusually elaborate country craftsmanship.

The chapel has rendered rubble walls and a slate roof. The exterior is plain, with round-arched windows and a wide doorway in the gabled S wall. The interior (36 ft by 31 ft) is trisected by two rows of octagonal oak posts with moulded capitals which support the gallery fronts and rise to a cornice at the ceiling. A segmental plaster barrel vault spans the central space and half vaults cover E and W galleries. The galleries, which have fielded-panelled fronts, extend round three sides, with the pulpit on the fourth side against the N wall.

Fittings – Baptistery: in floor in front of pulpit, with rounded ends and steps on W side. *Bootscrapers*: wrought-iron with elaborately scrolled standards, *c*.1785. *Communion Table*: small early 18th-century oak table with turned legs. *Monuments*: in burial-ground (1) Mary (Pepperell) wife of Henry Lippincott, 1753, *et al.*, table-tomb; (2) William Periom, 1769; (3) Daniel Meacham, 1721, and Daniel Slanderwick, 1784, table-tomb. *Pulpit*: back-board of former pulpit against N wall, with round-arched panel and swan-necked broken pediment with urn above elaborate cornice, 1785. *Seating*: in E and W galleries, benches with boarded backs and shaped intermediate supports, incorporating material from former chapel with graffiti and initials and dates 'NI 1719', 'WM 1721'.

Anon., *A Brief History of Prescott Baptist Church 1700 to 1922* (1922) four-page pamphlet.

(64) FRIENDS, Spiceland (ST 083139). Quakers have occupied this site since *c*.1680–3 at which period 'a close of ground called Spison' was placed in trust and a meeting-house erected for the use of 'the people of God called Quakers'. The present building, erected in 1815 on the site of the former house, is an outstanding specimen of its kind and retains a complete set of contemporary fittings.

(63)

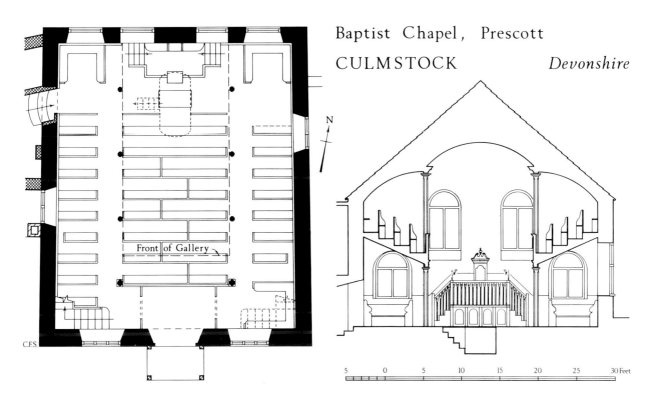

Baptist Chapel, Prescott
CULMSTOCK   *Devonshire*

Front of Gallery

C.F.S.

N

5   0   5   10   15   20   25   30 Feet

Baptist chapel, Prescott. (63)

Friends' meeting-house, Spiceland. (64)

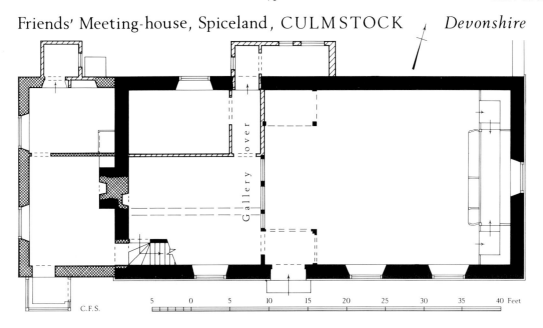

Friends' Meeting-house, Spiceland, CULMSTOCK   *Devonshire*

Gallery over

C.F.S.

5   0   5   10   15   20   25   30   35   40 Feet

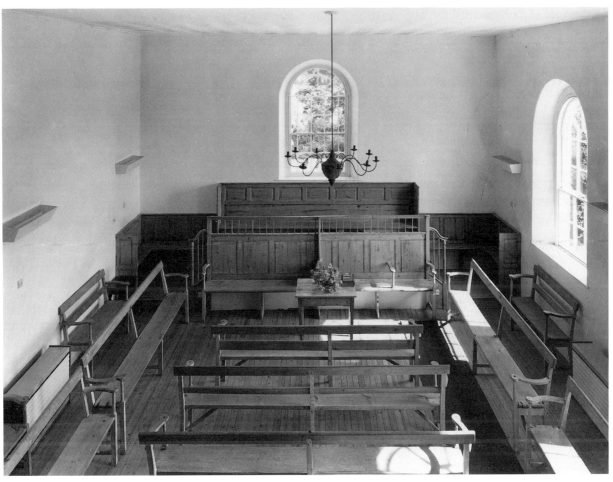

Friends' meeting-house, Spiceland.   (64)

The meeting-house stands a little over one mile W of the village. It has rubble walls and a hipped slate roof supported by six king-post trusses. The S front of four bays has a segmental-arched doorway between three round-arched windows, two of which light the large meeting-house to the E and one the small meeting-house and gallery to the west. Incorporated in the N wall is a tablet inscribed 'DANIEL HENSON BUILDER 1815'. A lean-to extension to the W forms part of a caretaker's cottage.

The interior (49 ft by 22 ft) is divided by a screen with vertically sliding shutters separating the two meeting-houses. The gallery above the small meeting-house, now partly enclosed, has an open-panelled front which is brought forward at each end.

Fittings – *Chandelier*: large turned-wood boss with nine thin metal branches. *Coffin Stools*: four, with turned legs, one stool dated 1783. *Monument*: in burial-ground, C. Stark, 1811; other stones later in spite of earlier dates (for mid 18th-century plan of burial-ground in County Record Office *see* DRO, 874, D/T5). *Seating*: eighteen loose benches with open backs and columnar supports to arm-rests. *Stand*: at E end, unpainted pine with two tiers of seats; steps at both ends to upper tier with ramped handrails and plain balusters; upper seat has fielded-panelled back, and panelled front with balustraded top.

Dymond (1899) 38–43.

DALWOOD

(65) BAPTIST, Loughwood (SY 253993). The Baptist church formerly meeting at Loughwood, then a detached portion of Dorset, was in existence by 1654; in 1832 a second chapel was built at Kilmington (*see* (105)). Regular services at Loughwood ceased *c*.1950 and the meeting-house was transferred to the National Trust *c*.1969; it has since been carefully repaired. The walls are of rubble with brick dressings, rendered to N and W, the roof was thatched *c*.1972, replacing 19th-century slates. Although claimed to date from the mid 17th century and probably in existence at least by 1700, the meeting-house contains no datable features prior to the early 18th century. It has been much altered in external appearance; a thatched cottage which stood against the E wall was removed in the later 19th century and some or all of the round-arched windows are alterations of that period. Two windows in the gabled S wall, with a brick chimney-stack between, replace a single central window with wooden lintel below a half-hip. The E wall, rebuilt in the early 19th century, has a round-arched doorway; two raking buttresses were added when the cottage was demolished. At an earlier date rounded buttresses were built against the W wall and at the ends of the N wall.

The interior (40¾ ft by 18¾ ft) has an entirely rebuilt segmental plaster barrel-vaulted ceiling. At the S end is a gallery with 18th-century fielded-panelled front; below it are two small vestries. The gallery staircase may have been re-sited in the 19th century, occupying the site of an earlier internal doorway. The seating comprises early 19th-century box-pews with a table-pew of similar date in front of the pulpit having a shallow baptistery beneath. The roof structure was completely renewed *c*.1972.

Fittings – *Clock*: on front of gallery, with striking mechanism, dial signed 'John Tratt, Colyton', and in smaller lettering 'George Major, Colyton'. *Monument*: on W wall, Rev. Isaac Hann, pastor, 1778, erected at expense of Baptist Western Association. *Pulpit*: octagonal, early 19th-century.

BHST IV (1914–15) 129–44. *BQ* XXXI (1985–6) 288–94.

Baptist chapel, Loughwood. Before 1972.

Baptist chapel, Loughwood. After restoration.   (65)

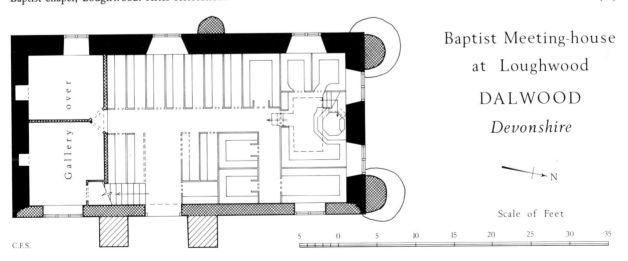

Baptist Meeting-house
at Loughwood
DALWOOD
Devonshire

N

Scale of Feet

5   0   5   10   15   20   25   30   35

C.F.S.

DARTMOUTH

(66) Former BAPTIST, Chapel Lane (SX 878510). The chapel has walls of rubble, partly rendered, and a slated roof. It was built in the late 18th century for a church formed *c*.1646 which numbered the engineer Thomas Newcomen amongst its pastors. A gallery was built at the S end in 1800 and side galleries, since removed, were added in 1839. The building was extended to the N and a schoolroom added in 1847 and the interior refitted *c*.1877–9. The front S wall has an altered entrance between two round-arched windows with intersecting glazing bars and a small circular window between.

Monuments: in chapel (1) Thomas Newcomen, 1729, modern tablet; (2) Rev. Edwin Harold Brewer, 30 years pastor, 1867.

Ivimey II (1814) 133–5.

(67) CONGREGATIONAL (SX 878515). The church, originally Presbyterian (now URC), originated with the ejection in 1662 of John Flavell, vicar of St Saviour's, Dartmouth. The meeting-house has been rebuilt at least twice; the penultimate building of 1841 was approached from Foss Street where an archway remains inscribed 'INDEPENDENT CHAPEL'. The present building, by E.H. Back, of stone with pointed-arched windows, was erected on an adjacent site in 1895.

Monuments: in chapel (1) John Flavell, 1691, with Latin inscription, removed by magistrates' order from St Saviour's Church and re-erected 1709 in the former meeting-house, brass in moulded wood frame incorporating explanatory tablet above; (2) Henry Cole, trustee, 1828, and Ann his widow, 1850; (3) Rev. Thomas Stenner, 39 years pastor, 1849. *Plate*: includes a pair of tankards of 1737, given 1738 (a standing-cup dated 1663 and associated with John Flavell, latterly in the possession of Pilgrim Church, Plymouth, was sold *c.*1971).

CHST III (1907–8) 153. CYB (1897) 170–1.

(68) Former WESLEYAN, Market Square (SX 877515). Wide rendered front of five bays in three storeys, with giant order of Ionic pilasters and three-bay pediment. Built 1816, subsequently much altered, largely rebuilt 1874–5 by John Wills and further altered 1938. (Demolition proposed 1988)

DAWLISH EAST

(69) CONGREGATIONAL, The Strand, Dawlish (SX 960768). Stone, prominent broach-spire, opened 1871. (URC)

Friend, D. R., *Notes on the Local Growth of Non-conformity and a Short History of the Dawlish Congregational Church* (1953).

DUNKESWELL

(70) WESLEYAN (ST 140078). Rubble with brick dressings, three-bay gabled front with lancets; opened 1845, altered or enlarged 1887.

EAST BUCKFASTLEIGH

(71) WESLEYAN, Chapel Street, Buckfastleigh (SX 737662). Rendered front of three bays with Doric porch and two tiers of sash windows; opened 1835.

EAST BUDLEIGH

(72) SALEM CHAPEL (SY 070851). The church originally meeting here was formed *c.*1709 as a Presbyterian society, later becoming Congregational but disbanding prior to 1975; in that year the chapel was reopened by an Evangelical, now Pentecostalist, congregation. The chapel, erected in 1719, is a square building with rendered walls probably of cob and a hipped slated roof. The E front has rendered quoins; the original central entrance was blocked and replaced in 1836 by two doorways on the site of former windows. The side and rear walls each have two segmental-arched windows; a small vestry projects from the W end of the N side. Detached to NE is a later building formerly used by a day-school.

The interior (34½ ft by 34 ft) has a vaulted plaster ceiling rising at the centre from an iron column (replacing a timber post, but retaining an original bracketed cornice) and from the walls above a moulded plaster cornice. An original E gallery with fielded-panelled front was extended along the adjacent sides *c.*1836 and is now supported by cast-iron columns of that date. Contemporary box-pews remain in the galleries but the body of the chapel was reseated in the late 19th century.

Fittings – Clock: on front of E gallery, with painted face, signed 'Jno. Murch, Honiton', 18th-century. *Monuments*: in chapel (1) Richard Baylie, 1732, John Waldron, 1740, and Mrs Elizabeth Bird, daughter of the first and widow of the second, 1762; (2) John Vinicombe, 26 years deacon, 1846, and Margaret his widow, 1847; in burial-ground N of chapel (3) Rev. Samuel Woolmers, Wesleyan minister, grandson of Rev. J. Hubbard of London, 1827; (4) Richard Gould, 1831, *et al.*; E of chapel (5) Henry Leatt, 1841, Jenny his widow, 1851, and Henry their son, 1876.

'Salem Chapel', East Budleigh.　　　　　　　　　(72)

EAST WORLINGTON

(73) BIBLE CHRISTIAN, Thornham Cross (SS 777149). 'Sharon Chapel'; three-bay front with pointed-arched windows. Opened 1849, enlarged and entrance re-sited 1908.

EXBOURNE

(74) Former BIBLE CHRISTIAN (SS 603018). Mid 19th-century; converted to house since 1975.

EXETER

(75) GEORGE'S MEETING-HOUSE, South Street (SX 921924). The importance of Exeter as an early centre of nonconformity is witnessed not only by the ejection in 1662 of no less than ten ministers from its pulpits but also by the number of dissenting congregations which flourished in the opening years of toleration. Three Presbyterian congregations emerged at this time, James's Meeting, the Bow Meeting, and the Little Meeting, between which close links were maintained. Of these, James's Meeting was pre-eminent. This society, formed about 1670 under the pastorate of Joseph Hallet, erected a meeting-house in 1687 which is said (Brockett (1962a) 54) to have remained standing in 1960, converted to dwelling-houses, in James Street, a lane between South Street and Coombe Street. The meeting-house was named in appreciation of King James's Indulgence of 1687. In 1760 the congregation removed to the present building where they were joined by the former members of the Little Meeting. In its early years the meeting maintained an orthodox position, dismissing a minister in 1719 who held Arian views, so occasioning the formation of the 'Mint Meeting' (see (76)), but it later supported a Unitarian ministry. (The society disbanded in 1982 and the building has since been converted to commercial use. Some fittings have been removed)

George's Meeting-house, named for its erection in the first year of the reign of George III, stands on the NE side of South Street. It has brick walls and a hipped roof covered with slates, having a half valley at the centre discharging to the rear. The front wall, with rendered quoins, stone plinth, moulded cornice and shaped parapet, is of three bays; the centre bay projects

slightly and has a pedimented porch with a pair of stone Tuscan columns. The upper windows throughout are round-arched and the lower ones have segmental-arched heads. The front windows have moulded wooden architraves and keystones. The side walls, of four bays, are without ornamentation; side entrances near the SW ends of these walls afford additional access to the gallery staircases. Two tall round-arched windows in the NW wall flank the pulpit.

The interior (65¼ ft by 45¼ ft) has a flat plaster ceiling with coved cornice. The ceiling is said to have been lowered by three feet in 1809 (Brockett (1962a) 172–3), but this is not confirmed by the evidence of the structure which appears to be unaltered. The corners of the walls above the galleries are rounded internally. Galleries around three sides have panelled fronts supported by square fluted wooden piers with Ionic capitals. The pulpit, centrally against the NE wall, is reported (ibid) to have been re-sited from a position ten feet SW in 1809, the alterations of that year being undertaken on the advice of the London architect, Charles Beazley, but structural evidence is again lacking and it is unlikely that the back panel and canopy have been moved. A Lecture Hall was built at the back of the chapel in the later 19th century. In 1881–4 the lower pews were altered and stone-flagged aisle floors replaced by wood.

Fittings – *Benefaction Board*: recording bequest from Francis Pengelly, 1700. *Chest*: iron, with elaborate locking mechanism inside lid, late 17th-century. *Clock*: on front of SW gallery, carved wood case in rococo manner with representations of sun and moon, late 17th-century. *Monuments*: in Lecture Hall, concealed behind matchboarded wall lining [subsequently exposed]

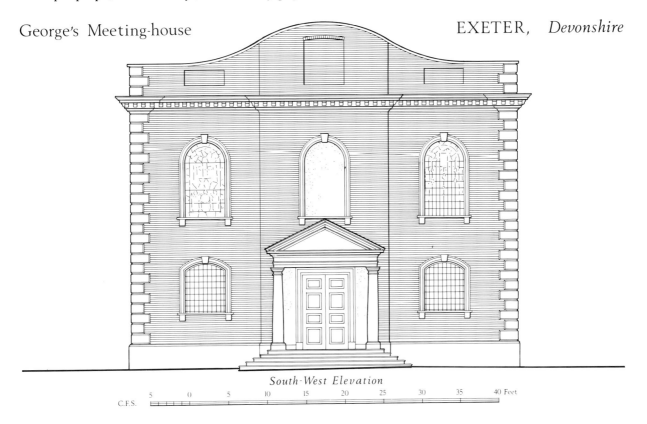

George's Meeting-house   EXETER, *Devonshire*

South-West Elevation

C.F.S.

5   0   5   10   15   20   25   30   35   40 Feet

George's Meeting-house, Exeter.

(75)

George's Meeting-house, EXETER
Devonshire

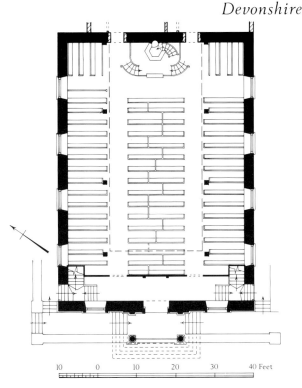

10   0   10   20   30   40 Feet

Former Wesleyan chapel, 'The Mint', Exeter.   (76)

include a large draped cartouche to Rev. James Peirce, 1726, re-erected here from 'Mint Meeting-house' in 1812, also five other monuments mainly of the early 19th century; in small burial-ground at rear, several early 19th-century stones said to include Joseph Priestly of Cradley, 1833, eldest son of Dr Joseph Priestley. *Organ*: in gallery, erected October 1813. *Plate*: includes two cups with baluster stems of 1660 and 1636, and two plates of 1705 and 1712 given in 1746 by John Vowler, all from James's Meeting. *Pulpit*: hexagonal, panelled front enriched with swags and ornamented with thin Ionic columns at the corners, segmental niche at back with scrolled side brackets, elaborate canopy carved with representation of bunched drapery; canopy late 17th-century, pulpit probably later. *Rainwater-head*: in NE wall, lead, with date 1759. *Seating*: in gallery, original box-pews; lower pews altered and lowered but incorporate original material.

A *burial-ground* at the corner of Magdalen Street and Bull Meadow Road (SX 923923) formerly used by this and other societies is surrounded by a brick wall; it contains several monuments of the 18th century.

Brockett (1962a) *passim*. Evans (1897) 83–5. Murch (1835) 372–452. *UHST* V (1931–4) 384–92; VI (1935–8) 253–6.

(76) WESLEYAN, Fore Street (SX 917925). The chapel built in 1813, enlarged 1867 and rebuilt in 1970, stands on the site of the 'Mint Meeting-house', opened in 1719 by Rev. James Peirce who had been dismissed from James's Meeting for Arianism; the original society united with George's Meeting in 1810.

Brockett (1962a) 193; Dolbey (1964) 137–8. Le Messurier, B., *A History of the Mint Methodist Church, Exeter* (1962).

(77) Former CONGREGATIONAL, Little Castle Street (SX 922929). The church formerly meeting here originated in 1794 when the largely orthodox members of the Presbyterian 'Bow Meeting' declined to accept a Unitarian nominee as minister and commenced separate services in the Wesleyan chapel, then in Musgrave's Alley. The Bow Meeting-house was thereupon closed and demolished. The new society bought the former County Gaol adjacent to the castle, demolished it and built the present meeting-house on the site in 1796. The building was altered in 1839, and in 1870, following the removal of the church to a new chapel at Southernhay, it was converted for Sunday-school use; it is now occupied by the Royal British Legion.

The chapel has walls of Heavitree stone, a pebbly red sandstone, and a hipped slated roof. It is rectangular ($45\frac{1}{2}$ ft by $64\frac{1}{2}$ ft externally) with a narrower projection added 1839 at the shorter SE end in which are two side entrances, that to the NE now converted to a window. All the openings have round-arched heads of brickwork, those to SE and SW with rendered keystones and imposts. The main front faces SW and has a moulded timber cornice (replaced *c*.1976), and four bays of windows at two levels, the centre pair replacing two taller windows which flanked the original site of the pulpit and with two original entrances in the end bays now converted to windows. In 1839 the pulpit was moved to the shorter NW end and the windows in that wall were also altered in consequence. *Monuments*: in burial-ground, many headstones and some table-tombs of the early 19th century.

The chapel at *Southernhay* (SX 924927), built 1868–70 in the Decorated style by Tarring and Son, was largely destroyed in 1942. The tower and broach-spire survive alongside a new building of 1956.

Brockett (1962a) *passim. CYB* (1870) 377.

(78) BAPTIST, South Street (SX 921924). The church, which was founded in 1656, has occupied the present site since 1725 when it was donated by Benjamin Heath. In the early 19th century the meeting-house became unsafe and was rebuilt in 1822–3. In 1855 houses lining the street frontage were removed. Apart from the front gable, little of the 1823 brick chapel remains visible behind a late 19th-century refronting.

Plate: includes a pair of two-handled cups of 1725 by John Elston junior, a church member.

Bickers, H. E., *A Brief History of the Baptist Church Now Meeting in South Street Chapel, Exeter, from the Year 1656* (1906). Brockett (1962a) *passim*. Gabb, A., *A History of Baptist Beginnings* ... (*c*.1950).

(79) Former BAPTIST, Bartholomew Street (SX 916924). The church, meeting since 1963 in Dorset Avenue, St Thomas's, was formed in 1817 by seceders from the South Street congregation and the chapel was erected in that year by the minister, Rev. George Baring, largely at his own expense. The chapel, sold in 1953, was reopened in 1978 by an evangelical congregation.

The chapel has rendered walls and a hipped slate roof with pediments above the middle bays of the two principal elevations. The E front is divided into three bays by tall pilasters and has a central porch with fluted Doric columns, three round-arched upper windows and two segmental-arched windows below. The S wall of four bays has two tiers of windows corresponding to

Former Baptist chapel, Bartholomew Street, Exeter. (79)

those in the front wall. A former Sunday-school to the N is dated 1876.

Anon., *A History of St Thomas Baptist Church (Bartholomew Memorial Church) Exeter, Ter-Jubilee 1817–1967* (1967). Brockett (1962a) *passim*.

(80) Former FRIENDS, Friars Walk (SX 921922). A meeting-house built in Wynards Lane, Magdalen Street (SX 923924) in

Former Friends' meeting-house and Salvation Army Temple, Exeter. (80)

1691, was superseded in 1836 by a larger building erected in Friars Walk. In 1868 the latter became a Temperance Hall; it was sold to the Salvation Army in 1882 who enlarged it in 1890; the Quakers eventually repurchased their original site and built their existing meeting-house there, a stone building in an institutional Gothic style, in 1876.

The former meeting-house has a rendered front wall of three bays with tall pilasters supporting a pediment and two tiers of plain sash windows. The interior has been altered. Adjoining to the NW is the wide red brick frontage of the Salvation Army Temple of 1890, architect W. Dunford, of five bays with central pediment, crowstepped gables in the adjoining bays, and corner towers.

Brockett (1962a) 62, 229. Dymond (1899) 1–10.

(81) WESLEYAN, Sidwell Street (SX 925931). Early design in reinforced concrete and brickwork, by Cottancin. Octagonal with domed lantern. Begun 1896, opened 1905, hall added 1924.

Concrete January (1977) 24–7.

(82) PROVIDENCE CHAPEL, Northernhay Street (SX 918929), was built in 1839 for Plymouth Brethren by Sir Alexander Campbell, one of their principal supporters; it was sold in 1851 to the Bible Christians. It remained in Methodist use until 1956 and is now occupied by the Elim Pentecostal Church. Large building with rendered walls and a hipped tiled roof. The broad front of five bays was embellished in the late 19th century; a school was added in 1894.

Bourne (1905) 322–3. Brockett (1962a) 200.

EXMOUTH

(83) CONGREGATIONAL (SY 003811). A small chapel, built 1777, enlarged 1800, was rebuilt in 1866–9; a stone incorporated in the N wall is inscribed 'GLENORCHY CHAPEL BUILT BY THE RT. HON. THE LADY VISCOUNTESS GLENORCHY 1777'. The present chapel of stone, with an octagonal bell-turret and spire above the SW entrance, is in the Gothic style by W. G. Habershon and Pite.

Wesleyan chapel, Sidwell Street, Exeter.   (81)

Monuments: in chapel (1) Rev. Robert Winton, first minister, 1818, oval marble tablet surmounted by urn in low relief; (2) Daniel Sprague, 1830, and Elizabeth his widow, 1847; (3) John Stacy and Sarah Osmet, 1831; (4) George Wilkinson of Meriton, 1812; (5) Thomas Harbottle, 1853.

CYB (1867) 362–3. Thompson, T. P., *Lady Glenorchy and Her Churches* (1967) 35–7.

(84) CONGREGATIONAL, Point-in-View (SY 008835). The chapel and almshouses, built and endowed in 1811 by Jane and Mary Parminter, were originally intended for the occupation of four single women, one to conduct a day-school for six poor girls, preference being given to converted Jewesses, and a minister 'holding and teaching the Doctrines of the Assembly's

Congregational chapel, almshouses and manse, Point-in-View, Exmouth.   (84)

Catechism'. The building is square with low rendered walls and a flat roof pierced at the centre by a steep pyramidal roof with triangular roof lights and surmounted by a weathercock; windows have triangular heads and crossed glazing bars. The chapel, a small central room 11½ ft square, was enlarged in 1829 by the incorporation of a room to the W which formerly accommodated the minister; a manse was built to the NE in that year.

Monument: on E wall of chapel, to Jane Parminter, 1811, and Mary Parminter, 1849. *Organ*: small instrument with hinged keyboard to convert as pulpit, by Rev. J. F. Guenett, minister, 1878.

Barber, D. R., *A Short History of the Mary Parminter Charity Known as The Point in View Trust* (nd). *CYB* (1890) 148–9.

FENITON

(85) Former WESLEYAN, Fenny Bridges (SY 114986). Centenary Chapel, built 1839 on land given by Edward Combe of Feniton Mills. (Now a farm building)

FILLEIGH

(86) Former BIBLE CHRISTIAN, Heddon (SS 652288). Small early 19th-century cob-walled outbuilding converted to chapel 1862, closed 1966. (Now a garage)

FREMINGTON

(87) CONGREGATIONAL, Bickington (SS 535325). Rendered three-bay front with two tiers of round-arched openings, 'built 1835, restored 1896'. (URC)

(88) Former BIBLE CHRISTIAN, Holmacott (SS 503289). Rendered walls, round-arched windows, gabled front with tablet 'HOPE/1843'; schoolroom added 1920. (Converted to house since 1973)

GREAT TORRINGTON

(89) BAPTIST, New Street (SS 493192). The chapel, built in 1829 for a church formed in 1820, has a rendered front wall with swept gable parapets and three bays of round-arched openings. In

Baptist chapel, Great Torrington. Before removal of cottage. (89)

the gable is a tablet with raised lettering bearing the name and date of erection. One of two contemporary cottages in front of the chapel flanking a narrow central approach was demolished *c*.1972 and the original wrought-iron gates and overthrow removed. Interior refitted 1879.

(90) WESLEYAN, Mill Street (SS 494191). Front wall with swept gable similar to the last but with two tall round-arched windows and circular window between. Pedimented tablet in gable inscribed 'WESLEYAN CHAPEL 1832'.

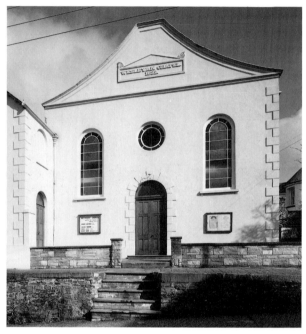

Wesleyan chapel, Great Torrington. (90)

HALBERTON

(91) WESLEYAN (ST 007131). Rendered front with narrow pediment between curved cheeks, columned porch and two round-arched windows; dated 1816.

Bagwell, F. H., *A Short History of Methodism in Halberton* (1960).

HALWELL

(92) Former INDEPENDENT, Moreleigh (SX 767529). Rubble with hipped slate roof, built *c*.1842. Front and one side wall slate-hung; round-arched windows.

Monuments: in burial-ground with dates from 1842 include (1) Henry Evens, 1846; (2) Betsy, wife of William Hockins, 1849, headstone signed 'Hannaford, Halwell'. (Disused 1973, derelict 1988)

HARBERTON

(93) ZION CHAPEL, Harbertonford (SX 785559), was built *c*.1799 for a Baptist congregation but now occupied by a Brethren assembly. The walls are of rubble, partly slate-hung, and the roof is hipped and slated. The entrance at the S end has a flat-arched head and wooden canopy supported by shaped brackets. In the N and S walls are small circular windows and at

Wesleyan chapel, Halberton. (91)

the sides pointed-arched windows with wooden Y-tracery. The interior (28 ft by 17½ ft) has a gallery at the S end entered externally and incorporating fragments of original seating. On the front of the rostrum pulpit is a small board inscribed 'Zion Chapel 1799'.

Monuments: in burial-ground (1) William Barrett Coyde, 1834; (2) Thomas Goodman, pastor, 1833, table-tomb; (3) Edmund Steer, 1839, *et al.*, table-tomb; (4) John Ford Bovey, 1836; (5) Thomas Braddon, 1836; (6) William Finch, 1838; (7) Thomas Haydn and John, sons of John and Lydia Treby, 1839? and 1841.

ZION CHAPEL, HARBERTONFORD

HEMYOCK

(94) WESLEYAN (ST 136132). Rubble and slate, three-bay gabled front with round-arched openings, dated 1838. Original gallery next to entrance.

HENNOCK

(95) Former WESLEYAN (SX 830810). Rendered walls with wide round-arched windows, opened 1835. (Closed 1976 and converted to house)

HIGHAMPTON

(96) BIBLE CHRISTIAN, Lydacott (SS 486035). 'Bethesda Chapel' with low walls and lancet windows is dated 1836; Sunday-school added and chapel altered 1879, enlarged 1891.

HOLSWORTHY HAMLETS

(97) BIBLE CHRISTIAN, Anvil Corner (SS 372042). Small chapel with round-arched windows and arched canopy to entrance. Opened 1854.

HONITON

(98) INDEPENDENT, High Street (ST 166008). The chapel, built in 1773–4, stands on the SE side of the street adjacent to the site of a Presbyterian meeting-house from which the orthodox members seceded in 1771. The parent society, in existence by 1687, had built its meeting-house in 1696; about 1788 it united with a General Baptist church, formed *c*.1715, using their meeting-house in Bridge Street, rebuilt in 1794, until its closure in 1863.

INDEPENDENT CHAPEL, HONITON

The Independent chapel has brick walls and a hipped slate roof reconstructed in 1836. The broad front with two tiers of round-arched windows is partly concealed by a wide gabled porch with organ chamber above added in 1862; rendered quoins and arched window-frames are all of this later period. The interior (32¼ ft by 42 ft) has a gallery around three sides with a panelled front of the early 19th century. The pulpit and lower pews were replaced in 1881–2 but some earlier seating remains in the gallery.

Monuments: in chapel (1) Rev. William Wright, 23 years pastor, 1852, and Georgiana Caroline his widow, 1864; in burial-ground (2) Mary Ann Darke, 1827, and Richard Rolle Darke her brother, 1844; (3) Rev. William Morton, former missionary in Calcutta for London Missionary Society, 1852.

Cooke, Rev. D. H., *The Independent Chapel, Honiton, 1771–1971; The Story of 200 Years* (1971). Murch (1835) 314–17.

ILFRACOMBE

(99) CONGREGATIONAL, High Street (SS 516476). A Presbyterian society which originated by 1687 under Rev. John Berry, an ejected minister, built a meeting-house on the present

site in 1728–9. In the early 19th century the church (now URC) was re-formed and in 1819 the chapel was rebuilt behind a fore-court which was subsequently occupied by further buildings. The present chapel, although basically of 1819, was extended to the front by R. D. Gould in 1866 and the interior was much altered in the late 19th century and after.

Monuments: (1) Ann, widow of George Clarke, 1837; (2) John Jones, surgeon, 1866, and Mary his wife, 1842; (3) John Fosse Croscombe, 1839, *et al.*; (4) Captain Charles Besley Gribble, 1831, *et al.*; (5) Powell Skinner, 1847. *Plate*: includes a cup of 1810 and a flagon of 1837.

Griffin, C. R. J., *A Golden Milestone: The Congregational Church, Ilfracombe, 1687–1955* (1955).

INSTOW

(100) WESLEYAN (SS 474304). Rendered three-bay front with round-arched openings, dated 1838. Schoolroom below.

INWARDLEIGH

(101) Former WESLEYAN, Chapel Lane, Folly Gate (SX 574979). Built *c*.1830–40 of rubble and cob, pointed-arched windows in the side walls, and a small later rear gallery. Superseded by a new chapel 1905. (Derelict 1975)

(102) BIBLE CHRISTIAN, Waytown (SX 547980). Bethany Chapel; small cob building with hipped slate roof, opened 1840.

Parsons (1972) 137–45.

KENTISBEARE

(103) BAPTIST, Saint Hill (ST 091082). The church, formed by separation from Cullompton in 1816, built the present chapel in 1830. Rendered walls with three pointed-arched windows in W wall facing burial-ground. Original S gallery.

Monuments: in burial-ground (1) Charles Baker, 46 years deacon, 1861, and Mary his wife, brick table-tomb; (2) David Temple of Traquair, Peebleshire, 1851; (3) Charles Baker, 'founder of the Baptist cause at Saint Hill', 1836, and Martha Rabjons his daughter, 1846, slate headstone set in brick pillar; (4) Joan Coombe, 1837.

Chalk, E. S., *Kentisbeare* (Parochial Histories of Devonshire: No. 3, 1934) 85–6.

KENTON

(104) Former WESLEYAN, Starcross (SX 977818). A pumping station built 1845–7 for the short-lived South Devon Atmospheric Railway, was refitted in part as a Wesleyan chapel in 1869 and continued in that use until 1958. The building of red pebbly stone in an Italianate style with prominent cornice has a tall tower at one corner, now partly removed.

Hadfield, C., *Atmospheric Railways* (1967) Pls XV, XVI.

KILMINGTON

(105) BAPTIST (SY 268983). The small chapel, built in 1832 for a branch of the Loughwood church (*see* Dalwood (65)), is concealed behind later outbuildings. The side walls to N and S have two pointed-arched windows, the former now covered by a later Sunday-school; two similar windows at the W end flank the pulpit. The interior has a segmental plaster barrel-vaulted ceiling and an original E gallery with arcaded front.

KINGSBRIDGE AND DODBROOKE

(106) BAPTIST, Baptist Lane, Fore Street, Kingsbridge (SX 734442). The Baptist church, which claims to have originated in 1640, appears to have met prior to 1688 in and around Loddiswell, acquiring a burial-ground at Venn (*see* Churchstow (49)) in 1673. A meeting-house built at Kingsbridge about 1705 stands 20 yards E of the present chapel which superseded it in 1799. The former meeting-house has rubble walls and a tall hipped roof covered with slates; two windows in the longer N and S walls and one in the W end have been altered, other openings added in the N wall, and the E wall has been rebuilt. The interior (approximately 24½ ft by 37 ft) has been divided into two storeys; the roof is supported by king-post trusses.

The present chapel, of stone with a gabled front, was much altered in 1852 when it was extended to the W but traces of earlier windows remain in the E front. The interior (originally 30 ft by 45 ft) has a gallery of *c*.1852 at the E end; other fittings are later.

Monuments: (1) to Leonard Kent, Philip Weymouth and Arthur Langworthy, early supporters of the cause, and pastors Samuel Hart, Martin Dunsford, 1713, and Crispin Curtis, 1768, 19th-century tablet; (2) Rev. H. Penn, 1802, 'By whose Exertions . . . this House was erected'; (3) Rev. John Nicholson, 1832.

Adey, W. T., *An Historical Account of the Baptist Church, Kingsbridge, 1640–1899* (revised 1940). Ivimey IV (1830) 303–4.

(107) BRETHREN, Fore Street, Kingsbridge (SX 735443). Gospel Hall built 1853, of coursed stone with a hipped slate roof. W front of three bays with tall upper windows and open porch with stone columns.

(108) Former FRIENDS, Fore Street, Kingsbridge (SX 734443). A Quaker meeting was in existence in Kingsbridge by 1676. In February 1703 a collection was made 'for expences of buying a plot and building a Meeting house' and the present building, although now devoid of early features, may be of this date. Meetings ceased in 1871 and the building was successively let to the Freemasons and the Salvation Army before being sold in 1917 to Roman Catholics for conversion to a chapel.

The meeting-house (originally 28½ ft by 26¾ ft) has rubble walls and a slate roof. The E wall is pierced by three pointed-arched windows of the 19th century; the W wall has been removed and the building enlarged at that end. Ten Quaker head-stones remain in a small burial-ground to the W, to the families of Balkwill, Fox and Prideaux. Another burial-ground in this vicinity, sold August 1879 to the trustees of the town lands, is described as 'The Quakers' Old Burying place situated at the [junction of] Duncombe Street with Fore Street in Kingsbridge, with the building formerly used as an engine house on the land'.

Dymond (1899) 27–37. MS records, Friends' Meeting-house, Plymouth.

(109) WESLEYAN, Fore Street, Kingsbridge (SX 734445). Built 1814, enlarged 1870. Rendered pedimented front of three bays with two tiers of round-arched windows and central doorway with fanlight. Interior with segmental barrel-vaulted plaster ceiling and original gallery around three sides supported by wooden columns; pews and pulpit have been renewed. Some

early 19th-century slate headstones remain at the sides of the forecourt.

LAPFORD

(110) CONGREGATIONAL (SS 734085). Built 1846 for a church formed in 1838; gallery added 1849. Stone with three-bay gabled front and tall lancet windows with original glazing bars.

(111) Former BIBLE CHRISTIAN (SS 733084). Built 1860–1, later occupied by Congregational Sunday-school and inscribed tablet replaced. Three-bay gabled front of rubble with brick dressings.

LODDISWELL

(112) CONGREGATIONAL (SX 720484). A former chapel, built in 1808, stood at one corner of the present burial-ground; a fragment remains incorporated into a shelter erected in 1929 and includes a tablet inscribed 'PROVIDENCE CHAPEL Erected by ye Reverend Geo DENNER 1808'. The existing chapel of rubble was built in 1864 on ground which slopes steeply down to the rear. The front and rear walls are gabled and the latter has flanking towers with shaped pyramidal roofs. All the windows have round-arched heads and brick dressings. The interior has a segmental barrel-vaulted plaster ceiling.

Fittings – In chapel, from former Congregational chapel, Kingsbridge, demolished since 1945 following war damage – *Chair*: square legs with horizontal bearers at base, arms, back with embossed leather panel, reputed property of Rev. Edmund Tucker, Presbyterian minister at Kingsbridge, d.1702, 17th-century. *Table*: four turned oak legs, 18th-century, top and rails later, associated with George Whitefield's preaching at Kingsbridge. The Kingsbridge church also possessed two mid 17th-century baluster-stem communion cups, sold *c*.1970.

The burial-ground, 100 yards NW, is surrounded by a rubble wall incorporating ogee-topped headstones. *Monuments*: reset in shelter, seventeen wall monuments including (1) Rev. John Hill, 48 years pastor, 1857; (2) Ann, wife of Rev. John Hill, 1843; (3) Rev. George Denner, first pastor 'by whose Exertions this Building was erected . . .', 1809; (4) Hannah, widow of Rev. George Denner, 1824.

LUPPITT

(113) Former BAPTIST, Beacon (ST 181053). Built 1859; dado of 18th-century fielded panels from pews, possibly brought from former Baptist chapel at Newhouse, Upottery. (Converted to house since 1983)

Former Bible Christian chapel, Lydford. (115)

LUSTLEIGH

(114) BAPTIST (SX 784812). Granite rubble with slate roof, pointed-arched doorway and windows, mid 19th-century. Small burial-ground in front.

LYDFORD

(115) Former BIBLE CHRISTIAN (SX 512849). Rubble with hipped slate roof and broad three-bay front, built 1839, superseded by present chapel opposite 1908.

MARWOOD

(116) Former WESLEYAN (SS 549372). Rubble with half-hipped slate roof and round-arched windows. Three-bay front with lunettes above principal windows; tablet dated 1829 removed. In use as Sunday-school 1873–1974, now converted to house. Present chapel to S, 1872–3 by A. Lauder.

Former Wesleyan chapel, Marwood. (116)

MARY TAVY

(117) WESLEYAN (SX 502796). Rubble and slate with three-bay gabled front, round-arched windows and large granite tablet above porch dated 1835. Interior nearly square; mid 19th-century gallery around three sides with original box-pews.

(118) Former WESLEYAN, Horndon (SX 519801). Small building of 1836 on N side of road, rubble and slate, narrow entrance in gabled front and two former windows to W; closed 1890, now used as barn.

MEMBURY

(119) Former FRIENDS (ST 274018). Minor building converted for use as a meeting-house *c*.1660–5, disused by mid 18th century, becoming a storehouse and latterly much altered to form a cottage. Walls of rubble, possibly with some cob, and a slate roof replacing thatch. Drawings of *c*.1870 indicate a covered external stair at the W end and a gallery, built 1686, along the W and S sides, possibly returning at the E end. The interior ($18\frac{1}{4}$ ft by $39\frac{1}{4}$ ft) now has no original features, but a wide outer doorway in the S wall and two enlarged windows to the W mark the sites of earlier openings.

Burial-ground (ST 273022). Triangular site adjoining Quakers' Lane, bounded by rubble walls and hedges, in use *c*.1660–1775, contains one headstone: Ann, wife of Edward Smith, 1755, and their children Thomas, 1719, and Ann, wife of Joseph Gillet, 1758.

Dymond, R., 'A Deserted Meeting-house and Burial Ground', in *Friends' Quarterly Examiner* XX (1886) 226–42. Dymond (1899) 104–8.

MILTON ABBOT

(120) WESLEYAN (SX 405793). Small chapel with three-bay front, four-centred arched openings and shield-shaped tablet of 1835.

MODBURY

(121) BAPTIST, Church Street (SX 657516). The church originated in 1791 by division from Kingsbridge; it occupied temporary premises, including the Presbyterian meeting-house, until the erection of the present chapel in 1807. Galleries were added in 1814, schoolrooms were built at the rear in 1844–5, the chapel was reseated in 1866 and the front altered and porch added in 1875. The chapel has rubble walls partly concealed by rendering and slate hanging, and a slate roof. The N front has a pediment surmounted by crudely Classical ornament. The E and W sides have each one wide round-arched window. The Sunday-school at the S end is of two storeys with two tiers of windows in the S wall.

The interior of the chapel has a segmental plaster barrel-vaulted ceiling with a late 19th-century panelled ceiling added beneath. The gallery around three sides is supported by thin cast-iron columns. The pulpit at the S end, flanked by two round-arched windows now internal and converted to doorways, was formerly approached directly from the upper schoolroom; stairs and an iron balustraded front were added in the late 19th century. Box-pews remain in the body of the chapel.

Monuments: in yard N of chapel, slate headstones, (1) Silvanus Gillard, 1840, and Emily Nicholson Smith his daughter, 1848, signed Crocker; (2) Sarah, widow of Silvanus Gillard, 1850, and Thomas their son, 1851.

(122) WESLEYAN (SX 659514). Rendered walls and hipped slate roof; two round-arched windows in front. Opened 1835.

MOLLAND

(123) Former WESLEYAN, Bottreaux Mill (SS 822265). Built 1850.

MONKLEIGH

(124) Former WESLEYAN (SS 454207). Tall and narrow with rendered walls and slate roof. Gable front with tablet dated 1833. (Closed 1975, walls lowered, converted to garage)

MORCHARD BISHOP

(125) BIBLE CHRISTIAN (SS 768077). Rubble and slate, gabled front with three tall narrow round-arched windows and central doorway with fanlight. Modern tablet in gable 'Emmanuel Chapel 1846'.

MORETONHAMPSTEAD

(126) Former GENERAL BAPTIST, Fore Street (SX 755861). The General Baptist church, in existence by *c*.1690, occupied rented accommodation until the erection of the present building in 1786. From 1818 the church shared a pastor with the Presbyterian congregation, both societies having adopted Unitarian doctrines, but the chapel remained in use for some time. In later years it became a workshop, but it was derelict by 1969 and the roof has since collapsed. The chapel, which stands concealed behind buildings on the N side of Fore Street, has walls of granite rubble with large roughly shaped quoins; the roof was hipped and

FORMER GENERAL BAPTIST CHAPEL, MORETONHAMPSTEAD   C·F·S· 1969

MORETONHAMPSTEAD, *Devonshire*

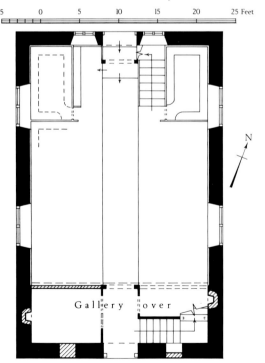

General Baptist Chapel, Fore Street

covered with slates. The S front has a central entrance from which a canopy has fallen away, flanked by two narrow blocked windows and two larger windows above; all the windows have plain timber lintels and renewed frames. Two windows in the N wall flank the pulpit and have between them a doorway giving access to a small later burial-ground at the back. There are pairs of larger windows in the E and W walls.

The interior ($37\frac{1}{2}$ ft by $22\frac{1}{2}$ ft) had a flat plaster ceiling. The gallery at the S end is supported by two square fluted columns with moulded caps and bases and retains a section of balustraded front concealed behind later fielded panelling. Two small vestries below the gallery have later fireplaces in the side walls. The former hexagonal pulpit stood at the N end above the rear doorway. The roof was supported by four king-post trusses.

Monuments: in chapel, on N wall (1) John Collier, 20 years pastor, 1780; in burial-ground, about ten memorials including (2) Dorcas Potter, 1812; (3) Elizabeth French, 1785, *et al*. *Seating*: two box-pews with fielded-panelled sides remain at N end.

Evans (1897) 177. Much (1835) 462–80

(127) PRESBYTERIAN, Cross Street (SX 755860). The congregation claims to have originated with the ejection in 1662 of Robert Woolcombe, who became the first minister of the Presbyterian society. About 1687 a house was converted for the use of the meeting. On Woolcombe's death in 1692 the congregation divided, the majority building a new meeting-house on the

Presbyterian chapel (Unitarian), Moretonhampstead.   (127)

present site where they were rejoined before 1721 by the other section of the church. The meeting-house was enlarged in 1718 but by 1801 it had become unsafe and it was replaced by the existing chapel in 1802. A fragment of the rubble walling of the former building remains as part of the boundary wall in the NW corner of the burial-ground. The society, which since 1818 has shared its pastor with the General Baptist congregation, has long supported a Unitarian ministry.

The chapel has rendered rubble walls and a hipped slate roof. The N front has a central doorway with a segmental-arched hood and blind fanlight; above is a small square tablet inscribed 'GW/ERECTED/1802'. Two small segmental-arched windows flank the entrance over which is a single round arched window. Two round-arched windows occupy each of the other walls.

The interior has a flat plaster ceiling with a moulded cornice. The N gallery has a panelled front with concave central section, supported by three turned-wood columns perhaps reused from the earlier building; the centre of the front is painted with the name *Yaweh* in Hebrew characters.

Fittings – *Chandeliers*: pair, brass, six branches, early 19th-century. *Clock*: Parliament clock from Bowden Hill Chapel (*see* Crediton (56)). *Glass*: in windows on E and W sides, with red border and sunburst above centre light, early 19th-century; also in N window of W wall small panel depicting Christ at the Last Supper. *Monument*: in chapel, Rev. John Smethurst, 42 years minister 'who for nearly the same space of time was also minister of the Unitarian Baptists in this town', 1859. *Plate*: includes a two-handled gadrooned cup of 1703. *Seating*: in gallery, some original plain high-backed pews.

Evans (1897) 176–7. Murch (1835) 471–9.

MORETONHAMPSTEAD, *Devonshire*

5   0   5   10   15   20   25 Feet

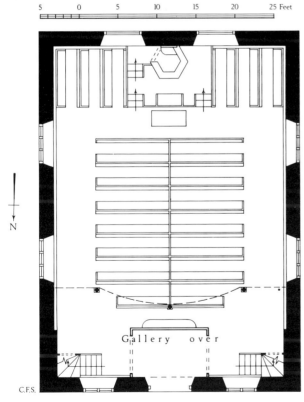

N

C.F.S.

Presbyterian Chapel, Cross Street

(128) Former WESLEYAN, Cross Street (SX 754860). Four round-arched windows in front wall. Dated 1817 but rebuilt or extensively repaired after a fire in 1866.

NEWTON ABBOT

(129) Former BAPTIST, East Street (SX 860711). A church which existed in 1697, with a chapel and burial-ground in East Street, was re-formed c.1818. The chapel, probably rebuilt at this time, continued in use after c.1860 by a Strict Baptist minority which disbanded about 1928; it is now used by a Spiritualist society. The rendered front wall has two round-arched windows and a circular window above a modern porch. The interior, which has been refitted, has a segmental barrel-vaulted plaster ceiling. In front is a small burial-ground with reset 19th-century headstones.

A new chapel 20 yards E, built c.1860 by the majority of the Baptist church, was extended to the front in 1894.

Oliver (1968) 120–1.

(130) Former CONGREGATIONAL, Wolborough Street (SX 856711). 'Salem Chapel' was built in 1836 on or near the site of Pound Chapel which had been opened in 1719 by one section of a formerly Presbyterian society originating with the ejection in 1662 of William Yeo, curate of Wolborough. The church became Congregational in the early 19th century; in 1876 it removed to a new chapel in Queen Street and the former building has since passed into commercial use.

The chapel has a broad rendered front of five bays, with a pediment, two tall windows above the former entrances and a series of lunettes at gallery level.

Huxtable, J., and Snow, A., *Our Fathers that Begat Us – The Story of the Protestant Dissenters of Newton Abbot, 1662–1984* (1985).

(131) Former CONGREGATIONAL, Queen Street (SX 862713). Built in 1875–6 to supersede (130). The chapel, in the Gothic style by Joseph Rowell, has walls of grey limestone with Bath stone dressings; it comprises a broad nave of five bays with an axial tower at the entrance flanked by staircase vestibules and an organ recess between vestries at the opposite end. The adjacent Sunday-school was built in 1881. A parapet and spire to the tower, although allowed for in the original design, were not completed until 1910. The church (now URC) united with a Methodist congregation in Avenue Road in 1984 and the building has since been converted to office use.

CYB (1877) 491–2. Huxtable and Snow, op. cit.

NEWTON TRACEY

(132) FRIENDS' BURIAL-GROUND, Loverings (SS 528268). Rectangular enclosure bounded by rubble walls. At S end is a slate tablet inscribed 'THIS PIECE OF LAND was given by RICHARD ADAMS to the SOCIETY OF FRIENDS For a burying ground BY WILL Dated 28th of 8th month 1782'. There are no monuments.

Dymond (1899) 59–71.

NORTHAM

(133) BAPTIST, Meeting Street, Appledore (SS 46453060). Three-bay gabled front of rubble with pointed-arched windows, built 1858 for a church founded 1833. The church formerly met in 'Ebenezer Chapel', Irsha Street, West Appledore, a building of

1835 later used (1858–1907) by Bible Christians but now demolished.

Thompson (1885) 68–76.

(134) INDEPENDENT, Meeting Street, Appledore, (SS 46403055). The church, formerly Presbyterian, claims to have originated in 1662 in which year Anthony Downe was ejected from the vicarage of Northam. The present meeting-house, built in 1816, has rendered walls and a slate roof. The N front, with two tiers of round-arched windows in four bays, has a central pediment flanked by swept parapets above the end bays. The central doorway is flanked by a pair of Roman Doric columns which support an entablature. Above the N gable is an hexagonal domed bell-cote and weathervane.

Monuments: in yard E of chapel (1) Jane Serjeant, 1847; (2) Ellen Fisher, 1846.

Independent meeting-house, Appledore.   (134)

(135) WESLEYAN, Richmond Road, Appledore (SS 462303). Rubble and slate, pointed-arched windows with intersecting glazing bars. Three-bay gabled front with large quatrefoiled tablet above entrance having modern painted inscription and date 1851.

NORTHLEW

(136) BIBLE CHRISTIAN (SX 504992). 'Hebron', built 1815, rebuilt 1858.

(137) BIBLE CHRISTIAN, Whiddon (SS 477001). Opened 1839, refurbished 1907. *Monument*: in burial-ground, Edward Rich Bickle, 1848, slate headstone.

Parsons (1972) 122–8.

FORMER BIBLE CHRISTIAN CHAPEL, NORTH MOLTON   C·F·S·1973

NORTH MOLTON

(138) Former BIBLE CHRISTIAN (SS 735298). Rubble and slate, broad three-bay front with wide pointed-arched openings; early 19th-century, now a workshop.

OKEHAMPTON

(139) Former CONGREGATIONAL, North Street (SX 589954). 'Ebenezer Chapel' built in 1822, has a rendered N front of three bays with a central pointed-arched entrance and blind oval recess above, flanked and surmounted by round-arched niches. The side and rear walls have each two wide pointed-arched windows with intersecting tracery. The interior, refitted in the late 19th century, has a single gallery next to the entrance.

Former Congregational chapel, Okehampton.   (139)

Monuments: in chapel (1) Sarah Underdown Burd, 1843; (2) William Burd of Goldburn, pastor, 1849; in burial-ground many slate headstones including, close to front entrance, (3) Nicholas Newcombe, 'first Calvinistic minister of Oakhampton', 1832. (Chapel closed *c*.1974, now in commercial use)

(140) Former WESLEYAN, High Street (SX 587951). Three-bay front with two tiers of lancet windows and date-tablet of 1841 above entrance. Schoolroom below chapel. Superseded 1904.

OTTERY ST MARY

(141) JESU STREET CHAPEL (SY 100954). The formerly Presbyterian congregation originated after the Restoration largely with the work of Robert Collins, ejected Rector of Talaton, and the meeting-house was built at the close of the 17th century. Towards the end of the following century the cause weakened and appears to have ceased for some years prior to its re-formation in 1812 as a Congregational church (now URC). The building was extensively repaired in 1842 and drastically refitted in 1899; the hipped roof, which retains its late 17th-century structure, was re-covered with large slates in 1922. The chapel has brick walls in Flemish bond with dark headers. In each wall is a pair of segmental-arched windows. An original porch with altered roof covers the principal entrance in the SE wall and has a small 18th-century window above, lighting the back of the former gallery; a second entrance in the NE wall is covered by a later brick porch. The NW wall is now obscured by a Sunday-school of *c*.1870 adjacent to it, and the two principal windows have been blocked, but two smaller windows remain at an upper level which lit a tall pulpit removed in 1876.

The interior (50 ft square) has four round timber posts supporting the roof structure between which the flat plaster ceiling rises to a square domed centre. An early 18th-century gallery along the SE side, removed in 1899, had a fielded-panelled front rising at its junction with the principal columns and supported between by two timber posts; a staircase at the S corner had turned balusters supporting a moulded handrail. Box-pews probably introduced in 1842 were removed at the same date.

Jesu Street Chapel, Ottery St Mary.   (141)

Fittings – *Clock*: on wall of lobby, formerly attached to gallery front, arched top and small secondary dial, signed 'John Pepys, London', early 18th-century. *Coffin Stools*: two, early 18th-century. *Hatchments*: two, on SE wall. *Monuments*: in burial-ground behind chapel (1) William Evans, 'who died while a student at Axminster', 1807, *et al.*, table-tomb; (2) Cornelius, son of Rev. J. B. Wildbore of Falmouth, 'who finished his course with joy at the late Rev. S. Buncombe's Academy at Ottery, April 15 1789, Aged 19'; (3) Rev. John Varder, ten years pastor, 1841, Mary his widow, 1850, her sister Elizabeth Lavington,

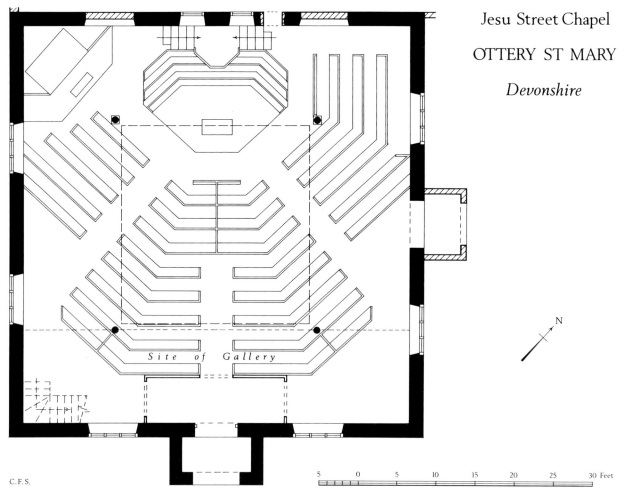

Jesu Street Chapel

OTTERY ST MARY

Devonshire

C.F.S.

5 0 5 10 15 20 25 30 Feet

1848, and their children Elizabeth Lavington Varder, 1844, and Mary Lavington Varder, 1861; (4) Susanna, wife of George Norrington, 1838; (5) William Palmer, 1823, and Elizabeth his wife, 1820. (All monuments uprooted and loose 1977, since laid flat as paths)

Tucker, G. M., *Ottery St Mary Congregational Church* (1962). Tucker, G. M., *Ottery St Mary United Reformed Church* (1988).

(142) WESLEYAN, Mill Street (SY 096953). Three-bay brick front with shaped gable, round-arched openings, and tablet dated 1829. Gallery around three sides, now attenuated. *Communion Cloth*: linen with repeated pattern of portraits of 'Rev. J. Wesley A. M.', secular, early 19th-century.

PAIGNTON

(143) Former CONGREGATIONAL, Cecil Road (SX 885610). 'The Independent Chapel in Spratt's Lane' (now Cecil Road), built in 1823, was sold to the Bible Christians in 1884 when the original congregation removed to a new building in Dartmouth Road; it remains in Methodist use. The walls are of red sandstone rubble with some brick dressings and the roof is hipped. The rendered front of three bays with pointed-arched windows was altered in 1903 by the addition of a gable formerly carrying a dated roundel and having below it a large decorative inscription; a wide triple-gabled porch was also added at this date.

Wesleyan chapel, Ottery St Mary. (142)

Wesleyan chapel, Lana. (144)

PANCRASWEEK

(144) WESLEYAN, Lana (SS 300073). The chapel has rubble walls rendered to the S and a hipped slated roof. E front with semi-circular-arched canopy above the entrance supported by two columns, three small upper windows with slate tablet between dated 1838. Pair of round-arched windows in side walls. Later schoolroom at rear with rebuilt porch dated 1894. Small original E gallery with panelled front and moulded capping, later rostrum pulpit opposite. Three ranks of pews with central dividing rail. Extensive burial-ground with slate headstones of late 19th century and after.

Dolbey (1964) 175–6. Shaw, T., *Methodism in Lana* (1955).

PARKHAM

(145) Former WESLEYAN, Holwell (SS 378231). Small chapel with rendered walls and slate roof. Three-bay gabled front with lancets. Opened 1823. (Converted to house since 1973)

PARRACOMBE

(146) WESLEYAN (SS 668448). Rendered walls and slate roof, gabled three-bay front with pointed-arched openings; dated 1839.

PLYMOUTH

(147) TREVILLE STREET CHAPEL (SX 482545). A society of Protestant Dissenters originating after 1662 under the influence of several ejected ministers built a meeting-house in Treville Street before the end of that century; this was replaced in 1832 by a chapel of five bays with a three-bay pediment which remained until 1941 when it was gutted by enemy action and subsequently demolished. The congregation, now Unitarian, has met since 1958 in a new chapel in Notte Street.

Plate: includes two cups of 1632 and 1660 and a footed plate of 1709.

Evans (1897) 199–200. Murch (1835) 496–524.

(148) SHERWELL CHAPEL, Tavistock Road (SX 481551). A congregation gathered by a follower of George Whitefield, Andrew Kinsman, a grocer living in Breton Side, later Essex Street, met from 1745 in 'The Tabernacle', a chapel built by Kinsman at the rear of his house. A 'New Tabernacle' was built in 1797 in Norley Lane for this congregation which formed itself into an Independent church in that year. Both chapels survived until 1941. The present building in Tavistock Road, erected in 1862–4 to the design of Paull and Ayliffe of Manchester, is in the Gothic style with walls of limestone rubble and a slated roof. The gabled front faces E and there is a tower and spire at the NE corner. The interior is divided into nave and aisles by arcades with paired iron columns and has a gallery around three sides. (URC)

Griffin, S., *The Sherwell Story, A History of Sherwell Congregational Church, Plymouth (1744–1964)* (Plymouth 1964).

(149) WESLEYAN, Eastlake Street (SX 480548). The Central Hall, originally 'Ebenezer Chapel', has rendered walls and two tiers of round-arched windows at the sides. It was built in 1816, subsequently much altered and in 1940 converted to its present use.

Rogers, A. H. E., *Count Your Blessings, 1816–1970* (1970).

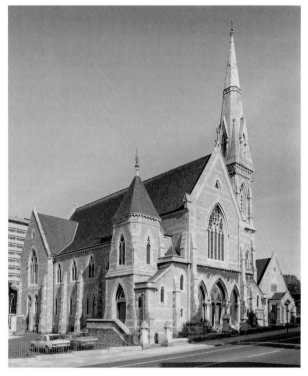

Sherwell Congregational chapel (URC), Plymouth. (148)

(150) Former WESLEYAN, Union Street, Stonehouse (SX 465544). Rendered walls and three-bay pedimented front; built in 1813 but altered and enlarged in the late 19th century.

(151) Former UNITARIAN, George Street, Devonport (SX 455545). The chapel, built in 1790 for a newly formed Unitarian congregation, was closed and sold in 1806, the result, in part, of opposition by the dockyard authorities to the supposedly subversive character of the denomination. The cause was later revived in other premises. The building, now The Old Chapel p.h., has rubble walls with brick dressings and a slate roof, gabled front and wide gabled porch with original date-stone

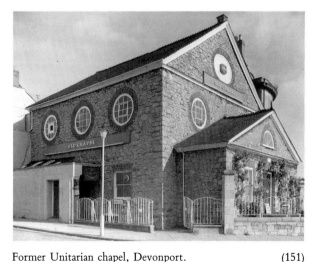

Former Unitarian chapel, Devonport. (151)

above the entrance, two circular upper windows above and a blind oval in the gable; there are three circular windows high in the SW wall. The chapel is approximately square (46 ft by 45 ft externally) and has vaulted cellars below.

Evans (1897) 69–70. Murch (1835) 526–32. *UHST* VI (1935–8) 148–9.

Two other 18th-century chapels in Devonport, demolished since 1950, were the *Methodist Chapel* in Ker Street of 1785–6, latterly a Drill Hall, and the *Moravian Chapel* in James Street of 1771, closed *c*.1917.

RACKENFORD

(152) BIBLE CHRISTIAN (SS 852184). 'Ebenezer Chapel', dated 1848, has rendered walls, gabled front with round-arched window above entrance and two pointed-arched windows in side wall. Small gallery over entrance. Detached schoolroom built 1891.

ROBOROUGH

(153) BIBLE CHRISTIAN, Ebberly Lodge (SS 570193). A pair of lodges flanking the N end of a former carriage drive half-a-mile NE of Ebberly House were built *c*.1810–20. They passed to the Bible Christians in 1839 after the construction of a new road had isolated them from the remainder of the drive. The NW lodge was converted for use as a chapel; it was enlarged in 1913 by the addition of a Sunday-school. Both lodges are square with rendered walls and slate-covered originally pyramidal roofs. The cottage doorways and adjacent windows remain facing the former drive.

BIBLE CHRISTIAN CHAPEL, EBBERLY LODGE   CFS·1973

SAMPFORD COURTENAY

(154) WESLEYAN, Sticklepath (SX 641940). Sticklepath was an important staging post in the mid 18th century for Methodist preachers travelling to and from Cornwall; here John Wesley and others enjoyed the hospitality of local Quakers whose *burial-ground* remains as part of the public cemetery 100 yards SW of the chapel. The chapel, built in 1816 and enlarged in 1838, has rendered walls possibly of cob and a slated roof. The N front is gabled and surmounted by a large granite cross of traditional pattern, possibly mediaeval. A small bell-tower with wooden superstructure and broach-spire, containing one bell, stands on the W side above a projecting gallery staircase. The interior has a segmental barrel-vaulted ceiling.

Dymond (1899) 109–11.

SAMPFORD PEVERELL

(155) WESLEYAN (ST 028143). Rendered front with round-arched windows, opened 1803. Porch later.

SHEBBEAR

(156) BIBLE CHRISTIAN, Lake (SS 448094). The first Bible Christian society was formed in 1815 by William O'Bryan at Lake Farm, the home of James Thorne. Shebbear College, 200 yards NE of the chapel, was founded in 1841 and became the principal school and training college for the denomination. The first chapel, built 1817–18, was rebuilt in 1841; the present building with rendered walls and slate roof has been drastically altered or rebuilt in recent years.

Monuments: in burial-ground, many slate headstones, including (1) Mary, wife of Samuel Thorne, printer, 'daughter of William O'Bryan founder of the Bible Christians among whom she was a minister sixty years', 1883; (2) Samuel Thorne, printer, 1873; (3) James Thorne, preacher, 1872; (4) Rebecca, wife of William Cobbledick, 1850.

Bourne (1905) 60–1, 266–7.

SIDBURY

(157) INDEPENDENT (SY 138916). The chapel, dated 1820, was built for a formerly Presbyterian church which claimed to have originated in 1662. It has rendered walls possibly of cob and a hipped slate roof. The broad E front of three bays has a central doorway, two-centred arched openings with moulded labels and intersecting tracery to the windows. There are two pointed-arched windows at the N end of the W wall and two small windows at the S end above and below a gallery.

Independent chapel, Sidbury.   (157)

SIDMOUTH

(158) THE OLD MEETING-HOUSE, High Street (SY 126876), built in 1710 for an existing Presbyterian congregation, now Unitarian, has rendered walls of cob on a rubble base. It was drastically altered in 1886 when traceried Gothic windows were inserted and a gable and porch added to the N side. The original front faced S and had a central doorway, now blocked, between four rectangular windows now with renewed frames. The interior (42¾ ft by 23¼ ft) has a boarded barrel-vaulted ceiling and an original W gallery with fielded-panelled front.

Fittings – Benefaction Boards: two, early 19th-century and later. *Clock*: on gallery front, inscribed 'The Gift of MS 1767' signed 'Wm Hornsey Exon.'. *Monuments*: in chapel (1) John Carslake, 1815, and Elizabeth his sister, 1816; (2) Rev. Edmund Butcher, 23 years pastor, 1822; (3) Ann Kiddell, 1847; in burial-ground to S, a few early 19th-century headstones. *Plate*: includes a cup of

The Old Meeting-house, Sidmouth.   (158)

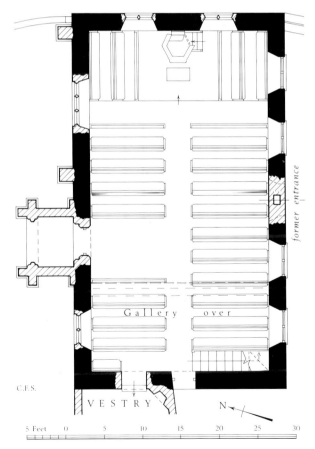

The Old Meeting-house
SIDMOUTH   *Devonshire*

Gallery   over

former entrance

C.E.S.

VESTRY   N

5 Feet   0   5   10   15   20   25   30

1807 and plate of 1749. *Pulpit*: hexagonal with flared base reduced in height, shaped back-board and ogee-section canopy surmounted by an urn, 1710.

Evans (1897) 225–6. Murch (1835) 344–52. *UHST* III (1923–6) 64–5.

(159) CONGREGATIONAL, Chapel Street (SY 126873). Lancet Gothic, c.1846, replacing the 'Marsh Chapel' built 1810 and demolished 1967. (URC)

(160) Former WESLEYAN, Mill Street (SY 127876). Rendered walls with tall round-arched windows; built 1837, superseded by present chapel in High Street 1884.

SOUTH MOLTON

(161) BAPTIST, New Street (SS 716258). A Baptist church which existed in the late 17th century dispersed c.1772. A new cause was formed in 1842 and the present chapel erected in the following year. The building has rubble walls and a slate roof. The E wall facing the street is of five bays with lancet windows and two-stage gabled buttresses.

Ivimey II (1814) 146. Thompson (1885) 113–18.

(162) Former CONGREGATIONAL, North Street (SS 714260). Several meeting-places for Presbyterians and Congregationalists were licensed in South Molton under the 1672 Indulgence. The present chapel, standing immediately W of the parish church and approached through the churchyard, was built in 1834 on the site of a formerly Presbyterian meeting-house of 1701; it was much altered in the late 19th century when the E front was reconstructed. The walls are of rubble and the roof, formerly hipped to the E, is covered with slates. The E front is of three bays with pilasters supporting a pediment above the central bay in which is the painted date 1662. In the front and side walls are tall round-arched windows and projecting on the N side is a brick vestry rebuilt in 1887, approached internally through a doorway of the early 19th century. The interior is lofty and retains traces of a former E gallery. (Chapel closed, proposed conversion to domestic use 1988)

Fittings – *Font*: stone, panelled octagonal bowl on square stem with double pilasters and chamfered base, inscribed 'ELIZTH THORN/GRILSTON/1846'. *Monuments*: in chapel (1) Mary,

Former Congregational chapel, South Molton.   (162)

wife of Rev. William Thorn, 1820, signed 'J. Gould, Barum'; (2) Rev. William Thorn, 1847; (3) Philip Wigery, 'Clerk in this place of Worship 51 years', 1820, erected by the congregation; (4) Elizabeth Richards Pyer, daughter of Rev. John Pyer, 1837; externally, in front of E wall (5) James, son of John and Frances Disney of North Molton, 1843, in railed enclosure.

(163) WESLEYAN, North Street (SS 715260). Stone, Gothic, with gabled porches and windows with cusped tracery, 1883 by A. Lauder, replacing a cob chapel of 1821.

STOKENHAM

(164) BIBLE CHRISTIAN, Chillington (SX 790428). Rubble and slate with three pointed-arched windows in the side walls, gabled N front with blocked doorway and oval tablet inscribed 'B.C./EBENEZER CHAPEL/1850'. Vestry at S end with schoolroom over; pulpit removed from S to N in late 19th century and new porch built on W side.

SWIMBRIDGE

(165) BAPTIST (SS 620300). Rubble and slate, pointed-arched windows with intersecting glazing bars, opened 1837.

Thompson (1885) 92–102.

TAVISTOCK

(166) ABBEY CHAPEL (SX 482743). The 15th-century Abbot's Hall of Tavistock Abbey was occupied from the late 17th century, by permission of the Earls of Bedford, by a Presbyterian society whose origin has been attributed to the work of Thomas Larkham, ejected from the parish church in 1660. This society divided in 1794, the heterodox, latterly Unitarian, element retaining possession of the Abbey Chapel until 1959 when they disbanded; the chapel is now used by a Brethren assembly.

The building has stone walls and a slate-covered roof. The original entrance was through a two-storeyed porch against the NW wall which has octagonal corner buttresses with crocketted pinnacles; the doorway has a two-centred arch with square moulded label and cusped spandrels; above the doorway is a two-light window. The present entrance in the NE gable wall is through a reset doorway with four-centred arched head and square label. On the SE side are three windows of two lights with massive two-stage buttresses between and the remains of a chimney-breast near the SW end.

The porch has an original ribbed vault with carved bosses and a small room above in which is a dado of 18th-century fielded panels. The chapel has been almost entirely refitted in recent years but some late 18th-century panelling remains at the top of the two gallery staircases at the NE end. The roof structure, rebuilt since 1960, was supported by arch-braced collar trusses and had a barrel-vaulted plaster ceiling below.

Monuments: a burial-ground NE of the chapel, in use from the late 18th century, has been partly cleared but some stones remain reset against the boundary walls including (1) Rev. William Evans, 1847; (2) Thomas Holmes, 1787, *et al.*; (3) Mary Moon, 1784. *Plate*: at Buckland Abbey Museum, two mugs, marks worn but probably pre-1679.

Christian Freeman (1869) 43–4. *CHST* IV (1909–10) 55–8. Evans (1897) 240–1. L.C.B., *Story of a Thousand Years, The Abbey Chapel, Tavistock* (1962). Murch (1835) 482–94.

(167) Former WESLEYAN, Barley Market Street (SX 482746). The chapel, opened in 1814 and superseded in 1858, is now used as a workshop; it has rubble walls and a hipped slate roof. Front wall of three bays with central entrance and fanlight in wide round-arched recess flanked by similarly arched windows, now altered, and three small windows above.

(168) WESLEYAN, Chapel Street (SX 479743). Rendered walls, corner buttresses with pinnacles, lancet windows. Built 1858.

Wesleyan chapel, Tavistock. (168)

(169) Former BIBLE CHRISTIAN, Bannawell Street (SX 479747). Built in 1847; in 1911 it passed to the Brethren; it is now in commercial use. Rubble and slate, front with wide eaves and round-arched windows in three bays; set back between a pair of two-storeyed houses intended for the use of ministers.

TAWSTOCK

(170) EASTACOMBE CHAPEL (SS 541297), built for a Baptist church in the early 19th century, is now used by the Brethren. It has rendered walls, a gabled front with two tiers of windows and tall windows in the side walls.

Thompson (1885) 143–4.

(171) Former BAPTIST, Hiscott (SS 549262). Rubble walls partly rendered and slate roof, gabled front with pointed-arched doorway and windows; early 19th-century. Subsequently used by Brethren, disused 1973 (converted to house 1982–4). *Monuments*: in burial-ground (1) Grace, wife of Thomas Ridd of Swannamoor, 1851; (2) John Parkhouse, 1853, and Mary his daughter, 1842; (3) John Cawsey, 1839; (4) John Cawsey, 1848; (5) Elizabeth, wife of John Moore, 1844; (6) George Leal, 1842.

(172) PROVIDENCE CHAPEL, Hiscott (SS 548261), believed to have been built in 1830 for a Baptist church, was sold to the Bible Christians in 1859 and remains in Methodist use. It has rendered walls and a slate roof, and a broad three-bay front with arched openings.

TEIGNMOUTH

(173) EBENEZER CHAPEL, Bitton Park Road (SX 938731), now the 'Gospel Hall', was opened 24 April 1824 by a Baptist church which in 1830 invited George Müller to the pastorate. During his short ministry Müller introduced practices characteristic of the Brethren to whom he and the congregation subsequently adhered. The building has rendered walls and a slate-covered roof; the front, of three stepped bays concealing a gable, has two ogee-arched windows with intersecting glazing bars, and an upper row of blind quatrefoils. The lofty interior has a former gallery next to the entrance, now converted to classrooms, but no other original fittings.

BM XVI (1824) 346. Broadbent, E. H., *The Pilgrim Church* (1931) 361–3. Rowdon (1967) 114 ff.

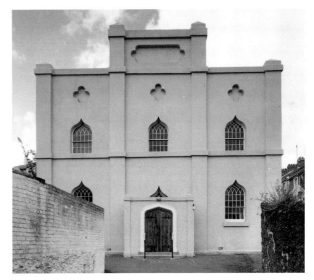

'Ebenezer Chapel', Teignmouth. (173)

(174) WESLEYAN, Somerset Place (SX 940728). Rubble and slate, opened 1845. Triple-gabled front with two-stage buttresses and lancet windows.

THORVERTON

(175) BAPTIST (SS 924020). Rendered walls and hipped slate roof, built 1833–4. Three-bay front with centre pediment and two tiers of four-centred arched windows; central bay rebuilt 1955 omitting one upper window. Refitted 1878, 1955.

Stoyle, I., *Thorverton Baptist Church 1832–1982, A Brief History* (1982).

THROWLEIGH

(176) BIBLE CHRISTIAN, Providence Place (SX 675893). Rendered rubble walls and hipped slate roof, end entrance with tablet on porch dated 1839, round-arched window over; pointed-arched windows to side walls; gallery at entrance.

THRUSHELTON

(177) WESLEYAN, Broadley (SX 462873). Rendered walls and hipped slate roof, rectangular windows; renewed date-tablet in front wall, 1836.

Bible Christian chapel, Providence Place, Throwleigh.   (176)

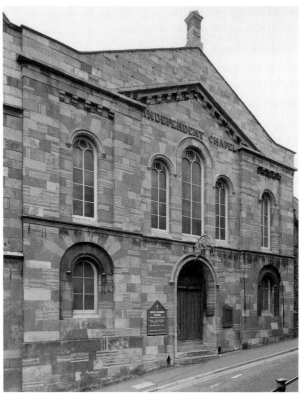

Congregational chapel (URC), Tiverton.   (179)

TIVERTON

(178) BAPTIST, Newport Street (SS 955128). Rubble with gabled front and staircase wings, round-arched plate-traceried window over central entrance, 1876–7 by G. S. Bridgman. Built adjacent to site of earlier meeting-houses of 1697 and 1730–2 for a church reputedly founded in 1607.

Case, H. B., *The History of the Baptist Church in Tiverton, 1607 to 1907* (1907). Ivimey IV (1830) 300–2.

(179) CONGREGATIONAL, St Peter's Street (SS 953126). The church (now URC) which originated with the ejection of the Rector of Tiverton, Theophilus Polwheile in 1660, has occupied the present site since 1687. In that year the 'Steps Meeting-house' was built, of irregular plan with a frontage of five bays with two tiers of windows and entrances in the two end bays. A secession c.1700 led to the erection of a second meeting-house also in St Peter's Street, which passed through a variety of uses and was demolished in 1844. A third congregation, which occupied the 'Pitt meeting-house', built c.1689, united with that at the Steps c.1787. The present chapel, built in 1831, has a grey ashlar front of three principal bays with a central open pediment and two tiers of round-arched windows. The interior, an irregular polygon, has a continuous gallery with a late 19th-century cast-iron front, at which period the pulpit and seating were also replaced.

Fittings – *Flute*: 'John Sharland's Flute played during services around 1833', signed 'L. Drouët, London, 537'. *Inscriptions*: on front wall below pediment, 'INDEPENDENT CHAPEL', applied ornamental lettering (removed before 1988); on front of gallery, painted legend 'This Church was founded *A.D. 1660* by

the Revd. THEOPHILUS POLWHEILE M.A.'. *Lamp Bracket*: over front entrance, cast-iron, mid 19th-century. *Monuments*: in chapel (1) Rev. W. E. Bailey, 1829; (2) Samuel Plumbe, ' . . . one of the four brethren who undertook on behalf of the people the pecuniary responsibility in the erection of this House of God in the year 1831', 1840; (3) William Stratton, 1841; (4) Robert Ellis, 1836.

Authers, W. P., *The Tiverton Congregational Church, 1660–1960* (1960) 85–91.

(180) WESLEYAN, St Peter's Street (SS 954126). Tiverton was frequently visited by John Wesley on his journeys to and from Cornwall. A Methodist society was formed c.1752 with a preaching-house converted from cottages 'behind the houses on the east side of Peter's Street'. The present chapel, on the same site, was built in 1814; it has brick walls covered with a later rendering; the front, of five bays in two stages with a three-bay pediment and swept parapets each side, was altered in the late 19th century by the addition of a wide porch but the original round-arched windows remain at gallery level and in the side walls. The interior has a gallery around three sides and an organ recess at the E end, with two Ionic columns *in antis*, added in the late 19th century.

Monuments: in chapel (1) William Henry Hodge, 1846, and his sister Emily Jane, wife of Rev. John Eglinton, 1848; (2) John Pratt, 1866, trustee, and Ann his wife, 1847; (3) William Worth Bennett, 1841, local preacher; (4) Sarah Sellick, 1845; (5) Rev. William Buckley Fox of Saddleworth, Yorks, circuit superintendent, 1834, erected by Sir John Kennaway Bart and others,

Wesleyan chapel, St Peter's Street, Tiverton.   (180)

signed 'Nash'; (6) Jane Ellen, wife of Rev. Robert Bond, Wesleyan minister, 1845; (7) William Brewer, 1848, and Mary his widow, 1851.

(181) Former CONGREGATIONAL, Bolham (SS 951149). Village chapel of rubble and slate, built 1849. Broad three-bay front with gabled porch and two windows of two cusped lights under a four-centred arch with moulded label. Gable wall to SW has a three-light window with four-centred arched head, and shield-shaped sundial above with date of erection; a bell-cote for one bell was removed from the SW gable c.1958. (Converted to house since 1975)

Authers, op. cit. 85–91.

(182) CONGREGATIONAL, Chapel Street, Elmore (SS 958128). Rubble and slate, built 1842–3. Two round-arched windows in side wall, entrance in NE gable wall with bell-cote above. (URC)

Authers, op. cit. 64–74.

TOPSHAM

(183) Former PRESBYTERIAN, Victoria Road (SX 966880). Four meeting-places were licensed for dissenters in 1662 and a regular society appears to have been established by c.1687. The meeting-house, which may have been built c.1700, was 'assigned to trustees' during the ministry of Daniel Cooper, 1723–7. A secession of Independents in 1804 left the increasingly heterodox meeting in an enfeebled state. The building was closed in 1888 and sold in 1892 to the established church for a Sunday-school and mission hall. It was transferred to the freemasons in 1930 who continue to use it.

The meeting-house stands on the SE side of the road, formerly a ropewalk. The walls are rendered and the roof is slate covered. The building is rectangular ($43\frac{1}{2}$ ft by $53\frac{1}{4}$ ft externally) with a double-gabled front to the NW and a roof valley at collar level. The original entrances may have been in the NE side, flanking a pair of closely set early 18th-century windows which could have

lit a former pulpit. The interior, now subdivided, has a segmental barrel-vaulted plaster ceiling.

Fittings – *Chandelier*: brass, sixteen-branch, c.1700. *Clock*: Parliament clock with octagonal face and oriental scenes on pendulum case, signed 'Cuthbert Lee, London', 18th-century. (The chandelier and clock are now in the parish church.) *Plate*: (since 1920 at Meadville Theological College, Chicago) included two late 17th-century cups and a footed plate dated 1705.

Delderfield, E. R., *The Raleigh Country* (1949, 5th edn 1960) 93, 149–50. Murch (1835) 366–9. *UHST* III (1923–6) 166–9; V (1931–4) 440; XVII (1979–82) 125–7.

(184) CONGREGATIONAL, Victoria Road (SX 967881). Built in 1839 for a church formed in 1804. Rendered front of three bays with pointed-arched windows and a small gable over centre with tablet inscribed 'RD : BROWN ARCHT.'. The original entrance in the end wall is partly covered by a school building of 1897. The interior has a gallery with Gothic panelled front and former pulpit recess opposite.

Brockett (1962b) 37–48.

TORQUAY

(185) BAPTIST, St Marychurch Road, Upton Vale (SX 914645). Large chapel of rubble with lancet windows and crow-stepped gables; built 1863 to supersede a chapel of 1837 in Temperance Street.

BM XXX (1838) 162. *Baptist Times* (11 March 1982).

(186) Former BRETHREN, Warren Road (SX 914640). Built 1852; rendered gabled front. Now auction rooms.

(187) Former INDEPENDENT, Lower Union Lane (SX 916640). When control of the proprietory 'Trinity Chapel' of 1831 in Meadfoot Road passed to the established church within a few years of its erection, Independents built a small chapel for themselves in Carey Street, now Lower Union Lane. The congregation divided in 1844, the seceders building a chapel, recently demolished, at the S end of Abbey Road, opened 1847. The former chapel, built in 1834, was sold for commercial use in 1877. The walls are rendered and the front of three bays has an altered pediment; the exposed side wall has wide bracketed eaves.

CYB (1847) 168–70; (1857) 182.

Free Church, Babbacombe Road, Torquay.   (188)

(188) FREE CHURCH, Babbacombe Road, St Marychurch (SX 922656). The chapel at Furrough's Cross was built in 1852–3 for evangelical Anglican seceders and paid for by Sir Culling Eardley Eardley Bart; a Congregational church (now URC) was formed in 1904. The building comprises a two-bay W chancel, a nave of three bays, N aisle and S porch with bell-cote formerly containing one bell. W of the chapel is a detached day-school built 1854.

(189) Former FRIENDS, Warren Road (SX 915639). Rendered gabled front of three bays with segmental-arched entrance; rubble sides. Built 1854.

(190) Former WESLEYAN, Babbacombe Road (SX 923637). Stone Gothic with tall corner spire; 1873–4 by Johnson of London. Now Elim Pentecostal Church.

(191) Former PRESBYTERIAN, Torwood Gardens Road (SX 923635). St Andrew's, built 1863 for the Presbyterian Church in England, is of stone with crow-stepped gables and a corner tower. Now First Church of Christ, Scientist.

TWITCHEN

(192) Former WESLEYAN (SS 788302). Small chapel of rubble with a slate roof built 1860 at one end of an existing house. Front wall of three bays with brick heads to doorway and two round-arched windows; basement below.

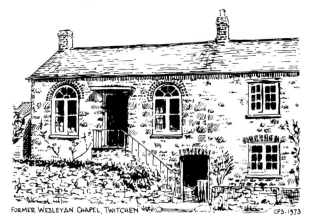

FORMER WESLEYAN CHAPEL, TWITCHEN   CFS.1973

UFFCULME

(193) BAPTIST, Chapel Hill (ST 067128). Rubble and slate, built 1815 to replace an earlier meeting-house, altered and enlarged in the late 19th century. Rendered front of three bays with round-arched windows and a quatrefoiled light above a pointed-arched doorway. *Monuments*: in burial-ground, include a table-tomb to Sarah Hill, 1781.

(194) CONGREGATIONAL (ST 063125). A Presbyterian congregation which originated in the late 17th century, and numbered amongst its ministers Samuel Short and John Chorly, appears to have occupied a meeting-house on this site at least since 1720. Existing tombstones attest to some continued use throughout the late 18th and early 19th century, although the history of the society at that period is obscure, as is the reference by Murch to the erection of the 'Bridewell Chapel' in 1792 by Richard Hall Clarke for Unitarians. The present chapel, built in 1862–3 to designs by George Bidlake of Wolverhampton, has stone walls

Former Wesleyan chapel, Torquay.   (190)

Former Presbyterian chapel, Torquay.   (191)

and a slate roof, plate traceried windows and a thin turret at the SE corner. *Inscription*: below turret, on cast-iron tablet, 'ERECTED 1720 REBUILT 1862–3'. *Monuments*: reset against S wall (1) Hannah, widow of Oliver Pyke, 1761; (2) Elizabeth, wife of Rev. John Chorly, 1776; S of chapel (3) Harriet, wife of Rev. Charles Williams, 1825; (4) James Parkhouse, 1817 and [　　] his wife, 1800.

　　CYB (1862) 319. Murch (1835) 305.

UPOTTERY

(195) BAPTIST, Newhouse (ST 197100). The church, regarded by Baptists as the mother church of the district, was founded at Luppitt in 1652; the present site, said to have been provided by Nicholas Clode, has been occupied by a meeting-house since the end of the 17th century. The chapel, rebuilt in 1859, stands on high ground close to the borders of Devon and Somerset. It has rendered rubble walls and a slate roof gabled to N and S with stone copings and ball finials, a gabled S porch and lancet windows; it retains its original box-pews. The Sunday-school and manse were built in 1913.

　　Monuments: in burial-ground (1) Nicholas Clode of Moon-hayes, 1698, table-tomb with black-letter inscription; (2) Thomas Meacham, 1739, *et al.*, table-tomb; also many unmarked burial-mounds.

　　Andress, W. T., *The History of Newhouse, Upottery* (1932). Ivimey II (1814) 139–45.

Baptist chapel, Newhouse, Upottery.　　　　　　　　(195)

WEARE GIFFARD

(196) WESLEYAN, Gammaton (SS 493243). Rendered walls and hipped roof, broad front with round-arched windows; built 1835.

WEST BUCKLAND

(197) WESLEYAN (SS 657314). Broad three-bay front with porch and round-arched windows; opened 1829. Interior refitted, seating formerly stepped up to left. *Monument*: in chapel, John Fairchild, 1834.

WESTLEIGH

(198) Former WESLEYAN, Eastleigh (SS 487279). Three-bay front with porch and round-arched windows; dated 1863. (Closed 1976, converted to house)

WIDECOMBE IN THE MOOR

(199) WESLEYAN, Dunstone (SX 714758). Rubble and slate. End entrance with arched gallery window over. Opened 1833.

WINKLEIGH

(200) BIBLE CHRISTIAN, Stable Green (SS 648115). 'Peniel Chapel' dated 1840. End entrance; three pointed-arched windows with intersecting glazing bars in side walls.

WITHERIDGE

(201) INDEPENDENT, Fore Street (SS 806143). Rendered walls and lancet windows; dated 1839. British School to N dated 1898.

WOODBURY

(202) Site of GULLIFORD CHAPEL (SX 996848). A dissenting congregation was formed here soon after 1662 by adherents of the Rev. Samuel Fones, ejected vicar of Woodbury. The first known minister, appointed in 1687, was the Rev. Samuel Tapper, sometime curate of Holsworthy, Devon, and later vicar of St Merryn, Cornwall, from which he was ejected at the Restoration. In 1689 the present site was acquired for 'erecting thereon a meeting for religious worship and the service of God of the people commonly called Presbyterians'. The first meeting-house was enlarged and the burial-ground extended about 1723. In 1774–5 the building was replaced by another, registered October 1775, which survived until the early 20th century. After 1820, when another chapel was built in the neighbouring village of Lympstone, Gulliford ceased to be used in the winter. Congre-

Gulliford Chapel, Woodbury. (*Christian Freeman*, 1871)　　(202)

gations, which by the 19th century had become Unitarian, rapidly declined and the chapel finally closed about 1888, responsibility for the site passing to the trustees of George's Meeting, Exeter. Its condition was described in 1907 as 'terrible', with 'windows broken, and walls tumbling down', although the books and minister's gown were still in place, and an old barrel organ (presented 1795) with several rollers remained in the gallery.

The S front had a low segmental gable, rusticated quoins, and a pedimented central porch; each side of the entrance were two tiers of round-arched windows, and a circular window above the porch. The site in Meeting Lane is surrounded by a stone wall with brick gate piers. Part of the brickwork of the N and W sides of the 1774 building remains to about five feet in height where it forms part of the boundary, and traces of rendered quoins are visible at the S end of the W wall. External size approximately 38 ft by 32 ft.

The burial-ground contains table-tombs and other monuments dating from the 18th century, including a table-tomb to the children of Worthington and Joan Brice, 1743–8.

Christian Freeman (1871) 24–5. Evans (1897) 96–7. Murch (1835) 344–64. *UHST* VI (1935–8) 385–6.

(203) CHRIST CHURCH (SY 012873). Built 1851 by seceders from the parish church; now used by a Brethren assembly. Brick and slate with pediments to N and S and four-bay sides with brick pilasters carrying segmental wall arches above tall round-arched windows. A former bell-turret has been removed. Interior altered 1968.

WOOLFARDISWORTHY

(204) BIBLE CHRISTIAN (SS 332210). E wall of three bays with pointed-arched openings and tablet over entrance inscribed '. . . 1857 Jehovah-nissi'. Schoolroom added to N 1887.

YARCOMBE

(205) BAPTIST, Four Elms (ST 250079). Rendered walls and hipped slate roof. E front with altered windows but original doorway with scrolled wooden brackets supporting a flat canopy; late 19th-century tablet inscribed 'BAPTIST CHAPEL OPENED AUGUST 20TH 1829'. N and S walls with two round-arched windows with stone Y-tracery; later vestry at rear. *Monument*: in vestry, to Abraham Spiller, 1834, and Elizabeth his wife, 1842, headstone.

More than sixty nonconforming ministers resigned their livings in the county in 1662; of these Bartholomew Westley, curate of Allington and previously rector of Charmouth, and his son John Westley, vicar of Winterborne Whitechurch, are amongst the best known. The latter, grandfather of the founder of Methodism, became, briefly, minister of a congregation in Poole.

By 1672 many groups of dissenters were active and numerous licences were issued, particularly for Presbyterian preachers and meeting places. The rebellion led by the Duke of Monmouth, who landed at Lyme Regis in June 1685, although calculated to receive support from the known strength of dissent in the south-western counties, was disastrous in its consequences. Monmouth's defeat at Sedgemoor was followed by the 'bloody assizes' of the infamous Judge Jeffreys to whom the least hint of dissent, whether religious or political, was equally obnoxious. Seventy persons were hanged at Dorchester alone, including Samuel Lark, the Baptist pastor of Lyme Regis.

Throughout these troubles many congregations maintained a form of existence, although it may have been some years after the Toleration Act of 1689 before they gained sufficient strength to erect permanent meeting-houses. At Charmouth (23) the conversion of a pair of cottages c.1689 sufficed until 1815, while in Weymouth (105) a similar conversion of three cottages c.1703–5 appears to have satisfied the needs of the church until 1803–4. At Lyme Regis, where Baptists and Presbyterians remained in considerable numbers, the latter (46) evidently had a regularly fitted meeting-house before 1683, but it, too, may have been in a converted building. The Old Meeting-house in Poole (68) of 1704, rebuilt in the 19th century, was clearly a building of some consequence for a substantial congregation. At Dorchester (27) the Presbyterian meeting-house of 1718–19 which, in company with Poole, passed into Unitarian use in its later days, survived for a longer period but has now also been demolished. The memory of a congregation at Blackdown (18) has faded almost to oblivion, whilst the re-building of the post-fire meeting-house at Blandford (9) and of the pre-fire chapel in Wareham (101) has left few traces of the buildings erected by orthodox dissenters before the mid 18th century. The one exception, at Bere Regis (7) of c.1730, though much altered, illustrates the basic requirements of a small village society.

Undoubtedly the grandest of mid 18th-century Dorset chapels is Lyme Regis (46), elegant in its external design and with its double roof typically supported by a pair of classical columns; the disappointing character of the interior is largely the result of unsympathetic 19th-century alterations, since compounded by further attrition and an eventual change of use. Of a similar date, though on a smaller scale, is Halfway House Chapel at Nether Compton (61), where the more traditional stone-mullioned windows continue to be employed; here, also, conversion has destroyed much of its previous interest. The Congregational chapel at Beaminster (5) also dates from the mid 18th century although some uncertainty remains over the extent of its 19th-century rebuilding. At Wareham (101) and Poole (69), of 1762 and 1777 respectively, both chapels of some size and importance, a resemblance is seen in their tripartite roof structure although they are otherwise dissimilar as is their historical background: the former housed an old society from which, exceptionally, Unitarians seceded, the latter a new foundation formed by seceders from the heterodoxy of the Old Meeting. The Old Meeting-house in Bridport (11), of 1794, is outstanding in the completeness of its fittings and an excellent unspoilt example of the work of the period.

Although Presbyterian and Independent congregations predominate in the history of Dorset dissent, the earliest surviving meeting-house is that built by the Quakers in Sherborne (86) about 1693. The interesting complex at Bridport (14), incorporating almshouses, is the conversion of an existing building. At Shaftesbury (82) a small but sophisticated meeting-house was built in 1746, but this and another at Poole (70), of the late 18th century, have been greatly altered in recent years. The sites of other Friends' meeting-houses at Corfe Castle (25) and Weymouth (108) were also noted.

Baptist congregations have never been numerous in this county, although that already referred to at Lyme Regis (45) is of great antiquity and occupies a meeting-house that may date from the 18th century. The only other Baptist building of that century is in Wimborne (113). It should, however, be remembered that the early Baptist meeting-house at Loughwood (Dalwood, Devonshire) stands in what was, until the mid 19th century, a detached part of Dorset.

The few Methodist buildings of particular note date principally from the early 19th century. Slightly earlier is the former Wesleyan chapel in Poole (71), of 1793, which is of interest as one of the benefactions of Robert Carr

Brackenbury of Raithby Hall, Lincolnshire, the friend of John Wesley, who is also credited with the introduction of Methodism into the Isle of Portland (74).

The humble origins of some country congregations of various denominations may still be recalled at Affpuddle (2) and Ashmore (4), whilst at Coryates (72) the combination of teaching and worship, here by Congregationalists, is an example of what was often a prelude to the erection of a separate chapel. At Cripplestyle (3) 'Ebenezer Chapel', with its cob walls, thatched roof and rustic fittings, was, until its collapse c.1976, an exceptionally moving relic of early 19th-century rural Independency. Of greater pretensions are Sydling St Nicholas (98), of 1834, with a shaped gable, and the chapels at Charmouth (23) and Uploders (43), both of which have the distinction of a bellcote. This feature is seen at its best at Longham (38) where the Congregational chapel of 1841 stands as proudly and prominently as any New England meeting-house, with its painted steeple rising high above a pedimented façade.

A more positive architectural style is to be found in several chapels of the early 19th century and later, particularly in the towns. The former Unitarian chapel in Wareham (103) of 1830, although set almost out of sight behind a row of shops and houses, has an Ionic colonnaded portico; a similar style was adopted in 1838 for the Wesleyan chapel in Bridport (15). A bold use of the orders continued into the later 19th century in the rebuilding of the Congregational chapel at Shaftesbury (81) by Andrew Trimen and the refronting of the Baptist chapel in Weymouth (104), both of 1859. Gothic elements appear remarkably early in the use of pointed arches for the windows at Skinner Street, Poole (69), in 1777. At Sherborne (85) the 'Strawberry Hill' Gothic of the doorways of the Congregational chapel, probably of 1804, is of a high quality. A more determined attempt to reproduce the elements of mediaeval decoration is seen in the Wesleyan chapel in Sherborne (87) of 1841–2 where 13th-century details are competently used, and at Wimborne (114) in 1846 where the result is rather less successful. The two examples of the work of Poulton and Woodman, at Bridport (13) and Dorchester (29), are typical of their extensive practice amongst Congregationalists. A local architect, R. C. Bennett, used the Romanesque style at Gloucester Street, Weymouth (105), of 1864, and the Baptists adopted a similar style when rebuilding their chapel in Gillingham (37) in 1858–9: both chapels were demolished during the course of this survey.

No single building material predominates in the county. Good building stones of various types abound, notably the limestones of Portland and the Isle of Purbeck, and the richer and warmer stones of the northern and western parts. Examples of the latter are in the chapels at Beaminster (5) and Nether Compton (61). Brick, available in the south east, appears at an early date in Dorchester (27), and later in the 18th century at Wareham (101, 102) and Poole (69, 70), where the cost of stone may have been prohibitive. At Bridport the use of red brick for the front of the Old Meeting-house (11), now colourwashed, is more clearly seen as the adoption of a fashionable material. The use of flints banded with brick is found in later work in the north east, at Ashmore (4) and Woodyates (64), but of the distinctive cob walling, still much in evidence in the cottages of south Dorset and used occasionally for small chapels, little remains; the most notable example of this was at 'Ebenezer Chapel', Cripplestyle (3), with its natural accompaniment of a thatched roof. Roofs formerly covered with thatch or stone slates have been generally re-covered with slate or tiles.

(Note: the volume and page number of monuments in the published Royal Commission Inventories of Historical Monuments in Dorset (1952–75) are given in square brackets at the end of each relevant entry.)

ABBOTSBURY

(1) Former CONGREGATIONAL, Back Street (SY 577854). Lancet Gothic by R. C. Bennett, 1870.
Densham and Ogle (1899) 1–4.

AFFPUDDLE

(2) Former WESLEYAN (SY 814929). Cottage of cob and thatch, possibly 17th-century, converted to preaching-house by removal of upper floor.   [II.8]

ALDERHOLT

(3) EBENEZER CHAPEL, Cripplestyle (SU 091121), was opened in 1807 by a congregation which had been meeting for a few years in private houses. After being several times enlarged, the chapel was superseded in 1889 by a new building nearby and the former retained for occasional services.

The old chapel is a long low building of cob with some later brickwork and a thatched roof. The original structure (22 ft by 13½ ft) has pairs of windows in the N and S walls, the former with square wooden frames of two lights, the latter with pointed-arched heads added in the later 19th century. Two periods of extension to the E are discernible in the side walls. In the extended N wall is a segmental-arched window. The E front, of cob faced with brickwork, has a round-arched doorway at the centre, perhaps originally with a fanlight but now blind and partly covered by a board painted with the name of the chapel; a large upper window of three principal lights serves the gallery.

'Ebenezer Chapel', Cripplestyle.

(3)

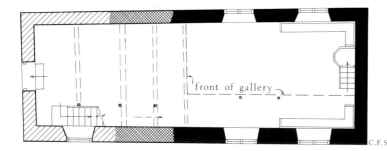

'Ebenezer' Chapel, Cripplestyle
ALDERHOLT *Dorset*

The interior (41¼ ft long) has a plaster ceiling at collar level to the earlier part but higher at the E end to allow head-room in the gallery. The E half of the chapel is occupied by a very deep gallery with boarded front divided into panels by applied mouldings; the gallery has stepped seating of a very primitive kind and provision at the front for a singers' pew. A narrow gallery added in the mid 19th century extends along the N wall of the original building and has a boarded front supported by two small octagonal posts. *Pulpit*: at W end, boarded sides with applied mouldings, early 19th-century, supported at the front by two turned baluster legs and approached by a plain staircase, all of later date. (Old chapel demolished after structural failure *c*.1976) [v.1–2]

Densham and Ogle (1899) 108–12.

ASHMORE

(4) WESLEYAN (ST 912177). A preaching-room at Manor Farm, now subdivided and converted to domestic use, was built *c*.1800 by Samuel Hall. A new chapel, 100 yards SE, built 1855 in banded flint and brick with stone dressings, has lancet windows and contemporary fittings.

Monument: in chapel, Samuel Hall, 'who first introduced Methodism into this parish', 1844, Elizabeth his wife, 1833, *et al.* [IV.2]

Uppleby, F. L., *Ashmore* (1949) 8.

BEAMINSTER

(5) CONGREGATIONAL, Whitcombe Road (ST 482012). A Presbyterian society which originated in the late 17th century had as one of its earliest ministers Thomas Crane, the ejected rector of Rampisham. After a heterodox ministry in the late 18th century the church was re-formed in 1798 and again in 1863. The chapel, first built in 1749, was enlarged or partly rebuilt in 1825 but probably stands on the earlier foundations and may incorporate 18th-century material, particularly in the side walls. The walls are of squared stone with ashlar dressings and the pyramidal roof, now covered with patent tiles, is surmounted by a ball finial. The S front has two tall round-arched windows of three lights with stone mullions; in the end bays are two arched doorways with fanlights and above them two circular windows. The N wall has two tall arched windows flanking the recent site of the pulpit, with doorways below to the vestry, and two tiers of windows in the end bays. The side walls have each two round-arched upper windows only.

The interior (30¾ ft by 37¾ ft) has been subdivided and entirely refitted since 1947. At that date it had galleries along the E and W sides with fronts divided by panelled pilasters.

Congregational chapel, Beaminster. (5)

Congregational Chapel, BEAMINSTER
Dorset

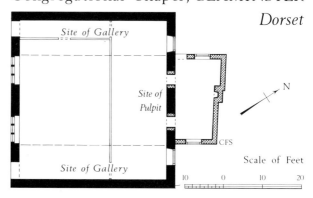

Fittings – *Monument*: on N wall over site of pulpit, James Daniel, 1711, recording his sufferings under religious persecution, erected 1835. *Organ*: small chamber organ, early 19th-century. *Panelling*: on W wall, fielded panelling, reset. [I.21]

CHST II (1905–6) 420–1. Densham and Ogle (1899) 5–16.

(6) WESLEYAN, Fleet Street (ST 481015). 'Centenary Chapel', opened 1854. Two round-arched windows below pedimental gable. (Reported closed 1979 and converted to houses)

BERE REGIS

(7) Former PRESBYTERIAN, Blind Street (SY 84989482). A society formed in the late 17th century, possibly under the

Former Presbyterian chapel, Bere Regis. (7)

influence of Philip Lamb, ejected vicar of Bere Regis, registered private houses as meeting places in 1711 and 1721. A meeting-house on a leasehold site in Blind Street was built c.1730 and remained in use until 1820 when it was converted to a house. Arian preaching in the late 18th century led to a Trinitarian secession and the opening of a new chapel in North Street in 1813 for Congregationalists with whom a remnant from the old meeting united in 1820. The second chapel, rebuilt in 1829, was sold in 1893 and is now 'Drax Hall', the church removing to their present chapel in Butt Lane (SY 846951), originally built 1871 for use as a schoolroom.

The old meeting-house, now no. 16 Blind Street, in a small lane off the E side of North Street, is a long rectangular building (46¼ ft by 20¼ ft externally), with brick walls rendered on two sides and a thatched roof with a half hip at the SW end. The end wall facing the street is rendered and has a bold plinth. The SE side, although refenestrated, retains traces of three regularly spaced wide windows with segmental-arched heads. The opposite wall, now rendered, may have had corresponding windows. The NE end is gabled and has two circular windows, now blocked, at an upper level. [II.20, monument 32]
Densham and Ogle (1899) 16–27.

(8) WESLEYAN, Bere Heath (SY 853928). Brick with hipped slate roof, broad three-bay front with two pointed-arched windows. Opened 1850.

BLANDFORD FORUM

(9) CONGREGATIONAL, Salisbury Street (ST 885066). A church which originated in the late 17th century, possibly under the influence of the vicar, William Alleine, ejected 1660, came in the 18th century to be described as Presbyterian. A barn at the rear of the present site was replaced c.1711 by the first regular meeting-house, rebuilt after its destruction in the town fire of 1731. The second meeting-house was a rectangular building of brick and tile with a broad ashlar front, having entrances in the end bays and two round-arched windows between with an open loggia below possibly of a later date; a large rear wing may also have been an addition. The present chapel, built in 1867, of white brick with red brick dressings, has a gabled front with a large wheel window over the entrance. (URC)

Fittings – Model: in paper and card, of 1731 meeting-house, late 19th-century. Monuments: externally against rear wall (1)

Jane, wife of James Salmon, collector of Inland Revenue, 1852; (2) William Henville, 1809, et al.; (3) Joseph James, 1812, and Sarah his wife, 1807; in burial-ground in front of chapel (4) Rev. Richard Keynes, 1853, Harriet his wife, 1837, et al., table-tomb, signed Simmonds; (5) William Henville, 1840, loose panels from table-tomb; also several reset headstones of the early 19th century. Plate: includes a pair of two-handled, gadrooned cups of 1714–15.
Densham and Ogle (1899) 27–45.

Congregational chapel (URC), Blandford Forum.
Model of 1731 meeting-house. (9)

BRIDPORT

(10) BAPTIST, Victoria Grove (SY 465931). Rendered pedimented front, with terminal pilasters and two tall round-arched windows flanking a central porch. A modern inscription over the entrance replaces a contemporary one in the pediment, dated 1841. [I.46]

(11) OLD MEETING-HOUSE, East Street (SY 468929). A society of dissenters, composed at first mostly of Independents, appears to have been in existence by 1672 under the leadership of Richard Down, the ejected rector of Winterborne Monkton. Before the mid 18th century the orthodoxy of the ministry was in question and in 1742 a major Trinitarian secession occurred for which a new meeting-house was eventually erected (see (12)). The old meeting, subsequently designated 'Presbyterian', was commonly regarded as Unitarian by the end of the 18th century.

The first meeting-house, dating perhaps from the late 17th century, stood behind a house in Barrack Street which has been claimed as the possible location of meetings in 1672. The meeting-house was demolished after 1794, although a fragment of its walling is said to survive. The present building, opened 9 March 1794, stands on the N side of East Street. The walls are of rubble with a front of red brick, now painted, and ashlar dressings; the roof is hipped and covered with slates. The S front of three bays has two tiers of round-arched windows, the lower ones blind, separated by a broad platband, and a central entrance with fanlight and narrow flanking lights. In front of the entrance is a semicircular porch with two Ionic columns and pilasters; the band above the porch is inscribed in bold lettering with the words 'UNITARIAN CHAPEL' added in 1821. Two tall round-arched windows in the N wall, now internal, flank the pulpit.

The interior (50 ft by 35¼ ft) has a flat plaster ceiling with moulded cornice. A gallery with panelled front extends around three sides and is supported by marbled wooden columns with

Old Meeting-house, Bridport.   (11)

Ionic capitals and tall bases; at the S end above the staircases are small raised galleries with iron-balustraded fronts; the space between them, formerly occupied by an organ, may have been the site of a small choir gallery reported by Murch (1835). Original box-pews remain throughout most of the chapel, together with a former table-pew with flanking seats in front of the pulpit; a separate railed communion area was formed in the mid 19th century and has two round-backed mahogany chairs of that period.

Fittings – *Books*: in vestry, several folio volumes inscribed 'The bequest of the late Rev. Thomas Howe for the use of future ministers', including Matthew Poole, *Synopsis Criticorum Aliorumque S. Scripturae Interpretum*, 4 vols. (1669–74), and Philip Limborch, *Theologia Christiana* (3rd edn 1700); also about 100 octavo volumes, the remains of an extensive early 19th-century lending library. *Clock*: on front of S gallery, signed 'Matthews, Bridport', mid 19th-century. *Monument*: in chapel, on N wall, Rev. Thomas Howe, 32 years pastor, 1820. *Plate*: includes a pair of plain two-handled cups of 1726–7. *Pulpit*: veneered wood, square with fluted corner pilasters and back-board.   [I.46]

Colfox, T. A., *History of the Bridport Unitarian Congregation* (1894). Densham and Ogle (1899) 45–59. Evans (1897) 32–3. *Inquirer* (22 June 1974). Murch (1835) 252–64. Short, B., *A Respectable Society* (1976). *UHST* IV (1927–30) 285–7.

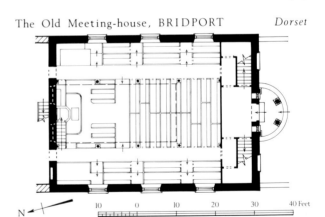

The Old Meeting-house, BRIDPORT   *Dorset*

N   10   0   10   20   30   40 Feet

(12) NEW MEETING-HOUSE, Barrack Street (SY 468930). Seceders from the Old Meeting in 1742 built a meeting-house on land in Stake Lane (now Barrack Street) given by Daniel Taylor which was replaced by the present building on the same site in 1776–7. This was twice enlarged, altered in 1837, and superseded by a new chapel (*see* (13)) in 1860. The building then passed to other uses, including, in 1886, a 'Liberal Hall', and carries a tablet with this inscription; it now serves as a dancing academy.

The walls are of coursed stone and the roofs are half-hipped

Old Meeting-house, Bridport.   (11)

THE NEW MEETING-HOUSE, BARRACK STREET, BRIDPORT   CFS 1983

and covered with slates. The original meeting-house of 1776–7, at the E end of the site (36½ ft by 40½ ft externally) has been re-fenestrated. The E front formerly had three upper windows and entrances below in the end bays, now replaced by a wide round-arched central doorway. The N and S end walls had two tiers of windows with flat-arched heads, converted in part to tall round-

arched windows in the early 19th century and partly obscured on the S by an adjoining house. The roof is supported by four king-post trusses.

In 1798 the building was extended to the W by about 17 ft with windows in the N and S walls matching the earlier work and similarly altered in early 19th century. Internally two Roman Doric columns replace the original back wall. A further extension to the W in 1815 has a curved end wall against which the later pulpit was placed.

Densham and Ogle (1899) 51–7. Hutchins II (1863) 32.

(13) CONGREGATIONAL, East Street (SY 468929). Built in 1859–60 to replace the foregoing. Gothic, by Poulton and Woodman, with gabled N front divided by pinnacled buttresses and two flanking gabled porches. Polygonal apse to S; hammer-beam roof. Modern glazed entrance pierced below front window c.1975. (URC/Methodist)

Pulpit: associated with the ministry of Bartholomew Westley at Charminster parish church (ejected 1662), whence it was removed c.1836 to the Wesleyan chapel, Bridport, and brought here c.1970 on the union of the two congregations; oak, semi-octagonal with three tiers of carved panels, early 17th-century.
[I.88]

CYB (1859) 244. Densham and Ogle (1899) 45–59.

Congregational chapel (URC), Bridport

(13)

Congregational chapel (URC), Bridport.   (13)

(14) FRIENDS, South Street (SY 466927). Meetings commenced in private houses in 1657 were transferred in 1690 to Daniel Taylor's barn. In 1697 this barn, together with the adjacent house and tenements of 15th and 16th-century date, were given to the society for use as a meeting-house and almshouses. The barn, possibly rebuilt c.1707, was fitted with galleries, benches and raised seats in 1720; it was much altered in 1958.

The buildings, of rubble with slate roofs, are ranged around a central courtyard, with an entrance passage through the former house on the W side, further almshouses to the N, the present meeting-house to the S and a smaller meeting-room of more recent date on the E side. A burial-ground behind contains uniform headstones of the 19th century.

The principal meeting-house has, in the W wall facing the street, a former central entrance blocked c.1720 when a new doorway was made to the N; the latter was replaced in 1958 by a window matching an older one to the right of the earlier entrance. The present entrance is at the opposite end of the building. The interior (average 40 ft by 19¼ ft) had a stand at the W end, now removed. A gallery at the E end supported by two turned columns of c.1720 has a panelled front. A gallery along the N wall with staircase opposite the former entrance has also been removed.   [I.46–8]

Lidbetter (1961) 60.

(15) Former WESLEYAN, South Street (SY 466928). Chapel of 1838 set back behind a forecourt bounded N and S by contemporary three-storeyed houses. Three pedimented bays with two tall Ionic columns flanking the entrance. There is an original gallery around three sides; the pulpit was replaced by a rostrum c.1900. Hall at rear built 1860 with tablet commemorating the establishment of Wesleyan Methodism in Bridport in 1808. Converted to 'Arts Centre' since 1970 and contemporary inscription on frieze obliterated.   [I.46]

Dolbey (1964) 168–9.

Former Wesleyan chapel, Bridport.   (15)

(16) WESLEYAN, West Bay (SY 463904). Gabled front of rubble with two round-arched windows flanking entrance. Square wooden porch with swept roof and small finial. Opened 1849.   [I.46]

BROADMAYNE

(17) WESLEYAN (SY 729866). Stone with brick dressings; three-bay gabled front dated 1865.

BROADWINDSOR

(18) Site of PRESBYTERIAN, Blackdown (ST 396031). A society, possibly originating with John Pinney, ejected 1661 as vicar of Broadwindsor, occupied a meeting-house on this site throughout the 18th century. Little is known about the building or congregation, although Joseph Paul, minister in 1775, was an Arian who used the 'Liverpool liturgy'. The site was sold c.1839 to Anglican seceders from Venn Chapel (see (19)) who erected a chapel-of-ease.

Monuments: in burial-ground (1) M . . ., daughter of Matthew and Mary Paull, 1729, headstone with winged cherub's head, symbols of mortality, and black-letter inscription; (2) square headstone, 18th-century.   [I.53]

Densham and Ogle (1899) 170, 331–2.

(19) VENN CHAPEL (ST 390040) was built in 1816 for a congregation at first of mixed denomination from which those preferring a liturgical service seceded c.1839; after a period of Baptist use it passed to Congregationalists c.1861 (now URC). The walls are of flint rubble with stone dressings, partly rendered, and the roof, originally thatched, was slated in 1893. The gabled W

front has a central entrance and three lancet windows; there is a wide round-arched window in each side wall.

Densham and Ogle (1899) 330–5.

(20) WESLEYAN, Netherhay (ST 414054). Built 1838, vestry wing added 1887; porch, decorative barge-boards and pottery finials added 1898.

Wesleyan chapel, Netherhay. (20)

BUCKLAND NEWTON

(21) CONGREGATIONAL, Duntish (ST 694063). Built 1867 on a new site, replacing a chapel of 1839.

Densham and Ogle (1899) 66–70.

BURTON BRADSTOCK

(22) Former WESLEYAN (SY 488896). Blocked central entrance with tablet dated 1825 between two altered windows; round-arched doorway inserted to left. An earlier structure converted.

CHARMOUTH

(23) CONGREGATIONAL (SY 366936). Two cob cottages adjacent to the Queen's Arms Inn (subsequently the manse but now reverted to its former use) were converted to a meeting-house in or before 1689 by John Brice, the first pastor of the church. Brice, ejected in 1662 as rector of West Chickerell, inherited the former inn and cottages from his wife, Eleanor, widow of Anthony Floyer of Whitchurch whom Brice had served as domestic chaplain. The property was transferred to a trust for Presbyterians in 1716 (now URC).

The present chapel, which stands on the site of the former meeting-house, was opened 30 August 1815; inscriptions on the front record 'restorations' in 1866 and 1963. The walls of the chapel are rendered. The N front has a simple pediment, narrow terminal pilasters and a central doorway flanked by two tiers of round-arched windows with Y-tracery. An octagonal wooden bell-cote with tall ogee cap and weathervane rises above the pediment; there is no bell. The side walls have each two round-arched windows. A small vestry projects on the W side.

The interior has a gallery at the N end, now inaccessible, supported by four Roman Doric columns with a bracketed cornice and panelled front curved forwards slightly at each end. Opposite the entrance is a tall segmental-arched recess but the contemporary pulpit, originally set centrally in front, and standing

Congregational chapel (URC), Charmouth. (23)

on tall columns, has been cut down and re-sited.

Monuments: in chapel (1) Rev. J. Brice, first pastor, 1716; (2) Rev. Peter Good, 21 years pastor at Havant, Hants., and later at Bishop's Hull, Som., 1807, and Rebecca his widow, 1818; (3) John Creed, 1817. [I.88]

CHST v (1911–12) 192. Densham and Ogle (1899) 79–89. *EM* (1815) 466.

CORFE CASTLE

(24) Former CONGREGATIONAL, West Street (SY 960820). The yard behind houses on the W side of the street, now Well Court, is claimed to be the location of John Wesley's preaching, 5 September 1776, to a small Methodist society which had commenced a few years earlier. It is possible that a house 'at the back of two dwelling houses' on the W side of West Street, registered for Presbyterians in 1774, may also be identified with this site. The former chapel on the W side of the yard, perhaps replacing the Presbyterian meeting-house, was built for an existing Independent congregation and opened 18 January 1815, being described as 'a neat chapel, built on the most economical plan capable of holding 200 or 300 persons'. It continued in use until 1834 when a day-school commenced *c.*1829 was forced to find new premises and the chapel was converted for use as a British School; a new chapel was then built elsewhere (*see* (25)). The building (34 ft by 22½ ft) is of rubble with a hipped stone-slated roof. The entrance is at the E end; two round-arched windows at the opposite end flanked the pulpit. [II.93, monument 118]

CYB (1871) 320. Densham and Ogle (1899) 104–8. *EM* (1815) 164.

(25) CONGREGATIONAL, East Street (SY 961819). The chapel, which stands behind houses on the W side of the street, occupies the site of a Friends' meeting-house built in 1691. By 1789 the meeting-house was only in occasional use and part was occupied as a dwelling-house; in 1793 the former burial-ground to the W was described as 'now in grass'. The property was later acquired by Congregationalists who erected the present chapel in 1835 in succession to the chapel in West Street.

The walls are of rubble and the roof is slated. The E and W walls are gabled and surmounted by tall finials. A small porch projects from the N side; in the W wall is a window of three graduated round-arched lights with columnar mullions. The pulpit is at the E end with a semicircular seating niche behind.

[II.55–6]

Densham and Ogle (1899) 104–8. Trust deeds.

CRANBORNE

(26) Former WESLEYAN (SU 054133), brick with gabled three-bay E front, round-arched openings and defaced tablet dated 1847. Later E gallery removed; vestry at W end added 1898. Patterned coloured glass in fanlight of front doorway and in lunette at W end, the latter including an *agnus dei*. *Monument*: removed from wall, George Ware, 1852. (Under conversion to secular use 1970)   [V.7]

DORCHESTER

(27) Former PRESBYTERIAN, Colliton Street (SY 691908). Several of the ejected ministers were resident in or active in the vicinity of Dorchester in the late 17th century; of these, William Benn, former rector of All Saints, Dorchester, and Joshua Churchill, former vicar of Fordington, are credited with being the originators and first pastors of this society. Meetings were first held in the Priory. The meeting-house on the N side of Colliton Street (formerly Pease Lane) was built in 1718–19 and registered 7 April 1719. Increasingly heterodox preaching in the 18th century led to a Trinitarian secession in 1776 (*see* (28)). The old meeting-house then continued in Unitarian occupation until the demise of the congregation in the mid 19th century. It later served as a Liberal club and latterly as a builder's store. (Demolished 1976)

The meeting-house has brick walls and a flat roof. According to Rev. Abel Edwards, minister 1769–1813, it originally 'had a double roof, tiled, and supported by two large and heavy looking brick pillars', but in 1808 the roof timbers 'were found to be so much decayed, that it became necessary to take down the whole roof and put on another. The new roof is single, covered with lead, and nearly flat, having a sky-light dome in the centre, which has a pleasing effect. At the same time the massy pillars, being no longer wanted, were removed, and sashes were substituted for casements' (Murch (1835) 272). The S front, set back from the road behind a small forecourt, is in Flemish bond brickwork with some glazed headers; it has a brick plinth and a moulded timber eaves cornice. A central doorway has been replaced by a wider opening, over it is a blocked segmental-arched recess with a platband arched above; two flanking

Congregational chapel, Corfe Castle.   (25)

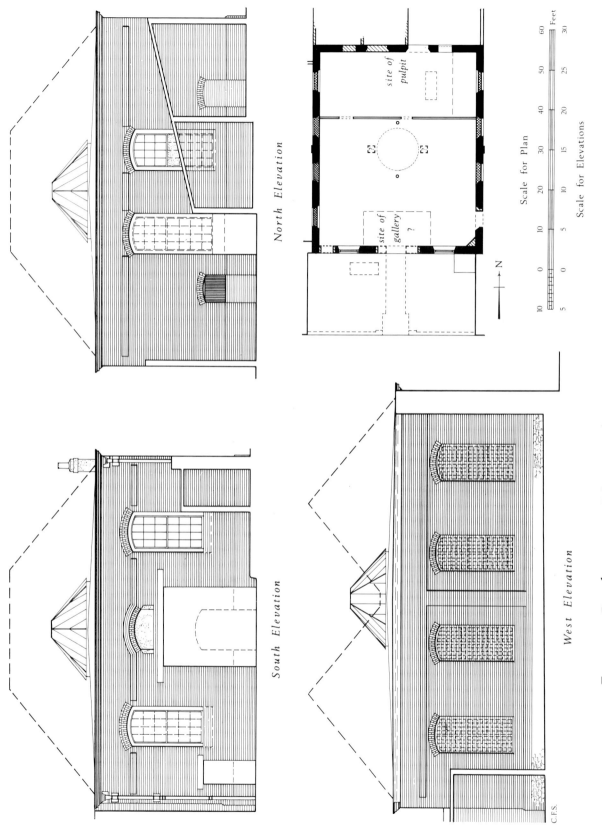

North Elevation

site of pulpit

site of gallery ?

Scale for Plan

Scale for Elevations

Feet

South Elevation

West Elevation

C.F.S.

Former Presbyterian Meeting-house, DORCHESTER, *Dorset*

windows have hung sashes of 1808. The N wall has a similar plinth, divided platband and cornice; two tall segmental-arched windows flank the site of the pulpit, E and W of them are the remains of two original doorways. The side walls are each of four bays with segmental-arched windows, all blocked in brickwork.

The interior (48½ ft by 40 ft) has a flat plaster ceiling with moulded cornice, four moulded roundels and a circular lantern with hexagonal glazed dome, all of 1808. A boarded dado to the side walls incorporates three earlier fielded panels. A 'small gallery' which existed in the early 19th century has been removed and no other original fittings remain. Murch (1835) records a floorslab to three ministers, Benjamin Spencer, 1755, Samuel Phillipps, 1761, and Timothy Lamb, 1772, 'In the aisle opposite the pulpit'. *Rainwater-head*: on front wall, lead, fluted, *c*.1719.
[II.112]

Densham and Ogle (1899) 113–22. Evans (1897) 74–5. Hutchins I (1861) 405. Murch (1835) 266–75. *UHST* VI (1936) 154–5

(28) Former CONGREGATIONAL, Durngate Street (SY 694907), built in 1776–7 by seceders from the foregoing, was superseded by a new chapel in South Street (*see* (29)) in 1857; it was later used by a British School and subsequently for storage. The walls are of brickwork and the roof is hipped and covered with slates except the N slope which is tiled. The S front is rendered, of three bays with a central altered entrance between two round-arched windows; above the entrance a small arched recess which rises through the cornice and blocking course may be the head of a former window. In the N wall are two round-arched windows with intersecting glazing bars and in the side walls near the N end two similarly arched windows have been blocked. The roof is supported by two king-post trusses.   [II.113]

Densham and Ogle (1899) 121–7.

(29) CONGREGATIONAL, South Street (SY 693904), built 1857 in the Gothic style by Poulton and Woodman for the church formerly meeting in Durngate Street. Gabled W front with traceried window of five lights and short tower and spire above principal entrance. Interior with polygonal E end and organ recess behind pulpit; small W gallery.

Fittings – *Floorslab*: externally S of chapel, reset from former building 1906, to R. Wellsteed, 180[?9], 'who erected this chapel in the Year of our Lord 1777'. *Seating*: pews with low doors and trefoiled ends with Roman numerals. (URC/Methodist)

CYB (1857) 237–8; (1858) 249–50. Densham and Ogle (1899) 121–7

(30) Former BAPTIST, Salisbury Street (SY 695907). Although Baptists were meeting in Dorchester in the mid 17th century very little activity took place in the following century. A new cause was begun *c*.1828 and a chapel was built in 1830 which remained in use until the removal of the congregation to a new site at 'Top of Town' in 1915. The former chapel, altered in the late 19th century, has a bowed E front with pediment and terminal pilasters. (Now 'Kingdom Hall' of Jehovah's Witnesses)
[II.112–13]

B.Hbk (1916) 506–7. Hutchins II (1863) 405. Jackman, D., *Three Hundred Years of Baptist Witness in Dorchester, 1645-1945* [1945].

Congregational chapel (URC), Dorchester.   (29)
(*Congregational Year Book,* 1857)

Congregational chapel (URC), Dorchester.   (29)

(31) Former WESLEYAN, Durngate Street (SY 693907), opened 1840 for a society formed c.1825. Brick with rendered S front, behind a small forecourt.   [II.113]

(32) WESLEYAN, South Street (SY 693907), immediately SW of the former, by W. S. Allardyce, was built in 1875 of rock-faced stone with ashlar dressings. The W front of three principal bays has an elaborately detailed open pediment. (Demolished 1983)

Wesleyan chapel, Dorchester.   (32)

EAST ORCHARD

(33) Former WESLEYAN, Hartgrove (ST 835183), built in the early 19th century, was superseded by the present chapel in 1876. The walls are of stone and the roof is slated. The original building (25 ft by 17 ft) has in the E wall two round-arched windows with wooden Y-traceried frames and cast-iron glazing panels and a single similar window centrally on the W side. The chapel has been extended by 11 ft to the front. In the S front is a segmental-arched doorway and upper window matching those in the side walls. Two tablets in the E wall of the extension, possibly reset from the original front wall, are inscribed 'Ebenezer, Sam:VII.12' and 'W.C. 1824'. A gallery at the S end with plain panelled front supported by marbled octagonal posts contains some simple open-backed benches. A later cottage adjoins to the north.   [IV.15]

EDMONDSHAM

(34) Former PRIMITIVE METHODIST (SU 064114). Tiny brick chapel of 1848 with defaced tablet above round-arched entrance in gabled end wall.   [V.17]

FONTMELL MAGNA

(35) WESLEYAN (ST 866171). Built in 1831 to supersede a chapel of 1797; schoolroom added to E in 1874 and the chapel largely refitted, re-roofed and a porch added at that period. The walls are of rubble with an ashlar front and the roof is tiled. The broad N front has two round-arched windows and a central doorway with a tablet above recording the dates of erection and 'enlargement'. There are three similar windows in the S wall. Rusticated gate piers with shaped capping but lacking the original finials are contemporary with the building. A gallery at the W end has been

WESLEYAN CHAPEL, FONTMELL MAGNA

Wesleyan Chapel, FONTMELL MAGNA   *Dorset*

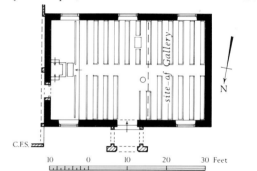

removed and the original pulpit in two sections is now in the schoolroom.

Monument: in chapel, James Edwards, 1843, Abigail his wife, 1830, their sons Josiah, 1822, John, 1827, *et al.*, signed Curtis, Poole.   [IV.23]

(36) WESLEYAN, Bedchester (ST 852175). Red and white brick, wheel window, 1879.

GILLINGHAM

(37) BAPTIST (ST 812263). A chapel built in 1839 but reported to be defective in construction was rebuilt in the Romanesque style

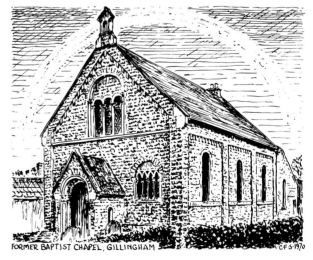

FORMER BAPTIST CHAPEL, GILLINGHAM

in 1858–9. The walls are of rock-faced stone. The gabled front wall is surmounted by an empty bell-cote and has a central porch flanked by windows with intersecting arcaded tracery. A new chapel was built alongside in 1892. (Former chapel demolished since 1970)

HAMPRESTON

(38) CONGREGATIONAL, Longham (sz 067986). Services which commenced in a small room were transferred to a new chapel in 1819 to which a large vestry with additional accommodation was soon added. A further increase in attendance attracted by the preaching of Joseph Notting, a boot manufacturer and tanner of Poole, led to the erection of the present chapel which was opened 29 December 1841. This building, designed by W. Gollop and executed at a cost of nearly three times the original estimate of

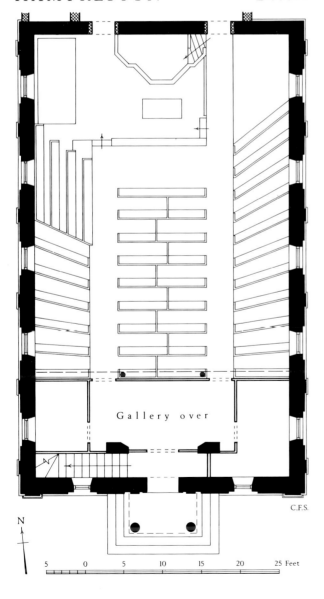

Congregational Chapel, Longham
HAMPRESTON   *Dorset*

Gallery over

N

5   0   5   10   15   20   25 Feet

C.F.S.

about £1,000, was undertaken on an exceptionally lavish scale in the misplaced belief 'that Longham was to be made a model village'.

The chapel (now URC) stands in a prominent position near the centre of the village. The walls are of grey brick with yellow brick and stone dressings and the roofs are slate covered. The S front (*see* frontispiece) of three bays has Ionic terminal pilasters, and an open pediment surmounted by a wooden octagonal bell-turret with eight columns to the upper stage and a slender copper-clad spire and weathervane; three round-arched bays enclose two tiers of windows and a central doorway with an open columned porch. The side walls are divided by brick pilasters into five bays, each bay with a single tall round-arched window. Two windows at the N end flank the pulpit.

The interior ($55\frac{1}{2}$ ft by $32\frac{3}{4}$ ft) has a segmental vaulted plaster ceiling. At the S end is a contemporary gallery through which rise two piers, arched above the gallery, to support the turret. The roof is carried by four bolted scissor trusses with added supports at their feet which penetrate the ceiling. The pulpit and seating were altered or replaced and two rooms constructed below the gallery in 1892.

Fittings – *Bell*: in turret, one, uninscribed, *c*.1841. *Clock*: in turret, external dial to S only. *Glass*: in central S window, white opaque glass with marginal and intermediate vertical bands of red, blue and green glass and occasional leaf paterae in yellow on a red ground. *Monuments*: in burial-ground E of chapel (1) William Carver, 1843, and Mary his widow, 1848; (2) Sarah, wife of Robert Morgan, 1843, and Hannah their daughter, nd; (3) Elizabeth Sims, 1844; (4) James Cripps, 1849, and Elizabeth his widow, 1857.   [v.27]

Densham and Ogle (1899) 135–8.

IWERNE MINSTER

(39) BAPTIST (ST 866144). Rendered walls divided by plain pilasters, round-arched windows, gabled front with tablet inscribed 'EBENEZER CHAPEL BUILT 1810 ENLARGED 1860'.   [IV.38]

(40) WESLEYAN (ST 866143), red and white brick, wheel window, 1879.

KINGTON MAGNA

(41) Former PRIMITIVE METHODIST (ST 765229). Gabled front of coursed stone in three bays with pointed-arched doorway;

FORMER PRIMITIVE METHODIST CHAPEL, KINGTON MAGNA   CFS 1970

tablet inscribed '1851 PRIMITIVE METHODIST CHAPEL
T. Tanner, Mason'.   [IV.42]

LANGTON MATRAVERS

(42) Former WESLEYAN (SY 995788). Three-bay gabled front to
N with gallery window above entrance; dated 1842. Contemporary railings. Present chapel alongside built 1875. [II.141]

LODERS

(43) WESLEYAN, Uploders (SY 504938). The chapel dated 1827
has rendered walls and a slate roof gabled E and W with a square
stone bell-cote with ball finial on the W gable. The entrance at
the E end has an open porch with Roman Doric columns and
entablature and two round-arched gallery windows with wooden
Y-tracery. There are two similar windows in the N and S walls.
A gallery at the E end with contemporary seating has a splayed
front and is supported by two wooden columns.

Wesleyan chapel, Uploders.   (43)

Fittings – Bell: loose, uninscribed. Clock: loose in chapel,
inscribed '1828. The Gift of Dr Robinson & Mr Geo[rg]e Brown
to the Wesleyan Chapel Burton'. Pulpit: at W end, panelled
front with bowed centre bay, c.1827.   [I.139]

LONGBURTON

(44) WESLEYAN (ST 650121). Stone with shafted lancets; 1878 by
Thomas Farrell of Sherborne 'Architect & Builder'.

LYME REGIS

(45) BAPTIST, Silver Street (SY 340922). The church claims to
date from 1653. The chapel, which has rendered walls and a
hipped slate-covered roof, may date from the 18th century. The
SW wall has two tiers of round-arched windows separated by a
platband. The entrance at the SE end is covered by a late 19th-
century porch of red brick and has two gallery windows above.
Later buildings adjoin the other sides.

The interior (approximately 52 ft by 25 ft) was almost entirely
refitted in the late 19th century with a gallery of that date at the
SE end. The NE wall is lined with reused mid 18th-century
panelling incorporating fluted pilasters and a moulded cornice
(covered or removed since 1970).

Fittings – Clock: on panelling of NE wall, circular brass face

BAPTIST CHAPEL, LYME REGIS

signed 'Frans. Pile, Honiton', mid 18th-century. Monuments: in
burial-ground to SE and E, 18th and 19th-century.

BQ VIII (1936–7) 44–8. Ivimey IV (1830) 291–5. Richards,
W. R., Lyme Regis Baptists, 1653–1953 (1953).

(46) COOMBE STREET CHAPEL (SY 342923). A society initially
regarded as Presbyterian but latterly Congregational originated
with the ejection of the vicar, Ames Short, who became the first
pastor; he was preaching in 1672 in his own house and later in a
meeting-house in George's Court. His meeting was disturbed by
constables in 1682 and on 7 July 1683 the seats and pulpit in the
meeting-house were destroyed. Arian preaching in the late 18th
century led to divisions and a decline in the congregation which a
reversion to earlier doctrines failed to repair; the church was re-
formed in 1821 and again in 1859.

The chapel stands on a site leased from the corporation in 1745.
Work on the new building was adversely affected by a sudden
decline in trade due to the French wars and the chapel was not
opened until 23 November 1755. The work is reputed to have
been supervised by the minister, John Whitty, who is credited
with the construction of the pulpit and gallery fronts. The walls
are of squared grey stone rubble, with later rendering to the S
front and E end, and ashlar dressings; the roof which is hipped
and has a central valley is covered with slates. The broad S front is
of five bays with rusticated quoins, plinth, platband and coved
eaves cornice. The central entrance, which has a timber doorcase
with fluted pilasters and entablature, and the flanking windows
have round-arched heads; above are three oval windows, two of
which are blocked; the windows have wide softwood glazing
bars. The E wall has two lower and two gallery windows
matching those in the front. The N wall has two tall round-
arched windows flanking the pulpit. The W end is covered by a
Sunday-school room built in 1912 in place of earlier buildings; no
evidence was found for original windows at this end.

The interior (36½ ft by 45 ft) has a flat plaster ceiling. The
valley-beam of the roof is supported by two square cased timber
columns of the Roman Doric order carrying entablature blocks.
A gallery around three sides, denuded of seats and attenuated at
the NW corner to accommodate an organ installed in 1911, has a
panelled front supported by square columns with a continuous
entablature: the upper surface of the front is painted with seat
numbers [1] – 45. The gallery floor is boarded and stepped; no
traces remain of internal staircases but a doorway, now blocked,
at the S end of the W wall allowed access from an adjacent
building. The pulpit, until recently centrally against the N wall,
was lowered by about 3 ft and altered in 1897. The former pews,

Coombe Street Chapel, Lyme Regis.   (46)

Coombe Street Chapel, Lyme Regis. Interior before 1896.   (46)

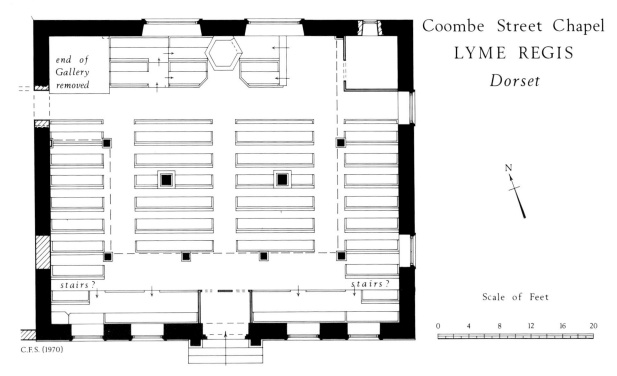

end of
Gallery
removed

stairs ?   stairs ?

Coombe Street Chapel
LYME REGIS
Dorset

N

Scale of Feet

0   4   8   12   16   20

C.F.S. (1970)

reduced in height in 1843, were replaced by the present seats in 1896 which were ordered to be 'similar to those at the Baptist chapel but the book rests like those of the Wesleyans'.

Fittings – *Clock*: on gallery front, circular brass dial in octagonal frame, signed 'Francis Pile, Honiton', mid 18th-century. *Glass*: in N windows, broad borders with large panes of variously coloured glass, mid 19th-century. *Panelling*: dado around walls, mid 18th-century. *Pulpit*: hexagonal with fielded-panelled front, mid 18th-century; the contemporary pulpit door, fielded-panelled back-board (except its carved and scrolled cheeks, lost since 1952) and the hexagonal pulpit canopy, together with the lowest flight of the pulpit staircase (renewed or altered in the 19th century), remained loose in the gallery in 1986; the canopy, surmounted by a carved urn from which 'flames' formerly issued, is constructed around a central hexagonal shaft rising from a hollow double-boarded soffit; below the concealed upper level of boarding is painted in red and white a six-pointed star as a possible design for an inlaid or painted soffit.

(The pulpit was further re-sited prior to the disbandment of the church *c*.1984. The chapel was converted to a private museum in 1986)   [I.144]

The Builder (21 April 1922) measured drawing by Austin Durst. Densham and Ogle (1899) 143–56. Paull, J. R. W., *One of the Two Thousand* (1962).

(47) WESLEYAN, Church Street (SY 343922). Stone with brick dressings, rendered front, sides and rear slate-hung. Tall narrow round-arched windows with iron frames. Opened 1840. (Demolished since 1972)

LYTCHETT MATRAVERS

(48) WESLEYAN, Wareham Road (SY 947955). Built 1824;

rebuilt 1853 with large round-arched windows in side walls. Extended to front 1910.

LYTCHETT MINSTER

(49) UNION CHAPEL (SY 957928). The first chapel on this site was built in 1824 for Independents and Baptists on the union of their two congregations at Organford and Lytchett Minster. A schoolroom was added in 1851. The present building of polychrome brickwork appears to date from the late 19th century. (URC)   [II.158]

Densham and Ogle (1899) 156–9.

MAIDEN NEWTON

(50) Former WESLEYAN (SY 596977). Gabled front, tall round-arched windows with borders of coloured glass. Dated 1871.

MARNHULL

(51) Former CONGREGATIONAL (ST 776193). Built 1852, replacing an earlier meeting-house which was then converted to cottages; porch added 1893. Stone with gabled front and rusticated quoins.

Densham and Ogle (1899) 165–8.

(52) Former WESLEYAN, New Street (ST 777186). Three-bay gabled front with wheel window; dated 1904. Earlier chapel further E, now cottage next to The Retreat Inn, with traces of two lancets above former entrance in gabled front, *c*.1860.   [III.156]

(53) PRIMITIVE METHODIST, Pilwell (ST 781191). Dated 1899. Former chapel 100 yards SE, now cottage; stone with recent brick dressings, altered fenestration and defaced stone tablet, *c*.1870.

Primitive Methodist chapel, Moorside.   (54)

(54) PRIMITIVE METHODIST, Moorside (ST 798195). Inscribed 'erected 1873 by the kind liberality of Mr James Hunt'. Stone with brick dressings and tiled roof.

MELBURY ABBAS

(55) Former PRIMITIVE METHODIST, Cann Common (ST 882208). Coursed rubble with three-bay gabled front and defaced tablet dated 1846.

FORMER PRIMITIVE METHODIST CHAPEL, CANN COMMON   CFS 1968

MOTCOMBE

(56) Former PRIMITIVE METHODIST (ST 848256). Now cottage 'Brookside' on W side of road; built c.1828, much altered.

(57) WESLEYAN (ST 847259). Dated 1870.

NETHERBURY

(58) Former CONGREGATIONAL, Netherbury (SY 469993). In village on W side of road. Built or converted c.1840. Rubble with a hipped slate roof; broad front with central entrance and three pointed-arched windows with traces of earlier windows below the eaves. Now a workshop.
   Densham and Ogle (1899) 355–65.

(59) Former CONGREGATIONAL, Salway Ash (SY 456961). Small chapel of coursed stone with round-arched doorway and windows. Tablet in front gable inscribed 'Independent Meeting 1841'.
   Densham and Ogle (1899) 273–5.

FORMER CONGREGATIONAL CHAPEL, NETHERBURY   CFS 1970

Former Congregational chapel, Salway Ash.   (59)

(60) Former WESLEYAN, Salway Ash (SY 456963). Closely similar to the foregoing, dated 1846. Now a farm store.

NETHER COMPTON

(61) HALFWAY HOUSE CHAPEL (ST 602164). The former Congregational chapel stands high above the main road S of the village equidistant from Sherborne and Yeovil. The congregation appears to have been gathered by Robert Bartlet, ejected in 1660 as rector of Over Compton, who ministered to a society here and later jointly at Yeovil until his death in 1710. After the lease of the first meeting-house expired, in the mid 18th century, the present site in Upping Stock field was acquired and the new meeting-house erected with the assistance of Trinitarian seceders from the then Arian meeting in Yeovil.

The chapel, built c.1750, has walls of coursed stone and a pyramidal roof originally thatched but replaced by slates in 1881. The S front has a plinth and moulded eaves cornice; two doorways in the end bays have moulded jambs, four-centred arched lintels and straight moulded labels, between them are two windows of three lights with hollow-chamfered mullions and transoms and moulded labels. In the E wall is a small wood-framed window serving one end of the gallery. The N wall is covered by a lean-to vestry and shed built in 1888; two windows at gallery level have been blocked.

The interior (27¾ ft by 29 ft) was altered in 1888 when a new floor and seating were provided and the pulpit lowered. The flat plaster ceiling has exposed tie-beams on the two main axes with braces at each end rising from moulded stone corbels, perhaps

'Halfway House Chapel', Nether Compton. Before conversion to house.   (61)

Halfway House Chapel, NETHER COMPTON, *Dorset*

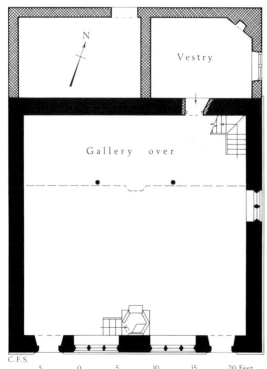

indicative of a more extensive alteration to the roof in the late 19th century. A gallery at the N end has a panelled front with moulded capping and is supported by two octagonal posts.

Fittings – *Coffin Stools*: pair, mid 18th-century. *Monuments*: in chapel, on W wall (1) Rev. William Vaugh[a]n, 1791, painted on wall plaster; on E wall (2) Rev. J. Vickery, 33 years minister, 1843, marble tablet. *Pulpit*: centrally against S wall, hexagonal with fielded-panelled sides, moulded cornice, back-board and matching canopy, mid 18th-century, reset lower and staircase renewed 1888. *Seating*: loose benches; also some decayed fragments of early 19th-century pews in gallery.   [I.101]

(Chapel closed *c*.1970; converted to house *c*.1976, all internal fittings removed and new windows pierced in side walls)

Densham and Ogle (1899) 92–104.

(62) DISSENTERS' BURIAL-GROUND (ST 603170), in use by the foregoing congregation since the early 18th century, lies $\frac{3}{8}$ mile N of chapel. The site is of irregular shape surrounded by walls of coursed rubble and with an elaborate pedimented gateway of Ham Hill stone on the N side. This figures in the will of John Hopkins of London who died in 1732 leaving £100 'to repair the wall and make a gateway to the burial place of the Dissenters, near Sherborne, Dorsetshire'.

Monument: William Fooks, 1841, Mary his wife 1835, Mary their daughter, wife of George Easton, 1817, *et al.*, table-tomb.   [I.102]

Densham and Ogle (1899) 103–4.

OKEFORD FITZPAINE

(63) WESLEYAN (ST 804111). The chapel, dated 1830, stands on a

roadside encroachment. Red brick front with rendered sides and half-hipped slate roof. Stone dressings added to N doorway and windows and a centre window blocked in late 19th century.

[III.203]

NETHER COMPTON, *Dorset*

Entrance to Dissenters' Burial Ground

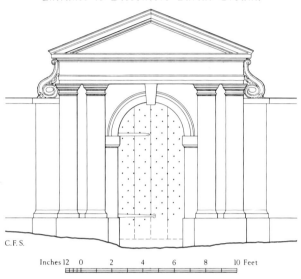

C.F.S.

Inches 12   0   2   4   6   8   10 Feet

PENTRIDGE

(64) PRIMITIVE METHODIST, Woodyates (SU 028194). Ebenezer chapel dated 1852 has walls of flint banded with brickwork.

PIDDLETRENTHIDE

(65) WESLEYAN (SY 708994). Opened 1894. Former chapel adjacent, now Sunday-school, dated 1856; stone-traceried windows inserted.

PIMPERNE

(66) Former WESLEYAN, Chapel Lane (ST 904089). Opened 1847, much altered.

POOLE

(67) BAPTIST, Hill Street (SZ 011907). Although several Particular Baptist converts were made c.1646 by Thomas Collier no separate congregation remained by the early 18th century. A new cause was commenced in 1735 and a meeting-house erected in West Butts Street, but by c.1790 this, too, had failed; the building was sold and demolished, and the proceeds applied to the General Baptist churches at Chichester, Downton, and Newport, Isle of Wight. The site (SZ 009908) is marked by a modern tablet. In 1804 a Particular Baptist church was formed which in 1806 opened a meeting-house in Bowling Green Alley and in 1815 built the present chapel on the NW side of Hill Street.

The E front of red brick has a central doorway covered by a later porch; traces of two former entrances remain alongside. The chapel has been altered externally by the addition of yellow terra-cotta dressings and refitted internally, the SE gallery has been

rebuilt, and an organ chamber and vestries added c.1879.

Fittings – *Monuments*: in chapel, Samuel Bulgin, 46 years pastor, 1854; externally in front of chapel are several reset head-stones from former burial-ground in West Butts Street, late 18th and early 19th-century. *Organ*: case with Classical enrichment, by T.J. Duncan, London, 1839, removed from St Paul's Church, Poole, 1879.

[II.199, 201]

Crosby III (1740) 52. Ivimey II (1814) 149–50. Short (1927) 56–9.

(68) THE OLD MEETING-HOUSE, Hill Street (SZ 010906). An orthodox paedobaptist congregation was in existence in 1663 with John Westley as its pastor. The necessity for separation from the established church was, however, reduced by the continuance

The Old Meeting-house, Poole. Before rebuilding.   (68)

The Old Meeting-house, Poole. Rebuilt 1868.   (68)

in office of Samuel Hardy as curate, in spite of his nonconformity, until 1682. Thereafter Independents and Presbyterians met in increased numbers and in 1704 erected the first regular meeting-house at the SW corner of Hell Street (now Hill Street). In 1721 the meeting-house was enlarged to double its size. A brief secession occurred in 1739 when the minister, Matthew Towgood, on being prevented from preaching, opened another meeting-house in Carters Lane. A more serious division occurred in 1759 when, after six years of unseemly internal disputes attributable to doctrinal differences, the minister, Samuel Philipps, was locked out of the pulpit and then withdrew with the orthodox members of the congregation to found a separate society (see (69)). The Arian and ultimately Unitarian members and trustees remained in possession of the meeting-house which was rebuilt on the same site in 1868.

The former meeting-house was described by Murch (1835) as 'now fifty feet square, having a double roof supported by four pillars in the centre'. It had brick walls and a tiled roof with a verge of stone slates. The broad SE front of five bays had two tiers of windows and wide segmental-arched doorways in the penultimate bays. The chapel of 1868, of white brick with polychrome dressings, has a staircase tower at the S corner with tall pyramidal roof and a single SE gallery. (Chapel closed 1967, demolished c.1970)

Fittings – *Clock*: Parliament clock, square dial with arched top and short pendulum case, inscribed 'The Gift of Severall masters of Vessells – Jos: Jackeman on London Bridge', mid 18th-century (now in Poole Museum). *Monuments*: in front of chapel, late 18th-century and after, illegible (Murch records a tablet above the pulpit in the former meeting-house to Joseph Stephenson, 45 years chapel clerk in succession to his father, 1810). *Pulpit*: upper stage of a former three-tier pulpit originally in Church Lane or South Parade Wesleyan Chapel, Halifax, Yorkshire, subsequently at St Paul's Wesleyan Chapel, Brighouse, Yorkshire (1885–1949), installed here 1950; oval mahogany desk with moulded cornice, possibly 1812 when Halifax chapel was enlarged, stairs and supports late 19th-century.   [II.202]

Densham and Ogle (1899) 180–96. Evans (1897) 201–2. Murch (1835) 288–98. Short (1927) 10–30.

(69) CONGREGATIONAL, Skinner Street (SZ 013905). When Samuel Philipps and his supporters withdrew from the Old Meeting in 1759 they acquired a building in Lag Lane (Lagland Street) which they fitted up, or possibly rebuilt, in 1760. That building, of brick and tile with a gallery and vestry, was enlarged in 1767. In 1776 the present site SE of the former was purchased from Mr John Skinner and a new meeting-house was erected at a cost of £1,400, registered 11 October 1777, which forms the

Congregational chapel (URC), Poole.   (69)

body of the present building. A vestry was added to the N in 1814, the chapel was enlarged to the rear in 1823, the front porch and an Infant School to the NW were built in 1833. In 1880 the interior was reseated and the vestries altered, and in 1886 changes were made to the galleries and the roof structure.

The chapel (now URC) has brick walls partly slate-hung and a half-hipped slated roof. The W front of five bays has a shaped gable with obelisks above the terminal bays. A wide semi-circular-arched central doorway of post-*c*.1833 replacing a circular window superseded the original pair of entrances in the penultimate bays. A timber porch with Doric columns and central pediment covers the three middle bays. Two tiers of windows have pointed-arched heads with keystones and impost blocks, with an upper row of three blind windows in the pediment. A cartouche above the central window is dated 1777. Two tiers of windows in the N and S walls have pointed-arched heads, those in the E wall of 1823 are round-arched.

The interior (originally 58 ft by 47½ ft) has a continuous gallery supported to N and S by circular timber columns, each with four attached three-quarter round shafts, which rise to moulded capitals and an arcade of elliptical arches below the wall-plates of the central roof trusses. The gallery appears to have been refashioned and widened and external staircases built *c*.1823. The seating in the body of the chapel was replaced by pitchpine pews and the pulpit enlarged in 1880. The roof of the chapel is said to have been altered in 1886; this probably refers to the removal of separate pitched roofs above the N and S aisles and the provision of a roof of a single slope to each side eliminating the intermediate valleys.

Fittings – *Chair*: in NE vestry, oak, with spirally turned side standards, late 17th-century. *Clock*: on front of W gallery, early 19th-century. *Monuments*: in chapel on E wall (1) Edward Ashburner M.A., pastor, 1804; in N vestry; (2) Thomas Durant, pastor, 1849; in burial-ground N of chapel (3) Edward Ashburner M.A., 1804, and Frances his widow, 1836, fragments of table-tomb; also in burial-ground remains of four early 19th-century table-tombs and other monuments. *Plate*: includes four two-handled cups, 1810. (Many monuments in burial-ground destroyed *c*.1960; Infant School demolished and residential development on burial-ground at E end proposed 1983)   [II.201]

Densham and Ogle (1899) 180–215. Short (1927) 26–55.

(70) Former FRIENDS, Prosperous Street (SZ 012906). A meeting gathered in 1655 by George Fox may have had a meeting-house on this site by 1678. This appears to have been rebuilt about 1731. In 1792 it was proposed to build 'a more convenient room' at Poole for the Quarterly Meeting and this project was completed by 7 September 1796 when M. Searle, the 'surveyor', presented his account for the work. The former building was still standing in 1803 when it was described as the 'old meeting house'. The present building is probably the room of 1795–6 which was extended to the S in the early 19th century, perhaps when the older building was demolished. The meeting-house has been much altered and extended to the E since 1946 on conversion to a boys' club.

The walls are of brick and the hipped roof was formerly tiled and had a verge of stone slates. The side walls have moulded wooden eaves cornices and round-arched windows with moulded

Former Friends' Meeting-house ,   POOLE
Dorset

Former Friends' meeting-house, Poole.   (70)

stone architraves; the E windows, now altered or blocked, were joined by a platband at impost level. The S porch, now rebuilt, had twin spiral staircases to the gallery.

The interior (originally 35½ ft by 27½ ft, enlarged to S by 22 ft) has a high plaster barrel-vaulted ceiling. A gallery at the S end has been removed. The stand at the N end had a plain panelled back and three tiers of seats; open-backed benches were of two types, with plank ends or shaped arm-rests – no fittings now remain. A burial-ground to the W which, in 1946, had plain uniform head-stones has been cleared.   [II.201–2]

Lidbetter (1961) 22. Short (1927) 6–9, pl. fcg 2.

(71) Former WESLEYAN, Chapel Lane (SZ 013908), of brick with hipped tiled roof extended in slate, was built in 1793 at the expense of Robert Carr Brackenbury; it was enlarged to the S and a two-storeyed wing added to the N in 1843. The S front was altered in 1956 but retains a dated oval tablet. The side walls have pointed-arched windows. The interior has a coved plaster ceiling with moulded cornice. There is a gallery in the S extension.

Present chapel adjacent to E in High Street, by Charles Bell, 1880.   [II.202]

Short (1927) 60–1.

PORTESHAM

(72) Former SCHOOL, Coryates (SY 629853). The school, dated 1845, was also used as a preaching station by Congregationalists from Upwey and Abbotsbury.   [II.243]

Densham and Ogle (1899) 326.

PORTLAND

(73) CONGREGATIONAL, High Street, Maidenwell (SY 684735). Rubble with lancet windows, built 1858 during the ministry of

James Cheney 'from plans of his own devising', on site of first chapel of 1827. Sunday-school 1874. (URC)

CYB (1859) 241. (1864) obituary of J. Cheney.

(74) WESLEYAN, Southwell (SY 688700). Methodism was introduced to Portland in 1791 by Robert Carr Brackenbury. The first chapel, since rebuilt, was erected at Fortuneswell in 1792. Land for a chapel at Southwell was acquired in 1836, the present small gabled building is dated 1849. Other former Wesleyan chapels are at Easton (SY 693719), of 1854, and at Maidenwell (SY 683736), of *c*.1860–70.   [II.250]

Pearce, R., *Methodism in Portland* (1898).

(75) Former PRIMITIVE METHODIST, Fortuneswell (SY 685736). Dated 1869, by James Kerridge. (In use in 1983 as theatre)

(76) Former BIBLE CHRISTIAN, Maidenwell (SY 685733). Gabled front with rusticated round-arched openings, dated 1865. *Monument*: in chapel, William Burden, 1896. (In use 1983 by Jehovah's Witnesses)

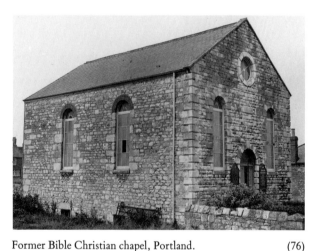

Former Bible Christian chapel, Portland.   (76)

PUDDLETOWN

(77) CONGREGATIONAL (SY 762942). Built 1866, with adjoining manse and later Sunday-school, 1886.

CYB (1867) 354–5. Densham and Ogle (1899) 221–5.

PUNCKNOWLE

(78) Former WESLEYAN (SY 533886). Simple rendered rectangle with gabled front dated 1849. (Converted to house since 1970)

RAMPISHAM

(79) Former CONGREGATIONAL, Uphall (ST 558026). Rubble and slate, built 1844. The broad S front has a plain doorway between two contemporary mullioned windows of four lights with moulded labels. The interior has a semicircular plaster barrel vault.   [I.192]

Densham and Ogle (1899) 225–6.

SANDFORD ORCAS

(80) Former BRETHREN (ST 627204). Gabled three-bay front with altered entrance and lancet windows. Built *c*.1870, closed 1916, now used for storage.

FORMER CONGREGATIONAL CHAPEL, RAMPISHAM   CFS 1970

FORMER BRETHREN MEETING-ROOM, SANDFORD ORCAS   C·F·S·1970

SHAFTESBURY

(81) CONGREGATIONAL, Muston's Lane (ST 864231). This site was acquired in 1706 by a formerly Presbyterian church of late 17th-century origin; a meeting-house was registered 15 July 1707. The present chapel of 1859 by Andrew Trimen has a front of Bath stone with paired Corinthian columns supporting a pediment over the centre bay. The roof is supported by exposed queen-post trusses.

Congregational chapel (URC), Shaftesbury.   (81)

Fittings – *Font*: stone with gadrooned and fluted bowl on cylindrical stem and octagonal base, 17th-century, origin unknown. *Monument*: in chapel, Rev. James Merchant, 1797. *Painting*: in vestry, portrait in oils of a minister, 19th-century. *Plate*: pair of two-handled cups, 1751. (URC)   [IV.66]

CYB (1862) following 320. Densham and Ogle (1899) 227–42.

(82) Former FRIENDS, St James's Street (ST 861227). The meeting-house was built in 1746 for a meeting settled *c*.1699; it was derelict by 1950 and has since been converted to a cottage. The walls are of ashlar and the roof, now flat, was formerly hipped and covered with stone slates. The SE front of three bays has a wide central entrance with a pair of doorways formerly covered by a porch; a round-arched upper window has been removed. The flanking windows had round-arched heads with keystones which were dressed back and the heads of the windows made square in the late 19th century. The end walls have each one window, now blocked, at an upper level. The NW wall is blank.

Former Friends' meeting-house, Shaftesbury.   (82)

Former Friends' Meeting-house
SHAFTESBURY
Dorset

C.F.S.   10 Feet   0   10   20

The interior (20½ ft by 32½ ft) may have been divided into two rooms of equal size, but no old features remain. The original roof structure, removed since 1950, included three trusses.

Monuments: in burial-ground to SE, small headstones of early 19th century and later, including Robert Ackland, 1833.   [IV.73]

(83) WESLEYAN, Bell Street (ST 863231). The chapel of 1907 by Gordon and Gunton stands on the site of a preaching-house of 1766, rebuilt 1827. Former date-stone reset.

SHERBORNE

(84) Former STRICT BAPTIST, Finger Lane (ST 636166). 'Providence Chapel', built 1838–9, is now used by the Brethren as a Gospel Hall. Gabled front of three bays with stone Y-tracery in pointed-arched windows.   [I.211]

Oliver (1968) 119.

(85) Former CONGREGATIONAL, Long Street (ST 640167). A Presbyterian society formed in the late 17th century built a meeting-house in Newland which was placed in trust in 1709, and is described as 'bounded on the north side by the Quakers' meeting-house and burying ground'. The growth of heterodox preaching led to orthodox secessions *c*.1744 and 1753. The seceders erected a new meeting-house in 1756 on the S side of Long Street (ST 641166) which continued in use until the opening of the present chapel in 1804. The remnant of the Old Meeting joined the new society about 1792 when the original meeting-house had become structurally unsafe. The new meeting-house was subsequently used as a school and is now occupied by a social club. It is a long rectangular building with a hipped roof, concealed from the street behind a row of two-storeyed cottages.

'Union Chapel' on the N side of the street, named in commemoration of the reunion of the old and new societies, was built on the back garden of a house acquired in 1802. The chapel, dated 1803, was opened 14 November 1804, side galleries were added 1814, the house next to the street was demolished in 1816 and in 1821 the chapel was enlarged to the front by 21 ft. An organ gallery was added in 1824, a lecture-room built behind the chapel in 1858 and the interior refitted in 1883.

The chapel has rendered stone walls with ashlar dressings. The gabled S front of 1821, formerly surmounted by a finial, has two pointed-arched doorways with elaborate Gothic surrounds,

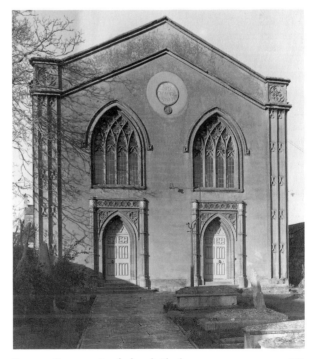

Former Congregational chapel, Sherborne.   (85)

possibly of 1803–4 but reset, and upper windows of four lights with intersecting cusped tracery. The original circular date-tablet, with amended inscription, is reset in the gable surrounded by a border of applied quatrefoils, now mostly fallen away. The interior has galleries supported by cast-iron columns. (Chapel converted to auction room c.1978; ceiling and lower seating removed)

Fittings – *Bell-cote*: on N gable, square, with finial and weathervane. *Monuments*: in chapel (1) Samuel Scott, 1836, Grace his wife, 1836, *et al.*, by King of Bath; (2) Rev. James Weston, 1823. *Plate*: includes a pair of two-handled cups of 1723. *Railings*: next to street, with wrought-iron gates and overthrow 1816. [I.211]

Densham and Ogle (1899) 243–73.

(86) Former FRIENDS, George Street (ST 638169). A meeting was in existence here in 1657. In 1693 a meeting-house behind The George Inn in Cheap Street was given to the society. Meetings ceased in 1835. The present building, which dates from the late 17th century, has more recently been used by the Salvation Army and latterly for amateur theatricals.

Former Friends' meeting-house, Sherborne. (86)

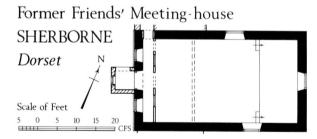

Former Friends' Meeting-house
SHERBORNE
Dorset

The walls are of rubble with a front of ashlar and the roof is hipped and tiled. The W front has an original central entrance with double doors, and an early 19th-century porch; small windows have been inserted each side of the porch and a wide upper window may also be later. Windows in the side and rear walls have timber lintels and renewed frames.

The interior (40½ ft by 20¾ ft) has a flat plaster ceiling. The room formerly had a deep gallery at the W end with shutters below the front, now removed. There is a dado of late 19th-century matchboarding around the walls.

Penney (1907) 86.

(87) WESLEYAN, Cheap Street (ST 638166). Built 1841–2 apparently at the expense of William Dingley to whose memory an apse was added at the W end in 1884. The walls are of ashlar with grouped lancet windows and buttresses in a 13th-century Gothic style. The interior of five bays has a canted ceiling with thin wooden arched supports decorated with cusped tracery rising from stone corbels. A gallery around three sides, rounded to the E, was rebuilt in the later 19th century.

Wesleyan chapel, Sherborne. (87)

Monuments: in chapel (1) Rev. Elijah Morgan, 1853; (2) Rev. John Lesson, 1850; in porch (3) Grace Dingley, 1858.

Densham and Ogle (1899) 266. Simon, J.S., *Methodism in Dorset* (1870).

SHIPTON GORGE

(88) WESLEYAN (SY 496916). Rubble walls, round-arched windows; date 1849 in gable. Conversion of earlier cottage.

SIXPENNY HANDLEY

(89) WESLEYAN, Woodcutts (ST 970173). Red brick with stone dressings, dated 1853.

SPETISBURY

(90) Former PRIMITIVE METHODIST (ST 915022). 'Ebenezer Chapel, built 1842, enlarged 1862'.

STOKE ABBOTT

(91) CONGREGATIONAL (ST 453006). Rubble with round-arched windows. Built 1838 superseding a chapel of c.1788 at Wood Mill, about 2 miles west. (URC)

Densham and Ogle (1899) 289–94.

Congregational chapel (URC), Stoke Abbott.   (91)

STOUR PROVOST

(92) Former CONGREGATIONAL, Stour Row (ST 819211). Built in 1843 for a congregation gathered in 1839 by the Rev. T. Evans of Shaftesbury. Ashlar walls and slate roof; gabled three-bay front with lancet windows and blind quatrefoil in circular frame above entrance. Now village hall.

Densham and Ogle (1899) 295–9.

STOURTON CAUNDLE

(93) CONGREGATIONAL (ST 714151). Small chapel, opened 13 October 1858. Rubble with ashlar dressings and slate roof. Gabled three-bay front with pointed-arched entrance, lancet windows and quatrefoiled ventilator in gable. Rostrum pulpit of c.1894; plain seating.   [III.267]

CYB (1859) 249. Densham and Ogle (1899) 299–302.

STURMINSTER NEWTON

(94) WESLEYAN, Church Street (ST 787140). Built 1832, rebuilt in brick and enlarged to front 1869; lower courses of first chapel remain in side wall.

SWANAGE

(95) CONGREGATIONAL, High Street (SZ 028788). The chapel of 1900–1, in a free Gothic style by Thomas Stevens, was originally designed to have a short tower above the principal entrance. Adjacent to it is the former chapel of 1837 which stands on the site of a Presbyterian meeting-house built in 1705.

The 1837 chapel is a plain structure designed by George Gollop. Its walls are of coursed rubble with ashlar facing to the front of a two-storeyed porch. Twin round-arched entrances give separate access to the lower floor and to a small gallery staircase within the porch. The interior has a gallery around three sides supported by cast-iron columns and an upper gallery at the S end. *Monument:* Samuel Marsh, 1841, deacon, Margaret his wife, 1807, *et al.* (URC)   [II.292]

Building News (20 March 1896). CYB (1901) 162. Densham and Ogle (1899) 306–14. Tatchell, L., *A Short History of the Swanage Congregational Church* (1951).

(96) WESLEYAN, High Street (SZ 029787). Gothic with tall octagonal turret to corner tower; 1886 by Bucknell and Jennings, Centenary Hall and school alongside 1907.

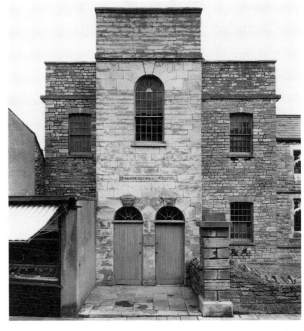

Former Congregational chapel, Swanage.   (95)

SYDLING ST NICHOLAS

(97) Former CONGREGATIONAL, High Street (SY 632994). House, on E side of street, used c.1790–1834 as a meeting-house by a society formed c.1770. The building later became a National School but is now in domestic use. Although said to have been 'erected' about 1790, it is probably the conversion of a late 17th-century cottage. The walls are of banded flint and stone and the roof is thatched. In the E wall facing the street are traces of three tall windows, now lowered and with semi-dormers added above. A floor was inserted in the 19th century.

(98) Former CONGREGATIONAL (SY 633999). N of village, built

Former Congregational chapel, Sydling St Nicholas.   (98)

Former Unitarian chapel, Wareham. Before conversion.

(103)

1834 to supersede the foregoing. Rubble and flint with dressings of brick and stone. The rendered S front has a shaped gable and pointed-arched windows. (Converted to house since 1970) [I.233]
  Densham and Ogle (1899) 315–18.

THORNFORD

(99) WESLEYAN (ST 603129). Three-bay gabled front with lancets, opened 1869.

TOLPUDDLE

(100) WESLEYAN (SY 797943). Built 1861; memorial gateway to 'Tolpuddle Martyrs' erected 1912.

WAREHAM LADY ST MARY

(101) OLD MEETING-HOUSE, Church Street, Wareham (SY 925874). The Presbyterian, subsequently Congregational, church (now URC), originated in the late 17th century. In 1672 the house of Dorothy, widow of Thomas Chaplyn, ejected minister at Wareham, was licensed as a meeting-house. The present site, formerly a garden, was acquired in 1694 and a new meeting-house erected which was rebuilt in 1747. On 25 July 1762 the new building together with much of the town was destroyed by fire; the existing structure dates from the subsequent rebuilding. Doctrinal differences within the congregation led in 1789 to a secession of some of the more orthodox members who built a chapel in West Street (102). Continuing differences resulted in a further division within the Old Meeting in 1828 when Unitarian supporters formed a separate society (103); the earlier seceders reunited with the parent body in 1849.

The chapel of 1762 has brick walls with some later rendering and a hipped tiled roof with verge of stone slates. The W front has three segmental-arched upper windows of c.1830 replacing windows of two lights with a central mullion. The lower openings, now covered by a continuous porch of c.1895, formerly comprised two doorways with outer porches and a window between. The E wall has a shallow gabled projection at the centre, of 1878, replacing two tall round-arched pulpit windows. The N and S walls are partly covered by wings added in 1860 and 1895.

The interior (41 ft by 45½ ft) is divided by two rows of tall timber columns, with moulded capitals supporting three parallel roofs with a coved plaster ceiling to the centre space. A gallery

with moulded panelled front extends around three sides. The chapel was altered and refitted in 1878 by W.J. Stent of Warminster, including, in the rebuilt centre of the E wall, a circular window with coloured glass given by the architect. Some earlier seating remains in the gallery. *Plate*: now lost, included two mugs of 1704. [II.314–15]
  Densham and Ogle (1899) 335–55.

(102) Former CONGREGATIONAL, West Street, Wareham (SY 922874). The chapel, built and probably designed by George Gollop and John Swetland, was opened 1 January 1790 for seceders from (101). After 1849 it became the British School.

The walls are of brick and the S front, rebuilt c.1849, is rendered in stucco. The front is of three bays with plain panelled pilasters supporting a pediment and two tiers of windows. The interior (45½ ft by 30 ft) formerly had a S gallery; a large room at the N end was originally a vestry. (Demolished and replaced by flats before 1988; façade remains) [II.315]
  Densham and Ogle (1899) 343–8, 354.

(103) Former UNITARIAN, South Street, Wareham (SY 923873), was built in 1830 by seceders from the Old Meeting (101). The walls are of brickwork, the E front is rendered in stucco. The front has a portico with four Ionic columns and blind round-arched recesses in flanking bays. The interior has a segmental plaster barrel vault. At the S end is a small gallery. The seating has been renewed but the pulpit, although remodelled, is original. (Chapel closed c.1975, now Conservative Club) [II.315]
  Densham and Ogle (1899) 349. Evans (1897) 248. Murch (1835) 278–85.

Old Meeting-house, Wareham, Rear before alteration. (101)

The Old Meeting-house, Wareham. Front before alteration. (101)

The Old Meeting-house, Wareham. (101)

WEYMOUTH

(104) BAPTIST, Bank Buildings (SY 68157878). Built in 1813–14 for a newly formed congregation by George Welsford, builder, and enlarged with the addition of galleries in 1828. It was re-fronted and extended to the S in 1859 and re-pewed in 1864. The walls are rendered and the roof is hipped and slated. The N front, now of three bays with two attached Doric columns *in antis* in the centre supporting a pedimented entablature, is described by Hutchins as formerly 'having a common house front, resembling but inferior to the adjoining buildings'. The interior has a gallery around three sides supported by cast-iron columns.

Monuments: in chapel (1) Thomas Butler, 1838; (2) Rev. Thomas Flint, two years pastor, 1819, signed C. Cooper, Canterbury; (3) Frances, 1833, and Jane, 1838, wives of George Welsford.   [II.335–6]

Hutchins II (1863) 461.

(105) CONGREGATIONAL, Gloucester Street (SY 679794). The church originated in the late 17th century as an Independent or Presbyterian society of which George Thorne, ejected rector of Melcombe Regis, was regarded as the founder. Until 1864, meetings were held in Nicholas Street where, in 1703–5, three

Congregational chapel, Gloucester Street, Weymouth.   (105)
(*Congregational Year Book*, 1862)

cottages were purchased and placed in trust for use as a meeting-house. The Great Meeting-house, probably a conversion rather than a rebuilding of the cottages, remained until 1803–4 when it was replaced by a new chapel on an enlargement of the same site. After 1864 the former building was sold and converted to a music hall; it has long been demolished.

The chapel in Gloucester Street, commenced November 1862 and opened 22 July 1864, is a large building of rubble with Bath stone dressings in the Romanesque style by R. C. Bennett, one of the deacons of the church. Two octagonal staircase towers with tall spires flank a gabled entrance front which has a wide round-arched doorway and above it a large wheel window filled with geometrical patterns of coloured glass. The ground floor is occupied by schoolrooms above which, approached by curved staircases from the S entrance, is the main body of the chapel. Galleries around three sides are supported by spirally turned cast-iron columns; at the N end is a small domed apse occupied by the organ with a circular stone pulpit in front. *Inscription*: tablet on SE staircase commemorates opening 1864. (Demolished 1980, inscription reset in new building on site)

CYB (1862) 315–16. Densham and Ogle (1899) 365–81. Hutchins II (1863) 459–60.

(106) CONGREGATIONAL, Hope Street (SY 681785). Orthodox seceders from the Great Meeting built a meeting-house in Old Weymouth in 1729 but reunited *c*.1744. A new congregation was formed in 1817 and in 1822 a warehouse was converted for their use. The present chapel, built on the same site in 1861–2 by Haggett and Pocklington, is of stone with an elaborate cornice and stilted arches to the windows. (URC)

CYB (1862) 320. Densham and Ogle (1899) 381–4.

(107) Former CONGREGATIONAL, Upwey (SY 666845). 'Upway Chapel', dated 1809, was built and at first maintained by George Wood and George, his son, later of Athelhampton Hall. It was superseded in 1880–1 by the present Gothic chapel (URC) on a new site (SY 670844) by R. C. Bennett. The former building is of stone with a hipped slate roof. Above the porch is a range of five pointed-arched windows of the late 19th century.   [II.366]

Densham and Ogle (1899) 321–6.

(108) FRIENDS' BURIAL-GROUND, Barrack Road (SY 683787). A meeting-house in Melcombe Regis near the SE end of St Thomas Street was converted from existing buildings purchased in 1721; it was closed *c*.1790 and then occupied briefly by Wesleyans. The building was sold in 1858 and subsequently demolished.

The *burial-ground* at The Nothe, acquired in 1719, is a walled enclosure also used, until 1834, by other dissenters. Hutchins records four monuments, including Rev. Joseph Wilkins, 1800, 45 years dissenting minister.   [II.336]

Hutchins II (1863) 461.

(109) Former WESLEYAN, Lower Bond Street (SY 678790), was built in 1805 for the society formed *c*.1790 which formerly met in the Friends' meeting-house. It was superseded in 1867 by the present chapel in Maiden Street (110). The former building, of brick and rubble with a hipped slate roof, had a N front of yellow brick of three bays with two tiers of pointed-arched windows; above the entrance was a shallow niche with urn and the date 1805. A burial-ground lay to the S. (Site of chapel and burial-

Former Wesleyan chapel, Lower Bond Street, Weymouth. (109)

Wesleyan chapel, Maiden Street, Weymouth.   (110)

ground redeveloped before 1983 for large shopping complex)   [II.336]

Hutchins II (1863) 461.

(110) WESLEYAN, Maiden Street (SY 68057878). Stone with brown brick front and ashlar dressings, in Italian Romanesque style by Foster and Wood; large wheel window above arcaded loggia. Opened 1867.

(111) Former WESLEYAN, Preston (SY 705831). Built c.1817. Brick with half-hipped slate roof, pointed-arched windows. N gallery with panelled front.   [II.362]

Former Wesleyan Chapel at Preston   WEYMOUTH Dorset   15 Feet

WHITCHURCH CANONICORUM

(112) CONGREGATIONAL, Morcombelake (SY 400942). Plain building with rendered walls and pointed-arched windows, opened 1832. The walls were heightened and a W gallery built in 1840 and a schoolroom added to the W in 1863. The pulpit at the E end, with flared base and panelled sides, has been lowered. (URC)   [I.263]

Densham and Ogle (1899) 169–75.

WIMBORNE MINSTER

(113) Former BAPTIST, Westborough (SU 009005). The chapel, built in 1788 for seceders from the Congregationalists, remained in use until the late 19th century; it is now used for storage. The walls are of brickwork and the roof is half-hipped and tiled. A two-storeyed house and shop were built against the W front in the late 19th century. The N and S walls have each one large segmental-arched window; smaller windows W of these came below the ends of a former W gallery. In the E wall are two windows flanking the site of the pulpit.

The interior ($27\frac{3}{4}$ ft by $16\frac{1}{4}$ ft) has a coved plaster ceiling with moulded cornice along the N and S sides. Below the chapel is a storage cellar with external access.   [V.85]

B.Hbk (1889) 139; (1893) 147. Densham and Ogle (1899) 395. Oliver (1968) 119.

(114) CONGREGATIONAL, Chapel Lane (SU 009004). The church, formed in the late 17th century (now URC), traces its origin to the Rev. Thomas Rowe, ejected rector of Lytchett Matravers, who was licensed as a Presbyterian preacher here in 1672. The present site was placed in trust in 1695 and a meeting-house was presumably in existence by that date. A new chapel built in 1788 and enlarged in 1829 was superseded by the existing building in 1846.

The chapel has rendered brick walls and a slate roof. The N front is divided by hexagonal buttresses which rise to plain pyramidal finials. The side walls have two-stage buttresses and lancet windows. The interior, much refitted in 1886 and later, has an original N gallery with later front and some contemporary seating. The roof is supported by hammer-beam trusses.

Congregational chapel, Winterborne Kingston. (115)

Monuments: in chapel (1) Rev. James Panton, 1778, and John his son, 1786, oval tablet; (2) Edward White, 1814, Mary his wife, 1804, Edward their son, 1818, and his two wives, Elizabeth, 1796, and Mary, 1813. [V.85]

    Densham and Ogle (1899) 385–99.

WINTERBORNE KINGSTON

(115) CONGREGATIONAL (SY 862977). Built 1846, enlarged to S 1884. White brick with red brick dressings and a slate roof. E side of four bays with segmental-arched windows, entrance

Congregational chapel, Winterborne Kingston. (115)

covered by extensions.

    Densham and Ogle (1899) 399–404.

WINTERBORNE WHITECHURCH

(116) WESLEYAN (ST 840002). Rendered walls, possibly of cob, and a parallel enlargement in brickwork at the rear. Plain pointed-arched windows. Built 1847, enlarged and a N gallery added in late 19th century. [III.311]

WOOL

(117) Former MEETING-HOUSE (SY 84658663). The former National School on E side of High Street is said by Hutchins to be 'a room originally built for the Dissenters and for some time used as their chapel'. Rendered walls with two arched windows, early 19th-century. [II.406]

    Hutchins I (1861) 364.

YETMINSTER

(118) WESLEYAN (ST 596109). Coursed stone and slate; gabled NE front with porch and three graduated lancets above. Opened 1850. [I.272]

Apart from a few notable exceptions, this county is not remarkable for the number or quality of its nonconformist buildings. The exceptions, of which the Old Meeting-house in Ringwood (50) is the most important, are, however, sufficiently outstanding to raise the interest of its monuments above a general level of mediocrity, if not quite up to a standard comparable with its better endowed neighbours.

Mainland dissent is dominated by Congregational churches, many of 17th or early 18th-century origin, either Presbyterian or Independent, and whose chapels account for two-fifths of the monuments recorded, but which, as for example at Andover (6), of 1700, have little if any recognizable early work. The Old Meeting-house at Tadley (62), of 1718, is a good but much enlarged example of a small village chapel, while at Havant (28) is a notable town meeting-house of contemporary date and modest size with a remarkably sophisticated brick façade. Of those Presbyterian meetings which followed a less orthodox theological path, the only monument remaining is at Ringwood; the former High Street Chapel in Portsmouth (49), again of 1718, was a major casualty of the bombing of 1941 which also swept away much that may have remained in Southampton. The Old Meeting-house at Ringwood (50), of 1727–8, is a building of great interest for the almost complete survival of its fittings and for the complex and masterly design of its structure which lies hidden behind an apparently dull exterior in what was until recent years an obscure back lane.

The scattered nature of early Baptist churches is exemplified in the origins of the cause at Broughton (14), but no chapels of any consequence remain from an early date. The Friends' meeting-house at Alton (3), of 1672, with its date proudly displayed in the brickwork of the boundary wall, although one of the earliest Quaker buildings to survive has been considerably altered. The Countess of Huntingdon's Chapel at Mortimer West End (42), built at the close of the 18th century and soon afterwards enlarged, is a much neglected building of great architectural charm, retaining a full set of contemporary fittings.

Most notable amongst 19th-century chapels are those Congregational buildings in which the use of the Gothic style was developed: of these, Fareham (21), of 1836, and Lymington (39), of 1847, may be particularly cited, while the unusual example of 1853 in Winchester (70), the work of Poulton and Woodman, is striking in its originality; the solution to the problem of a difficult site is seen at Romsey (55) in 1887–8, in the work of Paull and Bonella. Another chapel of this period, on a grand scale, is Richmond Hill, Bournemouth (11). Methodist chapels, though mainly of minor interest, include the Wesleyan garrison chapel of 1875–7 on a prominent site in the centre of Aldershot (1). The absence from contemporary Baptist chapels of a fully developed Gothic style is notable, plainer buildings such as Whitchurch (66), of 1836, and Middle Wallop (47), of 1841, being found sufficient for denominational needs and aspirations. The Baptist chapel at Hartley Wintney (27), of 1807 and later, is of greater interest for its historical development and the surviving gallery seating. The chapel at Poulner (53), of 1840 with cob walls and thatched roof, though disappointingly altered, is one of the most picturesque of Hampshire chapels besides being a rare example of the use of these building materials. The only other examples noted of cob walling are in the Methodist chapels of 1844 at Barton Stacey (9) and 1845 at Little Down (63) and at the Baptist chapel at Middle Wallop referred to above. The principal building materials used are brick for walling, with only occasional or late use of stone, and slate as the normal roof covering.

The *Isle of Wight* has only one monument of the 18th century, at Newport (86), where the General Baptist chapel retains some structure of 1774–5, although in a greatly altered state. Of the early 19th-century chapels, the former Wesleyan of *c*.1831 at Cowes (81) is notable but the principal feature of Methodist interest is the number of Bible Christian chapels on the island, such as Brook (78), of 1848, which, although they are small and some of late date, represent a significant and successful local missionary operation by this predominantly Devonian denomination. The use of the Gothic style by Congregationalists is here repeated at Brading (76), of 1847, while Baptists at Niton (96) also made a distinctive use of it in 1849 when removing from their former malt-house chapel. The front of the Baptist chapel in Castlehold, Newport (87), a rare and striking essay in the Classical style, probably dates from 1872. Brick and stone are both in common use for walling and slate again predominates for roofing.

ALDERSHOT

(1) Former WESLEYAN, Grosvenor Road (SU 861507). The whole site between Queens Road and Upper Union Street was developed between *c.*1875 and 1893, including a large chapel of 1875–7 at the SE corner, a church hall to the W and another hall to the N dated 1893 and inscribed 'in affectionate regard for the highest welfare of the British Army'.

The chapel, of rubble with ashlar dressings and exposed brickwork to the N, comprises a nave, N and S transepts, polygonal W chancel and a tall SE corner tower. The interior is subdivided by arcades supported by groups of slender cast-iron shafts. This served as the Wesleyan 'Garrison Church' from 1881 and was held by trustees under a unique military trust until the 1960s; it was closed in 1988.

Methodist Recorder (13 October 1977).

Friends' meeting-house, Alton.   (3)

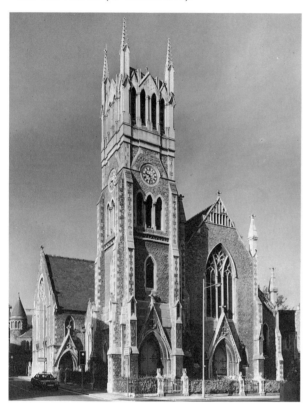

Former Wesleyan chapel, Grosvenor Road, Aldershot.   (1)

ALTON

(2) CONGREGATIONAL, Normandy Street (SU 720396). The church originated in the late 17th century. The chapel, which replaces a building of 1794, is dated 1834 on a tablet in the back wall; it was registered 10 January 1837 as 'lately erected'. The walls are of brickwork covered with a later rendering. The front is gabled, of three bays with a central porch and two tiers of windows, the upper ones with four-centred arched heads and moulded labels; the corners are angled. Probably by James Fenton.

(3) FRIENDS, Church Street (SU 717397). The meeting-house and adjacent cottage form a long low range with walls of brickwork

in English bond rendered at the front and a half-hipped tiled roof; an original brick chimney-stack between the two parts has been demolished.

The building was erected in 1672, the date being prominently displayed in glazed headers in the contemporary boundary wall next to the road. A second cottage was added at the N end of the range in the late 18th century; the two cottages have now been combined and two small dormers inserted in the roof.

The meeting-house at the S end has been much altered on several occasions, most recently in 1964–5; it has a single sash window in the W wall with entrance to the right, and two similar windows at the rear. The interior ($40\frac{1}{4}$ ft by 20 ft) is believed to have had galleries at N and S ends erected in 1690, but only the S gallery remains; this has an open-balustraded front, closed behind and below by shutters. The roof trusses have tie-beams and collars with V-braces and clasped purlins with wind-braces. *Seating*: 18th-century benches with shaped supports and added backs, loose outside 1967, also 19th-century benches with open backs and arm-rests.

Lidbetter (1961) Pl. XXXVII. Southall (1974) 14–16.

(4) WESLEYAN, High Street (SU 716391). Rubble with brick dressings, rendered front, and slate roof. Pedimented front wall with terminal pilasters, three round-arched windows with rusticated surrounds and central doorway; dated 1846. (Demolished 1977)

ANDOVER

(5) BAPTIST, High Street (SU 36524555). Stock brick with bands of red brick and large wheel window. Built 1866 by C. G. Searle and Son.

(6) CONGREGATIONAL, East Street (SU 36654565). The church (now URC) originated in the late 17th century and initially combined both Presbyterians and Independents. The latter seceded *c.*1700 from the original Lower Meeting in Soper's Lane and erected the present chapel or 'Upper Meeting-house' in that year. Side galleries were added in 1814 and the building was extended to the front in 1839. The interior was almost entirely refitted in the late 19th century.

The walls are of brickwork covered with stucco and the roof is hipped and slated. The original structure is visible on the N and S sides which are of three bays and have each a platband between two tiers of windows. The W front of three bays has a pedimented centre with a wide central entrance flanked by Roman Doric columns and a Venetian window above. The interior (originally 40¼ ft by 42 ft) has a gallery around three sides supported by cast-iron columns. At the E end of the S wall is a blocked doorway to a former vestry.

Fittings – *Fontlet*: white-glazed pottery model of font at St Mary Magdalene, Oxford, cover with gabled finial, mid 19th-century. *Gates* and *Railings*: in front of chapel, wrought-iron, between rendered piers with debased urns, *c*.1839. *Monuments* and *Floorslabs*. *Monuments*: in chapel (1) Anna, widow of Rev. John Cumming D.D., 55 years minister, 1810, and Martha Piper her niece, 1824; in vestibule (2) Samuel Shaw, 1843, *et al*.; (3) Benjamin Wiltshire, 1856, and Martha his wife, 1843; (4) Benjamin William Cockings, 1842, and Ann Jane Cockings, 1845; (5) Sarah Gue, 1860, *et al*.; in forecourt on S wall of house; (6) Martha, wife of Robert Tasker, 1843, and Joseph Tasker their nephew, 1854; also several early 19th-century headstones reset at sides of forecourt. *Floorslabs*: in N aisle (1) John Cumming D.D., minister, 1790, *et al*.; (2) Martha, wife of Jacob Bunney, 1741, and five children; in S aisle (3) illegible. *Organ*: with five ranks of pipes, from St George's Chapel, Windsor, late 18th-century.

Baptist chapel, Andover.   (5)

(7) FRIENDS' BURIAL-GROUND, Winchester Street (SU 365451). A meeting-house built in 1713 was sold in 1880 and has since been demolished. The burial-ground, on the W side of the street, is a square enclosure dominated by two tall ash trees; it contains two monuments (1) Mary, wife of Edmund Walderne, 1701, ledger stone; (2) Thomas Heath, 1842, Mary his wife, 1839, and Sarah Pink Heath their daughter, 1830.

(8) Former WESLEYAN, Winchester Street (SU 365452). Built in 1819, sold to the Salvation Army in 1925. Brick with hipped slate roof. Originally of three bays with windows in round-arched recesses; blocked doorway in N bay on E side, gabled extensions at S end.

BARTON STACEY

(9) Former PRIMITIVE METHODIST (SU 435407). Cob with hipped slate roof. E doorway with flat canopy on shaped wooden brackets, tablet above dated 1844. Chapel closed *c*.1942. (Derelict 1980)

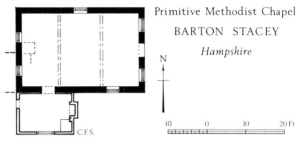

BASINGSTOKE

(10) CONGREGATIONAL, London Street (SU 639519). The church (now URC), which originated in the late 17th century, traces its origins to John Hook, ejected as rector of King's Worthy in 1661. The first known meeting-house, in Cross Street, was opened in 1695 and superseded by the present building in 1800–1; this was enlarged in 1839, refronted in 1860 and refitted in 1882. The chapel has brick walls; the S front is rendered, of five bays with a three-bay pedimented centre having two giant Roman Doric columns *in antis*. The side walls are of five bays with two tiers of windows set in tall round-arched recesses. The three rear bays, which date from 1800–1, are in blue-glazed brickwork in Flemish bond with red brick recesses and glazed brick aprons below the upper windows. The two front bays of 1839 are in red brick. The interior (originally about 35½ ft by 28½ ft) has a semicircular arch at the N end with a shallow rounded apse behind to enclose the pulpit and organ. The gallery, around three sides, has an open cast-iron front of 1882.

Inscriptions: on two stones in W wall with dates 1800 and 1839 of erection and first enlargement. *Monuments*: a few burial-vaults remain below rooms at N end of chapel; also a loose ledger stone to John Hook, 1710, with Latin inscription, removed from Holy Ghost Chapel, Basingstoke.

BOURNEMOUTH   *Dorset*

(11) CONGREGATIONAL, Richmond Hill (SZ 085914). The congregation, which was formed in 1848, occupied a privately built chapel in Orchard Street from 1849. The first chapel on the present site was built in 1854–9, its completion delayed by legal disputes over the title to the land. The existing building which replaced it in 1890–1 is a large and elaborate Gothic structure by Lawson and Donkin, with a choir apse at the N end, E and W

Congregational chapel (URC), Richmond Hill,
Bournemouth. (*Congregational Year Book*, 1890) (11)

transepts and a tall tower and spire at the SW corner. (URC)

CYB (1890) 213–14. Davies, J. T., *Richmond Hill Story* (1956).

(12) CONGREGATIONAL, Muscliff Lane, Throop (SZ 107960).
The chapel has brick walls, rendered at the front, and a hipped
roof. It was built and enlarged in the early 19th century for a
church (now URC) formed in 1828. A Sunday-school at the rear,
built in 1830, was rebuilt in 1866. The front and side walls of the
chapel are of three bays with two tiers of pointed-arched
windows. The chapel was refurbished and a wide Gothic porch
added across the front *c*.1877.

Monument: in front burial-ground, Anna, Martha and
Elizabeth Aldridge, 1848, 1849, 1853, table-tomb.

BROCKENHURST

(13) BAPTIST (SU 302024). The chapel, described as 'lately
erected', was registered 20 September 1792. The original
building, which has a contemporary cottage at the N end, was
enlarged by the addition of a parallel range next to the road in the
mid 19th century. The walls are of brick and the roof is tiled with
double gables at each end. The original doorway at the S end,
now internal, has a round-arched head; a similarly arched
window above now lights the roof space. Three pointed-arched
windows in the later W wall face the road and there are two
round-arched windows with iron frames in the opposite wall.

The interior (originally about 30 ft by 15½ ft) has been refitted;
the line of enlargement is marked by two iron columns which
support the intermediate valley. A baptistery in the floor at the N
end of the earlier part may indicate the original location of the
pulpit.

BROUGHTON

(14) BAPTIST (SU 306332). The church meeting here originated
in the mid 17th century as part of a church then gathered at
Porton, Wiltshire. In 1710 the meetings were transferred to
Broughton where they were held in two cottages converted to a
meeting-house. The present chapel, which dates from 1816, was
enlarged to the rear *c*.1840, re-fenestrated and a porch added
c.1900. The walls are of brick and the roof is slated. The front is
gabled and has two upper windows, each of two round-arched
lights below square labels, and a wide porch with arched
entrance. *Library*: an extensive collection of books bequeathed in
the early 18th century by John Collins was sold in 1977.

Baptist Times (22 December 1977). Chambers (1952) 88–91.
Ivimey IV (1830) 310–13.

CHRISTCHURCH

(15) CONGREGATIONAL, Millhams Street (SZ 159929). The
chapel, built 1866–7 by Kemp-Welch and Pinder of Bournemouth in an Italian Gothic style with corner tower, replaces a
meeting-house belatedly licensed in 1834 after disturbances. The
church (now URC) dates its origin to the ejection of the vicar,
John Warner, in 1661.

Monuments: in burial-grounds, include a row of matching
table-tombs with fluted corner pilasters, of 1806 and later.

CHRISTCHURCH EAST

(16) CONGREGATIONAL, Burton Green (SZ 166948). Adjacent to
earlier house; brick and slate, rendered front wall with semicircular gable parapet. Probably early 19th-century, perhaps the
result of the labours of Rev. Daniel Gunn, minister at
Christchurch 1816–48, who 'found one chapel and left seven in
Christchurch and the neighbouring villages'. A painted date of
1875 in the gable records the subsequent formation of the church.
(URC)

CYB (1848) obituary of Rev. Daniel Gunn.

COPYTHORNE

(17) Former CONGREGATIONAL, Cadnam (SU 295138). Brick
and slate with gabled front and lancet windows with cast-iron
frames. Built *c*.1833, possibly rebuilt 1849. Now in Methodist
use. *Monuments*: in burial-ground (1) Frances Tomlin, 1835, and
Ann Lockyer, 1858; (2) Rufus Young, 1833, and his parents
William, 1863, and Jane, 1871.

CRONDALL

(18) Former CONGREGATIONAL (SU 795488). Independents took
out several licences in the late 18th century and in 1798 a 'new
building' was registered for dissenters. The chapel of *c*.1798 is
now used by an Evangelical congregation. Brick and slate; gabled
front with high segmental-arched window above open gabled
porch. Rear gallery of late 18th century with turned balusters to
corner staircase.

FAIR OAK

(19) BAPTIST, Horton Heath (SU 494173). 'Union Chapel' dated 1862; plain building behind mixed style façade partly concealed by recent utilitarian glass porch.

Baptist chapel, Fair Oak. (19)

FAREHAM

(20) STRICT BAPTIST, Lower Swanwick (SU 496094). Brick and slate; gabled front with two blind windows above central doorway. Built 1844 to supersede a boat-house converted for use in 1835.

Chambers (1952) 99–100.

(21) CONGREGATIONAL, West Street (SU 580062). Built 1836, by J. Adams of Gosport, for a congregation formed in the late 17th century. Three-bay gabled N front in yellow brick with

Congregational chapel, Fareham. (21)

angle buttresses to each bay; projecting centre with Tudor doorway and three-light upper window with cusped tracery under a four-centred head and cast-iron patterned frames. (URC)

EM (June 1837) 272.

FORDINGBRIDGE

(22) CONGREGATIONAL, Salisbury Street (SU 149144). The formerly Presbyterian congregation (now URC) originated in the late 17th century. The present chapel is of early 19th-century date, much altered c.1900. Red brick with yellow brick gabled front, two tiers of round-arched windows and central entrance. Vestry added 1887. Monuments: in front of chapel (1) Jonas Wilt, 1855; (2) William Oates, 1831, and Mary his widow, 1835.

(23) CONGREGATIONAL, Stuckton (SU 160132). The church, earlier known as 'Hungerford' (¾ mile SE), was formed in 1827 and registered a meeting-house in that year. The present chapel, on a new site, was built c.1855 after the congregation had been dispossessed of their previous building. The walls are of brickwork in four bays with stepped buttresses and round-arched windows with widely splayed reveals. Monument: in burial-ground, Thomas Grant, 'for 22 years the ordained pastor of the church assembling in the adjoining chapel', 1867.

CYB (1868) 276, obituary of Thomas Grant.

(24) WESLEYAN, West Street (SU 144141). Rendered walls and slate roof. Opened 1836 but front altered and semicircular porch added in late 19th century.

GREYWELL

(25) Former INDEPENDENT (SU 717512). 'Meadow Cottage', built as meeting-house, 1817. Brick with hipped tile roof, three-bay front with two tiers of segmental-arched windows; tops of pulpit windows remain in rear wall.

HARBRIDGE AND IBSLEY

(26) CONGREGATIONAL, Mockbeggar (SU 161094). Brick and slate with pointed-arched windows, dated 1851. Originally two bays, enlarged to N in late 19th century.

HARTLEY WINTNEY

(27) BAPTIST, High Street (SU 769570). The chapel, which stands on the SE side of the street, has brick walls with rendered dressings and a slate roof hipped to the rear. It was built in 1807 and a Strict Baptist church was formed in the following year. The building was enlarged at each end c.1830–40. The NW front, of three bays with an open pediment and plain pilasters, has a central arch enclosing two tiers of windows; set back to the left is a porch having an arched entrance with fanlight and a keystone dated 1807. The SW wall has two original round-arched windows which may originally have flanked the pulpit; the opposite wall formerly had three similar windows, altered to two and the pulpit transferred to that side when the building was enlarged.

The interior has a gallery at each end with a vestry below the SE gallery and a minor room below the other. Both galleries retain original seating of the date of the enlargement, comprising box-pews and, in the NW gallery, a central desk for the singers. A round arch between the NE windows marks the second site of the pulpit which was later re-sited in front of the SE gallery. The

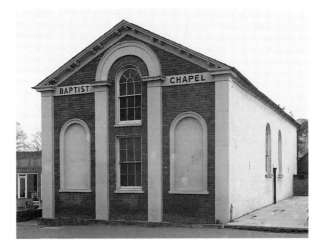

Baptist chapel, Hartley Wintney. (27)

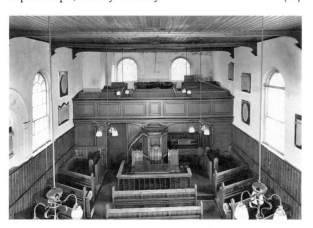

Baptist chapel, Hartley Wintney. Interior 1970. (27)

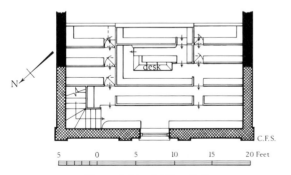

Plan of North-West Gallery

lower seats were replaced and the ceiling boarded in the late 19th century.

Monuments: in chapel (1) William James, pastor nearly 12 years, 1847, and Elizabeth his widow, 1870, signed W. Lee, Odiham; (2) Martha (White), wife of Freeman Roe, 1842; (3) Thomas Wells, 1821, Elizabeth his widow, 1842, and Eleanor Carter, 1832, signed Lee, Odiham; externally on SE wall (4) Thomas White, 1845, *et al.*; (5) William Crate, 1840, and Elizabeth his widow, 1847; (6) Susan (Crate) wife of Robert Hewett, 1838; (7) John Cooper, 1837; (8) Maria Hasker, 1838; in burial-ground behind chapel (9) William Jones, 1820. *Pulpit*: hexagonal with panelled sides and applied mouldings, early 19th-century. (Chapel much altered internally *c.* 1980)

Chambers (1952) 78–82.

HAVANT

(28) Former PRESBYTERIAN, The Pallant (SU 719063). The Presbyterian, latterly Congregational, society formerly meeting here claims to have been formed in 1710. The cause is said to have 'sensibly declined' during the late 18th century due to heterodox preaching but revived after 1800 with the appointment of an Independent minister. The meeting-house is dated 1718 although a certificate issued 14 October 1729 for a building 'newly erected in Pallant Lane on N side of East Street' may indicate a later date. It was enlarged to the rear in 1816 and a second certificate, for 'the meeting-house occupied by William Scamp, minister, and others', was taken out in 1821. A new Congregational chapel (now URC) by A. E. Stallard was built in North Street in 1891 and the former meeting-house has passed into commercial use.

The walls are of brick and the roof is hipped and tiled. The N front in Flemish bond with glazed headers has a plain stepped brick cornice surmounted by a panelled parapet having at its centre an elaborately detailed blind Venetian window of rubbed brick with pulvinated frieze and moulded cornice to the side panels but a narrow architrave only around the semicircular arched centre. The central doorway has a semicircular arch with keystone and impost blocks and is flanked by similarly arched windows with renewed frames. Above the entrance is an oval tablet bearing the inscription, now much obscured by paint,

Former Presbyterian meeting-house, Havant. (28)

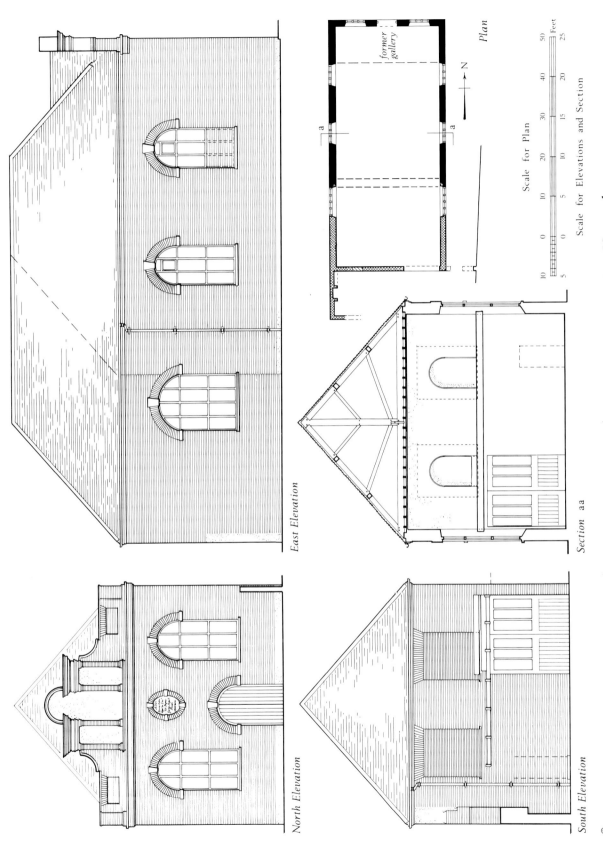

East Elevation

Plan

former gallery

N

Scale for Plan

0   10   20   30   40   50

Scale for Elevations and Section

5   0   5   10   15   20   25

Feet

a

a

Section aa

North Elevation

South Elevation

© C.F.S. 1967

Former Presbyterian Meeting-house, HAVANT, *Hampshire*

'ÆDES/Divino Cultui/Vigon^{le}Sac Liber^{tate}/Sub Imperio/Georgij Augusti/Dicata/MDCCXVIII'. The side walls have each two windows similar to those on the N and in the rearward extension one wider segmental-arched window of otherwise similar details. The S wall of 1816 has two flat-arched windows, now blocked, which formerly flanked the pulpit; a small vestry against this wall has been demolished.

The interior (originally 39½ ft by 27 ft extended 21 ft to S) has no original fittings; a floor has been inserted at mid-height and the plaster ceiling is covered by boarding. There are slight evidences of a small gallery at the N end, possibly inserted, and at the S end two shallow round-arched recesses in the blocking of the end windows which indicate a mid 19th-century alteration. The roof is supported by three king-post trusses of oak with double-braced principals to the N part and three similar but single-braced trusses of pine to the extension; the half ties below the centres of the hipped N and S ends are forked at their junction with the end trusses.

Inscriptions and *Scratchings*: on bricks in S part of E wall, several initials, some with date 1816, including name I. Gray, also 'WH 1843' repeated on brick in S wall. In E boundary wall near S end, stone inscribed 'TN 1730'.

CYB (1861) 238–9 obituary of William Scamp; (1891) 216.

HOUGHTON

(29) FREE METHODIST (SU 342320). Rendered walls, probably timber-framed, on brick and flint plinth, with hipped slate roof. Three-bay front with tablet dated 1833 above entrance. (Disused 1974)

FREE METHODIST CHAPEL, HOUGHTON   C F S 1974

HURSTBOURNE TARRANT

(30) Former CONGREGATIONAL (SU 385535). Rendered walls and slate roof with wide eaves and gabled three-bay front, dated 1840. Four-centred arched windows with Y-tracery, later porch.

KINGSCLERE

(31) PRIMITIVE METHODIST, Ashford Hill (SU 556622). Three-bay gabled front of glazed brick in header bond; built 1838, rebuilt 1856.

KING'S SOMBORNE

(32) PRIMITIVE METHODIST (SU 364311). Red brick with yellow brick dressings, dated 1871.

(33) Former WESLEYAN METHODIST ASSOCIATION (SU 365311). Rendered walls and hipped slate roof. Three-bay front with tablet dated 1826 above blocked doorway, entrance re-sited.

(34) Former WESLEYAN METHODIST ASSOCIATION, Upper Somborne (SU 396325). Low building of brick and flint behind earlier cottage. Dated T.H.1843 on brick next to entrance. Superseded 1902 by United Methodist chapel on adjoining site.

LOCKERLEY

(35) Site of BAPTIST (SU 299246). Cottage meetings were commenced in 1751 by James Fanch, Baptist minister at Romsey, and a church was formed in 1752. A larger building was then acquired, fitted up as a meeting-house and registered 6 October 1757; this, or a subsequent chapel on the site, was demolished in 1967.

Monuments: in burial-ground, many headstones of mid 18th century and later, reset against N boundary, include James Fanch, 1767.

Ivimey IV (1830) 500–4.

LONG SUTTON

(36) Former CONGREGATIONAL (SU 740473). The church formerly meeting here, which had links with the Countess of Huntingdon's Connexion, claimed to have been formed in 1815; in that year John Sury, labourer, certified his house as a meeting-house. The chapel, believed to have been erected in 1816, was registered 3 July 1818. It ceased to be used for services by the early 20th century, becoming, subsequently, a village hall and latterly it has been incorporated into an adjacent house. The walls are of brick and the roof hipped and tiled. The S front is of three bays with a doorway with flat canopy between round-arched windows. The interior (28¼ ft by 18 ft) has a round-arched recess behind the site of the pulpit.

LYMINGTON

(37) BAPTIST, New Street (SZ 323956). The church, formed in the late 17th century, built a new meeting-house 'on the E side of New Lane', in 1769. The present chapel on this site, rebuilt or greatly altered in the early 19th century and later, is a tall building with rendered walls and a slate roof. The front wall of three principal bays with two tiers of round-arched windows and a wide central doorway has a pedimented centrepiece with four attached Ionic columns to the upper stage.

Ivimey IV (1830) 497–9.

(38) Former BAPTIST, Ashley Lane (SZ 324954). Seceders from the foregoing built a new chapel on the W side of Ashley Lane which they registered for Baptist use 31 October 1791. It closed in the mid 19th century and was subsequently used as a National School. 'Providence Chapel' has brick walls and a hipped slate roof. The E, W and S walls have each two pointed-arched windows. The N wall has two round-arched doorways, now internal, and two tall lancets between, partly blocked. The interior (34 ft by 24 ft) has an inserted N gallery. Between the S windows the outline of the back-board of the pulpit remains visible.

(39) CONGREGATIONAL, High Street (SZ 323954). The church (now URC), which originated c.1700 as a Presbyterian congregation, erected the present chapel, on the S side of High Street, in 1847 to replace the 'Old Town Chapel', described as 'small and inconveniently situated'. The chapel, designed by W.J. Stent of

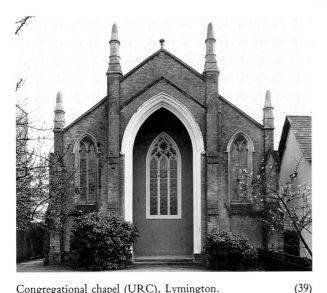

Congregational chapel (URC), Lymington.   (39)

Warminster in the Gothic style, with grey brick walls, stone dressings and a slate roof, has a three-bay gabled front divided by stepped buttresses rising to pinnacles intended to be finished with carved finials. In the centre bay is a tall two-centred arched opening with a traceried window of three lights at the back forming a recessed vaulted entrance with doorways at each end. The interior has a canted ceiling divided by moulded ribs into square panels with cusped intersections. The N gallery retains some contemporary seating, including singers' seats, but the remainder of the seating has been renewed.

Fittings – *Clock*: on gallery front, signed 'Sparks, Lymington', 1847. *Glass*: in tracery lights of N window, formal roses and leaf decoration including anthemion, *c.*1847. *Monuments*: a few reset 19th-century headstones remain S of the chapel. *Painting*: portrait in oils of Rev. David Everard Ford, pastor 1821–41. *Pulpit*: front of original pulpit incorporated into low rostrum, with three tiers of panels with cusped and pointed-arched ornament.

Cliffe, J., *A Brief History of the Congregational Church, Lymington, Hants.* (1901). *CYB* (1847) 164.

LYNDHURST

(40) GENERAL BAPTIST, Chapel Lane (SU 294079). The chapel, of red brick and slate rebuilt in the late 19th century, replaces a meeting-house registered in 1790. Several 18th-century headstones remain loose in the burial-ground, including one to Henry Steele, 1766, and Mrs Elizabeth Cox his sister, 1769.

Ivimey IV (1830) 499. Wood (1847) 232.

MARTIN

(41) PRIMITIVE METHODIST (SU 064199). Rendered walls gabled N and S, pointed-arched windows, porch dated 1829.

MORTIMER WEST END

(42) COUNTESS OF HUNTINGDON'S CHAPEL (SU 617642). Non-denominational cottage meetings began after *c.*1778 under the patronage of John Whitburn, a turf cutter. The meeting-house was built in 1798 on land provided by Whitburn and registered for 'Seceders' on 7 September in that year, the cost being largely met by John Mulford who also financed an enlargement of the

Countess of Huntingdon's Chapel, Mortimer West End.   (42)

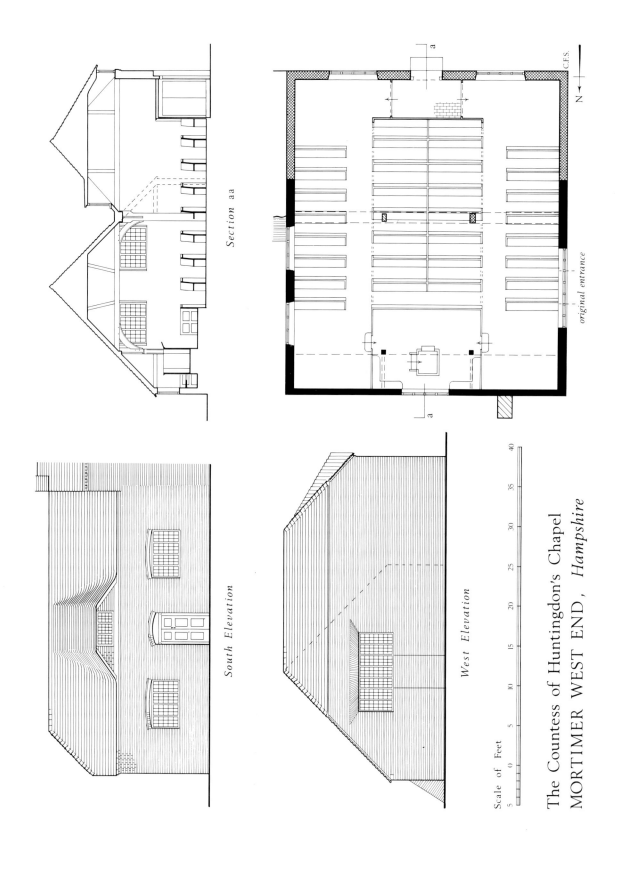

Section aa

South Elevation

West Elevation

original entrance

N

C.F.S.

Scale of Feet
5   0   5   10   15   20   25   30   35   40

The Countess of Huntingdon's Chapel
MORTIMER WEST END, *Hampshire*

Countess of Huntingdon's Chapel, Mortimer West End.   (42)

building about 1805. The congregation was formed into an Independent church in 1818, with the support of the Reading Evangelical Society, but in 1826 the property was transferred to the trustees of the Countess of Huntingdon's Connexion. The chapel has brick walls and tiled roofs. It was originally entered at the W end below a wide flat-arched window of seven lights and the pulpit was set between two windows at the opposite end. The roof was supported by two trusses with timber posts forming narrow N and S aisles. The *c*.1805 enlargement to the S provided a new entrance front of three bays with a low dormer above the entrance; the interior (originally 33¾ ft by 25½ ft) was re aligned with the pulpit centrally in the former N aisle. (Since *c*.1965 the chapel has been disused but services continue in an adjacent timber-framed Sunday-school building)

Fittings – *Inscriptions*: on bricks above W window, initials and date 1798. *Monuments*: in burial-ground, W of chapel (1) John Mulford, 1814, and John Whitburn, 1803, headstone; N of chapel (2) Tryphosa, wife of Thomas Goddard and third daughter of Rev. A. Pinnell, 1839, headstone; (3) James Spratley, 1866, and David Spratley, 1867, wooden 'leaping board'. *Seating*: box-pews, early 19th-century, doors removed.

Summers, W. H., *A Centenary Memorial of the Congregational Church at Mortimer West* (1898). Summers (1905) 133–6.

NETHER WALLOP

(43) WESLEYAN (SU 302365). Brick and slate, opened 1819. Gabled three-bay front with pointed-arched windows and blocked window above later porch. Principal side to left is of three bays with round-arched recesses enclosing rectangular sash windows.

NEW ALRESFORD

(44) Former CONGREGATIONAL, Pound Hill (SU 585326). The chapel, built for a newly formed church in 1825, was enlarged to the front *c*.1840. The walls are of brick and the roof is slated and

Former Congregational chapel, New Alresford.   (44)

hipped to the rear. The S front of three bays with two tiers of sash windows has a pediment with dentil brick cornices enclosing a reset tablet 'ALRESFORD CHAPEL 1825'. The side walls of the original structure have each three windows at the upper level with cills lowered and corresponding windows below now blocked. The interior remains at its original size with a S gallery supported by two cast-iron columns; the S extension comprises two storeys of minor rooms; two blocked upper windows are visible in the former S front. The chapel was in Methodist use from c.1965 to 1980 when a new chapel was erected on another site.

ODIHAM

(45) Former CONGREGATIONAL (SU 743511). The church formerly meeting here appears to have originated in the late 17th century. The meeting-house, registered as 'repaired and rebuilt' in 1794, was enlarged in 1820; it stands behind other buildings on the S side of the main road. It is now used as a hall by All Saints Church. The walls are of brick and the roof is slated. The N front is of three bays with a fourth bay added to the W, each with a wide round-arched recess enclosing a window; the window in the E bay above the entrance has a segmental-arched head, the others are round-arched. The S wall is rendered and has windows corresponding to those on the N side but without the decorative recesses. A window centrally in the W wall has been blocked and a deep gallery at the E end has been altered to provide minor rooms.

Inscription: flat slab in paving in front of N porch inscribed 'THE CHAPEL ENLARGED 1820'. *Monuments*: in burial-ground to S, several 19th-century slabs reused as paving, and a sarcophagus-shaped table-tomb.

OVERTON

(46) Former CONGREGATIONAL, Winchester Street (SU 515495). Built 1836. Red brick gabled front with graduated lancets and central porch, by James Fenton of Chelmsford. In Methodist use since c.1966 following the closure of the 1842 Wesleyan chapel (SU 514496) which survives only in a much altered state.

EM (January 1837) 30.

OVER WALLOP

(47) Former BAPTIST, Middle Wallop (SU 294377). The Baptist

BAPTIST CHAPEL, MIDDLE WALLOP   CFS 1973

church meeting at Broughton (14) included some members living at Wallop. It is possible that these constituted a separate church when the present chapel was built in 1841. The chapel has rendered cob walls on a brick and flint plinth, and a slate roof. Gabled front with brick porch; two upper windows at front and three windows in each side wall, all with four-centred arched heads, external moulded labels and cast-iron frames. A gallery at the entrance was added in the mid 19th century. The pulpit has been replaced but the original panelled back-board and octagonal canopy remain. *Monuments*: in burial-ground, table-tomb, uninscribed, mid 19th-century, and four wooden headboards.

Ivimey IV (1830) 310–13.

PETERSFIELD

(48) CONGREGATIONAL (SU 749236). Gothic with gabled front faced with polygonal masonry. 1883 by John Sulman on site of 1801 meeting-house. (URC)

CYB (1882) 407–8.

PORTSMOUTH

(49) HIGH STREET CHAPEL (John Pounds Memorial) (SZ 634995). The chapel, rebuilt in 1955 to replace a Presbyterian meeting-house of 1718 destroyed by bombing in 1941, now houses the united Presbyterian and General Baptist congregations, both of which adopted Unitarian sentiments in the late 18th century. The General Baptist meeting-house in St Thomas's Street, also destroyed in 1941, was first built c.1694 and rebuilt 1715 and 1865 for a congregation originating c.1640. The Presbyterian society, which was formed following the ejection in 1662 of the vicar Benjamin Burgess and his assistant Thomas Bragg, built its first meeting-house in 1691 in Penny Street. The 1718 building had a shaped gable facing the street. The interior was divided into nave and aisles with a plaster barrel vault over the central space.

Fittings – *Monuments*: in a small memorial garden SW of the chapel, several decayed 19th-century headstones, and a monument to John Pounds 'The Philanthropic Shoemaker of St Mary's Street, Portsmouth', 1839. *Plate*: from Presbyterian Meeting (now in Portsmouth City Museum) comprises three two-handled cups of 1659, 1668 and 1669 with repoussé decoration of flowers and beasts of the chase, and one two-handled gadrooned cup of 1698.

Evans (1897) 202–5. Ivimey II (1814) 210–11. Richards, J. M., *The Bombed Buildings of Britain* (1942) 100. Ridout, F., *The Early Baptist History of Portsmouth* (1888). Taylor I (1818) 294–6. *UHST* I (1917–18) 315–17; III (1923–6) 53–9, 71–4. Wood (1847) 206, 224.

RINGWOOD

(50) OLD MEETING-HOUSE, Meeting-house Lane (SU 147053). The Presbyterian society formerly meeting here appears to have owed its origin to the proximity of Moyles Court (2¼ miles NE), the paternal home of Alice Lisle, who, following the death in 1664 of her husband John Lisle, the regicide, retired there and encouraged the continuance of nonconformist preaching. In 1672 a meeting was established in Ringwood at the house of John Hancock to which the Rev. Compton South, ejected minister of Berwick St John, Wiltshire, travelled weekly from Donhead St

The Old Meeting-house, Ringwood.   (50)

Andrew; on those occasions, until Alice Lisle's death in 1685 at the hands of Judge Jeffreys, the preacher 'was constantly entertained at Moyles Court'. In the early 18th century the Ringwood congregation numbered five hundred and included one gentleman, probably Sir Jeremiah Cray, with an income of £3,000 per annum and votes in three counties: he was also one of the principal subscribers to the building of the meeting-house in 1727–8 which replaced one of *c*.1700 which stood 'in the south-west corner of the Furlong'. The new building 'in Batson's Close' was placed in trust 16 April and registered 21 June 1728. During the 18th century the Old or Upper Meeting as it came to be called lost some support to the more recently opened Lower Meeting (51), and by the 19th century the leadership had passed into Unitarian hands. Services were suspended *c*.1976 following union with similar congregations in Bournemouth and Poole. The meeting-house has since been surrounded on three sides by a large shopping precinct.

The meeting-house stands on the S side of Meeting-house Lane, about 200 yards ESE of the parish church. The walls are of brick and the roof, half-hipped with a double ridge returned N and S, is covered with tiles. The principal entrance is in the N wall, with subsidiary entrances in the slightly longer E and W sides, and the pulpit is set between a pair of tall windows at the S end. The N wall has a central gablet, rendered and bearing the date 1727; the segmental-arched central entrance has a pedi-mented stone surround set in a panel of finely jointed brickwork

with flanking Tuscan pilasters having moulded capitals of the same material. Two segmental-arched windows with stone frames, central mullions and rectangular leaded glazing flank the entrance above which is a similar but shorter window, now blocked and rendered. The E and W walls are alike; each has an entrance with segmental-arched stone surround flanked by two windows similar in design to those in the N front, but shorter, with two above at gallery level and one single-light window, also segmentally arched, above the doorway. The S wall has two windows similar to those in the N front and a smaller window between them at a high level; the walling between the main windows is here given additional thickness and a raking buttress has been built centrally against it.

The interior (45 ft by 40 ft) has a gallery around three sides with a front of square fielded panels with coved and moulded capping; it is carried on the E and W sides by three pairs of round wooden columns with moulded capitals which form the inter-mediate supports for the roof, and additionally on the N side by two smaller plain circular posts which do not rise above gallery level. The gallery is approached by staircases in the NE and NW corners. The ceiling, of plaster on laths, comprises a central segmental barrel vault with E and W cross vaults above the side galleries. The seating, partly reconstructed *c*.1912 when the boarded floor was largely renewed, remains essentially in its 18th-century form, the plain panelled woodwork and the door hinges being mostly of *c*.1727 although the height of the pew divisions

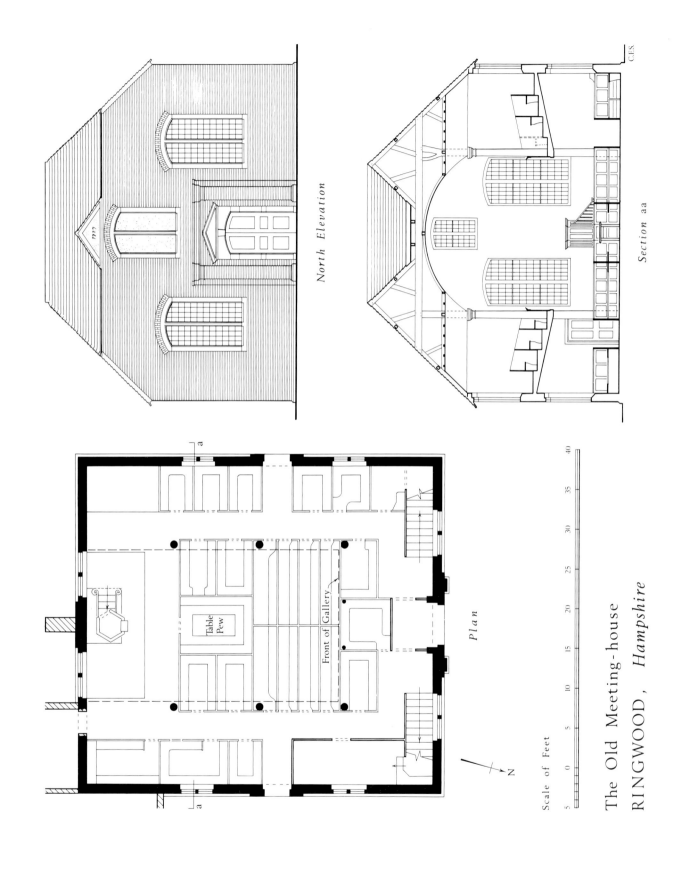

North Elevation

Section aa

C.E.S.

Table Pew

Front of Gallery

Plan

N

Scale of Feet

5 0 5 10 15 20 25 30 35 40

The Old Meeting-house
RINGWOOD, *Hampshire*

The Old Meeting-house, Ringwood.   (50)

appears to have been reduced. The side pews below the galleries are in their original form; the central rank has been partly changed although retaining a central table-pew aligned along the longer axis of the building. The original communion table is plain and has a renewed top; a large drawer has been added. The original gallery seating also survives except at the N end where an organ has been inserted. The hexagonal pulpit is a replacement of the mid 19th century. (Pulpit and side pews have been removed since c.1980)

The roof is carried by three pairs of principal posts, finished as columns where below the ceiling, supporting collar-beams from which rise twin trusses with V-braces; tie-beams from the E and W wall-plates join the posts at a lower level. One of the posts includes a natural fork near its apex.

Fittings – *Clock*: on front of N gallery, Parliament clock with wooden case, arched top, quadrant-indented lower corners and arched door to pendulum case, painted in black and gold with winged cherubs' heads and a Chinese scene, signed 'Dav[id]/Compigne/Winchester', early 18th-century, circular dial repainted black on white c.1800. *Monuments*: externally, to W (1) Benjamin Warn, 1762, *et al.*; (2) Flower Fryer, 1801, and Joseph Fryer, 1802; (3) Hannah, wife of Thomas Geare, 1750; to N (4) Harry Tilly, 'many years Clerk of this Chapel', 1815, and

Hannah his wife, 1803; to E (5) William [   ], and Mary his wife, 1784; (6) John Barnes, 1770, and Mary his wife, 1769?; to S (7) Sarah Conway, 1806, Elizabeth Conway, 1807, *et al.*, table-tomb.

Evans (1897) 209–10. Little, R.H., *Historical Review of the Roman Catholics and the Nonconformists in Ringwood following the Reformation* (typescript, c.1965).

(51) CONGREGATIONAL, Christchurch Road (SU 150051). About 1740 a second Presbyterian or Independent congregation was formed which included some members from the Old Meeting. It maintained an erratic existence until c.1772 when it reunited with the older society under their minister John Crisp. On his removal in 1781 the societies again separated and the Lower Meeting-house which had been erected in 1766 'in a field called Chandlers Close' was reopened. This continued in use until 1866 when it was superseded by the present chapel; it was then used as a British School and for other purposes until 1958 when it was demolished.

The Lower Meeting-house stood immediately behind the present chapel. It had brick walls with a continuous dentil eaves-cornice and the roof was hipped and covered with slates. The SW front had, at gallery level, a central Venetian window between two segmental-arched windows with keystones; the lower part was covered by a large single-storeyed extension of the late 19th century. The longer side walls were each of two bays with two tiers of segmental-arched windows.

The chapel of 1865–6, by T. H. Hellyer, has walls of yellow brick with stone dressings. The front of three bays is divided and terminated by massive buttresses with ponderous stone finials and has a wide four-light window with uncusped tracery in the centre bay. (URC)

Little, R. H., *Ringwood Congregational Church 1866–1966* (1966).

(52) FRIENDS, Christchurch Road (SU 150049). A meeting-house on the S side of the road 100 yards S of (51), built 1692, closed 1823, was demolished *c.*1965.

(53) BAPTIST, Poulner (SU 170066). Small chapel with rendered cob walls and half-hipped thatched roof. Tablet externally on E wall inscribed 'Poulner Chapel 1840'; entrance at S end with open thatched porch and small circular window above. Two windows in each side wall with renewed frames. Interior refitted.

Chambers (1952) 94–5.

Baptist chapel, Poulner.   (53)

ROMSEY INFRA

(54) BAPTIST, Bell Street, Romsey (SU 353211). Pedimented front with two tiers of altered windows and large shield-shaped tablet dated 1811. Tall round-arched windows to side walls. Extension to rear 1889.

(55) CONGREGATIONAL, The Abbey, Romsey (SU 351211). The church, formerly Presbyterian (now URC), originated in the late 17th century under the ministry of Thomas Warren, ejected rector of Houghton, Hampshire. A meeting-house opposite the present site was superseded in 1804 by one named the 'Abbey Chapel'; this was replaced in 1887–8 by the existing building, designed by Paull and Bonella, which stands on an irregular site adjacent to the Abbey precincts and incorporates a much restored mediaeval gateway with room above. The chapel is of stone and flint with low battlemented parapets and a clerestory with four-centred arched windows of three lights with Perpendicular tracery.

The interior has N and S arcades, a gallery around three sides and an organ at the W end supported on stone arches with an octagonal stone pulpit in front.

Congregational chapel (URC), Romsey.   (55)

Monuments: in chapel (1) Rev. James Bennett D.D., 17 years pastor, 1862, erected 1888; (2) Rev. John Reynolds, son of Dr Henry Revell Reynolds, physician in ordinary to George III, 1862, erected 1888; (3) Rev. Thomas Warren M.A., ejected 1662 as rector of Houghton, erected 1862; in former burial-ground to SE, site of first meeting-house now public garden, a few early 19th-century ledger stones.

Building News (6 November 1885). *CYB* (1886) 225–6. Stirling, I., *The Church by the Arch, An Outline of the Abbey United Reformed Church, Romsey, 1662–1974* (1974).

ST MARY BOURNE

(56) Former BAPTIST (SU 417509). Mid 19th-century, altered.

(57) PRIMITIVE METHODIST (SU 415509). Rendered walls on brick and flint plinth, gabled front with barge-boards and small circular window over porch. Dated 1859.

SELBORNE

(58) Former CONGREGATIONAL (SU 744334). Typical small village chapel with polygonal masonry facing to walls, brick dressings and slate roof. Gabled front with porch and paired lancets. Built 1860, 'the design was kindly given by Mr John Boggast, Sen.'; closed by 1967.

CYB (1861) 270.

FORMER CONGREGATIONAL CHAPEL, SELBORNE

SOUTHAMPTON

(59) CONGREGATIONAL, Pear Tree Green, Itchen (SU 439116). Brick and slate with yellow facing brick to front and exposed side. Gabled front with prominent apex finial and a widely splayed window of three lights with cusped tracery above the central doorway. Opened 1838. (URC)

STEEP

(60) Former PRIMITIVE METHODIST, Bowyers Common (SU 763260). Dated 1869.

FORMER PRIMITIVE METHODIST CHAPEL, BOWYERS COMMON   C.F.S. 1971

SWANMORE

(61) FRIENDS' BURIAL-GROUND (SU 578172). Small rectangular enclosure bounded by hedges. In use 1657–1703. No monuments.

TADLEY

(62) OLD MEETING-HOUSE, Doe's Lane (SU 606609). The Independent meeting in Tadley was formed in the late 17th century following the ejection of Thomas Kentish, rector of Overton. The meeting-house was registered in 1718 as 'new built on land of Robert West, senior'. It was considerably enlarged to the rear in 1828 and in the later 19th century a Sunday-school was built alongside and the front wall altered.

The meeting-house has brick walls and a tiled roof half-hipped at the sides. The broad NW front originally had two windows with cross-frames and external shutters, with a doorway to the right and platband below the eaves; the doorway has now been placed centrally between altered windows and the brickwork rendered.

The Old Meeting-house, Tadley.   (62)

The Old Meeting-house, Tadley.   (62)

Inside the chapel two iron columns support the wall-plate on the line of the enlargement. There is a gallery around three sides with fielded-panelled front and moulded capping. The pulpit set between two segmental-arched windows opposite the entrance is hexagonal with two tiers of fielded panels and a moulded cornice, panelled back-board with cornice, and staircase with turned balusters and square newels with knob finials. There is an extensive burial-ground. (URC)

B[enham], D., *Some Account of the Village of Tadley in Hampshire, and of the Independent Church There* (1862).

VERNHAMS DEAN

(63) PRIMITIVE METHODIST, Little Down (SU 350580). Rendered walls and slate roof, gabled W front with pointed-arched doorway and circular tablet dated 1845. The walls although comparatively thin (about 16 in.) are of cob, except on the S side which has been rebuilt or refaced in brickwork.

WEST END

(64) WESLEYAN, Burnetts Lane (SU 485156). Red brick with dark-glazed headers. Gabled front dated 1845 with later brick porch. Three plain sash windows in each side wall. Open-backed benches and late 19th-century rostrum pulpit.

WHERWELL

(65) WESLEYAN, High Street (SU 390409). Gabled front of brick in three bays with pointed lancets, four-centred arched entrance in later porch, and tablet dated 1846. Side walls of flint with brick banding. (Demolition proposed 1981)

WHITCHURCH

(66) BAPTIST, Newbury Street (SU 462482). The church, which seems to have originated in the 17th century, built a meeting-house in 1726 in Wood Street (later Bell Street). The first meeting-house on the present site was erected c.1770 and was replaced by the existing chapel in 1836. This has walls of red brick with glazed brick dressings and a hipped slate roof. The broad E front of three bays has two tiers of windows with splayed lintels separated by brick pilasters paired at each end; the window frames have been renewed and the lower end windows blocked. The S wall is covered by a later hall which incorporates the present entrance. The interior, largely refitted in 1901, has a S

gallery retaining some fragments of its original seating. *Monuments*: in chapel (1) Philip Davies, pastor, 1840; (2) Martha, wife of George Thorne, 1813; the burial-ground in front of the chapel has been cleared of monuments.

Chambers (1952) 92–3. Fancutt, W., *A Brief History of Whitchurch Baptist Church, 1652–1952* (1952).

(67) WESLEYAN, Winchester Street (SU 463480). Rendered front of three bays with two tiers of pointed-arched windows with stone Y-tracery. Two round-arched windows in side wall. Opened 1813 but now largely of mid 19th century or later.

WIELD

(68) Former PRIMITIVE METHODIST, Upper Wield (SU 629387). Small chapel with brick walls laid to rat-trap bond, dated 1848. Now Independent.

WINCHESTER

(69) BAPTIST, City Road (SU 480299). Brick with rendered front, tall pilasters carrying entablatures over side bays flank arched centre with thin pediment overall. Built 1865, altered internally 1978.

Baptist Times (20 July 1978).

(70) CONGREGATIONAL, Jewry Street (SU 480296). The Independent formerly Presbyterian congregation (now URC/Methodist) originated in the late 17th century and in 1704 built a meeting-house in Parchment Street which was rebuilt in 1807. The present chapel, opened 11 October 1853, stands on part of the site of the prison. The design by Poulton and Woodman of Reading closely followed one by the same architects for St Helier, Jersey. The front wall of yellow bricks with stone dressings has a gabled centre with three graduated lancets above a triple entrance flanked by octagonal buttresses

originally surmounted by tall pinnacles; to each side are narrow bays, angularly splayed, incorporating subsidiary entrances. The interior is an elongated octagon with a continuous arcade of pointed arches in front of a low narrow gallery with passages below the side galleries to allow access to rooms at the rear; the possibility of an upper gallery was envisaged but not carried out. Lighting is by a lay-light in the roof and by windows at the front of the building only. The original seating of pews with low doors remains complete. *Clock*: on back gallery, gabled Gothic surround, by Knowles, Winchester. (Internal subdivision proposed 1986)

Carpenter, F., *Winchester Congregational Church Tercentenary, 1662–1962* [1962]. *CYB* (1855) 262–3; (1856) 256–7.

(71) Former PRIMITIVE METHODIST, Parchment Street (SU 482296). The chapel of 1903 stands on the site of the Presbyterian Meeting-house of 1704, rebuilt 1807, which was sold to the Primitive Methodists after the erection of Jewry Street Chapel.

WOODGREEN

(72) WESLEYAN (SU 171174). Brick with rendered gabled front. Opened 1832, much altered.

ISLE OF WIGHT

ARRETON

(73) Former WESLEYAN, Blackwater (SZ 506862). Small building of brick, partly rendered, believed to have been built in 1824. Gabled S front with porch, two pointed-arched windows in W wall and one opposite.

(74) WESLEYAN, Merstone (SZ 526851). Brick and slate, gabled front with lancets and central porch, dated 1848. Partly refitted but with original square *pulpit* with columns at front corners, reset on platform, and octagonal wooden *font*.

(75) BIBLE CHRISTIAN, Niton Road, Rookley (SZ 507841). Rubble and slate, gabled three-bay front with pointed-arched openings, shaped kneelers, ball finial at apex. Dated 1859.

Congregational chapel (URC), Jewry Street, Winchester. (70)

Bible Christian chapel, Rookley.   (75)

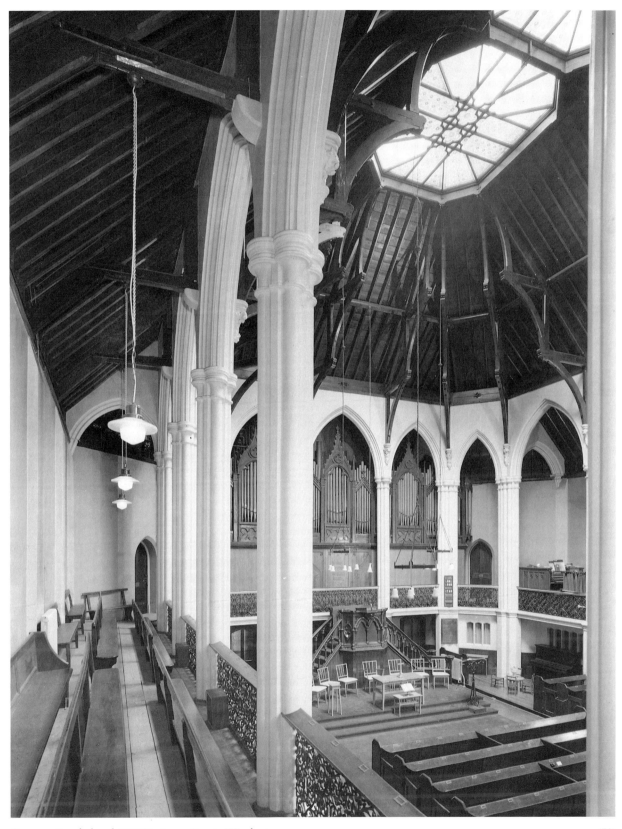

Congregational chapel (URC), Jewry Street, Winchester.　　　　　　　　　　　　　　(70)

BRADING

(76) CONGREGATIONAL (SZ 605865). Rubble and slate with gault brick dressings and rendered reveals to lancet windows. Built 1847 for a church formed 1832 (now URC). The chapel stands above a basement storey and has a gabled front and sides of four bays with stepped buttresses. *Monuments*: in burial-ground, Rev. Samuel Barrows, 1848, triangular pillar; also several table-tombs of mid 19th century and later.

Congregational chapel (URC), Brading.   (76)

BRIGHSTONE

(77) BIBLE CHRISTIAN, Brighstone (SZ 421831). Brick and slate, gable end to road with two narrow round-arched windows and tablet with remains of painted inscription and date 1836.

(78) BIBLE CHRISTIAN, Brook (SZ 390839). Brick and slate, gabled three-bay front with round-arched openings and traces of lunette-shaped inscription panel. Built 1848.

   Woolcock (1897) 84–6.

CALBOURNE

(79) Former CONGREGATIONAL, Porchfield (SZ 447912). The chapel was built in 1846 for a church formed in 1810. The walls are of coursed rubble with gault brick dressings and the roof is slated. The gabled front of three bays with round-arched openings has a large tablet inscribed 'BETHEL CHAPEL 1846'.

Two round-arched windows with blind tympana in the side wall facing the road are matched by two segmental-arched windows in the opposite wall. The interior, partly refitted in the late 19th century, has a gallery next to the entrance with open cast-iron balustraded front. The square pulpit is supported at the front corners by two dwarf columns and has an ogee-topped back-board. Monuments in the burial-ground date from the mid 19th century. (Derelict 1974)

Former Congregational chapel, Porchfield.   (79)

COWES

(80) Former CONGREGATIONAL, Union Road (SZ 494561). A place of worship at Sun Hill was registered 8 September 1803. Although dated 1804, the chapel is largely of the mid 19th century with brick walls with rendered dressings and a slate roof. Three-bay pedimented front with two tiers of round-arched windows and central entrance. Sunday-school opposite, 1876, by T. L. Banks, now used as chapel; former building closed and for sale 1974.

Former Wesleyan chapel, Cowes.   (81)

(81) Former WESLEYAN, Birmingham Road (SZ 497959). Built c.1831, superseded c.1901, now the 'Alexandra Hall'. Three-bay pedimented front of Portland stone ashlar with terminal pilasters and slightly projecting centre bay with altered entrance; two tiers of four-centred arched windows with intersecting glazing bars. The rear wall has been mostly rebuilt.

(82) Former CHAPEL, St Mary's Road (SZ 495959). Brick and slate, three-bay pedimented front with projecting centre bay, terminal pilasters, and tall four-centred arched windows with intersecting glazing bars. Built c.1830–40.

FRESHWATER

(83) GENERAL BAPTIST, Colwell (SZ 331877). 'Ebenezer Chapel', built 1836 for seceders from a Particular Baptist church, is a long low building with rendered walls and a slate roof; it originally had two segmental-arched windows on the W side, enlarged to N by one bay in later 19th century.

Wood (1847) 232.

GODSHILL

(84) BAPTIST, Roud (SZ 515803). Brick with pointed-arched windows. Dated 1859.

(85) WESLEYAN (SZ 530817). Coursed rubble and slate, gabled front with lancet windows and later porch, oval tablet dated 1838. Square pulpit with fluted columns at the corners, dwarf columns below front, panelled back-board.

Wesleyan chapel, Godshill.   (85)

NEWPORT

(86) GENERAL BAPTIST, High Street (SZ 502892). A Baptist meeting was in existence by 1728 when a meeting-house was erected in Pyle Street. The present site was acquired in 1774 and the chapel was registered 20 October 1775; the building was enlarged to the front in 1825, greatly altered internally in 1875 and further refitted in recent years. From the late 18th century the church came to accept heterodox preaching, notably under Richard Aspland, 1801–5, which soon after resulted in the formation of a separate Particular Baptist society; the General Baptist church thereafter came to rely entirely on Unitarian support and ministry.

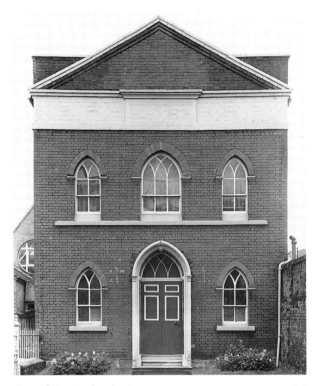

General Baptist chapel, Newport.   (86)

The chapel stands at the rear of a narrow site on the S side of the street. The walls are of brickwork. The N front is of three bays with two tiers of pointed-arched windows and has an arched doorcase with Gothic details; the upper part of the front appears to have been heightened in the late 19th century and has a pediment above a deep tiled frieze. The E and W walls have each two pointed-arched windows of 1775 with renewed frames, and in the S wall two smaller but similarly arched windows flank the site of the pulpit.

The interior (originally 40 ft by 20 ft), now entirely refitted, has a coved plaster ceiling with original moulded and bracketed cornice. In the N extension (18 ft deep) is a small vestry next to the entrance, on the first floor is a schoolroom and a gallery which has been extended into the N end of the original building, above is an upper room concealed behind the front pediment with three shuttered openings to the chapel.

Fittings – *Library*: bequeathed by Sarah Silver Sparks, 1847, now dispersed. *Monument*: loose in chapel, Abraham Clarke, 1813, and Rebecca Major his sister, 1829, marble tablet. *Plate*: includes a gadrooned mug of 1724 and a plated communion set given 1862 as a bicentenary memorial to the ejected ministers.

Aspland, R. B., *Memoir of the Life, Works and Correspondence of the Rev. Robert Aspland of Hackney* (1850) 104 ff. Evans (1897) 185–7. Ivimey IV (1830) 499–500.

(87) PARTICULAR BAPTIST, Castlehold, High Street (SZ 496891). Although a Particular Baptist church existed in the early 18th century it did not survive; the present congregation appears to have been formed in 1809, partly as a result of the doctrinal changes which took place in the General Baptist meeting. The

Particular Baptist chapel, Newport. (87)

chapel was built in 1812 and enlarged in 1872. The S front of 1872, of yellow brick with rendered dressings, is in five bays with a three-bay pediment supported by a giant order of attached Corinthian columns. (Interior altered 1982)

Ivimey IV (1830) 499–500. Roberts, W.J., *A Short History of the Baptists of Newport, Isle of Wight . . .* (1959).

(88) CONGREGATIONAL, St James's Street (SZ 498892). The formerly Presbyterian congregation was formed in the late 17th century following the ejection of the Vicar, Robert Tutchin, and the first meeting-house is believed to have been erected in 1699. On 7 October 1777 a 'newly erected building' on the E side of St James's Street was certified for Independents, and that was replaced by the existing building in 1848. The chapel, in the Gothic style by Francis Pouget, has walls of random rubble. The W front is of three bays divided by stepped buttresses, the middle bay is gabled and has a window of four traceried lights above an arched entrance. The interior, of four bays with a gallery around three sides, has an organ apse at the E end.

Roberts, W.J., *A History of Three Hundred Years of Congregationalism in Newport, Isle of Wight* (1962).

(89) Former CONGREGATIONAL, Nodehill (SZ 498889). Seceders from the St James's Street meeting in 1803 built a chapel at Nodehill which was opened February 1804, described as 40 ft by 29 ft with an end gallery. It was enlarged and a vestry added in 1828, further altered or enlarged c.1842–50, classrooms added 1866 and reseated 1867. The church reunited with St James's Street in 1881 and the building was used as an assembly hall; it is now in commercial occupation.

The walls are of brick and the roof is slated. The side wall facing Chapel Street was originally of three bays with two tiers of windows, the upper ones round-arched; it has been extended to the rear in banded brickwork and at the front is a rendered addition of two storeys, probably of 1866. The interior has a gallery with panelled front around three sides curving inwards towards the site of the pulpit which was flanked by two round-arched windows, now internal. *Monuments*: behind site of pulpit (1) Rev. Daniel Tyerman, first pastor, 1828, died at Madagascar when returning from a missionary tour; (2) Elizabeth, wife of Rev. Daniel Tyerman, 1809.

Roberts (1962) op.cit.

(90) Former FRIENDS, Castlehold, High Street (SZ 497891). A meeting-house built in Pyle Street in 1694, with a burial-ground attached, continued in use until the late 18th century, but in 1804 it was reported to be ruinous and a proposal was made to demolish it and to let the site. Meetings were being held in a building in High Street in the mid 19th century. The present building, now 'Holyrood Hall', dating from c.1860, was used by Quakers until c.1922 and subsequently occupied by Brethren. It is now used as a hall by the Roman Catholic Church. The walls are rendered and the roof is slated. The front wall of three bays has a central segmental-arched doorway with blind pointed recess above and a flanking pair of pointed-arched windows with Y-tracery; all openings have moulded labels.

(91) Former WESLEYAN, Pyle Street (SZ 50058915). The chapel, registered 23 January 1804, has walls of red brick and a pedimented front of three bays with an arched centre bay rising into the pediment. The central entrance has two fluted Doric columns supporting an entablature. The chapel was closed and converted to a theatre c.1970. Prior to conversion the interior, enlarged to the rear in 1830, had a gallery around three sides with early 19th-century pews, and a pulpit in a domed semicircular apse approached from below.

(92) BIBLE CHRISTIAN, Quay Street, (SZ 500893). Gothic with asymmetrical turret, 1879–80, by Frederick Mew, replacing a chapel of 1844.

Bourne (1905) 475. Woolcock (1897) 57–60.

(93) WESLEYAN, Wootton Bridge (SZ 546920). Stone walls and hipped slate roof. Three-bay front with rebuilt parapet, three small round-arched windows above wide central entrance and tall windows to side bays. Dated 1840.

(94) Former CHAPEL, Wootton Bridge (SZ 546920). Early 19th-century chapel, E of above, now St John's Ambulance Hall. Gabled front of three bays in header-bond brickwork.

NITON

(95) Former BAPTIST (SZ 507767). An 18th-century malt-house was bought in 1823 by a deacon of the Particular Baptist church in Newport; it was used as a meeting-house until 1849. It is a long low building with rubble walls and a slate roof; five windows face the road and have former entrances between the end pairs. Now Village Hall.

(96) BAPTIST, St Catharine's (SZ 507766). 'St Catharine's Chapel', named after the surrounding district, was built in 1849 to replace (95). It stands on rising ground and has walls of coursed rubble and a slated roof. The SE front is of five bays with a central porch and lancet windows. At the NE end an original single-storeyed vestry has been enlarged and a room added above it in 1904. The interior has been re-pewed. The pulpit at the NE end with cast-iron balustraded front was formerly entered directly from the vestry by a door at the back.

RYDE

(97) CONGREGATIONAL, George Street (SZ 594926). The first meeting-house on this site, built 1815–16, was superseded 1854–6 by a large chapel with rendered rubble walls having a Corinthian portico and octagonal turret. A fire in 1869 or 1870 destroyed all but the Sunday-school at the rear, which has a pedimented front

Former Wesleyan chapel, Pyle Street, Newport.   (91)

facing Melville Street. The subsequent Gothic chapel, built 1870–2 of rubble with ashlar dressings, having a corner tower and spire, designed by R. J. Jones, son of a member of the congregation, was demolished in 1974.

King, J. W., *The Independent Church of Christ Assembling in George Street Chapel, Ryde . . .* (1946).

(98) Former WESLEYAN, Nelson Street (SZ 594927). Registered 3 January 1844. Front of three bays with slightly higher recessed centre bay, tall round-arched windows and wide porch.

SHALFLEET

(99) BAPTIST, Wellow (SZ 385882). Brick and tile, built 1805 for a church formed 1801. Gabled front with lancet windows and later rendering, one bay added to rear *c*.1830–40. *Monuments*: in chapel (1) Rev. William Read, nearly 60 years pastor, 1857, and Anna his wife, 1838, 'by whose joint efforts under the auspices of the late Thomas Hollis Esq. of Lee, the first Baptist Church and Sunday School in the Isle of Wight were founded at Wellow, 1801'; in burial-ground (2) Anna Read, 1838, signed 'Stratton, Newport'; (3) William Rowlands, late of Naunton, Glos., 1838.

(100) BIBLE CHRISTIAN, Newbridge (SZ 411876). Built 1836, enlarged to rear and refronted 1881. Rubble walls with brick dressings and slate roof, pointed-arched windows with intersecting glazing bars. Three-bay gabled front of yellow brick with red brick dressings.

Woolcock (1897) 86–8.

YARMOUTH

(101) WESLEYAN (SZ 354896). Stone, with small corner turret and spire, elaborate tripartite window with crocketted gablets and sharply cusped tracery; foundation tablet 1881.

Baptist chapel, Niton.   (96)

SOMERSET

A county as varied topographically and socially as Somerset, with fashionable towns and remote upland hamlets, may reasonably be expected to furnish a corresponding diversity in its architectural heritage. Chapels and meeting-houses of all periods and all the principal denominations are to be found, from the simplest room to the most sophisticated composition, sufficient to illustrate the whole history of nonconformist building. The conversion of an existing structure, which has often been the first means of a congregation acquiring a regular meeting-house, was seen in the faded splendour of the mediaeval manor house at Croscombe (60), used by a Baptist church from the early 18th century but now restored to domestic use; the conversion of a house at Trudoxhill (163) by Congregationalists in 1717, by the removal of an upper floor, indicates the minimum alteration necessary to provide sufficient room for a moderately sized congregation.

Larger meeting-houses built for the very considerable numbers attracted to some nonconformist meetings remain from the late 17th century, the earliest being in Cowl Street, Shepton Mallet (136), of 1696. The most remarkable for the sophistication of its architecture is Rook Lane Chapel, Frome (74), dated 1707. Of more traditional appearance is Middle Lambrook Meeting-house (92), of 1729, with its round-arched mullioned windows at the front, a pattern repeated at Crewkerne (58) in 1733 and at Broadway (34) in 1739 as well as in later chapels such as Hatch Beauchamp (80) of c.1785. The Old Meeting-house at Ilminster (87) of 1719 may have had comparable features but it is now of interest more for the manner of its enlargement. Although the grander meeting-houses of the early 18th century were generally built for congregations originally styling themselves Presbyterian, a notable exception is Mary Street Chapel, Taunton (153), built about 1721 for an old established Baptist church. It has been much altered externally but the interior, with the traditional two-column support for the roof, is the best preserved of its period in the county. Friends' meeting-houses, too, include buildings of unusual charm. Long Sutton (99) of 1717, although in essence only a single room, stands in prominent witness to the simplicity of perfection, while the meeting-house at Claverham (194), of 1729, with its flanking wings, appears to emulate on a small scale the magnificence of a country house. Compared with these, the early meeting-houses at Portishead (132) and Sidcot (185) are primitive indeed.

The later 18th century also includes many buildings of note and of greater denominational variety. Christ Church Chapel, Bridgwater (30), although a rebuilding of 1788 on an exceptionally confined site, makes its mark with a façade to the street of unusual refinement. Two former Methodist chapels of the late 18th century were recorded: of these, the Octagon at Taunton (158), of 1776, is one of the later examples of the type much favoured by John Wesley; the former preaching-house at Midsomer Norton (118) represents the more basic requirements of a large urban society. Outstanding amongst the chapels of the period is that built in Bath by the Countess of Huntingdon (13) in 1765, with a small house adjacent, in a Gothic style which drew the approbation of Horace Walpole. Bath also provides examples of the chapels of several other denominations of which the Presbyterian, latterly Unitarian, chapel in Trim Street (7) of 1795 is the earliest, but most date from the following century.

Walcot Chapel, Bath (17), of 1815–16 is an exceptionally fine specimen of Wesleyan architecture, designed by the Rev. William Jenkins, a prolific architect in this denomination, whose work, or that of his copyists, is to be found at Bridgwater (33) in 1816 and Shepton Mallet (138) in 1819. Some of the smaller Wesleyan chapels such as Rudge (25), of 1839, and Somerton (142), of 1845, also merit attention, as does the existence of a few Bible Christian chapels of which Zion Chapel, Somerton (143), has a recognizably Devonian ancestry. The unusual bow-fronted Congregational chapel in Glastonbury (79), of 1814, is without parallel in the county, and the Gothic front of Ebenezer Chapel, Bath (9), of 1820, is similarly unique. The pedimented fronts of the Baptist chapels in Bridgwater (31), of 1837, and Chard (46), of 1842, and of the New Church (Swedenborgian) chapel in Bath (20), of 1844, follow contemporary fashion, while the simple but effective application of Gothic details in the Wesleyan chapels at Somerton (142), of 1845, and Huntspill (177), of 1851, presage the more elaborate chapels favoured later in the century. The Quaker meeting-houses at Street (152), of 1850, and Yatton (195), of 1866, are typical of the continued simplicity in design favoured by the Society of Friends. The former Catholic Apostolic chapel in Bath (12), of 1840, in the Romanesque style, is an interesting early building of that denomination, while the Agapemonite chapel at Spaxton (148) must, at least, be regarded as a curiosity.

The majority of the buildings recorded have stone walls, principally of rubble although ashlar was freely used where it was readily available in the vicinity of Bath. Little use was made of brickwork prior to the 19th century, the most notable earlier example being at Christ Church Chapel, Bridgwater (30). Roofs, where not covered with slate or modern materials, are usually pantiled, a material commonly found in the region of Bridgwater; a few examples of thatch still survive at Portishead (132), Chard (45), and on the small Methodist chapel at East Coker (68).

ABBAS AND TEMPLECOMBE

(1) CONGREGATIONAL, Temple Combe (ST 710225). A Presbyterian society was in existence here by the early 18th century, and a meeting-house was registered in 1717. A Congregational church (now URC) is said to have been formed in 1800. The chapel, opened 21 October 1834, has rendered walls and a hipped slate roof. In the W wall are two tall round-arched windows and a doorway to the left.

Thomas (1896) 61–2.

ASHCOTT

(2) WESLEYAN, Pedwell (ST 424366). Rendered walls and hipped pantiled roof; pointed-arched doorway, lancet windows at side. Opened 1827, altered or rebuilt 1882.

ASHWICK

(3) WESLEYAN, Oakhill (ST 635474). Rubble with ashlar front and hipped slate roof. Three-bay front with two tiers of pointed-arched windows; three tall windows with intersecting glazing bars face the road. Built 1825, replacing a chapel registered in 1800.

WESLEYAN CHAPEL, OAKHILL   C·F·S·1970

AXBRIDGE

(4) WESLEYAN, West Street (ST 429546). Random rubble with ashlar dressings and slate roof. Gabled front with hexagonal corner buttresses and pinnacles, gabled porch with scrolled panel over doorway, lancet windows. Opened 1850.

BACKWELL   Avon

(5) WESLEYAN, West Town (ST 484684). 'Zion Chapel'; rubble with ashlar quoins, gabled front with quatrefoil tablet dated 1853.

BARTON ST DAVID

(6) Former CONGREGATIONAL (ST 540322). 'Ebenezer Chapel' was built in 1804 and a two-storeyed annexe built alongside to S in 1871; it is now used for farm storage. The walls are of rubble and the roof is hipped and pantiled. E front with porch and gallery window above. Pointed-arched window at W end formerly with stone Y-tracery. The annexe has shutters to the lower storey opening to the chapel and three classrooms above. There is a small burial-ground in front of the chapel.

BATH   Avon

(7) TRIM STREET CHAPEL (ST 74906487). A Presbyterian society originating in the late 17th century occupied a variety of meeting places until 1692 when the first regular meeting-house was provided in Frog Lane (now New Bond Street). In the 18th century the society suffered from the secession, in 1726, of members professing Baptist sentiments and later by the proliferation of other denominations. By the end of that century the meeting was regarded as Unitarian. The chapel closed in 1969. Since 1971 a floor has been inserted at gallery level, the ground floor and cellars have been converted to a restaurant (c. 1978–80), larger windows have been pierced in the lower part of the W wall and a doorway inserted at the N end. The following account describes the chapel as it existed in 1971 prior to alteration.

The chapel, designed by John Palmer, was built in 1795; some alterations were made in the early 19th century and more sweeping changes carried out in 1860. The walls are of ashlar and the roof is hipped and slated. The S and E sides are covered by adjacent buildings. The exposed walls have a rusticated lower stage pierced on the W side by four square windows and by a doorway at the S end; the N wall facing Trim Street is blank. The upper stage to the W is of five bays with round-arched windows separated by pilasters. The N wall has an apsidal projection of 1860 with a pediment and low flanking wings.

Trim Street Chapel, Bath.   (7)

The interior (49¾ ft by 34½ ft) was entirely rearranged in 1860. Murch (1835) describes the building as oblong and very lofty with a single gallery occupied by the organ and a vestry next to the entrance. There is now a gallery at the S end with a small vestry below it in the SE corner and narrow galleries along the E and W sides. The ceiling has a coved plaster vault and a more elaborate ribbed vault in the N apse. The gallery fronts are continued as decoration around the apse with pilasters below and columns above from which the vaulting ribs spring. Barrel-vaulted cellars below the chapel, approached from an adjacent public house, have long been leased for the storage of wines and spirits.

Fittings – *Monuments*: in chapel (1) Rev. John Morell LL. D., 1840; (2) Sir Jerom Murch J. P., D. L., 13 years minister, 1895, and Anne his wife, 1893; (3) Henry Edward Howse, 'nine years Chamberlain of this city', 1834; (4) Rev. Robert Wallace, 25 years minister at Chesterfield, 4 years here, 1850; (5) Rev. Theophilus Browne M. A., rector of Hinton, Cambs., later a Unitarian minister, 1835, and Ann his wife, 1834; (6) John Osborn, sculptor, 1839. *Plate*: includes a pair of two-handled cups and three plates of 1744. *Pulpit*: fronts of two-tier pulpit remade as pulpit and reading desk, late 18th-century.

Burial-ground, at Lyncombe Vale (ST 755636), given to the society in 1819 by H. E. Howse. It has a high boundary wall next to the road and a small mortuary chapel near the centre which has thin ashlar walls and a low-pitched slate roof. *Monument*: in chapel, Henry Edward Howse of Lyncombe Villa, 'the donor of this cemetery to the Unitarian Church in the City of Bath', 1834, Anna his first wife, 1805, Elizabeth his second wife, 1847, Experience Noble, eldest daughter of Daniel Noble, many years elder of the Seventh-day General Baptist Church in Mill Yard, London, and sister of Sarah Weald, 1849, *et al*.

Evans (1897) 10–11. Murch (1835) 138–54. *UHST* IV (1927–30) 64. Wiard, H. D., *Some Notes on Unitarianism in Bath* (1951).

(8) Former BAPTIST, Somerset Street (ST 750644). Seceders from (7) who left the Frog Lane meeting in 1726 gathered first at a house in Widcombe and subsequently in a room and later a meeting-house close to Southgate Street. The meeting-house in Somerset Street, formerly Garrard Street, was opened 25 December 1768 and later enlarged. The church, formed in 1752, removed to its present chapel in Manvers Street in 1872.

The former meeting-house, now used as a printing works, has a broad ashlar front of eight bays with a moulded cornice, two tiers of plain sash windows and porches in bays three and six. The interior has been entirely altered and a floor inserted at gallery level. The pulpit was against the longer back wall.

Murch (1835) 142. Oliver (1968) 83–7.

(9) EBENEZER CHAPEL, Widcombe (ST 755642), was built in 1820 for an Independent congregation which had liturgical services. On the failure of the original proprietors the chapel passed in 1849 to the present Particular Baptist church. This originated in a secession from Providence Chapel, Lower Bristol Road, which had been built for a faction of the Somerset Street church.

The chapel has walls of ashlar and a pyramidal roof covered with slates and formerly surmounted by a ball finial. The N

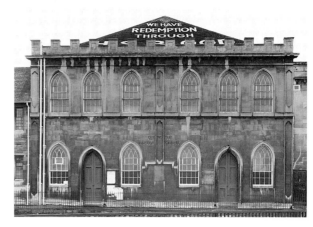

'Ebenezer Chapel', Widcombe.   (9)

front, facing the Kennet and Avon canal, has a battlemented parapet and two tiers of pointed-arched windows. The elevation is in two parts, each of three bays bounded by panelled pilasters and with a doorway central to each section. The S wall has been much altered but four original pointed-arched windows remain at the upper level. The side walls are partly covered by adjoining buildings.

The interior (53¼ ft by 50½ ft) has a continuous gallery supported by wooden columns of quatrefoil section. The S gallery has been altered and a vestry built below. The seating and rostrum pulpit date from the late 19th century. Below the chapel are twenty numbered rows of former burial-vaults and some early 19th-century wall monuments.

Bath Guide (1825). Oliver (1968) 90–1.

(10) THOMAS STREET CHAPEL (ST 75286581), dated 1830, is said to have been built for a Baptist congregation, passing eventually to the Church of England as a chapel-of-ease to St Swithin's, Walcot. It is now used for storage. Rubble walls, ashlar front and hipped slate roof. The front of three bays has a moulded cornice and shaped parapet with dated inscription. The lower stage is rusticated and has a central porch with two columns; the upper windows have round-arched heads.

Bath Chronicle (2 July 1938) letter.

(11) KENSINGTON CHAPEL (ST 754658), opened 4 January 1795 as an Independent proprietary chapel, was designed by John Palmer. When the chapel was transferred *c*.1866 to the Church of England as a chapel-of-ease to St Saviour's Church, dissenting members built a Baptist chapel at Hay Hill (ST 750653), opened 1869. The chapel is now in commercial use.

The walls are of rubble with an ashlar front. The N front is of three bays with a broad pediment, the lower stage is rusticated, the upper stage has three round-arched windows joined by moulded entablatures and flanked by pilasters in the manner of Venetian windows. The entrances are in arched bays in the adjacent terraces.

The interior (62 ft by 43¼ ft) has been much altered, with two inserted floors, and the roof has been rebuilt. At the S end is a short chancel (12 ft by 20½ ft) with a large lunette window above a tripartite reredos with Ionic pilasters. The body of the chapel had a gallery around three sides with staircases in the front corners. A coved plaster ceiling remains above the chancel but the main ceiling, which may have had a central barrel vault, has been removed. There is a basement storey below the chapel.

Reredos: against S wall, three bays with recessed centre, Ionic pilasters and entablature; the side panels have traces of inscriptions, including the Lord's Prayer, and are decorated at the head with palm leaves in oval frames; cherubs' heads above centre bay.

B. *Hbk* (1875) 283–8. *Weekly Chronicle* (10 September 1966) 5.

(12) Former CATHOLIC APOSTOLIC, The Vineyards (ST 75006541), in the Romanesque style by George Philip Manners, was built in 1840. It is now a social club. It comprises a nave of three bays with a small chancel and apsidal sanctuary at the N end. The chancel has an elliptical barrel-vaulted ceiling but the roof trusses in the nave are exposed. The chancel arch of a single order rises from detached shafts.

(13) COUNTESS OF HUNTINGDON'S CHAPEL, The Vineyards (ST 75006535). The site, on the W side of the street, was bought in 1765 by the Countess of Huntingdon who built a house facing the street for her occasional use, and as a residence for visiting ministers, and a large chapel behind. The Calvinistic Methodist society which met here was greatly reduced in numbers by the early 20th century and in 1922 it united with a congregation of the Presbyterian Church of England formed in 1900 which required a more suitable place of worship. The chapel was reopened by the united church on 2 April 1922 and renamed 'Trinity' in 1932. The church, then URC, joined that at Argyle Chapel (14) in 1981 and the Countess's chapel passed to the Bath Preservation Trust in 1983.

The chapel has walls of squared stone and a slated roof hipped to the east. The principal wall faces S towards a courtyard, formerly 'Harlequin Row', once in mixed occupation with houses and shops on the S side but which were replaced by a school house in the mid 19th century. The S wall, which has a low stone plinth, cornice and rusticated quoins, is of five principal bays with round-arched windows of three lights, except that at the centre which is of four lights, with stone mullions, intersecting tracery and moulded labels. The entrances were originally below the windows of the end bays, that to the W is now internal, the E doorway has been re-sited to the right. A sixth bay at the E end of this wall, concealing an internal apse, has two tiers of small windows only. The N wall has similar fenestration to that described but with three tiers of windows in the E bay and the only entrance in the adjacent bay covered by a porch. This porch, and a similar porch at the W end of the S side, has a pair of ogee-arched entrances with jambs of triple shafts with annular bands, one entrance serving the lower floor, the other opening to gallery stairs. The W end of the chapel has four round-arched windows of three lights with intersecting tracery.

The house at the E end of the chapel, of similar materials, is of two storeys with a two-stage bay window to the E having ogee-arched lights and a battlemented parapet. Single-storey wings N and S have paired former entrances of a similar design to the side porches of the chapel, but now partly blocked and with windows inserted.

The interior of the chapel (59½ft by 39¾ft) was described shortly after its erection in a letter from Horace Walpole to John

The Countess of Huntingdon's Chapel
BATH   *Somerset*

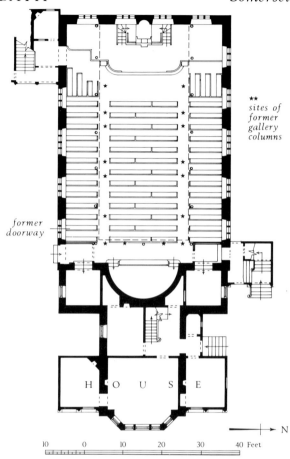

★★ *sites of former gallery columns*

former doorway

H O U S E

N

10 0 10 20 30 40 Feet

Based on a measured drawing by Richard Neville   (13)
of Aaron Evans Associates.

Chute, 10 October 1766, following a service taken by John Wesley. He writes: 'the chapel is very neat, with true Gothic windows . . . they have very neat mahogany stands for branches, and brackets for the same in taste. At the upper end is a broad *hautpas* of four steps, advancing in the middle: at each end of the broadest part are two of *my* eagles, with red cushions for the parson and clerk. Behind them rise three more steps, in the midst of which is a third eagle for the pulpit. Scarlet armed chairs for all three. On either hand, a balcony for elect ladies. The rest of the congregation sit on forms. Behind the pit, in a dark niche, is a plain table within rails.'

The pulpit and reading desks stand at the W end; in the wall behind the pulpit is a shell-headed niche. At the E end is a large apse forming a communion recess below the gallery and an organ chamber above. A gallery extends along the N, S and E sides with decorative fronts and supporting columns of cast-iron. The gallery is not original but may date in part from the early 19th century; earlier galleries were enlarged in 1783 but in 1811 the *Original Bath Guide* recorded that 'A handsome gallery has been added by the present proprietors, which nearly surrounds the

Countess of Huntingdon's Chapel, Bath.   (13)

Countess of Huntingdon's Chapel, Bath. Interior from west.   (13)

chapel' (*see* Medd (1965)). In 1891 the gallery fronts were set back by 18 in. to give more light. The sites of former gallery supports are visible in the floor, paired to each side of the wider central windows. The E gallery formerly continued into the NE corner where low benches for children remain behind a false wall flanking the apse. The ceiling has a wide coved cornice which continues around the apse. The roof is supported by five trusses with scissor bracing between king and queen-posts.

Fittings – *Monuments* and *Floorslabs*. Monuments: on W wall (1) Rev. John Owen, 30 years pastor, 1858; two other monuments have been removed since 1945. *Floorslabs*: at E end (1) Mrs Rachel Rose, 1799, and Benjamin Barber, 1827; also two slabs with decayed inscriptions, early 19th-century. *Pulpit* and *Lecterns*: desks supported by artificial-stone eagles with outspread wings, 18th-century on late 19th-century bases; original panelled pulpit front incorporated into later rostrum. *Seating*: late 19th-century. (Lower seating removed since 1981)

[Medd, B.G.] *A Bicentenary Record, 1765–1965, Trinity Presbyterian Church Formerly Countess of Huntingdon's Chapel, Vineyards – Bath* (1965). Murch (1835) 143. Seymour I (1839) 466–88.

(14) CONGREGATIONAL, Argyle Street (ST 75236500). A few former adherents from the Countess of Huntingdon's chapel who objected to the restriction of its use to episcopally ordained preachers left about 1780 and eventually opened a 'Tabernacle' in Morford Street in 1783. In 1785, after one further removal, they built Hope Chapel on the site of a Roman Catholic chapel in St James's Passage which had been destroyed by rioters in 1780; that building (ST 74986459), now occupied as a printing works, was greatly altered or rebuilt in the late 19th century. The present chapel, known successively as the 'Independent Chapel', Laura's Place, 'Jay's Chapel', and 'Argyle Chapel', was built in 1788–9 to designs by Thomas Baldwin, enlarged to N and S in 1821 by H. E. Goodridge and further altered in 1861. (Now URC)

The front wall is of ashlar but the original side walls are built of coursed rubble. The S front of three bays is in two stages; the lower stage, of 1821, has an open porch at the centre with two Ionic columns *in antis*, a large axial doorway at the back of the porch and smaller side doorways in the front and return walls of the flanking bays. The upper stage originally comprised the centre bay only which terminated in a pediment; in 1861 the whole of the frontage was raised to two storeys and finished with a balustraded parapet.

The interior (60 ft enlarged to 92½ ft, by 45½ ft), partly refitted in the late 19th century, has a gallery around three sides supported by cast-iron columns. Beneath the chapel is a stone-vaulted cellar with a late 18th-century iron gate at the N entrance; it was originally intended to be let for storage.

Fittings – *Monuments*: in chapel (1) Rev. William Jay, over 62 years pastor, 1853; (2) William Henry Dyer, 21 years pastor, 1878. *Pulpit*: arched front flanked by paired Ionic columns supporting dentil cornice, early 19th-century, altered and lowered.

Wills, A. W., *The History of Argyle Congregational Church, Bath, 1781–1938* (1938).

(15) Former CONGREGATIONAL, Charlotte Street (ST 74656495). 'Percy Chapel' was built in 1854 in the Lombardic

Former Congregational chapel, Charlotte Street, Bath.   (15)

style to designs by H. E. and A. S. Goodridge. The congregation originated in a division from Argyle Chapel following the contrived resignation of Rev. William Jay from the pastorate, after whose residence in Percy Place the new chapel was named. The broad S front has a gabled centre bay with a wheel window and narrow entrance bays at each end rising to short turrets. The interior has a continuous gallery, and ten columns carrying arches below a large decagonal clerestory formerly surmounted externally by a prominent ventilator (removed since 1945). The chapel has been used since 1955 by Elim Pentecostal Church.

CYB (1855) 259–60; (1876) 438.

(16) FRIENDS, York Street (ST 75186470). A meeting-house built in 1697 was sold in 1866 when Friends removed to the present building. This was erected in 1817–19 to designs by William Wilkins for use as a Masonic Hall and appears to have been used from 1841 by Baptists and others, at which period the date '1842' was added to the front. The front is of three bays with a central pedimented portico with two Ionic columns and blind doorway.

Oliver (1968) 92.

(17) WALCOT CHAPEL, London Road (ST 752657). The first Methodist society in Bath was formed in 1741. A chapel built in New King Street and opened by John Wesley in 1779, of similar

Walcot Chapel, Bath. (17)

design though smaller in scale than the chapel in City Road, London, was regarded as a model for others. It was rebuilt in 1847 and demolished in 1958 following wartime damage. 'Walcot Chapel', on the SE side of London Road, was built for a second Wesleyan society in 1815–16, to designs by the Rev. William Jenkins. The front is of five bays with two tiers of round-arched windows and a raised three-bay pediment. The lower stage is rusticated and has a wide central porch with paired Doric columns; the upper stage is punctuated by Corinthian pilasters. On the frieze above the centre bay are inscribed the words 'DEO SACRUM'. The side walls are of five bays and include basement windows.

The interior (66 ft by 46½ ft) has a gallery around three sides, rounded at the back, with a panelled front supported by wooden columns. Behind a late 19th-century rostrum pulpit is a large arched organ chamber with a vestry beneath, probably on the site of a communion recess; the original vestry appears to have been on the floor below.

Fittings – *Monuments*: loose in gallery (1) brass, 1914–18 war memorial from 'Westgate Buildings' Primitive Methodist Chapel; (2) Rev. Samuel Taylor, 1821; (3) Joseph Pearson, who 'established the first Wesleyan Sunday School in this city', 1844, and Martha his wife, 1830. Several monuments on the wall flanking the pulpit have been removed since 1945. In the burial-ground behind the chapel are many monuments of the early 19th century and later. *Seating*: original box-pews remain throughout but with doors removed.

(18) Former MORAVIAN, Monmouth Street (ST 74656472). John Cennick formed a society here in 1744 which was revived after 1752 and re-formed in 1757. A chapel was built in 1765 which continued in use until 1845 when a new chapel was built in Charlotte Street. The former chapel was subsequently used by the Brethren and latterly by the Salvation Army who demolished it c.1970 and built a new Hall on the site. It had a broad front of

five bays with round-arched windows and doorways in the end bays.

England II (1886–7) 5–6, pl. XVII.

(19) Former MORAVIAN, Charlotte Street (ST 74606501). The chapel, built 1845 to designs by James Wilson, is now in secular use. Three-bay front with two tiers of windows and pedimented centre with two giant Corinthian columns *in antis*. The chapel is behind two bays only; the left-hand bay is occupied by a house.

England, op.cit.

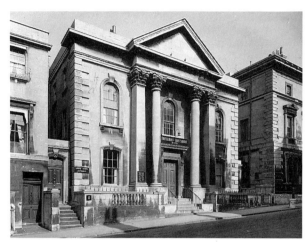

Former Moravian chapel, Charlotte Street, Bath. (19)

(20) Former NEW JERUSALEM CHURCH, Henry Street (ST 75206455). A congregation loyal to the writings of Emanuel Swedenborg was formed c.1827. The chapel, built in 1843–4 to designs by H. Underwood, is now occupied by the Bath Christian Fellowship. The front has a three-bay pediment with attached Ionic columns. The interior was entirely altered in the late 19th century and subsequently.

Hindmarsh (1861) 502.

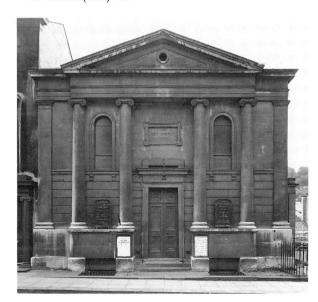

Former New Jerusalem Church, Bath. (20)

(21) PEOPLE'S MISSION, Corn Street (ST 74956450). The chapel was built in 1786 for Roman Catholics following the destruction of their former chapel in St James's Passage (*see* (14)); on the removal of the original congregation in 1809 to a former theatre in Orchard Street, now the Masonic Hall, the chapel was used by various groups including Baptist seceders from Somerset Street chapel *c*.1830–6, as a mission chapel for St Paul's parish church until 1936 and from *c*.1947 by the 'Peoples' Band Mission' which originated in a secession from the local branch of the Salvation Army. The chapel is a low building with segmental-arched windows at the sides and an apsidal sanctuary. The front is covered by a forebuilding of two storeys, possibly an addition of the early 19th century.

Little, B., *Catholic Churches Since 1623. A Study of Roman Catholic Churches in England and Wales to the Present Decade* (1966) 38.

BAWDRIP

(22) CONGREGATIONAL, Knowle (ST 339399). 'Sion Chapel', dated 1830, said to have been built at the expense of James Collings, is a small low building of rubble with narrow round-arched windows.

Thomas (1896) 68–9.

Congregational chapel, Knowle. (22)

BECKINGTON

(23) BAPTIST, Frome Road (ST 799518). The chapel was built in 1786 for a congregation which originated with the defection of a Calvinistic Methodist society. It was registered in 1788. The walls are of rubble with some ashlar dressings; the roof, rebuilt in the late 19th century, is hipped and slated. The SE front of three

bays divided by pilasters has a pedimented centre bay and balustraded parapets to each side. The central doorway has a pediment above a segmental-arched opening with keystone.

The interior ($35\frac{3}{4}$ ft by $33\frac{1}{2}$ ft) was drastically refitted in the late 19th century, including the renewal of seating and pulpit and the provision of open cast-iron gallery fronts. A Sunday-school at the back was built *c*.1840.

Communion Table: with turned baluster legs and carved upper rails, early 18th-century. *Monuments*: in chapel (1) Rev. John Hinton, 20 years pastor, 1822, and Rev. James Viney, 13 years pastor, 1838; (2) Elizabeth, widow of James Carpenter, 1831, and Jane their youngest daughter, 1828; (3) Samuel Dainton, 1839; (4) Ezit Pepler, 1820, Thomas Moody 'brother of the above', 1838, and Anna his wife, 1810; all monuments signed 'Chapman', or 'Chapman & Son, Frome'.

Coombes, A. H., *History of Badcox Lane Church, Frome* [*c*.1925] 17. Oliver (1968) 122.

(24) BAPTIST, Lower Rudge (ST 828518). Rubble and slate; rendered gabled front with rusticated quoins and round-arched windows, dated 1839. A low vestry wing projects to the left. Inside is a contemporary rear gallery and polygonal pulpit; the seating has been renewed. There is a small burial-ground behind.

Oliver (1968) 123.

BAPTIST CHAPEL, LOWER RUDGE

(25) WESLEYAN, Rudge (ST 829520). Gabled front with central pedimented doorway and round-arched windows with keystones; dated 1839. Interior refitted. *Monument*: in front of chapel, Meshach Wedlock, 1836, and Mary his widow, 1843.

BICKENHALL

(26) WESLEYAN, Abbey Hill (ST 279179). The chapel, built in 1824, was largely rebuilt, widened and extended in the mid 19th century. In one gabled end wall is a blocked doorway, and tablet above inscribed 'TM Wesleyan Chapel 1824'. A small detached building with central doorway between two lancets and chimney-stack at one end may have served as a schoolroom. *Monuments*: in burial-ground (1) Christopher Grabham, 1848, and Rebecca Grabham, 1858, table-tomb; (2) Thomas Murliss, 1844; (3) Sarah Flood, 1836, and Jean Flood, 1854.

BISHOP'S HULL (WITHOUT)

(27) CONGREGATIONAL (ST 203246). The church, originally Presbyterian, was formed in the late 17th century; a meeting-house registered in 1719 was described as a 'new erected house

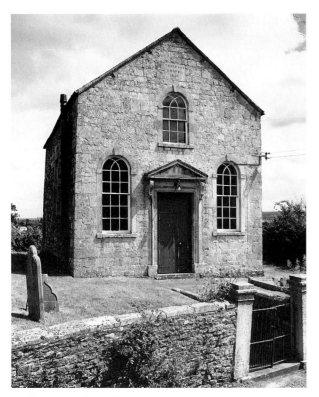

Wesleyan chapel, Rudge.   (25)

called The Trinity at Byshoppshull'. The present chapel, which appears to date from the early 19th century, was greatly altered and refitted in 1868. The windows have ogee-arched heads and wooden tracery.

Monuments: in chapel (1) Rev. Peard Jillard, 21 years pastor, 1799, *et al.*; (2) Rev. Robert Winton, 1822, *et al.*; (3) Rev. Samuel Greatheed F.S.A. [1823], and Jane Dorothea his wife, nd; (4) Robert Haskoll Jillard, eldest son of William Peard and Mary Jillard, 'interred by his own request in the burial-ground belonging to the Lewins Mead Unitarian Society in Bristol', 1826; (5) Peard Jillard, son of William Peard Jillard, 1824; in porch (6) Sarah, wife of Charles Barrington, 1843, and Selina his second wife, 1846.

Thomas (1896) 43.

BLAGDON   *Avon*
(28) Former WESLEYAN (ST 502588). Rendered rubble with pantiled roof; gabled front with pointed-arched doorway and gallery window over, both with brick arched heads. Early 19th-century.

BRENT KNOLL
(29) BIBLE CHRISTIAN (ST 333507). Rendered walls with pantiled roof; round-arched windows. Opened 1840 but much altered.

BRIDGWATER
(30) CHRIST CHURCH CHAPEL, Dampiet Street (ST 29953690). The Presbyterian, latterly Unitarian, congregation traces its

origin to the preaching of John Norman who was ejected as Vicar of Bridgwater in 1660 and imprisoned 1663–4 for nonconformist preaching. Ten of the ejected ministers are named as active here in 1669. The first regular meeting-house on this site was built in 1688 and rebuilt in its present form in 1787–8. The former building was noticed by Defoe as 'a fine new meeting-house' with 'an advanc'd seat for the mayor and aldermen, when any of the magistrates should be of their Communion, as sometimes has happened'.

The chapel stands on an irregular confined site. The side walls, which may survive from the earlier building, are concealed by adjoining properties. The N and S end walls are of brickwork with a rubble plinth at the rear. The roof is covered with patent tiles. The N front is set back slightly from the line of the neighbouring houses and screened by short return walls at each end. It is of three bays with two tiers of windows with stone dressings; the centre bay projects and is carried up to an open pediment. A wide central doorway has a large shell hood supported by brackets and there is a simple Venetian window to the upper stage. The S wall has a larger Venetian window between two side windows. A schoolroom or vestry was added to the SW in the early 19th century.

The interior (average dimensions 66 ft by 34 ft) tapers towards the S end and the S wall is at a marked angle to the front. Apart from lay-lights inserted into the roof in the 19th century, it is lit entirely by the windows in the end walls. The roof is supported by two pairs of stone columns with Attic bases and Roman Doric capitals which carry two N–S beams decorated with guttae from which springs a plaster barrel-vaulted ceiling over the central space. A singers' gallery at the N end, with panelled front supported by four wooden columns, is approached by a narrow winding staircase.

Fittings – *Inscriptions*: externally on N wall, two tablets inscribed '1688', 'REBUILT 1788'. *Monuments*: in chapel, on E wall (1) George Lewis Browne, captain R.N., 1856, and Ann (Pyke) his wife, 1846, 'during many years of active service Captain Browne obtained the trust and Highest Commendation of Admiral Lord Nelson under whose immediate command he distinguished himself at the Battle of Trafalgar', signed 'H. Cade, Bristol'; on W wall (2) William Browne, 1837, and Mary his wife, 1835, signed 'H. Wood, Bristol'; (3) Thomas Osler, 1825, 'interred in this chapel', and Mary (Cole) his wife, 1792; in schoolroom (4) Rev. Thomas Watson, nearly 38 years pastor, 1793, Mary (Codrington) his wife, 1774, and three children. *Plate*: includes a pair of two-handled gadrooned cups of 1692, acquired 1755. *Seating*: in body of chapel, three ranks of box-pews, the centre rank reduced in height by 9 in. but the side pews remain at their original height of 4 ft 2 in. above floor level, late 18th-century. The pulpit and S end have been refitted; Murch (1835) refers to a 'low gallery or long pew' at that end, 'extending from side to side, originally erected for the use of the corporation, but now appropriated to the Sunday scholars', with the pulpit 'at some distance from the end wall'.

Evans (1897) 30–2. Murch (1835) 176–90. *UHST* IV (1927–30) 280–5.

(31) BAPTIST, St Mary Street (ST 29803695). The chapel, of brick with an ashlar front, was rebuilt in 1837 to designs by

Christ Church Chapel, Bridgwater.

Edwin Down for a congregation which originated in the mid 17th century. The front wall of three bays with a pediment has a recessed central porch with two Ionic columns *in antis* and gallery staircases in the flanking bays. The interior has a gallery around three sides with an open cast-iron front. The chapel was greatly refitted and extended to the back in 1902. Iron railings and gates at the boundary of the forecourt have been removed since 1950.

B. *Hbk* (1903) 371–4. *BM* XXX (1838) 162. Hamlin, H.J., and Whitby, A.J., *Baptists in Bridgwater, Three Centuries of Witness* (1937).

Baptist chapel, Bridgwater, *c*.1950. (31)

(32) FRIENDS, Friarn Street (ST 29803690). This site was acquired in 1722. The meeting-house, which stands at right angles to the street with a cottage alongside sharing a uniform frontage, was built in that year. It was much altered in 1801 and additional rooms were built *c*.1971–2. The walls are of brickwork, with some rubble at the back, and the roof is pantiled. The street frontage is of two storeys with a wide segmental-arched passage leading to the rear. The meeting-house (66½ ft by 23½ ft) is divided into two rooms by 19th-century counterweighted shutters. The larger room to the S has two octagonal posts in line with the back wall of the cottage which support the roof; the platform of a former stand remains at the end next to the street with two blind windows behind. The smaller N room, with a stand at the opposite end, was refitted in the 19th century.

(33) WESLEYAN, King Street (ST 300370). Brick and pantile. Five-bay front with two tiers of round-arched windows and raised three-bay pediment; lower stage concealed by late 19th-century loggia. The date of erection, 1816, is cut on the upper platband; a large tablet below the pediment inscribed 'RAISED AND ENLARGED 1860' refers to a lengthening of the chapel and some heightening to the side walls and ceiling, but not greatly affecting the front. Interior refitted 1860. (Closed 1980)

BROADWAY

(34) Former CONGREGATIONAL (ST 320155). The chapel was built in 1739 for a section of the Ilminster Presbyterian society which had seceded following disagreement over the choice of a

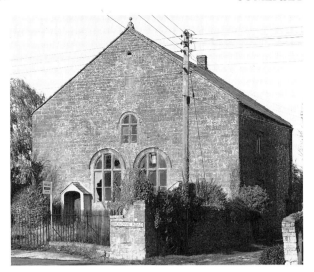

Former Congregational chapel, Broadway.
Before conversion. (34)

minister (*see* (87) below). The building (originally 26¼ ft by 40½ ft externally) was enlarged to the rear in 1852 and heightened in 1870; it was closed *c*.1960. The walls of squared brown stone were originally gabled on E and W sides. The S front has two segmental-arched doorways and two closely set round-arched windows of three lights with mullions and transoms and moulded labels. The wall was heightened above the level of the principal windows with a large gable and the insertion of a small window at the centre in 1870. The older parts of the E and W walls have mullion windows of two lights at gallery level and below. *Doors*: two, in S wall, wide-boarded and nail-studded, early 18th-century. *Monument*: in front burial-ground, Eleanor Upstill, 1839.

(Converted to house 1984–6; four small upper windows added in front, monument and one door removed)

CHST III (1907–8) 357–63. Murch (1835) 232. Thomas (1896) 55–6.

BRUSHFORD

(35) WESLEYAN, Oldways End (SS 870249). Rendered walls and hipped slate roof; two pointed-arched windows at side. Opened 1845.

WESLEYAN CHAPEL, OLDWAYS END C·F·S 1973

BRUTON

(36) Former CONGREGATIONAL, High Street (ST 683347). 'A large building in the High Street with a portico, erected by Sir Charles Berkley about 1750' and described as 'a disused factory' was converted into a chapel and manse about 1803. This has a broad stone frontage of five bays with early 19th-century Y-traceried windows and an altered centre bay. It was later converted to schoolrooms; a new chapel was built at the rear in 1836 at a cost of about £450 which, when opened, 'all agreed that they had never seen a cheaper chapel'. (Closed by 1970)

EM (1836) 565. Phelps, W., *The History and Antiquities of Somersetshire I* (1836) 246. Thomas (1896) 61.

(37) WESLEYAN, West End (ST 680347). Opened 1848, greatly altered and enlarged.

BUCKLAND DINHAM

(38) WESLEYAN, High Street (ST 753513). Rubble with ashlar dressings and pantiled roof. Three-bay front with two tiers of segmental-arched windows and pedimental gable. Central doorway with triple keystone and segmental-arched pediment on brackets in early 18th-century style. Oval tablet in gable with name and date 'Ebenezer' 1811. Interior ($30\frac{3}{4}$ ft by $20\frac{1}{2}$ ft) has early 19th-century rear gallery with contemporary box-pews. Lower seating and pulpit replaced in late 19th century.

BURNHAM-ON-SEA

(39) WESLEYAN, Berrow (ST 299517). Rendered walls with round-arched windows, opened 1850.

CAMERTON   *Avon*

(40) WESLEYAN, Red Hill (ST 682582). Coursed rubble, gabled front with central entrance and two segmental-arched gallery windows. Opened 1820.

CANNINGTON

(41) CONGREGATIONAL (ST 254395). Three traceried windows between turreted corners; 1869 by Habershon and Brock, replacing a chapel of 1823. (URC)

CYB (1869) 316. Thomas (1896) 66.

CARHAMPTON

(42) WESLEYAN (ST 007426). The first preaching-house, converted in 1796 from an existing building, now serves as the village post office (ST 008427). The present chapel, built in 1839, has rendered walls and a hipped slate roof. The front, concealed by a later cottage, has a central entrance and two small gallery windows.

Allen (1974) 44, 46.

CASTLE CARY

(43) Former CONGREGATIONAL, South Street (ST 638319). 'Zion Chapel', built 1815–16 and enlarged to NW in 1839 and later to provide Sunday-school rooms, is of brick with stone quoins and has a hipped slate roof. The entrance, formerly at the SE end between pointed-arched windows with Y-tracery, was re-sited and the interior entirely rearranged in 1893–4. (Closed before 1985, interior gutted)

Gass, D.J., *The Days That Were, A Short Historical Sketch of Zion Chapel, Castle Cary* (1943).

(44) WESLEYAN, North Street (ST 643324). Built 1839. Rubble with ashlar front and slate roof. Three-bay front with octagonal corner buttresses rising to bulbous finials, gabled centre bay with swept side parapets and bell-shaped inscription panel. Two tiers of round-arched windows above basement storey. A Tuscan-columned porch in front of the entrance has been removed.

CHARD

(45) Former INDEPENDENT, South Chard (ST 328053). The chapel has rubble walls with stone and brick dressings and a thatched roof. Although the structure may date in part from the 17th century, and even earlier dates have been claimed, little evidence remains of its former history. It was converted for use as a meeting-house in the early 19th century. In 1836 the congregation was formed into a Strict Baptist church which continued to worship here until 1909 when a new chapel was built 100 yards SE and the former adapted for Sunday-school use.

Former Independent chapel, South Chard. After conversion. (45)

The E and W end walls are gabled and have stone copings. The E end of the building is occupied by a two-storeyed cottage, which has a brick chimney-stack on the gable, and a second lower cottage has been added beyond. The S front of the cottage is rendered; that of the chapel is of exposed rubble with ashlar quoins at each end. A central doorway with round-arched head and keystone has been blocked; to either side is a window with semicircular brick arch and keystone, and Y-traceried frame. The N wall of the chapel has two windows with timber lintels and frames of the early 19th century. In the W end wall is a central doorway and above it is a window with brick dressings and round-arched head, probably inserted in the late 19th century; immediately over the doorway is the lower part of a narrow loop with chamfered jambs possibly of 17th-century date. Traces of a wide window remain in the W gable.

The interior ($34\frac{3}{4}$ ft by $21\frac{1}{4}$ ft) has an early 19th-century W gallery with panelled front supported by two wooden posts and approached by a staircase in the NW corner. The pulpit at the E end with rounded front and reeded side panels also dates from the early 19th century, but the seating is later. The roof structure has purlins with tusk-tenon joints. *Almsbox*: built into wall at base of gallery stairs, wooden with painted inscription 'Free will offering for the support of the Gospel in this place. *The labourer is worthy of his reward . . .*'.

(Converted to cottage before 1985; S doorway reopened)
Oliver (1968) 124–5.

CHARD BOROUGH

(46) BAPTIST, Holyrood Street, Chard (ST 322085). The church, which was in existence by 1653, had a meeting-house in Crinchard Lane (Coombe Street) and subsequently in East Street. The latter, rebuilt on a new site in 1786, stood on the S side of the street (ST 32750870) but has now been demolished. About 1799 several members seceded and in 1803 opened 'Broadlake Chapel' on the W side of Holyrood Street which closed in 1902 on the expiry of the lease. The present chapel, on the E side of the street, was built in 1842 for the congregation which has remained at East Street. The walls are of flint rubble at the sides, slate-hung to S, and the front is faced in ashlar. The W front has a pediment supported by four elongated pilasters, a central doorway in the rusticated lower stage, and simple round-arched window above with Grecian surround.

Oliver (1968) 125–6.

(47) CONGREGATIONAL, Fore Street, Chard (ST 323087). A Presbyterian society originating in the late 17th century, apparently with the support of some Independents formerly in membership with the Axminster church, built a meeting-house in 1700–2. This remained in use, although much enlarged *c*.1820–30, until the present chapel was built in front of it in 1868; the earlier building was then converted for the Sunday-school.

The former meeting-house has rubble walls with some brick dressings and a hipped roof slated to S but otherwise covered in patent tiles. The S front prior to 1868 was of early 19th-century character with a low gable, central porch with paired doorways and three round-arched upper windows with Y-tracery. The E wall retains one window of this form and traces of a second; there is another in the W wall but most of the windows are of the late 19th century. The meeting-house was extended to the N in the early 19th century and two tiers of blocked round-arched windows remain in the N wall. The interior (43 ft, extended to 51¼ ft, by 34 ft) was refitted *c*.1867 with a gallery around three sides, partitioned to form separate recesses for individual classes.

The present chapel, adjacent to S, of rubble with ashlar dressings, was designed by W. J. Stent. The S front is gabled and has a five-light traceried window above a wide porch, tower with octagonal spirelet to the W and a lower wing with gallery stair to the east. A gallery around three sides is supported by cast-iron columns which rise above to carry the hammer-beams of an open roof.

Monuments: in chapel (1) Robert Brine James, surgeon, 1812, Mary his wife, 1797, *et al.*; (2) Rev. John Gunn, 20 years pastor, 1836; (3) Henry Trenchard, 1830, Sarah his wife, 1828, and John their son, 1815; in forecourt (4) Rev. John Gunn, 1836, Rebecca his widow, 1864, their son Henry Mayo Gunn, minister at Warminster, 1886, *et al.*, obelisk.

(Chapel demolished *c*.1983)
CYB (1869) 318. Gunn, H. M., *History of Free Churches in Chard and the Neighbourhood* (*c*.1867). Howard, K. W. H. (ed), *The Axminster Ecclesiastica 1660–1698* (1976) 192–4.

(48) Former WESLEYAN, Fore Street, Chard (ST 32350800). Gabled front with three pointed-arched windows with intersecting glazing bars. Built *c*.1814, passed to Wesleyan Reformers *c*.1850, re-purchased by Wesleyans 1880, superseded *c*.1894.

Temple (1974) [20].

CHEDDAR

(49) BAPTIST, Lower North Street (ST 458533). Rendered walls, three-bay front dated 1831 with round-arched windows, later porch formerly with Corinthian columns, and stepped gable with scrolled and crested stone panel at apex.

CHEWTON MENDIP

(50) Former CHAPEL (ST 600532). Rendered walls, gable front with ball finial and blocked window over altered doorway. Early 19th-century.

CHILCOMPTON

(51) WESLEYAN, Bowden Hill (ST 649515). Simple Romanesque details to front with later battlemented porch; opened 1850.

(52) Former BRETHREN, Shell House (ST 649522). A mid 18th-century outbuilding converted for use as a meeting-room in the 19th century. (Demolished *c*.1977)

CHURCHILL　　　　　　　　　　　　　　　　　　*Avon*

(53) WESLEYAN (ST 444598). A chapel of 1834, with an adjoining Sunday-school of 1852, was replaced in 1880–1 by the present building at the expense of Sidney Hill of Langford House as a memorial to his wife. The chapel of stone in the Perpendicular Gothic style was designed by Foster and Wood of Bristol. It comprises a wide nave with a more elaborate S porch of 1906 by Silcock and Reay, E and W transepts and a N chancel. It is linked on the E by a corridor and vestries to a public hall of 1879 which remained in a separate secular trust until 1978.

Monuments: in burial-ground, SW of chapel (1) Charles Knowles, 'a liberal donor towards the erection and support of this place of worship', 1864, wall monument from former chapel; S of hall (2) Sidney Hill, 1908, Mary Ann his wife, 1874, *et al.*, tall monument with crocketted spirelet.

Leeming, C. F., *Churchill Methodist Memorial Church, Centenary Souvenir* (1981). *Methodist Recorder* (Winter Number 1897) 90–2.

CHURCHSTANTON

(54) BAPTIST, Churchingford (ST 213128). Small chapel built *c*.1837 for a branch of the church at Newhouse, Upottery, Devon. Rubble and slate with broad three-bay rendered front, pointed-arched doorway and windows, and rebuilt bell-cote on SW gable. Original SW gallery with panelled front; matching pulpit.

Bell: in bell-cote, one, *c*.1837. *Sundial*: over SE doorway, signed John Blackmore, 1846.

Andress, W. T., *The History of Newhouse, Upottery* (1932) 23–4.

Baptist chapel, Churchingford. (54)

CLUTTON
Avon

(55) CONGREGATIONAL (ST 624592). Gothic, late 19th-century. The adjacent British School, dated 1862 on later porch, could be the former chapel of 1810. This has a broad three-bay front with pointed-arched windows and clockface above entrance, ball finials on end gables.

(56) WESLEYAN, Upper Bristol Road (ST 619591). Rubble with rendered front, arched doorway with fanlight, 1810.

COMPTON MARTIN
Avon

(57) WESLEYAN (ST 544571). Plain rendered walls, opened 1848.

CREWKERNE

(58) HERMITAGE STREET CHAPEL (ST 441094). The Presbyterian society, latterly Unitarian, is thought to have originated about 1665 when James Stephenson, ejected vicar of Martock, removed to Crewkerne. Three other ejected ministers were also active here in 1669. The chapel, on the E side of the street, was built in 1733,

Hermitage Street Chapel, Crewkerne. (58)

altered in 1811 when it was re-roofed and re-pewed, and further altered in 1900. The walls are of coursed rubble and the roof which is half-hipped is covered with slates. The original front faced S and probably had two large round-arched windows of three lights with a transom flanking the pulpit and doorways at each end. An extension of 1900 has left only part of the wall intact with one large window remaining, the other is reset in the wing; the site of one doorway remains with a two-light gallery window above. The present entrance and windows in the W wall date from 1900 and a tablet with the dates '1733, 1811' has been reset above the new entrance. The N wall has a central window of three lights similar to that remaining in the S wall and former gallery windows at each end.

The interior (24 ft by 42 ft) was entirely altered in 1900. It originally had separate E and W galleries, both now removed. The pulpit, centrally against the S wall, was re-sited at the E end in the mid 19th century during an earlier refitting; the outline of the back-board and shaped canopy is visible in the wall plaster at both locations.

Fittings – *Clock*: in chapel, signed 'Thos. Cottell 1782'. *Monuments*: in chapel (1) Hannah, first wife of Rev. William Blake, 1810, and Hannah their daughter, 1822; (2) Rev. William Blake, son of Rev. William and Hannah Blake, 25 years minister, 1821, Elizabeth his second wife, 1835, and Malachi their son, 1820; (3) Rev. William Blake, 1799, Hannah his wife, 1777, and Hannah their daughter, 1791; (4) Elizabeth, wife of George Stuckey, 1750, also William Jolliffe, 1790, and Grace his widow, 1810, erected by Samuel Sparks, grandson of the first and nephew of the second; (5) to 'the numerous family of Fitchett who were inhabitants of the town more than two centuries and regular attendants in this place of Christian worship', marble tablet dated October 1835, signed 'Payne, Beaminster'.

Evans (1897) 62–3. Murch (1835) 240–8. *UHST* VI (1935–8) 54.

(59) BAPTIST, North Street (ST 441100). The chapel, built in 1820, has walls of coursed rubble with ashlar quoins and a hipped slate roof. Broad front with doorways in end bays and round-arched windows over. A large central projection was added in 1880.

CROSCOMBE

(60) Former BAPTIST (ST 591445). Meetings of Baptists were being held in private houses in 1669 and 1672 and the site of a meeting-house and burial-ground is said to have been located on a neighbouring hillside. The early history of the congregation is obscure but it seems probable that the present building was occupied as a meeting-house from the early 18th century. The former chapel, which stands 50 yards N of the parish church, was built in the 15th century as a hall of the manor house of the Palton family. The estate passed through the Pomeroys to the Fortescues, of which Hugh Fortescue was created Baron Clinton in 1721 and raised to the earldom in 1746; he was responsible for the sale of most of the Croscombe estates, which presumably included the remains of the manor house. The conversion of the building did not involve any major structural alteration to the mediaeval fabric. The chapel was largely refitted during the early 19th century, at which period a burial 'near or under the table

Baptist Chapel , CROSCOMBE

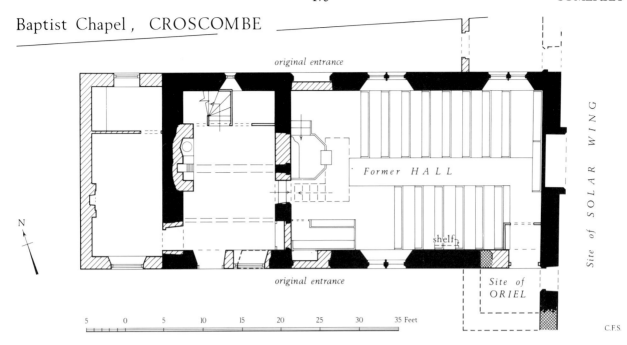

original entrance

original entrance

Site of SOLAR WING

Former HALL

shelf

Site of ORIEL

N

5   0   5   10   15   20   25   30   35 Feet

C.F.S.

Former Baptist chapel, Croscombe.   (60)

Former Baptist chapel, Croscombe. Lamp bracket.   (60)

pew' was recorded, and in 1824 an internal baptistery was constructed. About 1864 a new floor, seating and rostrum pulpit were provided. The church, which long continued in a feeble state, was finally disbanded *c*.1974 and the chapel restored to domestic use. The following describes the building as it was in 1970.

The chapel, of stone with a pantiled roof, comprises the only remaining parts of the manor house, being the hall, which became the chapel, and the service rooms to the W which were formed into a cottage and extended by a further room to the W in the early 19th century. In the N and S walls the doorways at the ends of the former screens passage remain visible although blocked internally; there are two windows in the N wall and one in the S, each of two lights with cusped tracery in a two-centred arched head with moulded label. A doorway at the E end of the S wall dates from the 19th century but replaces a wider doorway, possibly of the early 18th century, in the blocking of the opening to a former oriel window.

The interior (32½ ft by 20 ft) has a rostrum pulpit at the W end and a stone-lined baptistery in front. Three doorways from the former screens passage remain partly blocked in the W wall. A flat plaster ceiling was inserted in the 19th century. The original 15th-century roof structure comprises five trusses with arched-braced collars, curved struts above and three purlins to each side with arched wind-braces, the braces being paired in the two lower tiers.

Fittings – *Lamp Bracket*: on S wall, stone shelf with battlemented top, with a shield-of-arms of six roses for Palton between two shields impaling this coat; on upper surface, site of four iron holders for rushlights, one of which remains, 15th-century. *Monument*: in chapel on N wall, Joseph George, gent., 1770, and Elizabeth his wife, 1739, white marble tablet with moulded cornice surmounted by urns.

Collinson, J., *The History and Antiquities of the County of Somerset* III (1791) 469–70.

CURRY RIVEL

(61) CONGREGATIONAL (ST 391251). Stone with hipped slate roof, three-bay front with lancet windows and narrow projection to right for gallery stair. Built 1840, enlarged to rear 1867. (URC)

Thomas (1896) 66–7.

(62) Former BIBLE CHRISTIAN, Hambridge (ST 394213). Three-bay gabled front with round-arched windows and porch, dated 1855.

DINNINGTON

(63) Former BIBLE CHRISTIAN (ST 402129), rubble with ashlar dressings, gabled front with narrow round-arched doorway and window above. Built *c*.1840–50, closed 1956 but since used as 'Gospel Mission'. (Disused and most fittings removed 1986)

DULVERTON

(64) CONGREGATIONAL (SS 913277). A Presbyterian society formed in the late 17th century built a meeting-house here in 1710 which was closed by the early 19th century and then occupied by Independents. The present chapel, dated 1831, of rubble with a rendered gabled front and slate roof, was extended by the addition of a Sunday-school at the side in 1897.

Allen (1974) 50–1. *CYB* (1877) 417. Thomas (1896) 51.

DUNKERTON *Avon*

(65) BAPTIST, Withyditch (ST 703594). Stone and slate with narrow gabled front, round-arched windows and wooden acorn finial; storage cellar below. Dated 1830. Large detached Sunday-school and cottages to N, mid 19th-century.

DUNSTER

(66) Former WESLEYAN, Mill Lane (SS 990434). 'Ebenezer Chapel', dated 'Sept. 2 1811', has rendered rubble walls, perhaps with some cob, and segmental-pointed windows. A Wesleyan Day School at one end, built in 1825, was rebuilt in 1855. Now a builder's workshop.

Allen (1974) 54.

(67) Former WESLEYAN, West Street (SS 990436). Built 1832, rebuilt 1878, has an elaborate front with scrolled gable and large central window with rusticated surround. By S. Shewbrooks of Taunton. (Closed 1968, now a studio)

EAST COKER

(68) WESLEYAN (ST 541124). Small chapel attached to back of large 17th-century house. Rubble with a thatched roof. Opened 1841.

ELM

(69) Former WESLEYAN, Great Elm (ST 750494). 'Providence Chapel' dated 1835, stone with hipped slate roof, three-bay front with gabled porch and large pointed-arched windows. (Converted to house since 1970)

EXFORD

(70) Former WESLEYAN (SS 853384). Opened 1838. Plain rendered walls with two round-arched windows to front and back. *Glass*: in rear windows, pair of angels playing musical instruments, *c*.1890 by Sir Edward Burne-Jones, originally in the Haweis Chapel, Marylebone, London, reset here 1949. (Chapel closed 1979 and glass removed)

Allen (1974) 55–6.

FRESHFORD *Avon*

(71) WESLEYAN, Sharpstone (ST 786598). A Methodist society was in existence in Freshford by the late 18th century and a new

WESLEYAN CHAPEL, SHARPSTONE C·F·S·1974

preaching-house was opened by John Wesley on 15 March 1782. A chapel was built on ground close to Sharpstone House in 1827 and a new chapel erected alongside it *c*.1860–70. The early 19th-century chapel of stone with a pantiled roof has a broad three-bay front with an ogee-arched lintel to the central entrance and two pointed-arched windows with stone Y-tracery; there are two similar windows in the back wall. The interior has a coved plaster ceiling. The later chapel has a gabled front with lancet windows.

Former Wesleyan chapel, Great Elm. (69)

FROME

(72) Former BAPTIST, Catherine Street (ST 774480). 'Badcox Lane Chapel' was built for a congregation in existence by 1669. The site was acquired about 1710 and a meeting-house erected shortly afterwards. That building was a parallelogram (about 38 ft by 45 ft) with a double roof supported internally by two pillars and having a gallery around three sides. A *burial-ground* was provided *c*.1748 in Wayland's Close where an open baptistery and vestry were also constructed for the use of several

Former Baptist chapel, Badcox Lane, Frome.   (72)

congregations. A baptistery was made in the meeting-house in 1763.

The present chapel, built in 1813–14 on the site of the former, is a plain building of rubble concealed from the street behind a schoolroom built in 1845–6. The latter has an ashlar wall to the N with a portico of four Greek Doric columns at the centre. The chapel was closed in 1962.

Coombs, A. H., *A History of Badcox Lane Baptist Church, Frome* [c.1925]. Ivimey II (1814) 556–7. Oliver (1968) 80–1.

(73) BAPTIST, South Parade (ST 774479). 'Sheppard's Barton Chapel' was built in 1850 for a congregation of General Baptist tendency formed in 1705. Five-bay front with rusticated ashlar dressings, arcaded entrance and two tiers of windows.

Coombs, op. cit. 17.

(74) ROOK LANE CHAPEL, Bath Street (ST 77504785). The church formerly meeting here traced its origin to the work of several ejected ministers. Richard Alleine, rector of Batcombe, is named as preaching at Frome in his own house in 1669, and in 1672 John Sheppard's house was licensed for Presbyterians. Meetings were later held at the house of Robert Smith where Alleine spent his last years. The Presbyterian society owed much to the benevolence of Robert Smith, a substantial clothier, and to his immediate successors on whose land the chapel was built in 1707 and who may have contributed largely to the cost of its erection. It remained a part of their personal estate until 1778 when it was conveyed to trustees for the use of Presbyterians or Independents. In the early 18th century the society was reported to be one of the largest in the county with one thousand adherents but it appears to have suffered a severe decline in the latter half of the century. A secession occurred in 1744 to form a separate meeting at Starveacre and in 1773 another Independent congregation was organized at Zion Chapel (75). The 19th century saw a revival in the church and in 1862 a major refitting and repair of the chapel was carried out under William Stent of Warminster. After a further decline the Congregational churches at Rook Lane and Zion united in 1967 at the latter place. The chapel has since undergone extensive and protracted repairs for conversion to secular use, but in 1989 it remained in a semi-derelict condition.

Rook Lane Chapel stands on the NW side of the street behind

a lengthy forecourt. The street, originally named Rook Lane, was formerly aligned much closer and parallel to the front of the chapel. The builder is said to have been James Pope. The walls are of rubble with an ashlar front and the roof is hipped and covered with tiles. The SE front of seven bays, with two tiers of round-arched windows, has a central entrance with broken pediment and urn and is surmounted by a parapet with a pediment over five bays having a tablet bearing the date of erection. Lower flanking wings were added in the early 19th century to provide side entrances and gallery staircases outside the main body of the chapel. In 1862 the central doorway was blocked internally and the window-frames were replaced by patterned frames of cast-iron. The NW wall, now largely obscured by additional rooms behind the chapel, has two large round-arched windows flanking the pulpit; these were partly blocked and circular windows inserted in the mid 19th century. The end walls are of four bays with two tiers of windows matching those in front but with the windows in the end bays blocked or converted to entrances and the cills of the centre windows raised.

The interior (39½ ft by 54½ ft) was entirely refitted in 1862 with the exception of the two pillars supporting the roof, parts of the gallery structure, and some of the smaller fittings. The gallery, around three sides with angled corners, is supported by cast-iron columns; the front has bolection-moulded fielded panels, perhaps incorporating or reproducing earlier work. The gallery structure, exposed during recent work, appears to have been altered on several occasions and no trace of the sites of earlier staircases remained. In the W corner the floor has been cut through to insert a large organ. In the N corner and centrally on the SE side the stepped gallery floor is interrupted by lower platforms, perhaps the earlier sites of organs.

The roof structure is concealed by a panelled plaster ceiling of 1862 (removed c.1978). Two supporting columns of stone have Attic bases on tall fluted octagonal sub-bases, and Roman Doric capitals carrying entablature blocks. There is no continuous central valley but two inverted pyramidal valleys above the columns discharge by pipes to a gutter behind the front parapet. Beams extend from the heads of the columns to the end walls but not across the central space which seems to have had a plaster vault coved on four sides. Although the roof carpenters evidently experienced some difficulty in matching the formwork of the roof to the required shape of the ceiling, its early date is confirmed by the nickname 'the cupola' originally given to the building.

Fittings – *Clock*: on gallery front, signed 'Vincent, Frome', 18th-century. *Gate Piers*: next to road, four, rusticated masonry surmounted by urns, two of stone, two cast-iron. *Monuments*: in chapel on NE wall (1) Rev. John Sibree, 30 years pastor, 1820, Ann his widow, 1852, and their sons Robert, 1800, and Benjamin, 1817; (2) Sampson Payne, 1843, Mary Payne, 1826, and Sampson, son of Robert and Matilda Payne, 1845, tablet with canopied Gothic surround and black-letter inscription; on SE wall (3) Sarah, wife of William Chinnock, 1845; (4) William Adams, 1746, Lydia his daughter, 1748, Joseph Davis her husband, 1750, Mary their daughter, wife of Thomas Morgan, 1811, Elizabeth, daughter of Thomas and Mary Morgan, 1831, and Thomas Morgan, 1835, white marble on black marble

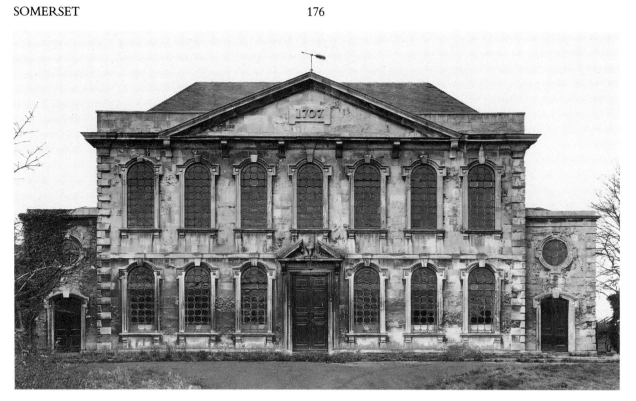

Rook Lane Chapel, Frome.

(74)

Rook Lane Chapel, FROME

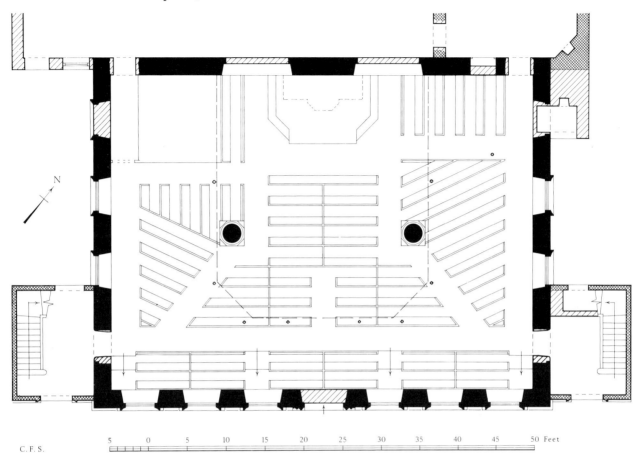

C.F.S.

5   0   5   10   15   20   25   30   35   40   45   50 Feet

backing with two-handled urn in low relief above and shield-of-arms below, signed 'J. Chapman, Frome'; (5) Rev. John Jones, 1851, and Isaac Benjamin his son, 1844; on SW wall (6) Robert Moon, 1852, Mary his wife, 1841, and their daughters Mary Ann Wheeler, 1833, and Matilda, 1834, signed 'Chapman, Frome'; (7) Edward Harris, woolstapler, 1772, 'He was an Instrument of restoring the light of Divine Truth in this place, after a long season of Darkness and Error', Mary his widow, 1798, and Thomas their son, over 40 years deacon, 1830, signed 'J. Chapman, Frome'; on NW wall (8) Rev. Isaac Tozer, son of Rev. Isaac Tozer of Taunton, 1822, tablet with panelled and scrolled sides surmounted by cross, shield and anchor against obelisk-shaped backing with urn finial; (9) bicentenary monument to four ejected ministers, Rev. John Humfry, 1719, Rev. Richard Alleine, 1681, Rev. Henry Albin, 1696, and Rev. Humphrey Phillips, 1707, also Rev. Walter Singer, 1719, and Mrs Elizabeth Rowe his daughter, 1736; (10) William Fussell, 1891, and Harriett his wife, 1876, brass; (11) Charles Tucker, 20 years deacon, 1855, Mary his widow, 1871, Edwin George Tucker, 1840, and Charles Rowsell Tucker, 1840, tablet with pedestal and kneeling female weeper; externally, in boundary wall S of chapel (12) James Moffat, ?1810; (13) Rev. John Bowden, 17[50]; (14) [   ] Cook, 1707. *Weathervane*: on roof,

large feathered arrow on scrolled support above ball finial, *c.*1707.

CYB (1847) 156; (1863) 335. *Somerset Standard* (21 April 1972).

(75) ZION CHAPEL, Whittox Lane (ST 775481), was built in 1810 for a Congregational church formed in 1773. The walls are of rubble with an ashlar front and dressings. The gabled front was refaced and a wide porch added in 1888 in the Romanesque style. An arched entrance from Catherine Hill is dated 1893. (URC)

(76) Former FRIENDS, South Parade (ST 774479), on N side of street, rubble with hipped slate roof, segmental-arched windows, high boundary wall around burial-ground on E side. Built 1821, sold 1955, now British Red Cross Society.

(77) WESLEYAN, Wesley Slope (ST 775477). Occasional Methodist meetings began in 1747 and by 1761 regular services were being held in private houses. The first preaching-house on the present site was opened in 1779 and supplanted by the existing chapel in 1810–12. The chapel has rubble walls with an ashlar front and hipped slate roof. The front of five bays and the sides of six bays have two tiers of windows, round-arched above and segmental below gallery level, separated by a stone platband. The central entrance has an open porch with two Tuscan columns. The interior has a continuous gallery with original seating; the staircases are in external wings. The lower seating was replaced in 1860 and coloured glass inserted in the windows in 1889. A

Wesleyan chapel, Frome. (77)

segmental apse behind the pulpit marks the site of the communion area with singers' gallery above.

Frome Wesley Methodist Church 150th Anniversary 1812–1962 (1962). Tuck, S., *Wesleyan Methodism in Frome* (1837).

(78) Former PRIMITIVE METHODIST, Sun Street (ST 774481). Rubble with gabled ashlar front, built 1834 but altered in late 19th century. Sunday-school behind dated 1851.

GLASTONBURY

(79) CONGREGATIONAL, High Street (ST 502390), built in 1814 for a formerly Presbyterian society (now URC) which originated in the late 17th century, has rubble walls with an ashlar front and hipped pantiled roof. The N front of three bays has a bowed centre with Venetian window above a later porch. Stone mullions and arched tracery were added to the windows *c*.1898. At the opposite end is an apse matching the outline of the front.

HATCH BEAUCHAMP

(80) BAPTIST (ST 301202). A church was in existence here in 1654. The present site was acquired in 1782 and the chapel built soon afterwards was registered in 1785. It was extended to the E in 1832 and a large lecture-room with classrooms above was built against the N side in 1883. The walls are rendered over stone rubble and the roofs are slated. The W front is gabled with a date-stone of 1783 at the apex; there is a central entrance with flat

canopy and arched window above of three lights with wooden tracery; decorative barge-boards applied in 1883 have been removed since 1971. The S wall has two original windows of four lights with round-arched heads and stone mullions and transoms. Two windows of two lights in the E wall flank the present site of the pulpit. Two windows inserted in the N wall have been blocked.

Baptist chapel, Hatch Beauchamp. (80)

The interior (20½ ft by 29 ft extended to 44 ft) has a W gallery of 1824–5. The seating was renewed in 1870; the original site of the pulpit was probably between the two S windows.

Coffin Stools: two, 18th-century. *Monument*: in chapel, Rev. Robert Fry, 13 years pastor, 1828, signed 'Pearse & Son, Sculptor, B. Hull'.

BQ XII (1946–8) 34–40. Wigfield, W. M., *The Baptist Church at Hatch Beauchamp, Somerset (from the 17th Century to the Present Day)* (1970).

HEMINGTON

(81) Former BAPTIST, Steps Lane (ST 775534). The chapel, built in 1836 for a church formed in 1814 which ceased to meet *c*.1960, has two tiers of windows about a central S entrance and lower flanking wings which serve as a cottage and Sunday-school. The interior has a very deep gallery above the entrance with original straight-backed pews. A rostrum pulpit between two windows at the N end is also of the early 19th century.

Former Baptist chapel, Steps Lane. (81)

Monuments: in chapel (1) Joseph Parsons, 1837, and Elizabeth his widow, 1844, signed 'J. Chapman Jnr. Frome'; (2) William Hosier, 1826, and Sarah his widow, 1853.

(82) WESLEYAN, Faulkland (ST 740546). Gabled front with columnar porch between segmental-arched windows, round-arched gallery windows above and tablet dated 1842. Gallery at entrance with original box-pews. Room below chapel with separate access.

Monument: in chapel, John Battle, 1852, and Susanna his wife, 1852.

HIGH HAM

(83) CONGREGATIONAL, Henley (ST 439319). 'Zion Chapel' dated 1841, refitted and schoolroom built 1896.

Thomas (1896) 70.

(84) CONGREGATIONAL, Low Ham (ST 435296). Built 1884 superseding a former Wesleyan chapel of 1815 in use from 1827. Rusticated quoins and round-arched windows with keystones.

Thomas (1896) 68.

HINTON CHARTERHOUSE   *Avon*

(85) Former WESLEYAN, High Street (ST 772581). Concealed behind houses and approached by a narrow passage on the E side. Gabled S wall with oval tablet dated 1814.

HORSINGTON

(86) WESLEYAN, South Cheriton (ST 694247). Gabled front with two lancets and circular tablet dated 1844, porch added 1894.

ILMINSTER

(87) THE OLD MEETING-HOUSE, East Street (ST 363145). The Presbyterian society originated in the late 17th century, meeting initially in private houses. The present building was erected in 1718–19 and registered 7 April 1719 as a 'new built house... lately erected on a Plott of Ground... called Tuckers Plott'. About 1738 a portion of the congregation seceded and built a new chapel at Broadway (34). By the late 18th century the society was depleted in numbers following the proliferation of other places of worship; it has since had a Unitarian ministry.

The meeting-house stands at the E end of a sloping site with a burial-ground in front. It has been considerably enlarged and altered. It was widened to the E in the mid 18th century to provide a gallery. In 1846 a schoolroom was built against this to the E and extended in 1907. The front of the chapel was altered or partly rebuilt in 1851, the interior refitted and reorientated in 1894 and further alterations made in 1913, including the addition of an organ chamber at the N end.

The walls are of stone and the roofs are covered with slates. The broad W front has two original doorways, each with a segmental-arched head below a four-centred arched outer moulding; pedimented stone surrounds were added in 1851. The centre bay was brought forward slightly in 1851 and given a moulded pediment and finial; two wide windows have four-centred arched heads and moulded labels but no mullions. Murch (1835) describes the front as having 'two gothic windows' but these may have been the traditional round-arched mullioned windows, perhaps indicating a more extensive rebuilding of part of the wall. The S wall is gabled and has one upper and two lower windows each of two lights with hollow-chamfered mullions and square moulded labels; the mid 18th-century extension has at this end a lower gable, altered in 1846, and a

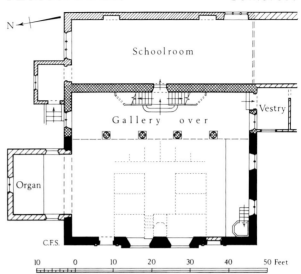

The Old Meeting-house,
ILMINSTER   *Somerset*

Schoolroom

Gallery over

Vestry

Organ

C.F.S.

10   0   10   20   30   40   50 Feet

two-light window on the line of extension. The N wall was similar to the S before the addition of the organ chamber in which some details from the former N windows have been reused. The N wall of the schoolroom has a three-light window with moulded label.

The interior ($25\frac{1}{2}$ ft enlarged to $36\frac{1}{2}$ ft, by $46\frac{1}{4}$ ft) has been greatly altered. The pulpit was formerly between the two windows on the W wall and the seating, partly visible in an old photograph, was of box-pews with a table-pew centrally in front of the pulpit. The original E wall was removed in the mid 18th century and replaced by four massive stone piers which support the ends of the roof trusses and carry the front of a gallery along that side of the building; the piers have square moulded capitals above and below the gallery. The gallery front has fielded panels with an outer framework added in the late 19th century. Although the intention to erect end galleries may be presumed from the fenestration, no trace of their existence has been found. The seating now faces south. The schoolroom has a plaster barrel-vaulted ceiling; above the doorway from the chapel is a niche formerly containing a statue.

Fittings – *Chest*: oak, with two chip-carved front panels, early 18th-century. *Clock*: on gallery front, octagonal face, 18th-century. *Coffin Stool*: one, early 18th-century. *Glass*: in W windows, dated 1901, 1917, replacing mid 19th-century glass with coloured borders. *Inscription*: on E wall of schoolroom, recording the erection of the room by Mrs Collins of Ilminster 'for the uses of the Sunday schools and congregation 1846'. *Monuments*: in chapel (1) Robert Collins, 1796, *et al.*; (2) John Collins, 1851, Mary his widow, 1852, and their children Malachi Blake, 1817, John Blake, 1862, and Hannah Maria, 1863; in burial-ground to W (3) John ?Pool [   ], early 18th-century, table-tomb with arched panelled sides, later inscriptions on panels to E and N sides record dates of erection and alterations to chapel including 'A new front & other repairs made in 1851' with date

The Old Meeting-house, Ilminster. (87)

recut from 1825; (4) John Thorne, 1739, and Hannah, daughter of John and Ann Thorne, 1734, headstone with Corinthian pilasters; (5) headstone with two winged cherubs' heads and draped sides, early 18th-century; (6) Elizabeth [   ], headstone with winged cherub's head, 18th-century. *Plate*: includes two beakers *c*.1671 and 1701, and flagon, 1770. *Sculpture*: formerly in niche in schoolroom, plaster statue of child with open book inscribed 'Evangelism'.

(Chapel closed and several headstones removed and loose against building, 1986)

Evans (1897) 112–13. Murch (1835) 230–7. *UHST* VII (1939–42) 71.

ISLE ABBOTTS

(88) BAPTIST (ST 349207). 'Bethesda Chapel', dated 1815 but registered 1817, repaired 1874, has plain rendered walls with round-arched windows.

Wigfield, W. M., *A Short History of the Baptist Churches at Isle Abbotts and Fivehead* [1968].

KEINTON MANDEVILLE

(89) WESLEYAN (ST 549308). Dated 1843, coursed stone with pointed-arched windows, rooms below.

KEYNSHAM   *Avon*

(90) BAPTIST (ST 654687). 'Ebenezer Chapel' built 1834 has a rendered front of three bays with recessed centre and two tiers of round-arched windows. The interior, drastically altered 1975–6, formerly had a complete set of box-pews. *Monument*: behind pulpit, Rev. Thomas Ayres, 1853.

Baptist Times (18 March 1976).

KILMERSDON

(91) WESLEYAN (ST 697524). The chapel of *c*.1850 and its predecessor stand adjacent E of the parish church. The earlier building which stands above a basement is said to have been built as a cider house and converted to a chapel in the early 19th

Wesleyan chapel, Kilmersdon.   (91)

century. It has walls of coursed rubble and the roof is tiled and slated. The S wall has traces of two former windows and the gable is surmounted by a stone Lorraine cross, possibly mediaeval. The entrance is at the N end. The interior (21 ft square) has an early 19th-century N gallery. The later chapel of rubble with an ashlar front and hipped slate roof has three bays of windows in two tiers to the front and tall windows in the side walls. The interior has an original N gallery and box-pews with doors removed.

Monument: in chapel John Steeds, 1844, Ann his widow, 1854, and their children Mary Bush, 1819, William, 1842, and Betty Beachim, 1856.

KINGSBURY EPISCOPI

(92) MIDDLE LAMBROOK MEETING-HOUSE (ST 423185). A Presbyterian society was in existence by 1681 and a marriage in an earlier meeting-house was recorded in 1688. That building was registered in 1689 and the present meeting-house on a new site, under construction when the land was acquired in 1727, was registered in 1729. From the end of the 18th century the church was Congregational (now URC).

The walls are of squared rubble with an ashlar front and the

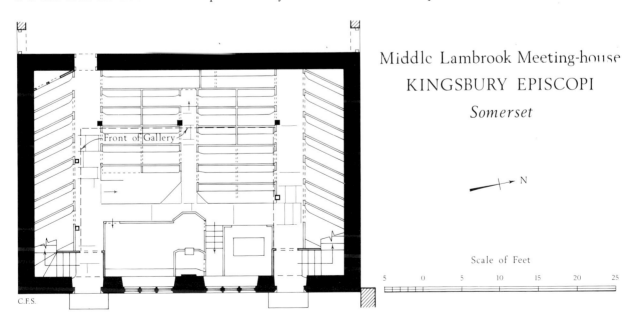

Middle Lambrook Meeting-house
KINGSBURY EPISCOPI
Somerset

N

Scale of Feet

5   0   5   10   15   20   25

C.F.S.

Middle Lambrook Meeting-house. (92)

roof, formerly thatched, has been covered with slates since 1888. The broad E front is dated 1729 on a small tablet between the windows. It has two segmental-arched doorways with moulded jambs and lintels and two round-arched windows of three lights with mullions and transoms and moulded labels. There is a small mullioned window of two lights near the N end of the wall. The rear wall is covered by a modern building with lean-to roof; it formerly had a gallery window at the centre. The N and S walls are gabled and have each one mullioned window of two lights at gallery level.

The interior ($25\frac{3}{4}$ ft by 40 ft) retains its original arrangement of fittings with pulpit against the E wall between the front windows and a gallery around three sides. It is possible that the W gallery was built first and the end galleries added shortly afterwards; all have fielded-panelled fronts supported by six irregularly spaced wooden posts. The floor is paved with stone flags in the aisles and boarding below the pews.

Fittings – *Clock*: on front of W gallery, with shaped dial and short pendulum case, signed 'Reuben Lamude, Chard', dated 1734, with the initials E:A: and M:S:. *Gate Piers*: in front of chapel, square with moulded cornices and ball finials, 18th-century, with mounting steps adjacent. *Monuments* and *Floorslabs*. *Monuments*: in chapel (1) Elizabeth, widow of Henry England, 1815, and Edward their son, 1817; (2) John, son of Edward and Ann England, 1842; (3) Elizabeth (England), wife of William Haggett Richards, gent., 1822; (4) Stephen England, gent., 1821, and Mary his widow, 1829; (5) Henry England, 1848, and Elizabeth (Stuckey) his wife, 1847; (6) Robert England, 1851, and Mary his widow, 1867; (7) Stephen England, 1812, Sarah his widow, 1836, and their sons Francis, 1836, and Stephen, 1851; in burial-ground E of chapel (8) Robert England, 1851, Mary his widow, 1867, and Robert White their son, 1859; (9) Henry England, ?1848, and Elizabeth England, ?1847, panel from table-tomb; (10) Edward England, 1814. *Floorslabs*: in chapel (1) Stephen England, 1824; (2) Elizabeth, wife of Henry England,

Middle Lambrook Meeting-house. (92)

gent., 176[ ]; in N aisle (3) illegible, late 18th-century. *Pulpit*: with panelled front and back-board with cornice, *c.*1729, much reduced in height. *Seating*: early 19th-century box-pews to lower floor, some plain 18th-century seating with shaped arms in gallery.

Anon., *A Short History of Middle Lambrook Meeting 1668–1968* (*c.*1968). Thomas (1896) 53.

(93) Former WESLEYAN (ST 435210). Former chapel, behind present chapel of 1899 facing adjacent street, is inscribed 'built 1810 rebuilt 1852'. Gabled three-bay front with finials and pointed-arched windows with stone Y-tracery.

FORMER WESLEYAN CHAPEL, KINGSBURY EPISCOPI   C·F·S·1971

KINGSTON ST MARY

(94) Former CONGREGATIONAL (ST 216296). Rendered walls and hipped roof, built 1821; Sunday-school added 1864.
Thomas (1896) 64–5.

LANGPORT

(95) Former BAPTIST, Bush Place (ST 421267). Three-bay N front with round-arched upper windows, mid 19th-century.

FORMER BAPTIST CHAPEL, LANGPORT   CFS1975

(96) CONGREGATIONAL (ST 418268). Built 1828–9, refronted 1874 in brick with plate-traceried windows. (URC)
Thomas (1896) 67–8.

LEIGH-ON-MENDIP

(97) WESLEYAN (ST 690472). 'Ebenezer Chapel', rendered three-bay front with tablet dated 1811; Wesleyan School alongside dated 1820.

(98) Former PRIMITIVE METHODIST (ST 689472). Low three-bay ashlar front dated 1835, now a house.

LONG SUTTON

(99) FRIENDS (ST 467259). A meeting at Robert Ford's house at Knole was reported in 1669 and a meeting-house occupied by Richard Nowell was in use from 1670. This last is supposed to have stood N of the present building. The meeting-house, on the S side of the main road N of the village, was built in 1717 at the expense of William Steell (or Steele). It has walls of coursed grey stone and a hipped slated roof with a verge of stone slates. The walls have a low stone plinth, a moulded string-course and a moulded timber cornice below the eaves. The N and S walls have each two sash windows with flat-arched heads and external shutters, and near the E end a wide doorway with moulded timber frame and a segmental canopy. The E wall has upper and lower windows at the centre, the W end has a single window above the stand. A small detached meeting-room was added to W in 1985.

Friends' meeting-house, Long Sutton.   (99)

Friends' meeting-house, Long Sutton.   (99)

The interior (38 ft by 26¾ ft) comprises a single room. The ceiling has a plaster vault rising to collar level and is coved on all sides. A gallery at the E end has a fielded-panelled front closed above and below by shutters; the gallery staircase, enclosed in

Friends' Meeting-house, LONG SUTTON

5   0   5   10   15   20 Feet

Somerset

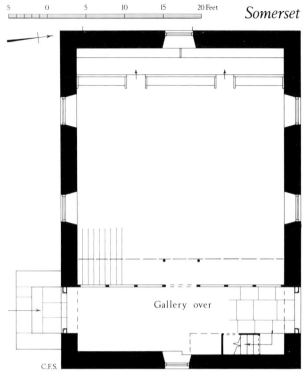

Gallery over

C.F.S.

later boxing, has original turned balusters and lower newel with knob finial. The stand has a panelled back and open-railed front. Benches have shaped plank ends and open backs.

Fittings – *Inscription*: on N wall, externally, 'Ex Dono Willmi Steell Anno Dom 1717'. *Monuments*: in burial-ground to S, Samuel Bull, 1732, headstone; also many uniform headstones of 19th century and later.

Arnold (1960) 98–101.

MARKSBURY   *Avon*

(100) WESLEYAN (ST 667626). Rubble with pantiled roof and ball finials to gables; opened 1838.

MARTOCK

(101) Site of POUND LANE CHAPEL (ST 45951915). A Presbyterian society formed in the late 17th century built a meeting-house on this site about 1722 in which year it was placed in trust. The society, which later became Congregational, was much reduced by the early 19th century and the building was subsequently used for a time by Particular Baptists. An attempt was made in 1906 to resume Congregational services but with no lasting success and by 1950 the chapel had been demolished.

The site is enclosed by stone walls with an entrance from Pound Lane on the N side with stone gate piers with moulded cornices and ball finials. Some fragments of the walls of the former building remain in the E and S sides. The chapel had stone walls and a thatched roof; the main body of the building appears to have been aligned N–S with a wing on the E side probably forming a vestry. The entrance was at the N end with a gallery window above. The interior had a polygonal pulpit at the S end

between a pair of cross-framed windows, side galleries with panelled fronts and central aisle between the pews.

Monuments: in burial-ground (1) William Judoe, 1724; (2) James Patten, 1810, and Rebecca his wife, 1801; (3) Susan, wife of John Rake, 1849, Elihu their son, 1849, John Horwood, 1837, Susan his wife, 1852, *et al.*

CHST III (1905–6) 244–50. Thomas (1896) 45.

(102) CONGREGATIONAL, Bower Hinton (ST 458182). An Independent society was gathered in the late 18th century by the Rev. Christopher Hull, a former student of the Countess of Huntingdon's College, and a church formed in 1830 (now URC). The chapel was built in 1791 and much altered in the late 19th century. The walls are of coursed stone with an ashlar front and the roof is hipped and covered with tiles but with a verge and hips of stone slates. The broad W front originally had a central round-arched entrance with lunette above between two pointed-arched windows of three lights with stone mullions and transoms. In the E wall are three similar pointed windows. In the late 19th century the W entrance was replaced by a third matching window, a new doorway, now covered by a porch, was made in the S wall below an original tripartite lunette and a chancel and vestry were added at the N end.

The interior (50 ft by 30 ft) has a flat plaster ceiling with moulded cornice and an early 19th-century S gallery with contemporary seating.

Fittings – *Clock*: in vestibule, circular brass face with swan-neck pediment and seated female figure above, signed 'Thomas Bray Next St Marg'ts. Church Westminster' and inscribed 'The Gift of Jno. Butler Esq', 18th-century, perhaps from Pound Lane Chapel. *Crockery*: commemorative cup and saucer with picture of chapel before alteration, inscribed 'EBENEZER CHAPEL BOWER-HINTON 1841', by Copeland and Garrett. *Monuments*: in chapel (1) Rev. Christopher Hull, 1814, 'He laid the first stone of this chapel 1791'; (2) Jesse Hopkins, 1848, *et al.*, recording two bequests of £100, signed Barber, Martock; (3) John Culliford, 1796, Mary his widow, 1839, *et al.*, signed Raggett, Weymouth.

Thomas (1896) 45–6.

(103) WESLEYAN (ST 462197). Gabled front with tall thin spirelet at corner, 1886–9.

(104) Former CHAPEL, Highway (ST 466208). Rubble with corrugated-iron roof replacing thatch. Gabled N end to road with tablet above altered entrance roughly inscribed with date 1763. E and W sides have each two round-arched windows of

FORMER CHAPEL, HIGHWAY nr. MARTOCK   CFS 1971

three lights with stone mullions and transoms. The interior
(31¾ft by 17ft) has a plaster ceiling. It is now used as a garage.

MIDDLEZOY

(105) BAPTIST, Burrow Bridge (ST 355308). 'Ebenezer Chapel',
dated 1836, of brick with a hipped slate roof, has a front of three
bays with two pointed-arched windows and a wide doorway
with blind fanlight and later stone porch. At the rear is a later
schoolroom above an open shelter for vehicles or animals.

MILBORNE PORT

(106) CONGREGATIONAL, Chapel Lane (ST 677185). A
Presbyterian society tracing its origin to the preaching of
William Hopkins, ejected vicar of Milborne Port, which fitted up
a meeting-house c.1700, was reorganized as a Congregational
church in 1743 (now URC). The first meeting-house on the
present site, erected in 1752, was 28 ft square with the pulpit
between two front entrances and a single gallery to which side
galleries were added in the early 19th century; it was enlarged to
the W about 1830. The existing chapel, built in 1844, is said to
incorporate the N wall of its predecessor. The walls are rendered
and the roof slated. The E front is gabled and of three bays with
two pointed-arched windows with stone Y-tracery; in the S wall
are three windows and in the W wall two windows, all of similar
design; the N wall is blank. There is a gallery with contemporary
seating around three sides supported by thin cinquefoiled wooden
columns.

Clock: signed 'Samuel Game, Milborne Port', 19th-century.
Monument: in chapel, William Carey King, 1818, Betsy his first
wife, 1791, Sarah his second wife, 1825, *et al.*

Densham and Ogle (1899) 256. Pitman, E. R., *Memorials of the
Congregational Church or 'Old Independent Meeting House', Milborne
Port* (1883). Thomas (1896) 46–7.

MILVERTON

(107) Former CONGREGATIONAL, Fore Street (ST 123258). Built
1821 for a church formed in 1784. Rendered three-bay front, two
tiers of round-arched windows with wooden Y-tracery below a
pedimental gable. Interior, refitted c.1880, has a gallery above the
entrance. (Closed and converted to house c.1975)

Thomas (1896) 57–8.

Former Congregational chapel, Milverton.   (107)

(108) Former FRIENDS, North Street (ST 123260). The meeting-
house, built in 1758 to replace an earlier structure, stands on the
W side of a courtyard off the N side of the main road. The walls
are of rubble and the roof is covered in patent tiles. The E front
has a doorway centrally between two windows and one window
above, all with renewed frames. One upper window remains
high in the N gable and two have lately been inserted in the W
wall. An earlier cottage adjoins to the south.

The interior (18 ft by 20 ft) was reported to have been still in its
original condition c.1950 although Friends' use ceased in 1855
and the building was sold in 1872. It has more recently been
entirely refitted and a gallery around three sides has been rebuilt
in modern materials.

Burial-ground: see Wiveliscombe Without (191).

(109) WESLEYAN, Silver Street (ST 125258). Rubble with three-
bay gabled front; narrow projecting centre bay with cusped-
traceried window above entrance and inscribed band dated 1850.

MINEHEAD

(110) Former BAPTIST, Periton Road (SS 954458). Built c.1817
for a church which moved in 1831 to The Parks. A wide
segmental-arched opening in the gabled end alone remains
recognizable as earlier work after c.1970 conversion to a house.

(111) BAPTIST, The Parks (SS 966462). Built 1831, greatly altered
and enlarged c.1901–2. Rendered walls, block cornice at eaves,
round-arched windows and Doric-columned porch. An

'attractively lettered' inscription above the porch has been removed.

NETHER STOWEY

(112) Former CONGREGATIONAL (ST 192399). Rubble with tiled roof; registered as 'new built' in 1808. Gabled S front with pointed-arched doorway and window with stone Y-tracery above. Two windows in E wall of three lights with plain intersecting tracery, moulded labels and brick relieving arches. One altered window in W wall. *Pulpit*: hexagonal with scrolled back-board and cornice supporting flaming urns and figure of angel, 18th-century. (Chapel demolished since 1971)

Thomas (1896) 63.

CONGREGATIONAL CHAPEL, NETHER STOWEY   CFS·1971

NORTH CADBURY

(113) WESLEYAN (ST 636276). Three-bay gabled front dated 1848.

NORTH CURRY

(114) BAPTIST (ST 315249). 'Ebenezer Chapel' dated 1825, square with pyramidal roof and two tiers of round-arched windows.

(115) WESLEYAN (ST 318251). Brick with hipped roof and tall round-arched windows, dated 1833.

NORTH WOOTTON

(116) PROVIDENCE CHAPEL (ST 563417). Built 1830 by Bible Christians but reopened 1848 by Baptists from Croscombe; now used as garage. Rubble with slate roof half-hipped to front. Shaped gable at front with modern rendering. Stone Y-traceried windows at sides.

NORTON FITZWARREN

(117) CONGREGATIONAL (ST 194259). The chapel, opened 1821, has a rendered three-bay front with a pedimented gable and two tiers of round-arched windows. Large extensions each side for Manse and Sunday-school. The interior, with a segmental barrel-vaulted ceiling, has a gallery next to the entrance approached from the Sunday-school. *Painting*: oil portrait of Rev. W. Gammon, minister c.1839–79. (URC)

Thomas (1896) 64.

NORTON-RADSTOCK   *Avon*

(118) Former METHODIST, High Street, Midsomer Norton (ST 667542). The preaching-house, now used as a hall by the Salvation Army, was occupied by the Wesleyan society until 1859

Former Methodist chapel, Midsomer Norton.   (118)

and subsequently served as a school. It was built or converted at the end of the 18th century and may be 'The Preaching House at the lower end of Midsummer Norton' which was registered in October 1791 'for Independents'.

The walls are of rubble and the roof is covered with slates. The S half of the building, which is rectangular, is part of an earlier structure which has been heightened and enlarged by a trapezoidal extension to the north. The N front is of three bays with two tiers of windows and a later porch. The front windows and two windows set high in the E wall have dressed stone surrounds; two taller windows in the W wall are later and without dressings. The interior ($34\frac{1}{2}$ ft by $41\frac{3}{4}$ ft) has been gutted but traces remain of a gallery around three sides with the pulpit probably against the S wall.

(119) WESLEYAN, High Street, Midsomer Norton (ST 666543). Gothic with corner turret, dated 1859.

NORTON ST PHILIP

(120) Former BAPTIST, High Street (ST 775558). 'Ebenezer Chapel', dated 1814, has a hipped roof and pointed-arched windows with intersecting glazing bars. Rear gallery with panelled front, otherwise refitted. (Now Brethren) *Monument*: in forecourt, William Short, 1831, Elizabeth Short, 1845.

(121) Former BAPTIST, Farleigh Hungerford (ST 803576). Gabled front with two pointed-arched windows flanking altered entrance. Inscribed 'Deo Sacrum 1850'.

(122) Former WESLEYAN, Bell Hill (ST 772559). Pedimented front of three bays with round-arched windows, dated 1836. (Derelict 1971; since converted to house, front windows sub-divided and pediment rebuilt as featureless gable)

NUNNEY

(123) WESLEYAN (ST 736457). Two pointed-arched windows with site of former entrance between, dated 1812.

OLD CLEEVE

(124) WESLEYAN, Washford (ST 047411). Built 1826, greatly altered and enlarged.

Allen (1974) 84–5.

OTTERHAMPTON

(125) BETHEL CHAPEL, Combwich (ST 258424). The chapel was built for Congregationalists in 1838 but occupied since 1879 by

Former Wesleyan chapel, Norton St Philip.   (122)

Wesleyans. The gabled front is rendered and has a central doorway and two upper windows, all with round-arched heads and keystones.

Thomas (1896) 71–2.

PAULTON   *Avon*

(126) BAPTIST (ST 653562). Rubble with ashlar dressings and slate roof. Three-bay gabled front with panelled corner pilasters and apex finial, two pointed-arched windows and ogee-headed doorway with open pediment supported by columns; quatrefoil tablet in gable with dates '1724, rebuilt 1827'. Sides of three bays with two tiers of ogee-arched windows.

(127) WESLEYAN, Park Road (ST 651564). The chapel, built in 1826 to replace a preaching-house of 1776, was enlarged to the front in 1894; the original cast-iron date-tablet of 1826 is reset in a side wall. The 'Wesleyan School' of 1843 adjacent to the rear has a five-bay front with two tiers of pointed-arched windows; the central doorway has been converted to a window.

Warfield, D. A., *A Lively People, the Story of a Village Methodist Society* (1960).

PEASEDOWN ST JOHN   *Avon*

(128) FREE METHODIST, Carlingcott (ST 698582). Rubble with ashlar front, three-light window with intersecting tracery above entrance. Dated 1851.

PILTON

(129) Former BIBLE CHRISTIAN, Pylle Road (ST 592404). 'Ebenezer Chapel' dated 1839, of rubble with a hipped slate roof, has a central doorway and two gallery windows all with intersecting glazing bars under arched heads. The interior, now converted to a house and studio, retains an original gallery with moulded panelled front.

Country Living, February 1990.

PITMINSTER

(130) CONGREGATIONAL, Blagdon Hill (ST 211188). Rubble and slate with pointed-arched windows. Built in 1837 for use as a school in connection with Fulwood chapel. Day-school use ceased in 1914. (URC)

Thomas (1896) 54–5.

(131) Former CONGREGATIONAL, Fulwood (ST 211203). A Presbyterian society in Pitminster, which originated in the preaching of the former vicar, Thomas Forwood, and other ministers ejected in 1662, subsequently had close links with several tutors at the Taunton Academy. The history of this society in the late 18th century is obscure. The cause appears to have revived *c*.1800 when the new chapel was built at Fulwood at the expense of Thomas Welman of Poundisford Park and other members of his family whose hospitality extended to some of the leading ministers of the day. The chapel was closed *c*.1956 and is now used for storage. The walls of brick and stone are rendered and the roof is hipped and slated. The front wall has two round-arched doorways with Tuscan columns supporting open

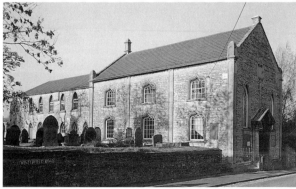

Baptist chapel, Paulton.   (126)

Former Congregational chapel, Fulwood.   (131)

pediments, and two windows above. The side walls are of three bays with two tiers of windows.

Monuments: in burial-ground (1) Rev. James Taylor, 33 years pastor, 1882; (2) Sarah, wife of Rev. James Taylor, ?1881.

Thomas (1896) 54.

PORTISHEAD   *Avon*

(132) FRIENDS, St Mary's Road (ST 465755). Although a building was given in 1669 for use as a meeting-house, the present structure could date from the early 18th century. It has rubble walls and a thatched roof. The original entrance was in the W wall, now replaced by a segmental-arched window, with a similar window to the right and the site of another window covered by a small extension to the left. The N front, partly covered by a late 19th-century porch, has a brick chimney-stack on the gable. The walling at the S end may have been rebuilt.

Friends' meeting-house, Portishead.   (132)

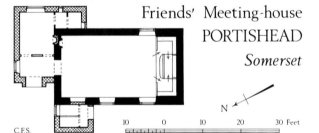

Friends' Meeting-house
PORTISHEAD
Somerset

C.F.S.   10   0   10   20   30 Feet

The interior (30 ft by 15½ ft), entered through an early 19th-century doorway at the N end, has a short stand at the opposite end with fielded-panelled front and dado.

Monument: in burial-ground, small headstone inscribed 'W.H.1687'.

Southall (1974) 7–9.

RODE

(133) BAPTIST (ST 805539). The chapel, built in 1786 for a church formed in 1783, has rubble walls with ashlar dressings; the roof, gabled to front and rear, is covered with slates. The NW front of three bays with two tiers of round-arched windows has a central entrance with flat canopy supported by moulded stone brackets; there is a coved stone band at the base of the gable. The side walls have each two windows at gallery level only. Two round-arched windows in the SE wall flank the pulpit.

Baptist chapel, Rode.   (133)

The interior (34¾ ft by 30¼ ft) has a gallery around three sides, rounded to the NW, supported by six turned wood columns; the panelled front is of early 19th-century character. The roof is supported by three king-post trusses with square-set purlins.

N of the chapel is a small detached building of rubble with a pantiled roof, dated 1839; possibly a school.

Fittings – Clock: on gallery front, early 19th-century. *Inscription*: loose in vestry, painted on board 'It is requested that no PERSON will wear pattens into this place of worship'. *Picture*: lithograph of baptismal scene in river at Rode, by R. Pocock after drawing by W. W. Wheatley. *Seating*: in gallery, early 19th-century; otherwise refitted in late 19th century.

Oliver (1968) 122–3.

(134) Former WESLEYAN, High Street (ST 804538). Gabled three-bay front with two tiers of round-arched windows, central doorway with pedimented surround, and circular tablet in gable dated 1809. The interior, largely refitted in late 19th century, has a rear gallery only. (Proposed conversion to house 1986)

SELWOOD

(135) Former PRIMITIVE METHODIST, Little Keyford (ST 778462). Gabled three-bay front with segmental-arched openings; dated 1854.

SHEPTON MALLET

(136) COWL STREET CHAPEL (ST 619441). The Presbyterian society meeting in Cowl Street, which by the 19th century supported a Unitarian ministry, was disbanded *c*.1961. The society originated in the late 17th century as a branch of a congregation meeting in the vicinity of Ashwick for which a meeting-house had been opened at Downside about 1689. In May

eaves; the centre bays were formerly occupied by two or possibly three bays of windows at two levels, some traces of which survived internally, but which were superseded in the mid 18th century by a pair of wide round-arched windows into which intersecting stone tracery was inserted early in the 19th century.

The N and S walls have each two upper and two lower windows matching those over the entrances. The W wall has no original features. The W wing, of rubble with a tiled roof, has a W gable with stone coping; a doorway approached from rising ground at the rear gives access to the former gallery, now an upper room, and has a window above; in the S wall is a stone mullioned window of three lights.

Former Wesleyan chapel, Rode. (134)

Cowl Street Chapel, SHEPTON MALLET *Somerset*

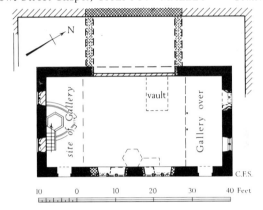

1696 the members living in Shepton Mallet bought the present site from the executors of Abraham Barnard, clothier, and by November of that year, when it was placed in trust, had erected a meeting-house. The building was greatly altered or enlarged in 1758. Further alterations were carried out in 1837–8 and an internal refitting in 1886.

The chapel has rendered rubble walls with ashlar dressings and a hipped slate roof. The main body of the building which faces E dates from 1696 but a wing symmetrically at the rear was added in the mid 18th century to provide additional galleried seating. The front wall has, in the end bays, pedimented doorways and gallery windows above with vestigial pediments close below the

The interior (22½ ft by 45¼ ft) originally had galleries at the N and S ends; the pulpit may have stood centrally against the rear wall but was brought to the front when the rear wing was added. In 1886 the pulpit was re-sited at the S end, the S gallery removed, and N gallery rebuilt with an external staircase, and the W gallery separated from the body of the chapel.

The main roof is supported by four trusses with tie-beams and collars, a diagonal ridge and butt-purlins, with an axial stiffening member between the collars. The tie-beams have housings for substantial oversailing joists, replaced in the 19th century by rafters lower down to provide a flat ceiling. The roof over the W wing has two trusses with collars and ridge-pieces apparently added. The lower purlin of the E roof is omitted at the junction of the two roofs.

Fittings – *Brass*: in chapel between E windows, reset from stone externally in front wall, William Hislop, native of Moffat, 1728. *Communion Rails*: in front of pulpit, late 19th-century, reproducing balusters of pulpit stairs. The communion table and chair referred to by Evans (1897) had been removed before 1970. *Monuments* and *Floorslabs*. *Monuments*: in chapel on E wall (1) Rev. Anthony Atkey, 1734; (2) Rev. Joseph Bull Bristowe, 60 years minister, 1854, marble tablet surmounted by crest, signed 'W. Rawlings'; (3) Elizabeth, wife of Richard Perkins, 1775; (4) Simon Browne, minister, 1732, with details of depressive malady; (5) Elizabeth, daughter of Thomas and Ruth Green, 1849, tablet in Gothic frame signed 'W. Rawlings, Shepton Mallet'; on W wall (6) Abraham Brodribb, clothier of Bowlish, 1804, and Betty his wife, 1803, signed 'H. Wood, Bristol'; (7) James Green, 1798, Ann his widow, 1830, William their son,

Cowl Street Chapel, Shepton Mallet.   (136)

1825, and Jane his wife, 1833, signed 'S. Rawlings'; (8) Thomas Green, gent., of Bowlish, 1817, and Ruth his wife, 1806, signed 'Reeves, Bath', later tablet below erected by their daughter, 1838, signed 'Rawlings, Shepton Mallet'; (9) Lucy, daughter of William and Lucy Cooper of Bowlish, 1835, *et al.*, signed 'Rawlings'; (10) Thomas, son of Thomas and Ruth Green of Bowlish, 1820, and George his brother, nd, signed 'S. Rawlings'; (11) Samuel Painter, 1821, Elizabeth his wife, 1790, and their children Charles, 1817, John, 1824, Sarah, 1829, Elizabeth, 1840, Henry, 1853, signed 'S. Rawlings'; (12) Rev. John Nayler, 1872, Ann his first wife, 1860, and Ann his second wife, 1868, signed 'W. Rawlings'; externally (13) Rev. John Evans, pastor, 1839, loose tablet. *Floorslabs*: above vault in chapel (1) John Watts, gent., 1721, Mary his widow, 17[ ]8, and Mrs Elizabeth Batten, their daughter, 1754; (2) John Watts, clothier of Bowlish, son of the above John Watts of Bodden, 1730, Katherine (Bennet) his widow, 1747, Samuel their son, 1806, Mercy (Bayly) his second wife, 1798, and John their son, clothier, 1785, with shield-of-arms and crest of Watts. *Plate*: includes a two-handled cup of 1799 and a footed plate of 1710. *Pulpit*: hexagonal with flared base above short post, panelled front with enriched mouldings and swags, fielded-panelled back-board with enriched cheeks, canopy with pedimented front and angle finials, stairs with turned and twisted balusters, *c.*1758.

Here lieth the Body of WILLIAM HISLOP *Born in the parish of* MOFFAT *in the County of* ANNANDALE *in* NORTH BRITAIN *Who departed this life* Apr: 25 1728 *Aged* XL *Years*

LONG while with Pains and Sickness sore oppreſt
The Traveller at last lies here at reſt
Reader in deep and awfull thought tread round
Fleſh mouldring into duſt lies underGround
But out of Duſt each saintſhall riſe again
In perfect Life that bars all death and pain

(Pulpit now in the St Nicholas Church Museum, Bristol. Chapel derelict and all fittings removed 1986)

Christian Reformer (1838) 144. Evans (1897) 221–2. Murch (1835) 166–74. *Protestant Dissenters' Magazine* IV (1797) 364–5.

(137) Former INDEPENDENT, Commercial Road (ST 618435). 'Providence Chapel' was built in 1800–1 for a recently formed church which had previously met in a converted workshop at Bowlish named 'Hepzibah Chapel'. The chapel, used since *c*.1960–70 by a Baptist congregation, is a large building of rubble with two tiers of segmental-arched windows with ashlar surrounds. It was extended to the rear in 1814, refitted and the front gable embellished with a shaped coping in 1877.

Thomas (1896) 60–1.

(138) WESLEYAN, Paul Street (ST 620435). 'Ebenezer Chapel', dated 1819, was built for a society which began about 1746 when John Wesley first visited the town; it superseded a preaching-house built in Park Road in 1762. The chapel, which stands on the site of the Tennis Court Inn, is of rubble with an ashlar front of five bays with a raised three-bay pediment, two tiers of round-arched windows and a porch with Tuscan columns. The side walls are of four bays. The interior was divided in 1968–9 when a floor was built at gallery level and all lower fittings apart from the supporting columns were removed. The original gallery seating remains.

Wesleyan chapel, Shepton Mallet.   (138)

Fittings – *Benefaction Tablet*: brass, recording bequest by Charles King, 1872. *Light Fitting*: in centre of ceiling, gas light with nine multiple burners and pierced ventilator, late 19th-century. *Monument*: in gallery on W wall, Eliza, wife of James M. Byron, minister, 1803, wooden tablet painted to resemble marble on dark surround surmounted by celestial crown.

Anon., *Shepton Mallet Methodist Church, 1819–1969* (1969).

SHOSCOMBE   *Avon*

(139) PRIMITIVE METHODIST, Single Hill (ST 721563). Built 1849 with three-bay front, greatly altered, heightened and enlarged 1878.

(140) FREE METHODIST, Upper Shoscombe (ST 711564). The chapel of 1892 and predecessor of 1859 stand adjacent.

SOMERTON

(141) CONGREGATIONAL (ST 489285). Rubble with hipped roof, built 1803 for a congregation which earlier occupied a former Presbyterian meeting-house, enlarged to front in late 19th century; oval tablet reset in front gable. (URC)

Thomas (1896) 55.

(142) WESLEYAN, West Street (ST 489286). Coursed stone with gabled front and three slender pinnacles (two lost since 1970); three pointed-arched windows with stone Y-tracery and central doorway; dated 1845. Interior has a gallery above entrance with original seating.

Wesleyan chapel, Somerton.   (142)

Fittings – *Clock*: on front of gallery, by W. Goodwyn, Taunton, mid 19th-century. *Communion Rails*: with chamfered balusters, mid 19th-century. *Monument*: in chapel, Samuel Barnard, local preacher, 1869.

(143) Former BIBLE CHRISTIAN, Sutton Road (ST 486285). 'Zion Chapel', coursed stone with a half-hipped slate roof and two round-arched windows above entrance, built 1841.

'ZION CHAPEL', SOMERTON   C.F.S.1970

SOUTH BARROW

(144) UNITED METHODIST (ST 601278). Coursed stone with half-hipped tiled roof, round-arched windows. Inscribed 'Pisgah Chapel 1857'.

SOUTH PETHERTON

(145) Site of PRESBYTERIAN, Palmer Street (ST 431170). The Presbyterian society formed in the late 17th century suffered from a doctrinal division after 1747 when the more orthodox members seceded; it was disbanded in 1842. The meeting-house, which stood E of Rock House, may have been built before 1700; it seems to have been demolished by 1881 when a change was made in the trust deeds where the size of the site is quoted as 55 ft by 45 ft and the burial-ground 22 ft by 48 ft.

The burial-ground is bounded to the N by an early 18th-century wall with stone gate piers and ball finials.

Monuments: against E boundary wall (1) George Tupp, 1799, Hannah Tupp, 1791, Ann Tupp, 1766, Elizabeth Chapman, 1764; (2) Henry Rutter (?), 1734, with decayed Latin inscription; (3) Hannah Ostler, nd, William Ostler, 1821, and Thomas Ostler, 1835; also several illegible stones, and one inscribed 'PP 1784'. *Plate*: now in Taunton Museum, two beakers with embossed decoration, 1691, 1697.

CHST III (1907–8) 25–6. Evans (1897) 113. Thomas (1896) 43–4.

(146) Former CONGREGATIONAL, St James's Street (ST 435169). The chapel, built in 1862 for a congregation derived from the foregoing, superseded a meeting-house of 1775. Three-bay gabled front with stepped buttresses and pinnacles. *Monuments*: (1) Richard Herdsman, pastor, 1815, brass; (2) Rev. Edward Paltridge, 1854. (Closed since 1980)

Thomas (1896) 43–4

(147) WESLEYAN, Palmer Street (ST 432170). Built 1882 as memorial to Thomas Coke, curate 1771–7, pioneer of Methodism in America.

SPAXTON

(148) Former AGAPEMONITE, Four Forks (ST 233369). Following the removal of the rector of Charlinch, the Rev. Samuel Starkey, and his curate, G. R. Thomas, one of the 'Lampeter Brethren', for irregular religious practices, a chapel was built *c*.1849 for the use of the latter. This was probably designed by William Cobbe, a civil engineer, who also preached

there. The chapel shortly afterwards became the nucleus of an Agapemonite settlement under the leadership of the Rev. H.J. Prince. It is now in commercial use.

The walls are of rubble with five bays of pointed-arched windows at each side and a gabled S front of three bays, formerly surmounted by a lion, and a porch with buttresses and octagonal finials. The interior, perhaps rearranged in the later 19th century, had a wide pointed arch at the N end enclosing a fireplace and overmantel, and a canopied rostrum towards the rear on the W side.

Glass: in leaded panes, with floral pattern in arched head and coloured borders, the pieces being of varying thickness, late 19th-century.

Dixon, W.H., *Spiritual Wives* I (1868) 226–331. McCormick, D., *Temple of Love* (1962). Montgomery, J., *Abodes of Love* (1962) 175–94, pl. fcg 128.

STOGUMBER

(149) BAPTIST (ST 097372). Square with pyramidal roof, front partly covered by adjacent manse, mid 19th-century. (Closed 1990)

STOKE ST MARY

(150) STOKE CHAPEL (ST 263223). The chapel, built for Independents in 1825 but subsequently occupied by Wesleyans, has a low gabled front of three bays with pointed-arched windows.

Thomas (1896) 65–6.

Former Agapemonite chapel, Spaxton. (148)

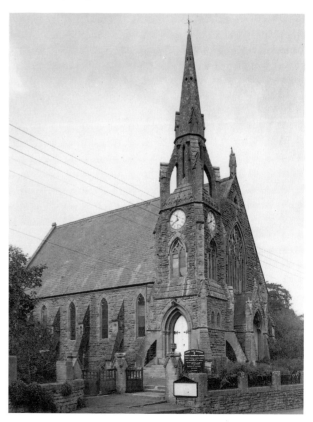

Congregational chapel, West Stoke. (151)

Friends' meeting-house, Street.   (152)

STOKE-SUB-HAMDON

(151) CONGREGATIONAL, West Stoke (ST 473176). Gothic chapel by R. C. Bennett of Weymouth, opened 1866. NE tower with spirelet supported by flying buttresses, five-bay nave above basement schoolroom and later four-bay pseudo-chancel to W of *c*.1889 with traceried end window and bell-cote on gable. The W extension is divided internally to encompass a two-bay chancel replacing the original semicircular organ-apse.

Monument: in chapel, Richard Southcombe, 19 years deacon, 1885, 'It was mainly through his efforts that this place of worship and the minister's house were erected'. (URC)

CYB (1867) 361. Thomas (1896) 74–5.

STREET

(152) FRIENDS, High Street (ST 485369). The meeting-house of 1850 by J. Frank Cotterell superseded a building in use from *c*.1718. Ashlar with rusticated plinth and quoins, hipped slate roof. The broad S front has a pedimented porch with Tuscan columns, two tall windows to the left and three to the right. The E end bay is divided internally into two storeys; the remainder comprises a large meeting-room at the W end and smaller room to the E divided by a screen with double shutters. The stand at the W end has an open-railed front; seating includes benches with turned supports below shaped arms, and wall-benches.

Books: library of 17th to 19th-century works, some inscribed 'Monthly Meeting of the Middle Division of Somerset', including George Fox, *Gospel Truth Demonstrated in a Collection of Doctrinal Books* (1706). *Monuments*: in burial-ground to W, uniform headstones of mid 19th century and later.

TAUNTON

(153) MARY STREET CHAPEL (ST 228242). The Particular Baptist church, in existence by 1646, gradually modified its theological position during the 18th century so that, by the beginning of the 19th century, it had come to accept Unitarian doctrines. In 1815 the church was joined by the remnant of a Presbyterian society whose 'New Meeting-house', built in Tancred Street *c*.1732, was then demolished. Mary Street Chapel is said to have been built in 1721 although a conveyance of the site and buildings 'to be used as a place of worship by Baptists' dated September 1730 could indicate a slightly later date.

The chapel stands on the S side of Mary Street, formerly part of Paul or Pole Street. The walls are of brickwork with later rendering at the front, and the roofs, hipped with a central valley, have been re-covered with patent tiles. The N front was greatly altered in the late 19th century when it was embellished with rendered decoration comprising two tiers of pilasters with entablatures in five bays; a wide pediment, removed *c*.1912, was placed above the three central bays. The lower windows and central doorway with pedimented surround have been altered but are on the sites of former openings; the three upper windows were originally oval. The S wall is unaltered and has two tall round-arched windows with a large oval window centrally above the pulpit. The W wall, now covered by later buildings, had three oval windows at gallery level, visible internally; the E wall is blank.

The interior (44¾ft by 49¼ft, slightly reducing in width to the S) retains many original fittings. Two cased timber posts supporting the roof structure have tall moulded plinths and bases,

Mary Street Chapel, Taunton. (153)

square fluted shafts, Corinthian capitals and entablature blocks. The flat plaster ceiling has a moulded modillion cornice. The gallery around three sides has a bolection-moulded fielded-panelled front supported by square columns; wide staircases in the NE and NW corners with turned balusters and newels probably date from 1826 when £600 was spent in repairs and alterations. The roof structure is in two parallel ranges, each with five trusses having king-posts with struts and a yoke or collar below the ridge; the central valley is partly covered by a later cross roof.

Fittings – *Baptismal Basins*: (1) artificial stone, octagonal with mediaeval ornament and angels with scrolls below bowl, height 7⅛ in. *c.*1850; (2) glazed pottery, 'St Mary's, Nottingham' type, lid with gabled finial, *c.*1870. *Chandelier*: brass, three tiers each of eight scrolled branches with dove finial, shaft with three spherical bosses, the lowest inscribed 'NATHANIEL WEBB 1728'; scrolled iron standard above. *Clock*: on front of N gallery, octagonal face, 18th-century. *Monuments*: in chapel, on S wall (1) Malachi Blake M.D., 1843, and Mary (Locke) his widow, 1844; (2) Richard Meade King (formerly Meade), 1866, Elizabella (Warren) his wife, 1825, and Frederick their son, 1834; (3) Rev. Theophilus Edwards, minister of the Mint, Exeter, 1833, Susan his wife, 1829, and Elizabeth Parr their daughter, wife of Rev. H. Davies, 1820; on W wall (4) John Warren M.D., 1789, *et al.*; (5) Bartholomew Rosselloty, native of Masdasil, Comté de Foix, 1824, and Jane his wife, native of La Rochelle, 1813, erected by Jane Dowlin their daughter; (6) John Noble, merchant, 1733, Jane his widow, 1777, their children Samuel, 1744, Mary Totterdell, 1780, *et al.*, marble tablet with moulded base and

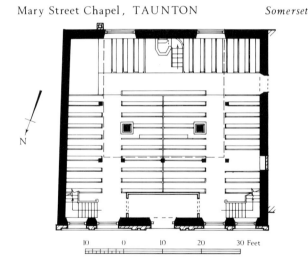

Mary Street Chapel, TAUNTON   *Somerset*

cornice, shaped apron with cherub's head, surmounted by scrolls, flaming urn and lamps, signed 'E. Osborn, Bristol'; (7) Samuel Daw, 1820, *et al.*; on N wall (8) Maria Mitchell, 1829; (9) Benjamin Cornish, 1860; (10) Thomas Gilbert, 1843, and Jane his widow, 1875; on E wall (11) Lieut. Robert Smith, 'died of a fever in the West Indies', 1796, erected by his father, Captain Smith, during the ministry of his uncle Rev. Dr Joshua Toulmin, inscribed 'Erected May 30th 1797, G. Hutchings, Mason'; (12) John Capon, 1806, Salome his widow, 1815, and John their son, 1801, signed 'M. Long'; (13) Mrs Joggett, 1813. *Plate*: includes a set of four cups, four plates and two flagons, 1746, given by

Mary Street Chapel, Taunton.   (153)

Samuel Noble 'Attorney at Law of Taunton to the Baptist Meeting of that Place', inscribed date 1744/5. *Pulpit*: polygonal with flared base, panelled sides with upper bands of carved ornament, back-board with scrolled cheeks and pediment with flaming urn, *c*.1721, all lowered by about 2 ft in late 19th century. *Seating*: to lower floor, reconstructed in 19th century using old material but reduced in height; seating in E and W galleries and at ends of N gallery early 18th-century.

Evans (1897) 238–40. Ivimey II (1814) 554–6. Murch (1835) 192–210.

(154) PAUL'S MEETING-HOUSE, Paul Street (ST 229243). The Presbyterian society, later Congregational (now URC), was formed about 1662 by Joseph Alleine, ejected curate of St Mary Magdalene, Taunton, and numerous licences for Presbyterian teachers and meeting-places were issued in 1672. A meeting-house is said to have been built in that year but to have been sacked at the time of the Monmouth Rebellion. In 1732 part of the congregation seceded to form a 'New Meeting' in Tancred Street which eventually united with the Baptists at Mary Street. The present meeting-house, built in 1797, has brick walls and a hipped slated roof. The W front of five bays has two tiers of windows with flat-arched heads and altered frames; prior to late 19th-century alterations it had a central entrance, now converted to a window, and subsidiary entrances with pedimented surrounds between the end pairs of bays, now concealed by brick porches; the cornice was formerly surmounted by urns at the centre and ends. At the rear is an early 19th-century Sunday-school and alongside is a Memorial Hall built in 1862.

The interior (50½ ft by 60 ft), refitted in the late 19th century, has a gallery around three sides. The pulpit centrally against the E wall is flanked by two round-arched windows, now blocked.

Fittings – *Clock*: on front of W gallery, late 18th-century. *Monuments*: in chapel (1) Henry Groves, 1737, with Latin inscription; (2) Josiah Peacock, 1775; (3) John Westcott, sergemaker, 1781; (4) Thomas Parsons, 1800, and Mary his wife, 1798; (5) Samuel Reed, wool merchant, 1770, Betty his first wife, 1756, and Mary his second wife, 1807; (6) Rev. Henry Addiscott, 1860; (7) George, son of Abraham and Elizabeth Sheppard, 1818; (8) Rev. Immanuel Harford, 1706, cartouche with Latin inscription; (9) Rev. Thomas Reader, 1794, signed 'M. Long'; (10) Rev. Isaac Tozer, 1820, signed 'John Long'; (11) James Bunter, 1848. *Paintings*: in library, portraits in oils of Rev. Joseph Alleine M.A., minister 1662–8, and Rev. George Newton M.A., minister 1670–81, dated 1670; also in vestry six portraits of former ministers. *Plate*: includes one cup of 1634, one two-handled cup with embossed decoration, 1667, given by Rollin Mallock, two two-handled gadrooned cups, 1703, 1705, and two plain two-handled cups, 1736, 1750. *Rainwater-head*: on N wall, dated 1797.

CHST III (1907–8) 116. Crippen, Rev. T.G., *The Story of Paul's Meeting, Taunton* (1969, unpublished typescript). *CYB* (1863) 334. Murch (1835) 193–4.

(155) BAPTIST, Silver Street (ST 232244). Particular Baptists from Wellington commenced a new cause in 1814. The chapel, opened 20 September 1815, was refronted and refitted in 1870. A gallery around three sides was built *c*.1830. *Paintings*: portraits in oils of Richard Horsey, pastor 1814–22, and Anna his wife.

Ivimey IV (1830) 302–3.

(156) CONGREGATIONAL, North Street (ST 228247). Built 1844 for seceders from Paul's Meeting. Gabled W front of rubble with corner buttresses formerly rising to tall octagonal pinnacles, lancet windows, gabled porches at ends of aisles. Interior with stone arcades to N and S, galleries added 1851. *Monument*: S of chapel, to Joseph Clarke, deacon, 1869, and Catharine his wife, 1844.

(157) FRIENDS, Bath Place (ST 226244). Built 1816; brick with hipped roof, five tall windows with altered frames high in W wall. Interior, much changed, has large meeting-room at N end and smaller room to S with gallery over.

(158) THE OCTAGON, Middle Street (ST 229248). The former Methodist chapel, latterly used by Brethren and subsequently as a social club, was opened by John Wesley on 6 March 1776. It remained in use until 1811 when the society moved to The Temple (159). The walls are of brickwork and the roof is tiled. The sides have each a single round-arched window with a circular window above. The entrance on the N was later covered by a double porch and a schoolroom was built to the rear; these additions were removed during a major reconstruction of the site in 1987.

Paul's Meeting-house, Taunton. Before late 19th-century alteration.	(154)

The Octagon, Taunton.	(158)

The Octagon, Taunton. Former gate piers. (158)

The Octagon, Taunton. (158)

The interior ($40\frac{1}{4}$ ft span) has a gallery around five sides with panelled front supported by six wooden columns. The roof structure includes a central king-post with eight lower struts, some now removed, and two upper struts. *Gate Piers*: at entrance from Middle Street, with panelled sides, cornices and vase finials, *c*.1776; have been removed since 1963.

(159) THE TEMPLE, Upper High Street (ST 226242). A building on this site erected 1808–9 by James Lackington, a London bookseller of unsettled but mainly Methodist persuasion, which was named 'The Temple', was sold in 1811 to the Wesleyan society formerly meeting in the Octagon. It was described in 1822 as 60 ft by 40 ft with galleries around three sides and a pulpit at the N end. The building was altered and schoolrooms added in 1840 to designs by James Wilson of Bath who probably built the present S front. A new school building was erected E of the chapel in 1868 and the chapel was partly rebuilt, extended to the W and the interior reorientated *c*.1870–4.

The walls are of brick with stone dressings and the roof is slated. The S front of 1840 is gabled and divided into three bays by stepped buttresses formerly rising to crocketted pinnacles and with a finial at the apex of the gable. At each end of the elevation is a square porch rising to an octagonal turret; the E turret was altered *c*.1870 by the addition of buttresses and by a tall open spire which has now been removed. The interior, now facing W, has galleries supported by tall cast-iron columns which carry an open timber roof.

Monuments: in chapel (1) William French, 1845, and Ruth his wife, 1839; (2) Rev. Francis Collier, 1851, and Prudence his wife, 1845; (3) Anna, daughter of Rev. Joseph Earnshaw, 1839, and Ann his wife, 1839. *Organ*: at W end, by James Philpott of Exeter, 1878. *Panelling*: reset on landing in Sunday-school, with applied Gothic tracery, perhaps from former gallery fronts, *c*.1840.

(160) WESLEYAN, Victoria Street (ST 236246). Gabled front with corner buttresses and pinnacles, gabled porch with traceried doors; grouped lancets. Built 1839, closed 1979. (Demolished)

TIMBERSCOMBE

(161) BIBLE CHRISTIAN (SS 957420). 'Providence Chapel' built 1836 has a rendered gabled front and a round-arched doorway. Below the chapel is a small cottage or schoolroom.

TIMSBURY   *Avon*

(162) WESLEYAN, South Road (ST 670586). Gabled ends with obelisk finials, tall round-arched windows, central doorway at W end. Opened 1805.

TRUDOXHILL

(163) CONGREGATIONAL (ST 749438). The formerly Presbyterian society formed in the late 17th century bought their present meeting-house in 1717. The building was erected or enlarged in 1699 by Robert Newport as a private house and retains its original domestic proportions. On conversion to a meeting-house the upper floor was removed; the roof was ceiled in 1776, the lower seating was renewed in 1847 and that in the gallery after 1853 when an additional window was inserted at the E end; a further internal renovation took place in 1892 and a schoolroom was built to the W in 1898.

The walls are of rubble and the hipped roof is covered with slates. The N wall facing the road is of four bays with two tiers of windows of two lights with ovolo-moulded mullions, and a moulded string-course above the heads of the lower windows. A tablet centrally between the upper windows is inscribed 'R^N_A 1699' for Robert and Ann Newport. The entrance at the E end has a square head and moulded jambs. A staircase wing and later vestry project to the south.

The interior (40 ft by 13 ft) has a gallery at the E end with three bolection-moulded panels at the front separated by pilasters; the staircase has shaped flat balusters. The pulpit is at the W end.

Congregational chapel, Trudoxhill.   (163)

Baptist chapel, Watchet.   (165)

original rear gallery supported by four timber columns; the gallery front has been replaced by an open iron balustrade.

Monuments: in chapel (1) John Palmer, gent., 1776, Julia [   ], nd, 'Mrs. B.P.N.', 1793, 'Mr. Jas. N. Min'r', 1806; (2) John Gimblett, 1867, and Isett his wife, 1831.

Allen (1974) 86.

WEDMORE

(166) BAPTIST, Grants Lane (ST 435477). The church was in existence by 1655 in which year it was represented at meetings of the Western Association of Particular Baptists; it joined the General Baptist Assembly in 1803. After 1811, when the formerly Unitarian minister changed his views, the church reverted to its earlier allegiance. The chapel was rebuilt in the early 19th century; the walls are rendered and the windows have four-centred arched heads and wooden frames.

Aspland, R. B., *Memoir of the Life, Works and Correspondence of the Rev. Robert Aspland, of Hackney* (1850) 297–302.

(167) BAPTIST, Crickham (ST 436499). Plain building with round-arched windows and porch with stone columns. Opened 24 October 1841.

BM XXXIII (1841) 642.

(168) WESLEYAN, Sand Road (ST 432476). Rubble walls and hipped slate roof. Broad three-bay front divided by pilasters, with central porch and round-arched windows. Dated 1817, refitted late 19th century.

WELLINGTON

(169) BAPTIST, South Street (ST 13952050). The chapel was built in 1833 to replace one of 1731–2; it has rendered walls and a

Fittings – *Benefaction Board*: wood, early 19th-century. *Coffin Stools*: pair, with turned legs and shaped upper rails, 18th-century. *Monuments*: on W wall (1) Rev. John Callaway, 1837, and Jane his wife, 1828, signed 'Chalker'; (2) Rev. David Watts, 1822, signed 'Chapman, Frome'. *Plate*: includes a two-handled cup, 1802. *Pulpit*: polygonal with bolection-moulded panels, early 18th-century.

WALTON-IN-GORDANO   *Avon*

(164) Former CONGREGATIONAL (ST 426732). Cottage of *c*.1800 in terrace of three, converted *c*.1849 by removal of floor and insertion of tall arched front window. Now used for storage.

WATCHET

(165) BAPTIST, Brendon Road (ST 071431). Meetings were commenced in 1770 by Countess of Huntingdon's ministers; two cottages, bought by John Palmer for use as a meeting-house, were registered for Independents in 1773. By 1806 the church had become Baptist. The present chapel, built in 1824, has rendered walls and a front of three bays with two tiers of round-arched windows and an arched gable. In the late 19th century a square porch was built in front and the interior refitted. There is an

Baptist chapel, Wellington.   (169)

hipped slate roof with wide eaves. The S front has a broad porch with attached columns and a dated inscription in raised lettering on the entablature. The chapel was enlarged and interior much altered in 1877.

Fittings – *Monuments*: in chapel (1) William Cadbury, 1847; (2) John Parsons, gent., 1816, *et al.*; (3) Thomas Elworthy, 1834, *et al.*; (4) Miss Elizabeth Cadbury, 1829; (5) John Cape, 1804; (6) Rev. Robert Day, 'first pastor', 1791; (7) Rev. Richard Horsey, 25 years deacon, and founder and first pastor of Silver Street Church, Taunton, 1831, and Anna his widow, 1842. *Painting*: oil portrait of John Cape, deacon, 1771–1804.

Ivimey IV (1830) 295–7.

(170) CONGREGATIONAL, Fore Street (ST 138205). The formerly Presbyterian congregation (now URC) in existence by the late 17th century built the first meeting-house on this site in 1730; 'The Presbyterian Meeting House' was registered in 1799 and superseded by the present chapel built in 1861. The walls are of rubble; the gabled front has massive stepped buttresses surmounted by pinnacles and three pointed-arched traceried windows above the entrance. The roof is supported by open scissor-braced trusses. There is a rear gallery. *Monument*: in burial-ground, John Vickrey, 1791, and Mary his widow, 1811. (Proposed conversion to mixed use 1987)

Thomas (1896) 53–4.

(171) FRIENDS, High Street (ST 141207). The first meeting-house was built in 1694. The present building, of 1844–5, standing behind no. 18 High Street, is of brick with a gabled N front of three bays and two tiers of segmental-arched windows. The interior has a gallery along the N and W sides, minor rooms below the N gallery flanking the vestibule, shutters below the front of the W gallery, and a stand against the E wall.

(172) Former BIBLE CHRISTIAN, Scott's Lane (ST 142205). Rubble with three-bay gabled front, round-arched windows with brick dressings. Built 1848 and superseded 1899–1900 by a new chapel in Waterloo Road. (Now Salvation Army)

WELLS

(173) Former CONGREGATIONAL, Union Street (ST 548457). The chapel, now in commercial use, was built *c*.1800 at the expense of a sister of the Rev. Rowland Hill. In 1917 the church,

of mid 18th-century origin, formed a United church with the Baptists at Ebenezer Chapel. The walls are of rubble with an ashlar front and the hipped roof, which has a central valley at collar level, is covered with patent tiles. The windows have pointed-arched heads and stone Y-tracery. No interior features remain.

Thomas (1896) 56.

FORMER CONGREGATIONAL CHAPEL, WELLS   CF·S 1970

(174) EBENEZER CHAPEL, Union Street (ST 548457), N of the foregoing, was built in 1827 for a Baptist church formed in 1814 with the assistance of members from Croscombe, with which

'Ebenezer Chapel', Union Street, Wells.   (174)

Congregationalists (now URC) united in 1917. The rendered front of three bays has a moulded cornice, central entrance with attached columns, and two tiers of round-arched windows.

(175) WESLEYAN, Southover (ST 548454). The chapel opened 1838, possibly standing on the site of a Presbyterian meeting-house registered in 1740, was 'enlarged 1865 and 1898'. Ashlar front, rendered sides and hipped slate roof. Three-bay front with panelled terminal pilasters, platband and moulded cornice, two tiers of round-arched windows and central entrance with attached columns and Doric entablature.

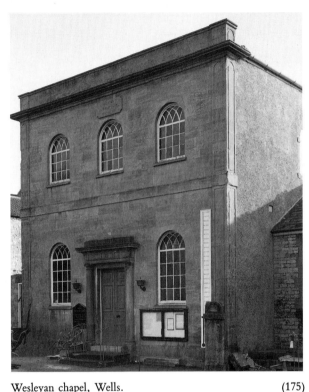

Wesleyan chapel, Wells. (175)

WEST CHINNOCK

(176) Former WESLEYAN, Higher Street (ST 467133). The chapel, built c.1825 and extended in 1913 by the addition of a schoolroom to the N, has rubble walls and a pantiled roof. The S wall has two round-arched windows of three lights with mullions and transoms and a similar window to the right which,

differing in minor details, may indicate a mid 19th-century enlargement to the east. The interior has a barrel-vaulted ceiling. (Closed c.1980)

WEST HUNTSPILL

(177) WESLEYAN, Huntspill (ST 310456). Brick with stone dressings and a dark-glazed pantiled roof. Front of three bays with stepped corner buttresses and crocketted pinnacles; slightly projecting centre bay with inscribed band above entrance dated 1851.

Wesleyan chapel, West Huntspill. (177)

WESTON-SUPER-MARE   *Avon*

(178) WESLEYAN, Uphill (ST 320588), with elaborate shield-shaped tablet dated 1841, greatly altered.

(179) EBENEZER CHAPEL, Lawrence Road, Worle (ST 355629), opened in 1813 probably by Wesleyans, was later used by Free Methodists. Rendered walls and slate roof, gabled front with round-arched doorway and upper windows; later schoolroom alongside.

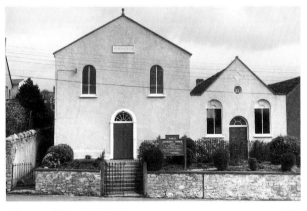

'Ebenezer Chapel', Worle. (179)

WEST PENNARD

(180) Former WESLEYAN, Piltown (ST 553390). The chapel, built c.1803 and converted to a house since 1970, has stone walls and a slate roof. The N front of three bays has a narrow pediment between curved parapets, pointed-arched windows and a blind quatrefoil above the entrance.

Former Wesleyan chapel, Piltown. (180)

WHATLEY

(181) Former PRIMITIVE METHODIST, Chantry (ST 717469). Rendered walls with wide pointed-arched windows. Mid 19th-century.

WINCANTON

(182) BAPTIST, Mill Street (ST 712286). The chapel, built 1832–3, has rendered walls; the front of three bays with tall round-arched windows has an open pediment to the centre bay. The interior was greatly altered and refitted in the late 19th century and the galleries removed. 'Baptist Schools' in front dated 1887.

(183) Former CONGREGATIONAL, Mill Street (ST 711286). Services conducted by Countess of Huntingdon's ministers began *c.*1770 and eventually a house in North Street was converted to a meeting-house. The present chapel was built 1799–1800 and much altered in the late 19th century, both internally and by the application of additional embellishment to the front. The walls are of brick with stone quoins and other dressings and the roof is slated. The S front has a central doorway between two pedimented windows and arched windows above; a wheel window has been inserted into the altered gable. 'Congregational Chapel Schools' in front dated 1859.

Thomas (1896) 56–7.

(184) FRIENDS, High Street (ST 715286). A late 19th-century meeting-house of brick and tile behind buildings on the S side of the street, W of the Dolphin Hotel, replaces a building of 1832. The burial-ground was in use 1833–1935.

WINSCOMBE
Avon

(185) Former FRIENDS, Sidcot (ST 427574). The meeting-house, built in 1712–13 to replace a building occupied since 1690, was superseded in 1817 and has been converted to a cottage, 'Harbury Batch'. It is approximately 28 ft square externally, with rendered walls, probably of rubble, and a hipped roof with short central valley at collar level now covered with patent tiles. The fenestration was entirely altered in 1818 and later and the front now faces west. The interior appears to have had a gallery along the N side of which the supporting beam of the front survives, and possibly a doorway centrally in the N wall.

The present meeting-house (ST 429575) of 1817 has been greatly altered and enlarged for the use of the Friends' School. *Burial-ground*: S of former meeting-house, dated 1690.

Knight, F., *A History of Sidcot School* (1908).

WINSHAM

(186) CONGREGATIONAL (ST 376065). The church, now URC, originated in the late 17th century. A meeting-house of 1760 was superseded by the present chapel, dated 1811. This has rendered stone walls with rusticated quoins and a hipped roof. The broad front of three bays has a central doorway and two tiers of round-arched windows. Two tall windows in the rear wall mark the former site of the pulpit. The interior has been refitted and reorientated and the galleries removed.

Monuments: in chapel (1) Rev. William Durnford, 20 years pastor, 1829; (2) Richard Chaffey, 1834, Ann (Trenchard) his wife, 1831, their sons Benjamin, 1849, and Richard Trenchard, 1854, and Grace Ann, widow of Benjamin Chaffey, 1877, signed 'Chislett, Beaminster'; in burial-ground at front (3) James Fowler, 1832, Ann his widow, 1866, and Robert their son, 1837; (4) Rev. Thomas Childs, 1832.

Thomas (1896) 51–2.

WITHYCOMBE

(187) Former BIBLE CHRISTIAN (ST 016412). Small chapel with rendered walls; gabled front with round-arched window over later porch. Built 1846, closed 1973 and since converted to house.

Allen (1974) 90–1.

WITHYPOOLE

(188) Former WESLEYAN, Withypool (SS 846356). Built 1881 (*pace* Dolbey *et al.*), closed 1967 and converted to house since 1973.

Allen (1974) 90–2. Dolbey (1964) 170–1.

WIVELISCOMBE

(189) CONGREGATIONAL, Silver Street, Golden Hill (ST 08152790). The formerly Presbyterian congregation traces its origin to the ejection of the vicar, George Day, who was preaching here in 1669–72. The chapel, dated 1708, was rebuilt in 1825. The walls are rendered and the hipped roof is covered with slates. The front is of three bays with two tiers of round-arched windows. The interior (50 ft by 29¾ ft) has an early 19th-century rear gallery and a later gallery along one side. The pulpit and seating were renewed in the late 19th century. An early 19th-century Sunday-school faces the front of the chapel across a small courtyard.

Monument: in chapel, Rev. Joseph Buck, 30 years pastor, 1837, and Anna his widow, 1851. *Organ*: Thomas (1896) reports organ in gallery formerly property of the Hon. Spencer Percival, lent to Napoleon, recovered 1817, installed here 1829. *Rainwater-heads*: two, on front wall, moulded lead, 1825.

Thomas (1896) 47–8.

(190) Former WESLEYAN, South Street (ST 081276). Rendered façade with steep central gable and lancets, 1845. (Closed c.1985)

WIVELISCOMBE WITHOUT

(191) FRIENDS' BURIAL-GROUND (ST 106260), S of 'Quaking House', is associated with the meeting at Milverton (see (108)). Long rectangular enclosure bounded by stone and earth walls, gateway with cast-iron plate dated 1681. A few flat rectangular stone tablets remain of the 19th century and later.

WOOLAVINGTON

(192) Former WESLEYAN (ST 348417). Stone with three-bay gabled front dated 1838; much altered or rebuilt 1865.

WRAXALL   *Avon*

(193) Former WESLEYAN, Lower Failand (ST 519736). Small three-bay chapel with dentil cornice and hipped pantiled roof. Built 1825, converted to cottage c.1965.

YATTON   *Avon*

(194) FRIENDS, Claverham (ST 453663). A meeting at 'Clareham' was in existence by 1672 in which year the present site was given by Robert Dawson for a burial-place and as the site for a meeting-house. A new meeting-house erected in 1729

Friends' Meeting-house, Claverham
YATTON   *Somerset*

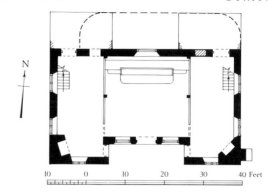

remained in use until 1866 when it was superseded by one at Yatton. The former building then served for occasional meetings but by 1950 it had fallen into decay; it was repaired c.1955.

The meeting-house has rubble walls, formerly limewashed but now covered with a harsh concrete rendering, and a hipped pantiled roof. It comprises a central meeting-house recessed

Friends' meeting-house, Claverham. Before refurbishment.   (194)

between two wings both now converted to cottages, but that to the E originally part of the public area. The S front has a central round-arched doorway between two windows and a smaller window above, all with widely splayed outer jambs and keystones; a stone pedestal above the entrance, carrying a sundial and urn, is inscribed 'This house rebuilt in the year 1729'. The wings have each a small doorway in the return walls and two tiers of windows at the front which, before 1955, had wooden casements with small panes. Chimney-stacks at the outer corners have curved parapets at the base.

The interior retains a central meeting-room (20¼ ft by 21½ ft) rising through the full height of the building with a stand at the N end and a window above. The W side has two tiers of shutters opening from the adjacent cottage. The E side, which formerly comprised a gallery with space below, has an open-railed gallery front now closed by a modern wall to the first floor and with fielded panelling below. The lower storey of the E wing, which has a corner fireplace, may originally have served as a women's meeting-house.

Fittings – *Doors*: in central doorway, panelled with wrought-iron hinges, early 18th-century. *Monuments*: in burial-ground behind outbuildings to N, flat marker-stones and nine re-sited stones, perhaps from Yatton, 19th-century. *Sundial*: above entrance, cube with dials on three faces, 1729.

Sholl, E. P., *Claverham Meeting, A Stronghold of Quakerism in Somerset 1673–1874* (1935).

FORMER FRIENDS' MEETING HOUSE, YATTON

(195) Former FRIENDS, High Street, Yatton (ST 432656). Built 1866 to replace the Claverham meeting-house. Rubble with round-arched windows; two meeting-rooms with shuttered passage between and lower vestibule between minor rooms against NW side. Now an Infants' School.

YEOVIL

(196) BAPTIST, South Street (ST 556158). Built *c*.1827–9, enlarged to front 1868. Side wall of three bays with two tiers of round-arched windows. (Demolition behind façade proposed 1987)
[Butt, A. W. G.] *Yeovil Baptist Church* (1938). Ivimey II (1814) 558.

(197) Former CONGREGATIONAL, Clarence Street (ST 555160), demolished 1979, stood behind the present chapel, in Princes Street, of 1877–8 by T. Lewis Banks (now URC); it was built 1791–3. The walls were of brick with stone quoins and there was a tall hipped roof; the interior (47 ft by 36 ft) originally had a gallery around three sides.

Denman, W. B., *Two Hundred Years at Congregational/United Reformed Church, Princes Street, Yeovil, Somerset* (1980).

(198) VICARAGE STREET CHAPEL (ST 557161). The Independent or Presbyterian society, formed in the late 17th century, supported Arian doctrines by the end of the 18th century. The Unitarian congregation now meet in the 'Unitarian Hall', a converted modern building at 122 Goldcroft (ST 558167). The site of the former meeting-house, on the N side of Vicarage Street, was acquired in 1704. The meeting-house built in that year was closed for a few years at the end of the 18th century, reopened in 1801 and rebuilt 1809. The latter had a gabled front of three bays with a central doorway and three pointed-arched windows with Y-tracery. It was demolished *c*.1950–60.

Fittings – *Monuments*: at Goldcroft (1) Rev. Samuel Fawcett, 1835; (2) John Ralls, gent., 1832, Elizabeth his widow, 1858, Samuel Ralls, 1878, Elizabeth his first wife, 1870, and Mary Ann his second wife, 1876; (3) Thomas Southwood Smith M.D., minister 1816–20, 1861, erected 1894; (4) Edmund Batten, descendant of Rev. Henry Butler, vicar, ejected 1662, 1836. *Plate*: includes a cup of 1798 and footed plate of 1724.

Evans (1897) 262–4. Murch (1835) 212–28.

Wiltshire is exceptionally rich in the number of early chapels and meeting-houses which have survived, particularly in the north-west part of the county around Bradford-on-Avon. Early industrial development in the 17th and 18th centuries gave rise to substantial nonconformist congregations whose buildings were more than sufficient for succeeding generations. Earlier groups of separatists, from one of which the Horningsham congregation may derive, have left no tangible evidence, and Horningsham Chapel (77) must share the laurels of a Presbyterian antiquity with the Grove Meeting-house in Bradford-on-Avon (13), the fragmentary remains of a meeting-house in Salisbury (New Sarum) (109) and the Old Meeting-house in Warminster (152), all built within a few years of 1700 and variously altered. In addition to these, the small and interestingly sited chapel at Avebury (6) is a rare example of a small country meeting-house of the early 18th century, while at Tisbury (140) the square chapel of 1726 represents a second generation of Presbyterian buildings.

The survival of a complete set of early 18th-century fittings at Monks Chapel, Corsham (51), is of exceptional importance in understanding the requirements of contemporary dissenting worship. The chapel is equally of importance as representing the earliest remaining Friends' meeting-house in the county, built in the vernacular style of the late 17th century, a period also indicated by the few remaining traces at Slaughterford (9). The meeting-houses in Devizes (61), of 1702, and much later in Melksham (101), of 1776, exemplify the more sophisticated designs preferred by urban meetings. None of these is now in use by the Society of Friends.

Particular Baptist congregations which originated in the 17th century in gathered churches deriving support from a widely scattered population later separated into numerous distinct societies, tracing their origin to such early causes as Porton (81) and Southwick (131). The oldest surviving Baptist meeting-house, at Grittleton (70), was built in the early 18th century, while at Bratton (23) the much altered chapel of 1734 retains its principal features and is exceptionally well documented. At Crockerton Green (87) the former chapel of the mid 18th century presents a typically broad elevation to the road and has an external baptistery, a feature evident at several other chapels in the vicinity. Later 18th-century Baptist chapels include large and refurbished buildings at Melksham (98), of 1776-7, and Westbury Leigh (155), of 1796-7; little of its original character remains in the much enlarged Old Baptist Chapel in Devizes (57), of 1780, but the similarly named chapel in Bradford-on-Avon (14), of 1798, secure from the gaze of the world behind a range of buildings, still has much of interest.

The few early General Baptist congregations have had little success in maintaining even a chequered existence. The memory of churches meeting at Downton (63) and Southwick (130) lingers on, but little else. The chapel at Rushall (122), of c.1743, was of denominational interest and comparable in size and appearance with General Baptist meeting-houses in other parts of the country. Trowbridge (142) is exceptional in having had a society which, in the early 18th century, so far outshone the usually affluent Presbyterians that it was reported to include four 'very rich' gentlemen amongst a congregation of six hundred strong; but its early meeting-house has not survived.

Many of the chapels of the late 18th century are attributable directly or indirectly to the Methodist revival and particularly to the successful if erratic labours of John Cennick. The Moravian church into whose care Cennick placed some of his societies is represented at East Tytherton (24) by the chapel, rebuilt in 1792-3, and several buildings of a typical settlement. The chapel at Malmesbury (92) of 1770 has been much altered. Contending forces which denied to the Moravians a secure tenure of buildings in which they had an interest were apparent at Brinkworth (27), in a chapel now demolished, and at Kington Langley (82), where this interest became reduced to a nominal share. The chapel at Bradenstoke or Clack (88), of 1777, is of particular architectural note besides affording an instance of an Independent congregation of Calvinistic Methodist origin which adopted Strict Baptist practices in the 19th century. Congregational chapels of a similar origin appear at Devizes (60) where the principal elevation, although of some quality, was concealed from general view, and at Bradford-on-Avon (18) which was for a time served by ministers of the Countess of Huntingdon's Connexion. Other late 18th-century Congregational chapels of importance are at Corsham (50), of 1793, and the former Upper Meeting-house at Westbury Leigh (157), of c.1790.

Early Wesleyan Methodism has left few monuments in the county, but one of particular note is the former preaching-house of 1756 in Bradford-on-Avon (20), entirely hidden from view but given some vestige of architectural character by a Venetian window above the site of the pulpit. The chapel at Seend (123), claimed to date from 1774–5, has been much altered. Two Wesleyan chapels of exceptional interest, both of which were abandoned for worship and partly or entirely demolished in recent years, were at Bradford-on-Avon (21), of 1818, and Trowbridge (148), of 1835–6. These were masterly essays in a restrained Classical manner and closely related in style, if not by the same architect.

Of the many chapels of the early 19th century the number built by small Strict Baptist churches is remarkable. 'Little Zoar' at Studley (38), of 1814, is a charmingly unspoilt building erected by voluntary labour; the equally small chapel at Upavon (151), of 1838, has the rare designation 'Cave of Adullam'. The Old Baptist Chapel in Chippenham (41), of 1804, is of greater interest than its location in a narrow street appears to promise, while Zion Chapel, Trowbridge (144), of 1816, does credit to the memory of its first pastor, John Warburton, in a town more than usually endowed with Baptist chapels of all descriptions.

Many of the early 19th-century chapels follow the standard arrangement of a gabled front of three bays with a central entrance and a minimum of additional decoration. At Tisbury (141) in the Congregational chapel of 1842 the theme is developed to produce a lively Gothic design free from the scholarly inhibitions of later years. Several later buildings in the Gothic style are by W.J. Stent of Warminster, but outstanding amongst those of the late 19th century is the Congregational chapel in Fisherton Street, Salisbury (111), of 1879, by Tarring and Wilkinson, who were sufficiently daring, especially in this cathedral city, to include a spire. The high quality of the chapel in Mere (103), of 1868, is of exceptional merit, which must be attributed to the patronage of a local manufacturer. The Classical style in various forms was used successfully in several towns, notably in Swindon (138) where the Baptist Tabernacle of 1886, now demolished, was particularly outstanding, and in the Wesleyan chapel in Melksham (102), of 1871–2; the former Primitive Methodist chapel in Wilton (160) of 1875, in a palatial style with the principal chamber at first-floor level, is highly remarkable.

The county has a considerable variety of building materials with much good building stone in the north and west as well as brick which is frequently used with stone quoins and dressings. The more localized sarsen stone is used at Avebury (6). Cob walling was noted at the formerly Independent chapel in Winterbourne Dauntsey (161) of 1799, and a late example of timber-framed construction in the Wesleyan chapel at Chute (46) of 1844. Slate and tile form the usual roofing materials although some stone slates survive as at Monks Chapel, Corsham (51), and examples of the continued use of thatching at Horningsham (77) and Winterbourne Dauntsey (161).

ALLCANNINGS

(1) STRICT BAPTIST, Allington (SU 068630). 'Bethel Chapel' built 1829; brick with stone dressings and hipped slate roof. Three-bay front with two tiers of stone Y-traceried windows between lower vestry wings.

Oliver (1968) 23–4. Paul VI (1969) 1–36.

Strict Baptist chapel, Allcannings.   (1)

ALLINGTON

(2) PRIMITIVE METHODIST (SU 205394). The chapel, with rendered cob walls and patent tile roof, forms part of a continuous range of building. It was converted in 1843 from an early 18th-century cottage. There is a large window inserted in the front wall and a gallery at the N end with a balustraded front. *Monument*: in chapel, John Young, 1818, Mary his widow, 1845, *et al.*

ASHTON KEYNES

(3) Former CONGREGATIONAL (SU 049943). 'Bethesda Chapel' built 1838, of coursed stone and slate. Gabled front with two round-arched gallery windows above porch. Contemporary wrought-iron railings. (Converted to house and windows altered since 1970)

(4) Former PRIMITIVE METHODIST, Gosditch (SU 044939). Built *c*.1840–50. Stone with brick dressings and slate roof. Two round-arched windows and defaced oval tablet in gabled front wall.

Oliver (1968) 32.

ATWORTH

(5) CONGREGATIONAL (ST 862660). The chapel was built *c*.1799 for a newly formed congregation. The walls are of coursed rubble with ashlar dressings; the hipped roof formerly covered with

Former Congregational chapel, Ashton Keynes.
Before conversion.   (3)

Congregational chapel, Atworth.   (5)

stone slates has been re-covered with patent tiles since 1971. The front wall has a pointed-arched doorway with a matching stone hood supported by moulded brackets and above it a pointed lunette lighting a small gallery. The side walls have each four windows with pointed-arched heads. The interior ($45\frac{1}{2}$ ft by 20 ft) formerly had a gallery at each end but that behind the pulpit has been replaced by a vestry. *Coffin Stools*: two, 18th-century.

AVEBURY

(6) CONGREGATIONAL (SU 103699). Nonconformist preaching by John Baker, ejected vicar of Chisledon, and others is recorded in 1669. The meeting-house, described as the 'new erected house built lately on the ground belonging to Samuel Morris's tenement in Avebury', was registered in April 1707. It stands in the village approximately at the centre of the prehistoric stone circle. The walls are of squared sarsen stone with later additions and alterations in brickwork and the roof is covered with tiles and slates. The building appears on Stukeley's plan of Avebury of 1724 as a small square structure with a double-gabled roof aligned approximately N–S, one window under each gable in the S wall and one centrally in the W wall. The E and W walls of the original building remain and are built of large blocks of sarsen, with one square window centrally in each wall. The windows have wooden frames and a centre mullion with a quarter-round moulding internally (both frames have been renewed since 1970).

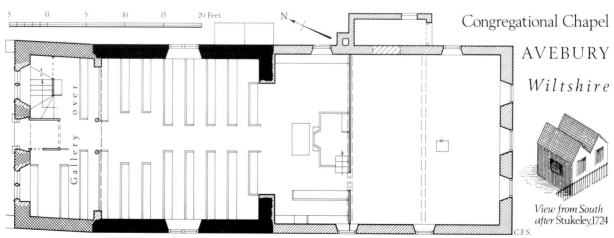

Congregational Chapel

AVEBURY

Wiltshire

*View from South
after* Stukeley, 1724

Congregational chapel (URC), Avebury. (6)

In the mid 18th century the meeting-house was extended by 10 ft to the N in similar materials, including a shallow gallery in the extension lit by a small window at each end. A second enlargement was made *c*.1830 to provide a schoolroom at the S end. In the late 19th century the N front was remodelled with a pointed-arched doorway and stone Y-traceried windows; the front gable, which is in brickwork, replaces a former double gable.

The interior (originally 20 ft square) has a N gallery with moulded panelled front supported by chamfered posts. The roof, replaced in the late 19th century, is supported by four queen-post trusses.

Fittings – *Monuments*: in chapel (1) Rev. William Cornwall, pastor nearly thirty years, 1847; in burial-ground (2) Ann, daughter of William and Elizabeth Cornwall, 1835, and Martha Cornwall, 1837. *Pulpit*: incorporates the fielded-panelled front of an 18th-century pulpit. *Seating*: pew W of pulpit incorporates fragments of 18th-century box-pews; in schoolroom, open-backed benches with shaped plank ends, 18th-century. *Hearing Aids*: in false back of front pew on E side, three speaking tubes formerly linked to pulpit, late 19th-century. (URC)

BERWICK ST JOHN

(7) BAPTIST (ST 944222). 'Ebenezer Chapel' dated 1828 has walls of snecked ashlar with pointed-arched windows. There is a small gallery above the entrance and an original pulpit.

BIDDESTONE

(8) BAPTIST (ST 862736). 'Ebenezer Chapel' dated 1832 has rubble walls with ashlar dressings and a hipped slate roof. Small circular window over later porch. In the side wall facing the road are two windows with four-centred arched heads.

(9) Former FRIENDS, Slaughterford (ST 844737). The meeting-house, now a roofless ruin overgrown by trees, was built or possibly converted from an existing cottage in the late 17th century. Friends' use ceased by 1775 and they agreed to sell the property in 1806 as being 'long out of use'. The meeting-house (30½ ft by 18¼ ft) was altered in the early 19th century and served

Former Friends' Meeting-house
Slaughterford, BIDDESTONE, *Wiltshire*

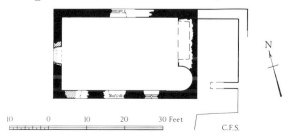

as a chapel for another denomination. The W wall of rubble with larger quoins is gabled and remains largely intact; a mullioned window of three lights was replaced in the early 19th century by a central doorway with a plain lintel and with a stone hood supported by shaped brackets; a window above has also been inserted. The S wall had a doorway at the W end, replaced by a window in the early 19th century, and two original windows of two lights with ovolo-moulded mullions. The N wall retains traces of a single similar window at the centre. At the E end was a wide fireplace of which no details remain.

A walled forecourt to the S may be the earlier burial-ground. In it are two later *monuments*: (1) Richard Holder, 1870, Jane his wife, 1862, and George their son, 1890; (2) Elizabeth, wife of Richard German, 1863, and three children.

(10) PRIMITIVE METHODIST (ST 861739). Coursed rubble with ashlar dressings and slate roof. Round-arched side windows. Opened 1834.

BISHOPSTONE

(11) Former PRIMITIVE METHODIST, Croucheston (SU 067255). The chapel, of brick and tile, was registered for use by Primitive

Former Primitive Methodist chapel, Croucheston.   (11)

Methodists in November 1833. The building may, however, be earlier and identical with the 'newly erected meeting-house for Independents in Bishopstone' registered March 1805. Gabled E front with round-arched doorway and small circular gallery window above. Two round-arched windows in each side wall of two pointed-arched lights. Earlier house attached at rear. Interior with traces of former segmental barrel-vaulted plaster ceiling but altered and refitted in the late 19th century. (Converted to house and altered since 1968)

BLUNSDON ST ANDREW

(12) BLUNSDON HILL CHAPEL (SU 141907). Small chapel with rendered walls and half-hipped roof, built for Independents *c*.1815. A Strict Baptist church was formed in 1834.

Oliver (1968) 18. Paul VI (1969) 121–39.

BRADFORD-ON-AVON

(13) GROVE MEETING-HOUSE, Middle Rank (ST 82356105). The Presbyterian society formerly meeting here originated in the late 17th century. The introduction of heterodox preaching in the following century led to a secession *c*.1740 to form an Independent church. By the end of the 18th century the congregation was reported to be very small and the meeting-house was let for a time to other denominations. A revival of the original society was attempted in 1822 by the Unitarian Richard Wright, then General Baptist minister at Trowbridge, but with little success and the work appears to have ceased by about 1870. The building is now occupied by the Baptist church formerly meeting in Zion Chapel which had for many years previously used it as a Sunday-school.

The meeting-house built *c*.1698 may be the 'new erected house of Anthony Methwen' registered July 1699. A further registration was taken out in 1793. The walls are of stone, faced to the SE in ashlar, and the roof, which is hipped at the NE end, is covered in patent tiles. The front wall of six bays with two tiers of windows separated by a moulded string-course has a stone

Grove Meeting-house
BRADFORD-ON-AVON
Wiltshire

Scale of Feet for Elevation

5   0   5   10   15

South-East Elevation

C.F.S.

Grove Meeting-house, Bradford-on-Avon.   (13)

plinth and moulded cornice at the eaves. Two doorways in the
end bays have bolection-moulded architraves and moulded
cornices; the doorway to the right is blocked in stone. The two
central upper windows have round-arched heads but may
originally have matched the other windows which have stone
mullions and transoms. The NE end has a central doorway
inserted in the 19th century and an upper window of four lights,
possibly of the same date.

The interior (23½ ft by 45¾ ft) may have had a pulpit centrally
against the front wall and a gallery at each end but it has been
entirely refitted.

Monuments: on SE wall (1) Rev. Roger Flexman D.D.,
minister 1739–47, 1795, painted wooden tablet; externally, loose
but formerly inside on SE wall (2) Elizabeth, wife of John Penny,
1726, stone wall monument with inscription panel flanked by
naked figures holding drapery, coloured and gilt, a crest formerly
above the monument has been lost.

Jones (1907) 154–8. Murch (1835) 64–8. *WAM* v (1859)
252–5.

(14) PARTICULAR BAPTIST, St Margaret's Street (ST 826608).
The 'Old Baptist Chapel', built 1798, stands on a site leased for
the erection of a meeting-house in 1689; the Baptist church was
formed in 1697. The chapel is approached from the street
through an arched entrance cut through an early 18th-century
house behind which it lies concealed; the previous meeting-house
was reached by a narrow passage at one side.

The chapel has rubble walls faced at the front in ashlar and has
a hipped slated roof. The NW front is of three bays with two
tiers of pointed-arched windows with stone Y-tracery. The
central doorway has a pedimented surround with attached Tuscan
columns. Two doorways to right and left, now blocked, were
inserted in the 19th century to give direct access to the gallery
stairs. The side and rear walls have windows matching those in
the front.

The interior (44 ft by 37 ft) has galleries around three sides,
possibly a few years later in date than the chapel, with panelled
fronts, and cornices with fluted dentils. The seating mainly dates
from a refitting in 1887 but some of the gallery pews at the rear

Old Baptist Chapel, St Margaret's Street, Bradford-on-Avon. (14)

incorporate late 18th-century fielded panels. In the side galleries
are box-pews of the early 19th century. The pulpit between two
large windows, now blocked, at the SE end is square with
splayed corners and has a fielded-panelled back-board.

Monuments: in chapel on NE wall (1) John Hale, commercial
traveller, 1830, signed 'Tyley, Bristol'; in small burial-ground
behind chapel (2) [   ] Head, 1825, table-tomb; also many
small square undated marker-stones.

Oliver (1968) 69–78. Oliver, R. W., *Baptists in Bradford-on-
Avon, The History of the Old Baptist Church Bradford-on-Avon
1689–1989* (1989).

(15) ZION CHAPEL, Middle Rank (ST 824611), dated 1823, was
registered in May 1824 as 'a chapel on ground called The
Conigree Newtown, Bradford'; it was built by seceders from the
Congregational Chapel (17) who from *c.*1813 had held services in
the Grove Meeting-house (13). In 1844 the congregation was
formed into a Baptist church following the addition of some
disaffected members from the Old Baptist Chapel; they
eventually returned to the Grove Meeting-house *c.*1950 which
they had long been using as a Sunday-school. Zion Chapel,
derelict in 1959, has since been demolished; it had a front of three
bays with pedimented centre, rusticated lower stage and round-
arched windows.

CHST XIV (1940–4) 45–7.

(16) PROVIDENCE CHAPEL, Bearfield (ST 824615), was converted about 1858 from part of an existing terrace of houses for use by a Baptist church formed in that year. Traces of two former doorways and other openings remain in the front wall. The interior (38¼ ft by 16¼ ft) has a deep gallery at the E end.

(17) CONGREGATIONAL, St Margaret's Street (ST 826607). The chapel, on Morgan's Hill (now URC), was built in 1740 by former members of the Grove meeting who had seceded following the introduction there of Arian doctrines; it was enlarged to the rear in 1798 and again in 1835 when the roof was raised and the interior refitted; a partial reseating was carried out in 1913. The walls are of stone with an ashlar face to the SW and the roof is hipped and slated. The SW front, formerly concealed behind houses, is of five bays with a central doorway and two tiers of plain rectangular windows. A platband marking the original height of the walls rises at the centre in a pedimental outline embracing a large oval tablet inserted in 1835 recording the dates of erection and enlargement. The upper windows appear to have been heightened and the centre window, which has a timber lintel, has been blocked but retains beaded jambs, a detail elsewhere replaced by chamfers. The central doorway supersedes a pair of entrances in the adjacent bays.

The NW side wall is partly covered by an early 19th-century annexe obscuring the original end wall in which is a central round-arched doorway, now a cupboard, a former window above, and an inscription (see below) recording the erection of the chapel in 1740. Beyond the annexe, towards the rear, two extensions of the building are clearly marked by lines of quoins, each added bay having a window at ground floor and at gallery level; a levelling course of stone in the first and second periods of building indicates the former eaves level. The SE wall is similarly fenestrated. The back wall to the NE has two segmental-arched windows flanking the pulpit.

The interior (originally 26 ft deep enlarged to 40 ft but now 52¾ ft, by 32½ ft) has a plaster ceiling rising in a wide cove from the original wall height; an early 19th-century gallery with panelled front continues around three sides and has contemporary box-pews.

Fittings – Inscription: on former outer face of NW wall, now internally in first floor of annexe, 'The Walls of this Meeting House|Were Erected in the year 1740|And that on the Eastern side had|Eighteen inches Left out of the Free Land|Purchased by Mrs Sarah Grant for|Eves Droping so the Trustees are not|To put up or keep up a Shute and the|Wall on the North Side belong to us|Witness our hands who built the walls|Edward Deverell|John Deverell'. Monument: in lobby on NW wall, Rev. Nicolas Phené, 19 years pastor, 1792, Sarah his widow, 1798, and four children, 1776, 1777, 1782, 1784. Pictures: two pairs of portraits in oils of an 18th-century minister and his wife, one pair badly damaged.

CHST XIV (1940–4) 40–7.

(18) BETHEL CHAPEL, Bearfield (ST 824614). A building 'in a field commonly known or called by the name of Berefield, the property of Caleb Hodges and others' was registered for Independents on 12 August 1790. The present chapel which may have succeeded this was built c.1800. Although the first pastor was an ordained minister of the Countess of Huntingdon's

Connexion, the chapel remained private property until after 1816; it was administered by the Connexion c.1824–79 but has since become Congregational.

The chapel has walls of rubble and a hipped roof covered with stone slates. At the S end is a stone porch with pedimented outer doorway. Above the entrance is a round-arched window; other windows have lintels and renewed frames. The interior (40¼ ft by 26¼ ft) was refitted in the late 19th century; there is no gallery.

Fittings – Monuments: in chapel (1) Sarah, wife of James Howard, 1818, and Thomas their son, 1825; (2) Rev. Thomas Watkins, first pastor, 1802, Rev. Joseph Rawling, eight years pastor, 1811, and Barbara his widow, former wife of Thomas Watkins, 1816, recording her gift of the property to trustees. Pulpit: with cast-iron balustraded front, late 19th-century. Sculpture: three eagles with outstretched wings formerly supporting a communion rail, artificial stone, c.1824.

(19) Former FRIENDS, St Margaret's Street (ST 825608). A meeting-house built in 1718 'in a court leading out of St Margaret's Street' was in use for a British School by 1817. The building was sold in 1902 and demolished 1963–4. The site of meeting-house and burial-ground is now covered by a car park.
VCH Wiltshire VII (1953) 32–3.

(20) Former METHODIST, Market Street (ST 826610). The preaching-house, registered for Methodists 13 July 1756 as 'lately erected, adjoining the dwelling-house of John Silby', stands concealed behind the premises of the Bradford-on-Avon Club on the NE side of the street. The walls are of rubble and the three parallel hipped roofs are covered with patent tiles. The SW front is masked by the adjacent building. The NE end, which is cut into rising ground, has an original Venetian window with keystone and roll-moulded jambs. The side wall to SE has four bays of windows in two tiers with a basement window near the SW end and an original doorway at the opposite end. The other side wall has corresponding upper windows but the lower openings have been altered.

The interior (41¼ ft by 26¾ ft) has been refitted. A gallery which remains at the SW end formerly extended along each side and was supported by two pairs of octagonal stone piers which were surmounted by two wooden Roman Doric columns to carry the roof; the NE pair of columns has been removed. Clock: Parliament clock by Thomas Bullock, Bath, 18th-century.

Gill, F. C., In the Steps of John Wesley (1962) 107–8.

(21) Former WESLEYAN, Coppice Hill (ST 827611). The former preaching-house in Market Street, earlier Pippett Street, may have been superseded by a chapel on Coppice Hill in 1790 of which the present building is the successor. This was built in 1818 and is similar in design and identical in size with the Wesleyan Chapel in Trowbridge (148) for which it may have served as a model.

The walls are of rubble faced with ashlar and the roofs are covered with slate. The S front of five bays has a three-bay centerpiece which rises above the flanking bays to an eared pedimental blocking-course on which is a dated inscription. The round-arched windows have incised borders and the central entrance has two columns supporting a Doric entablature.

The interior (56¼ ft by 43¼ ft) has a gallery around three sides

Former Wesleyan chapel, Coppice Hill, Bradford-on-Avon.   (21)

Former Wesleyan chapel, Coppice Hill, Bradford-on-Avon. (21)

rounded to the south. At the N end is a former communion recess (8 ft by 18 ft) with singers' gallery above, the lower part converted to a vestry in the later 19th century. In the N wall of the vestry is a circular window 4 ft in diameter to light the communion table and on the adjacent walls the remains of moulded plaster decoration. The roof is supported by trusses with king-posts and queen-struts. (Derelict 1971 after partial demolition, sold 1977, shell survives 1988)

(22) Former PRIMITIVE METHODIST, Sladebrook (ST 829614). Three-bay ashlar front with round-arched windows; pedimental gable with date '1845' at apex and large plain tablet signed 'WV Octr. 11'.

Petty (1880) 450.

BRATTON

(23) BAPTIST (ST 914525). A Particular Baptist church meeting at Erlestoke, three miles E, by 1669, appears to have held some meetings in Bratton from 1701 when the house of William Whitaker was registered for dissenters. With the erection of a meeting-house in Bratton in 1734 the focus of church activity moved away from Erlestoke which by the mid 18th century ceased to form part of the church's usual designation.

The chapel, registered 16 July 1734 as a 'house newly erected . . . on a piece of ground commonly known as Browns Plot lying at the north-east corner of . . . Browns Berry', has brick walls with stone dressings, and a half-hipped roof covered with stone slates, and hipped tiled roofs to the wings. The building has been much altered and enlarged at various dates. It was re-roofed in 1775. A vestry was built in 1784 and the chapel extended to the rear 'about 12 feet backward', in 1786. A 'front gallery' was constructed in 1807 and windows pierced in the side walls. In 1818 a schoolroom was added against the W side. More drastic alterations were made in 1858 when the walls were raised by about four feet and the present roof built, the interior was entirely refitted and schoolrooms, lecture-rooms and vestries built in flanking wings. The W schoolrooms were extended to the N in 1874 and in 1894 a baptistery was constructed inside for the first time and the principal windows were reglazed with cast-iron frames replacing leaded lights.

The original S front is of three bays bounded by plain stone pilasters; it was heightened and a circular window inserted in 1858. The central doorway has a semicircular stone hood resting on stone corbels; the windows have round-arched heads and moulded stone surrounds. The N wall repeats the fenestration of

Baptist Chapel , BRATTON, *Wiltshire*

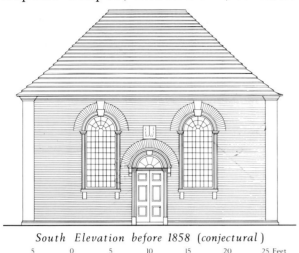

South Elevation before 1858 (conjectural)

5   0   5   10   15   20   25 Feet

C.F.S.

the front but with less elaborate details; a date-tablet of 1786 is reset in the heightening. The side wings are of two storeys with hung sash windows.

The interior (originally 20 ft enlarged to 32 ft, by $29\frac{3}{4}$ ft) has a flat plaster ceiling with coved cornice of 1858. The line of the 1786 enlargement is marked by two octagonal timber posts with moulded capitals and stone bases which rise behind the gallery fronts. The gallery around three sides is approached by staircases in the wings.

Fittings – *Bootscrapers*: pair, cast-iron portable with oval tray, dolphin standards and shell ornament, mid 19th-century. *Seating*: box-pews to lower floor and fragments in side galleries, 1858. In lower schoolroom sixteen benches with shaped plank ends, early 19th-century. *Sundial*: over S doorway, square stone dial, iron gnomon, 18th-century.

Ivimey IV (1830) 313–14. Reeves, E. S. W., K., and M., *A History of the Baptist Church, Bratton, Wilts* (1962). Reeves, M., *Sheep Bell and Ploughshare* (1978).

Baptist chapel, Bratton.   (23)

BREMHILL

(24) MORAVIAN, East Tytherton (ST 966750). The society meeting here originated in the work of Calvinistic Methodist preachers, notably John Cennick. By 1742 several societies had been formed in Wiltshire and on 14 November in that year Cennick preached for the first time at Tytherton in a house converted for that purpose. In the following year a new chapel

Baptist Chapel , BRATTON, *Wiltshire*

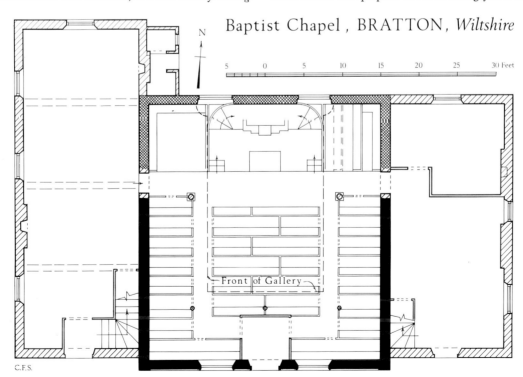

5   0   5   10   15   20   25   30 Feet

Front of Gallery

C.F.S.

Moravian Settlement, East Tytherton.   (24)

was built alongside and in 1744 the former house was rebuilt to serve as a manse. Further land was acquired in 1745 and when in that year Cennick resolved to join the Moravians the Tabernacle Society in London agreed 'that the society in Wiltshire that chose brother Cennick should be given up to him...'. The Wiltshire societies thereafter passed to the Moravians and on 9 May 1748 were united as 'The Wiltshire Congregation' with Tytherton as their principal meeting place. In 1751 one of the attributes of a regular settlement was acquired by the removal of the occupants of a Single Sisters' House at Kington Langley, opened 1748, to a 'house, orchard and garden, not far from the chapel'. A new Sisters' House was built in 1785–6, in 1792–3 the chapel and minister's house were rebuilt and in 1793–4 premises for a girls' day and boarding-school were erected. A detached building for Sunday-school and day-school use was built in 1871. The chapel was refitted in 1882.

The chapel of 1792–3 forms the centre section of a range of three buildings of brick with stone dressings and tiled roofs. The S front is of three bays with round-arched windows and a porch formerly gabled but rebuilt in its present form in 1882. In the rear wall are two tall round-arched windows flanking the former site of the pulpit. At the E end of the roof is a hexagonal wooden bell-cote. The interior (28 ft by 40 ft) has a late 18th-century gallery at the E end with fielded-panelled front and bowed centre supported by a pair of wooden columns. A gallery at the W end was removed in 1882 when the pulpit was re-sited at that end.

The former manse, adjacent to the W side of the chapel, is of two storeys and attic with windows of two lights with stone mullions. The house has been extended to the north. Adjacent to the E side of the chapel is the former girls' school of 1793–4; this now forms two separate units of which that to the E has been altered or partly rebuilt.

The former Sisters' House, a detached building NW of the front range, has walls of ashlar and a roof covered with stone slates. It is of three storeys separated by platbands; the S front is symmetrical with tripartite windows at each level either side of the central doorway. A round-arched window in its W wall is dated 1785. The house was converted for use by the girls' boarding-school in 1877. A small stable standing W of the front range, with brick walls and half-hipped stone slate roof, dates from the late 18th century.

Fittings – *Monuments*: externally on S wall of chapel, large stone tablet dated 1792 recording 20 burials in front yard 1743–7; in burial-ground N of former Sisters' House, many small unnumbered rectangular stones of late 18th-century and after, reset as common paving.

England I (1886–7) 7–10, pl. 9. *London Record Society Publications* XI (1975) 22.

(25) WESLEYAN, Foxham (ST 980773). Brick with stone dressings, porch, and two tiers of round-arched windows; dated 1855.

Wesleyan chapel, Foxham.   (25)

(26) WESLEYAN, Spirthill (ST 995755). Brick and pantile, windows with stone Y-tracery and surrounds, flat-arched entrance in gabled end wall with gallery window over; dated 1825, but registered as 'newly erected' 1829.

BRINKWORTH

(27) Former INDEPENDENT (SU 008847). A chapel was built in 1741 on land donated by 'a gentleman of Grittenham' for a congregation gathered as a result of John Cennick's preaching which passed with the other Wiltshire societies into the care of Moravians in 1745. In 1751 the trustees successfully reclaimed the building for use by Independents who continued to use it until c.1950. It has since been demolished.

The chapel was a low building of brick with a half-hipped roof covered with stone slates. The broad front of three bays had a central porch and two round-arched windows.

England I (1886–7) 7, 9, pl. 10.

(28) PRIMITIVE METHODIST (SU 018847). Dated 1860. The former 'P. M. School and Assembly Room' to the W, dated 1876, is probably a conversion of the original chapel registered December 1828; it has stone walls with segmental-arched windows and a central doorway with circular window above in the gabled front wall.

BROAD CHALKE

(29) CONGREGATIONAL (SU 039256). Gothic, 1862–3, by W. J. Stent of Warminster, superseding 1801 chapel. (URC)

CONGREGATIONAL CHAPEL, BROAD CHALKE   CFS 1988

BROMHAM

(30) WESLEYAN (ST 962651). Although largely rebuilt c.1860 and extended to the N, the chapel incorporates in the W wall part of the structure of an earlier building; this may be the chapel registered 15 June 1799.

BROUGHTON GIFFORD

(31) STRICT BAPTIST, Broughton Common (ST 875642). Meetings at the house of Elizabeth Clack culminated in the formation of a church in 1806 by members dismissed from Melksham. The chapel built c.1806 was registered 12 June 1809. The walls are of squared stone with ashlar dressings and the roof is hipped and slated. The front of three bays with two tiers of

Strict Baptist chapel, Broughton Common.   (31)

round-arched windows has a later porch. In each side wall are two tall segmental-arched windows with central mullions.

Oliver (1968) 53.

BULFORD

(32) CONGREGATIONAL (SU 167434). A 'newly erected' meeting-house for Independents was registered 15 July 1806. The chapel, which dates from the early 19th century, has rendered walls and a hipped slate roof with wide eaves. Windows have rectangular cast-iron frames with a semicircular pattern of glazing bars at the head. The interior, largely refitted and a schoolroom added to the N in the late 19th century, has an original gallery with some contemporary seating at the S end.

Fittings – *Clock*: on gallery front, inscribed 'Ex Dono Amici', early 19th-century. *Monuments*: in chapel (1) Henry Blatch, 'one of the founders of this place of worship', 12 years deacon, 1821, and Sarah his widow, 1837; (2) Sarah, 1852, Henry, 1855, and Elizabeth, 1870, children of Henry and Sarah Blatch.

CALNE WITHIN

(33) BAPTIST, Castle Street, Calne (ST 996709). The church formed in the mid 17th century had a meeting-house on or near the present site which was destroyed in a storm on 27 November 1703 and rebuilt in the following year. The present chapel, built in 1816–17, was refronted in the late 19th century. The walls are of stone with pointed-arched windows in the side walls having plain Y-tracery of the early 19th century. The interior has a gallery next to the entrance but has otherwise been refitted.

Monuments: in chapel (1) Rev. Isaac Taylor, 1810, oval tablet; (2) John Davis, 1786, recording legacies of £800 for the chapel and £50 to the Bristol Education Society; (3) John Mead, 1836, Mary his wife, 1831, *et al. Plate*: includes two gadrooned pewter mugs dated 1710.

Marsh (1903) 169–72. Oliver (1968) 47–8.

(34) STRICT BAPTIST, Zion Lane, Calne (ST 998712). 'Zion Chapel' was built in 1836 for a section of the earlier church which had seceded in 1813. Rubble walls and slate roof, pedimented W front with rebuilt porch and two gallery windows. The interior, reseated in the late 19th century, has an

Strict Baptist chapel, Calne.   (34)

original pulpit at the E end beyond which are later vestries and an upper schoolroom with two shuttered openings to the chapel.

    Marsh (1903) 172. Oliver (1968) 47–8. Paul VI (1969) 104–20.

(35) INDEPENDENT, Church Street, Calne (ST 998710). 'Calne Free Church' was formed by seceders from the parish church having a Congregational minister as its first pastor. Gothic chapel of rock-faced stone with corner tower, 1867–8, by W. J. Stent of Warminster.

    Marsh (1903) 179.

(36) Former FRIENDS, Wood Street, Calne (ST 997712). Small urban meeting-house built 1838 with burial-ground at rear. Ashlar front with moulded cornice, two sash windows to upper floor, central doorway between windows in rusticated lower stage replaced by shop front since 1960.

    Marsh (1903) 173–6.

(37) Former PRESBYTERIAN, Bollins Lane, Calne (unlocated). A meeting-house, built c.1695, closed 1835, was used intermittently by Primitive Methodists 1836–75. Reported demolished in 1962.

    Chandler, J. H. (ed), 'Wiltshire Dissenters' Meeting House Certificates and Registrations 1689–1852' *Wiltshire Record Society Publications* XL (1985) 5. Hague and Hague (1986) 44. Marsh (1903) 169, 177–8. Murch (1835) 56–62.

CALNE WITHOUT

(38) STRICT BAPTIST, Studley (ST 964710). 'Little Zoar' at Derry Hill was built in 1814 on the initiative of William and Martha

Strict Baptist chapel, Studley.   (38)

Wiltshire and the work was carried out by voluntary labour. 'Women dug out stone from the quarry during the day and their husbands moved them to the site in the evenings. Local farmers lent men and horses. Mr Wiltshire, himself, had a saw-pit made outside his house, where volunteers could work'.

    The chapel is a small building of rubble with ashlar dressings; the roof is half-hipped and covered with stone slates. The entrance is at the N end of the E wall and has a plain lintel inscribed with the name and date of erection. Centrally on both the E and W sides is a round-arched window with stone Y-tracery; two round-arched windows at the S end flank the pulpit and at the N end, above the lean-to roof of a later vestry, are two further windows to light the gallery.

    The interior retains its original fittings of N gallery with plain panelled front, pulpit with fielded-panelled sides, and open-backed benches with shaped arm-rests.

    Oliver (1968) 40–1. Paul VI (1969) 201–20.

(39) Former STRICT BAPTIST, Sandy Lane (ST 965679). 'Providence Chapel', of rubble with ashlar dressings and a slate roof, is dated 1817. The gabled E front has the denominationally unusual feature of a stone cross let into the masonry of the gable. Windows have three round-arched lights and transoms below square labels. (Converted to house since 1970)

    Oliver (1968) 51–3.

CHAPMANSLADE

(40) BAPTIST (ST 827479). Meetings of Independents and Presbyterians were in existence by the early 18th century for one of which a barn had been registered in 1699. Although a society with 'a rich endowment' appears to have survived at least until the end of the 18th century, a new and more 'enthusiastic' cause was commenced in 1777 and continued largely by Countess of Huntingdon's ministers and students and later by Baptists. A Baptist church was formed from this cause in 1788 and was joined in the early 19th century by the Independent congregation from the Old Meeting leaving their minister in possession of a sinecure from which he was with difficulty displaced. The old meeting-house was rebuilt as a Congregational chapel in 1867 and the Baptist church united with the congregation at that place c.1965.

    The Baptist chapel was built in 1799. The walls are of rubble with brick dressings and the roof is hipped and covered with tiles. The E front of three bays has a rubble plinth and two tiers of segmental-arched windows with hung sashes. The central doorway, obscured by a porch of utilitarian character, appears to have had ashlar dressings. The side walls are each of two bays with windows matching those at the front. The rear wall is rendered and has two tall segmental-arched windows flanking the pulpit; a later vestry stands against this wall.

    The interior (35 ft by 28 ft) has an original rear gallery; side galleries were probably added in the early 19th century for the enlarged congregation. The pulpit, supported at the front by two short columns, may have been altered in 1869 when the chapel was re-pewed. The roof is supported by two queen-post trusses.

    Fittings – *Baptistery*: in front of pulpit, with N and S steps. *Inscription*: stone on inner face of front boundary wall with initials AH. *Monuments*: in burial-ground, late 19th-century; Doel refers to a monument to John Marshman, 1818, and Susannah his wife,

1817, parents of Dr Joshua Marshman, the Baptist missionary. (Converted to house since 1970)

Doel (1890) 172–7.

CHIPPENHAM WITHIN

(41) OLD BAPTIST CHAPEL, Chapel Lane, formerly Gutter Lane, Chippenham (ST 921733). A Strict Baptist church formed in 1804 included some seceders from the Tabernacle. The chapel was opened 10 June 1804 and registered 1 December 1810. It stands in a narrow lane on the NE side of High Street. The front, of rubble with ashlar dressings, has a central doorway and two tiers of sash windows. The interior has a gallery around three sides and an original pulpit with panelled back-board; the seating was renewed in the late 19th century. An internal baptistery was constructed in 1818.

Oliver (1968) 39–40.

Old Baptist Chapel, Chippenham.   (41)

(42) THE TABERNACLE, Emery Lane, Chippenham (ST 922733). Although a Presbyterian society existed in the early 18th century, the present Congregational church (now URC) owes its origin to Calvinistic Methodist preachers, notably George Whitefield, who were active in the district from 1742. The new society, which was in association with the 'Rodborough Connexion', built its first Tabernacle on this site in 1770; a new and larger chapel replaced it in 1826. This has walls of rubble with squared stone and ashlar dressings to the front and a hipped slated roof. The front is of three bays with a pedimented centre and two tiers of windows separated by a platband. The interior was entirely refitted in 1889. *Monument*: in chapel, Rev. Benjamin Rees, 40 years minister, 1864.

Evans, D. E., *Tabernacle Congregational Church, Chippenham* (1970). Stribling (1897) 30–1. VCH *Wiltshire* III (1956) 131.

(43) Former WESLEYAN, The Causeway, Chippenham (ST 924729). Mid 19th-century, superseded 1908 by chapel at Monkton Hill; now in commercial use. Gabled ashlar front with flanking octagonal buttresses and pinnacles, three former doorways, two now converted to windows, and large upper window of four lights with plain intersecting tracery. Basement schoolroom below chapel.

(44) PRIMITIVE METHODIST, The Causeway, Chippenham (ST 923731). The first chapel, now schoolroom, concealed behind its successor of 1896, occupies the site of a Friends' meeting-house built in 1737 and sold to Primitive Methodists *c*.1832 who appear to have rebuilt it. Stone with hipped slate roof, two altered windows at rear, side windows inserted later.

Kendall, H. B., *The Origin and History of the Primitive Methodist Church* II [1905] 349.

CHRISTIAN MALFORD

(45) CONGREGATIONAL (ST 958792). 'Shecaniah erected AD 1836'. Stone, gabled front with ashlar corner pilasters, platband, and two pointed-arched windows with stone Y-tracery. (URC)

'SHECANIAH' CHAPEL, CHRISTIAN MALFORD   CFS 1971

CHUTE

(46) WESLEYAN, Lower Chute (SU 313532). Opened 1844. Rendered timber-framed walls, partly weatherboarded, and low hipped slate roof.

CODFORD

(47) Former CONGREGATIONAL, Codford St Mary (ST 970398). The chapel of 1812 was demolished *c*.1960–70; the adjacent brick Sunday-school with three-bay front of the early 19th century has been converted to a cottage since 1970.

COLLINGBOURNE KINGSTON

(48) WESLEYAN (SU 239556). The former chapel of the mid 19th century, with rendered brick walls and hipped slate roof, adjoins its 1914 successor.

CORSHAM

(49) BAPTIST, Priory Street (ST 870706). 'Ebenezer Chapel', built in 1828 to supersede a small building opened in 1824, has stone walls with an ashlar front and hipped slated roof. Three-bay front and sides with two tiers of four-centred arched windows with intersecting glazing bars. Single-storey Jubilee Memorial Hall of 1873 alongside. Interior, partly refitted in late 19th century, has a rear gallery with bowed centre.

BM XVI (1824) 444.

Baptist chapel, Corsham. (49)

(50) Former CONGREGATIONAL, Pickwick Road (ST 871703). The chapel was built in 1793 by a congregation which first registered a former malt-house for preaching in 1788. The walls are of rubble with an ashlar front; the roof is hipped and covered with stone slates. The E front has two round-arched doorways with arched canopies supported by moulded stone brackets. The keystones of the two upper circular windows and a tall central window have been cut back to receive external shutters, now removed. In each side wall are three windows with arched heads and keystones altered in a like manner. A schoolroom was built against the W end in 1902.

Former Congregational chapel, Corsham. (50)

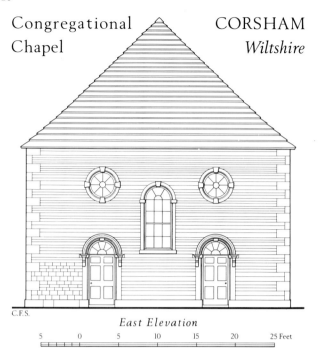

Congregational Chapel

CORSHAM
Wiltshire

C.F.S.

East Elevation

5 0 5 10 15 20 25 Feet

The interior (40 ft by 30 ft) has a flat plaster ceiling. A gallery at the E end which cuts across the central window was added in 1824; it is approached by two staircases and has panelled front with bowed central projection supported by two iron columns. The W wall has been pierced by a semicircular arch beyond which is a later organ chamber. The gallery seating has been removed, the lower seats were renewed in the late 19th century. The roof is supported by two queen-post trusses. (Converted to offices since 1971)

Stribling (1897) 22–3.

(51) MONKS CHAPEL (ST 876686), half a mile NE of The Ridge, was built in the late 17th century as a meeting-house for the Society of Friends. This is said to have been bought by Independents (now URC) in 1690; Friends registered a meeting-house in Corsham in 1690 and built a new meeting-house at Pickwick, near Corsham, in 1709. An Independent minister, Thomas Stantial, was reported to be preaching at 'Casham Ridge or Corsham' *c*.1715.

The walls are of rubble laid in narrow courses with ashlar dressings and the roof is covered with stone slates. The S front has a central doorway between two windows of two lights with ovolo-moulded stone mullions joined by a continuous moulded label. A wide segmental dormer of five lights with hollow-chamfered stone mullions was inserted *c*.1900. The E and W walls are gabled with stone copings. Centrally in the E wall is an original upper window of two lights with a moulded label. The W wall has an inserted upper window to the right of an internal chimney-breast. The N wall has three windows similar to those in the opposite wall, joined by a moulded label; the central window was partly blocked in the early 18th century and a small two-light pulpit window inserted above it, also with an ovolo-moulded mullion.

Monks Chapel, Corsham.   (51)

Monks Chapel, Corsham.   (51)

Monks Chapel, CORSHAM, *Wiltshire*

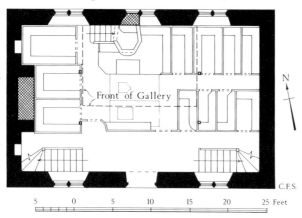

C.F.S.

5   0   5   10   15   20   25 Feet

The interior (18½ ft by 31 ft) has at the W end a wide chimney-breast and fireplace now blocked by the later fittings; most of the fittings date from the conversion of the meeting house to a place of Independent worship with the pulpit centrally against the N wall. The ceiling is plastered and rises to the collar-beams of two roof trusses which have been altered by the removal of tie-beams and their replacement by iron straps at a higher level. E and W galleries have panelled fronts supported by square wooden posts; a cross gallery on the S side may be of later date.

Fittings – *Communion Table*: with turned legs and moulded rails. *Hat Pegs*: variously situated, of turned wood, also of iron in gallery. *Inscriptions*: on sloping ceiling above pulpit, black-lined cartouche with coloured cherub's head above, enclosing text from Psalm 93:5, early 18th-century; inside S lunette, painted text from Psalm 92:1; on outer face of lunette, in raised letters, text from Ecclesiastes 5:1. *Monuments* and *Floorslabs*. *Monuments*: in burial-ground, of 18th century and later. *Floorslabs*: in front of

pulpit (1) Luke Filmore, minister of this place, 1753; (2) Ann Kington, 1775, and Bridget Filmore, 1782. *Pulpit*: fielded-panelled front, back-board with moulded cornice. *Seating*: to lower floor, box-pews with fielded-panelled sides, 18th-century and later; in gallery, open-backed benches. *Sundial*: over S doorway, with broken pediment and ball finial, 18th-century.

Stribling (1897) 22.

CORSLEY

(52) BAPTIST, Whitbourne (ST 826447). The chapel was built in 1811 for a congregation gathered by a preacher from Chapmanslade. The building was heightened, extended to the rear and a two-storeyed schoolroom wing added later in the 19th century; the interior was largely refitted in 1882. The walls are of rubble with a brick front and dressings, and a slated roof. The gabled front is of three bays with two tiers of short segmental-arched windows. The side walls were originally of two bays. The interior has a gallery around three sides.

Baptist chapel, Whitbourne.   (52)

Baptistery: externally at rear, circular, about 11 ft in diameter, with rendered brick sides. *Monuments*: in chapel, wood, repainted *c*.1882 (1) Mrs Elizabeth Eyers, 1841, recording a bequest of £500; (2) Richard Parsons, founder and first pastor, 1853.

Doel (1890) 178–80.

(53) WESLEYAN, Lane End (ST 812457). A society was formed in 1769 and a preaching-house registered in 1773. The present chapel, built in 1849, of stone with a hipped slate roof, has round-arched windows and a gallery next to the entrance. It was refitted in the late 19th century.

Davies (1909) 56–7, 89.

CRICKLADE

(54) Former STRICT BAPTIST, Calcutt Street (SU 103935). Built 1852, closed 1946, now used by Roman Catholics. Gabled stone front with one round-arched window above porch.

Oliver (1968) 31. Thompson (1961) 40–1.

(55) Former PRIMITIVE METHODIST (SU 101935). Gabled brick front with stone dressings, two round-arched windows and later porch. Oval tablet with name 'Pethahiah', dated 1855.

Former Primitive Methodist chapel, Cricklade.   (55)

DAUNTSEY

(56) STRICT BAPTIST (ST 996815). 'Providence Chapel' built 1824, largely rebuilt 1875, of brick with stone dressings but incorporating some of the earlier walling.

Oliver (1968) 46.

DEVIZES

(57) BAPTIST, Maryport Street (SU 006614). The 'Old Baptist Chapel' was built in 1780 for a church which originated in the mid 17th century and formerly met in a long narrow tenement behind buildings in The Brittox, N of the present chapel. The

Old Baptist Chapel, Devizes.   (57)

former building is reported to have been demolished *c*.1968; the site now serves as a car park. The chapel has brick walls, rendered at the front, and a hipped slate roof. The S front, originally of three bays with two tiers of windows, was extended by two bays to the W in 1818 and a porch covering the lower part of the wall was added in 1922.

The interior (originally 36 ft by $32\frac{1}{4}$ ft) has been greatly altered at various dates. Galleries around three sides were added in 1860 but the side galleries have since been removed. *Monuments*: reset in porch (1) John Handforth, minister, 1819, and Ann his widow, 1829; (2) James Pyne, minister, 1780; (3) James Dyer, minister, 1797.

Oliver (1968) 55–7. Waylen (1859) 574.

(58) BAPTIST, Sheep Street (SU 007614). The 'New Baptist Chapel' was built in 1851–2 on the site of a former Presbyterian

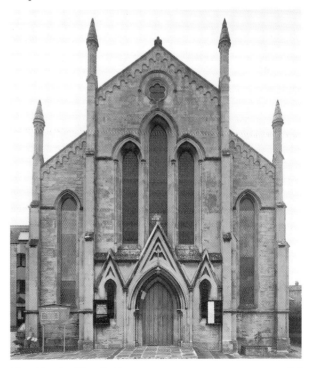

New Baptist Chapel, Devizes.   (58)

meeting-house of 1792. The Presbyterian meeting, in existence since the early 18th century, had been served by ministers of Arian views in its later years, but with the appointment of Charles Stanford as pastor in 1847 the society was re-formed as a Baptist church and a similar change effected in the trust deeds.

The chapel, designed by a Mr Hardick in the lancet style, is of stone. The W front has a projecting centre bay with triple-gabled entrance and angle buttresses rising to tall thin pinnacles. Interior refitted 1979.

B. Hbk (1887) 120–2. Loveridge, S. M., and Whiting, A., *New Baptist Church, Devizes, Centenary Souvenir, 1852–1952* (1952). Waylen (1859) 574.

(59) Former STRICT BAPTIST, New Park Street (SU 003617). 'Salem Chapel' was built in 1838 by supporters of George Wessley, a pastoral candidate at the Old Baptist Chapel to which the church eventually returned in 1892. It is now used by the Brethren. Brick with hipped slate roof. Three-bay front with three-centred arched doorway and two tiers of sash windows.

Oliver (1968) 58. Waylen (1859) 574.

the preaching of Robert Sloper. The meeting-house was placed in trust for Calvinistic Methodists but the society soon evolved into a Congregational Church (latterly URC, united with Methodists in Long Street, 1985, and chapel converted to workshop). The original building was enlarged to the SE about 1790, when the front wall was brought forward, and in 1792 when a Sunday-school was built against the SW side. In 1868–9 an extension was made to the NE presenting a new entrance front facing Northgate Street and including further classrooms; this was designed and built by Benoni Mullens. The interior was altered and refitted in 1876 under the supervision of J. A. Randell of Bath.

The original chapel of brick with stone dressings lies hidden from view behind the 19th-century forebuilding. The latter is of stone with a gabled front, paired doorways and a large pointed-arched window of four lights. The older SE front of *c.*1790, probably reproducing that of 1777, has a stone plinth, platband, cornice and rusticated quoins. Two doorways are blocked in

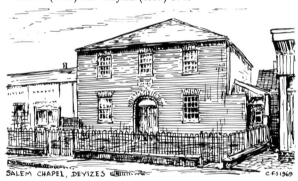

SALEM CHAPEL, DEVIZES

(60) ST MARY'S CHAPEL, Northgate Street (SU 002616), was built in 1776–7 for a society which originated about 1772 with

St Mary's Chapel, Devizes.   (60)

St Mary's Chapel

DEVIZES, *Wiltshire*

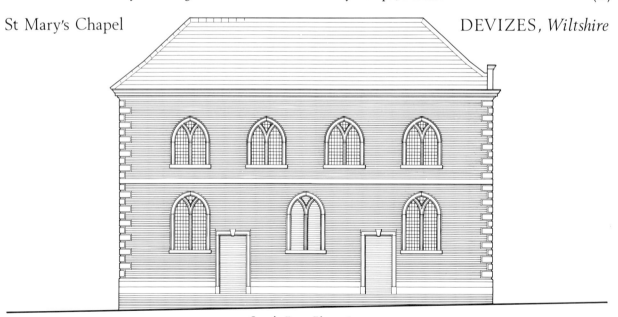

South-East Elevation

brickwork; the windows have simply moulded architraves and stone Y-tracery. The NW wall has two tall windows flanking the pulpit and two shorter gallery windows with details as in the opposite wall but with signs of a possible lowering of the cills.

The interior (originally $29\frac{3}{4}$ ft enlarged to $50\frac{1}{4}$ ft, by 45 ft), although much refitted, still has the pulpit in its original position against the NW wall. Side galleries of the late 18th century formerly continued along the SE wall but a section has been removed to accommodate an organ. The line of the *c*.1790 enlargement is marked by a substantial beam in the roof supported by a large circular column with moulded base and capital.

Fittings – *Books*: remains of a small chapel library, with printed bookplates, *c*.1840. *Monuments*: in chapel (1) Rev. Richard Elliott, 1853; (2) Rev. Robert Sloper, pastor nearly 40 years, 1818, signed 'T. King, Bath'; (3) Rev. William Priestley, pastor here and later at Fordingbridge, Hants., 1827, signed 'T. King, Bath'; (4) Robert Waylen, 1841, and Sarah his wife, 1841, signed 'Druitt, Mile End Road'; (5) Mary, wife of Robert Cale, 1812, and three children, signed 'T. Wood, Bath'; externally, against SW wall, four wall monuments much decayed. *Plate*: includes two tall two-handled cups of 1799.

Broster-Temple, F., *The Story of St. Mary's* [1971–2]. Waylen (1859) 574–5.

(61) Former FRIENDS, High Street (SU 00456140). The meeting-house, now used by Exclusive Brethren, was built in 1702. It stands concealed on the W side of the street behind a later screen wall and forecourt on which further rooms have been built. The walls are of brick with some stone dressings and the roof, hipped to the E, is covered with modern tiles. The E front has rusticated quoins and a coved plaster eaves cornice; the doorway is central with a small window above between two tall windows with flat-arched brick heads. In the roof is a single dormer. A staircase wing projects on the S side. The W wall is gabled and has an extension built against it.

The interior (originally $28\frac{3}{4}$ ft by $25\frac{1}{2}$ ft) comprises a single room to the ground floor with an exposed ceiling beam supported by timber posts against the N and S walls with braces at each end. The staircase rises to a landing with shutters overlooking the meeting-room and continues to an attic room; the uppermost flight has substantial turned balusters of the early 18th century.

Waylen (1859) 574.

DILTON MARSH

(62) BAPTIST, Penknap (ST 857497). 'Providence Chapel', built in 1810 by seceders from the church at Westbury Leigh (155), is a large building of brick with a slate roof. The gabled front of three bays has two tiers of pointed-arched windows filled with stone Y-tracery; in the gable is a pointed lunette with dated inscription. The interior, with a gallery around three sides supported by later iron columns, has been reseated. *Monument*: to Rev. George Phillips, first pastor, 1833.

Ivimey IV (1830) 315.

DOWNTON

(63) BAPTIST, South Lane (SU 175214). A General Baptist church was meeting in Downton by *c*.1670. Peter Coles, 'a Baptist

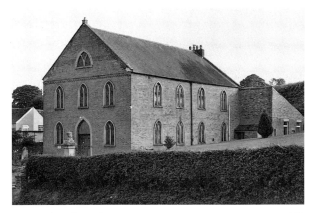

Baptist chapel, Penknap.   (62)

preacher at Downton', is named by Crosby as one of three Baptists kept for 'several years prisoners in the county goal at Sarum, for nonconformity', and John Sanger, 'who kept a writing and grammar-school, and was pastor of the church at Downton', is also named as suffering harassment for the same offence. A house in South Lane close to the present Baptist chapel, built in 1673 across the boundary between the Borough and Manor of Downton, is known to have been occupied from 1679 by a Free Grammar School founded by Sir Joseph Ashe; it is possible that Sanger may have served there as master and that the administrative boundary, clearly defined by stones marking the division across the principal ground-floor room, could have provided some measure of legal immunity to a dissenting conventicle meeting on the premises.

A dwelling-house registered for worship in 1706 during the eldership of Benjamin Miller (1699–1747) may have been intended for the use of General Baptists who built themselves a new meeting-house in 1715. This was superseded by a new chapel in 1835, enlarged 1845, which stood in Gravel Close and may survive as the art room of a school; it closed in 1892 on the amalgamation of the two Baptist congregations.

A Particular Baptist church was formed in 1735 by secession from the earlier society. It has occupied the present site in South Lane since 1794. The chapel, rebuilt in 1856 7, has brick walls and a slated roof with wide eaves supported by moulded brackets. The centre bay of the W wall projects and is surmounted by an elaborate stone acroterion. The interior was drastically altered in 1977.

Monuments: in burial-ground (1) John Taunton, 1841, *et al.*, table-tomb; (2) John Honeywell, 1845, and Elizabeth his wife, 1841; (3) John Barling, 1820, *et al.*, table-tomb.

Crosby III (1740) 126–7. Ivimey II (1814) 584–5. Oliver (1968) 25. Taylor (1818) I, 297, 352; II, 437–40. VCH *Wiltshire* XI (1980) 50. Wood (1847) 206.

EBBESBORNE WAKE

(64) CONGREGATIONAL, Ebbesbourne Wake (ST 993241). The chapel, of flint and stone with a tiled roof, gabled porch and paired round-arched windows, by W.J. Stent of Warminster, was built in 1857. It replaced a former coach-house in use from 1791. The first meeting-house, now a cottage, (ST 992239),

occupied 1782–91, was also the conversion of an existing building. It is square on plan with walls of rubble, ashlar quoins and a pyramidal thatched roof. Two tall windows with brick jambs, now altered, flanking the entrance, and other brick repairs appear to date from the original conversion. A tablet recording its former use was fixed to the SW wall in 1953.

CYB (1858) 253. Haynes (1956) 8–11.

EDINGTON

(65) WESLEYAN, Tinhead (ST 934532). Brick with hipped pantiled roof; dated 1828. Lengthened and refenestrated.

FOVANT

(66) CONGREGATIONAL (SU 004288). Built 1820. Gabled ashlar front with small lunette above round-arched doorway. End gallery added in mid 19th century. *Bootscraper*: wrought-iron with curled standards and urn finials.

CYB (1897) 201–2.

(67) Former FRIENDS' BURIAL-GROUND (ST 99552910). NE of Poplars Inn, seven perches of land with apple tree at centre. Unenclosed, no monuments.

GRAFTON

(68) WESLEYAN, Wilton (SU 266615). 'Bethel Chapel' of brick and slate, was built in 1811; it was much altered *c*.1860–70 when the walls were heightened and a porch and upper window were added to the front. Late 19th-century 'Wesleyan Schools' at side.

GREAT SOMERFORD

(69) Former PRIMITIVE METHODIST, Startley (ST 944824). Three-bay gabled front with round-arched windows; dated 1834. 'Jubilee' schoolroom at rear, 1860. Now studio.

GRITTLETON

(70) Former STRICT BAPTIST (ST 862800). A Baptist conventicle in Mr Greene's house at Grittleton was reported in 1669. The present chapel, although said to have been built in 1720, a date also given for the formation of the church, figures in an undated meeting-house certificate for a 'building newly erected on a close now in the occupation of Joseph Houlton, gentleman', which could date from 1709. The chapel stands on a remote site once part of the grounds of the adjacent Grittleton House. The walls are of rubble with ashlar dressings and the roof is hipped and covered with pantiles. The entrance at the S end has a segmental-arched head with continuous roll-moulded jambs and flush keystone, and a short moulded label above. Two tall mullioned and transomed windows in the W wall, with segmental-arched heads and moulded labels, flank the original site of the pulpit. The E wall has four bays of windows in two tiers separated by a string-course; all are of two lights with segmental-arched heads, the lower taller windows have transoms. The N wall is blank.

The interior ($20\frac{1}{2}$ ft by $40\frac{1}{4}$ ft) has at the S end a gallery with fielded-panelled front supported by two columns, of the mid 18th century. At the N end is a gallery built or altered in the mid 19th century below which is a vestry with a partly glazed screen

Former Strict Baptist chapel, Grittleton.   (70)

Former Strict Baptist chapel, Grittleton.   (70)

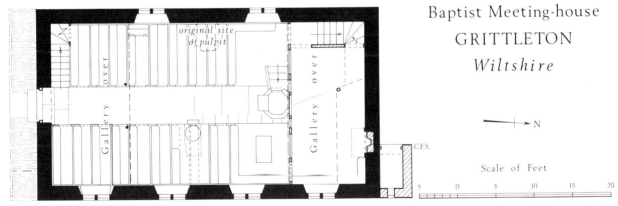

Baptist Meeting-house
GRITTLETON
Wiltshire

towards the chapel, formerly with a doorway in the centre; in the N wall is a small fireplace with 18th-century surround. The roof is supported by king-post trusses of pine with painted date 1916 possibly of repair or renewal.

Candle Sconces: on pulpit and N gallery two pairs each with double arms, brass, 19th-century. *Clock*: on front of S gallery, signed 'J. W. Gantlett, Sherston', 19th-century. *Graffiti*: externally at SE corner, initials and date 1722. *Monuments*: externally on E wall (1) Jacob Bourne, minister, 1857, and Clement, son of Jacob and Emma Bourne, 1857; (2) Robert Smith, 1839, *et al.*; in burial-ground E and N of chapel are several monuments of 18th century and later including (3) Sarah, wife of Daniel Farr, 1740; (4) Elizabeth (May), wife of Thomas Leonard, 1834. *Pulpit*: reset in front of N gallery, octagonal with two tiers of fielded panels, early 18th-century; the outline of the former

pedimented back-board remains on the wall between the W windows. *Seating*: in SE corner, three 18th-century box-pews with fielded-panelled doors, rear pew remains to full original height; other box-pews to lower floor are of mid 19th-century date and include a child's seat on W side; in S gallery, boarded seats, 18th-century; in N gallery, 19th-century. *Miscellaneous*: 'Rules and Regulations for Burial Ground', inscribed on back 'Drawn by John Gerrard, Grittleton, March 1854'.

(Chapel closed 1980, candle sconces and clock removed; reopened *c.*1986 by an independent congregation)

Oliver (1968) 34–5.

(71) CONGREGATIONAL, Littleton Drew (ST 832801). Small chapel with rendered walls and slate roof, registered January 1816 as 'lately erected', superseding the house of Samuel Chappell in use from 1800. Original W gallery with contemporary seating.

Chair: in pulpit, with carved back panel, 17th-century. *Coffin Stools*: two, early 18th-century.

HANKERTON

(72) Former STRICT BAPTIST (ST 974906). Registered 19 October 1837. Rubble with hipped slate roof; entrance at S end with blocked window above, two sash windows in E side, one opposite.

Oliver (1968) 30.

FORMER STRICT BAPTIST CHAPEL, HANKERTON   CFS 1971

HIGHWORTH

(73) CONGREGATIONAL, High Street (SU 201924). 'Zion Chapel erected 1825'; gabled ashlar front of three bays with two tiers of round-arched windows, formerly surmounted by a bell-cote. Interior refitted. Music rolls for a *barrel-organ* reported found in gallery, now removed. (URC)

Beck, R. A., *Highworth United Reformed Church, A Short History, 1777–1977* (1977). *CHST* IV (1909–10) 371–83.

HILPERTON

(74) STRICT BAPTIST, Church Street (ST 873595). Built 1806. Three-bay ashlar front with two tiers of plain sash windows below gable.

Oliver (1968) 67.

HINDON

(75) CONGREGATIONAL (ST 913327). The chapel is said to have been built 1827 for a church formed 1810. Walls of squared stone and a tiled roof. The gabled E front has a pointed-arched doorway and small round-arched gallery window over. Windows in the side walls are of three lights with intersecting tracery in two-centred heads. The seating of plain benches with later backs is of early 19th-century date; the E gallery was also added at that period.

HOLT

(76) CONGREGATIONAL (ST 861618). Chapel built 1880 by W. J. Stent of Warminster. Former chapel, now Sunday-school, may be the meeting-house registered in 1810. It is of stone with a hipped slate roof and pointed-arched windows with intersecting glazing bars.

HORNINGSHAM

(77) THE OLD MEETING-HOUSE (ST 812411) has been described as 'the oldest nonconformist chapel in England'. The date 1566 and the story that the building was provided for the use of Scottish Presbyterian masons then working on Longleat House

have, however, been found incapable of proof from available sources. It can only be said with certainty that a very considerable meeting of Presbyterians or Independents was in existence here in 1669 and that there are some indications that a substantial body of separatists was to be found in this part of the county by the late 16th century. The Horningsham church, regarded as Presbyterian throughout the 18th century, came to be described as Congregational by 1828.

The oldest part of the meeting-house probably dates from *c*.1700 in which year a 'newly erected building standing in a close of pasture or garden ground in possession of George French' was registered for worship. The meeting-house was enlarged to the E in 1754 and greatly extended to the W in 1816. The walls are of stone and the roof is thatched with half hips at each end. The earliest walling in the N and S sides is of small roughly squared and carefully laid rubble. The S side had a central entrance, now blocked and covered by one of two buttresses built in 1925, between two windows with square wooden frames of two lights with leaded glazing. There is a pair of dormer windows above the former doorway. In the corresponding N wall symmetrically about the axis of the entrance are two lower windows with dormers above. The later E wall, which is thinner than the previous work, has a central doorway between two blocked windows. The W extension, in similar materials to the foregoing but with some brick dressings, included a doorway in the N side,

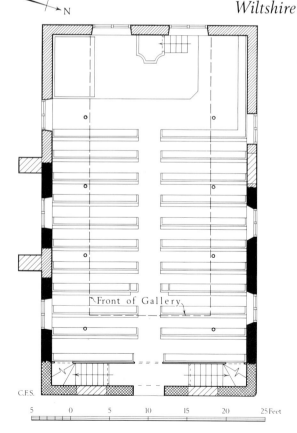

Old Meeting-house, HORNINGSHAM
Wiltshire

Front of Gallery

C.F.S.

The Old Meeting-house, Horningsham. (77)

blocked c.1863. At the W end are two large wooden-framed windows of two lights with a transom.

The interior (originally about 25 ft by 21 ft, now 44 ft by 25 ft) has a gallery around three sides with panelled front of the early 19th century. The E gallery dates from the mid 18th century but was widened when the side galleries were added. The gallery seating is of c.1816 but the lower pews were renewed in 1863. The pulpit at the W end in the style of the 18th century is of more recent date. The roof is supported by braced collar-beam trusses which are concealed above an irregular barrel-vaulted plaster ceiling.

Fittings – *Hat Rails*: in N gallery, with wooden hat pegs, c.1816. *Inscription*: externally on W wall, stone tablet with raised numerals '1566' set between bands of brickwork, erected and perhaps cut in 1816 to celebrate the supposed 250th anniversary of the building. *Monuments*: in chapel (1) to former ministers, Dr Cotton, Rev. J. Driver, Rev. J. Russill, 1791, and Rev. J. Gould, 1813, with later names added, painted wooden tablet; externally on W wall (2) 'IN MEMORY OF WILLM BARNES who died of the HYDROPHOBIA: he was Bitten by a Dog on the 18 of May and was Dipped in the Salt Water on the 19 and Died on the 31 of July following after a few HOURS *of Strong* PAROXYSMS: aged 28 years 1820', stone tablet with decayed painted inscription.

Banton, A. E., *Horningsham Chapel* (1952). *CYB* (1855) 258–9. *PHSJ* I (1914–19) 73–87. Stribling (1897) 12–14. VCH *Wiltshire* III (1956) 99–100.

HULLAVINGTON

(78) STRICT BAPTIST (ST 895820). 'Mount Zion Particular Baptist Chapel', dated 1843, small building of rubble with ashlar quoins.

Oliver (1968) 33.

(79) Former CHAPEL (ST 895824). Rubble with half-hipped roof covered with stone slates, pointed-arched windows. Early 19th-century, possibly the chapel registered as 'lately erected' August 1821 and held in trust for Baptists and Independents.

(80) Former FRIENDS, Watts Lane (ST 897822). A meeting-house built in 1697 and closed in 1812 was used as a school from 1818. In 1842 Primitive Methodists applied for the use of the building, eventually purchasing it in 1902. The Methodist chapel, which occupies the same site and may incorporate some of the material of the meeting-house, is a low building of rubble with red brick dressings; it was rebuilt or extensively repaired in the late 19th century. Burial-ground to W with single headstone only of 1905. (Chapel sold 1988)

IDMISTON

(81) BAPTIST, Porton (SU 187364). A Particular Baptist church was formed at Porton in 1655 including members from as far as Broughton, Hampshire, and Salisbury. The Salisbury members formed a separate church in 1690 and meetings at Porton ceased about 1710 when two cottages at Broughton were converted to a meeting-house. Ivimey (1814) says that 'there is at present no trace of a dissenting interest at Porton excepting the burying-ground; nor is there a baptist or dissenter of any kind in the place'. Earlier meetings were held 'in a large hall of a farm-house,

belonging to Mr. Andrews', Bird-Lime Farm (SU 185368), next to which was the burial-ground. The present chapel, of c.1860–70, has rendered walls and paired lancet windows.

Doel (1890) 8. Ivimey II (1814) 580–4; IV (1830) 310–13. Oliver (1968) 88–91. White II (1973) 107 n.26.

KINGTON LANGLEY

(82) UNION CHAPEL (ST 922768). A society gathered by John Cennick c.1742 first met in a barn. The principal conduct of the services soon passed to the Moravians who in 1748 opened a Single Sisters' House. This was transferred to East Tytherton (24) in 1751 but the meeting-house remained in use.

Union Chapel, Kington Langley. (82)

The present chapel was built in 1835 and placed in trust for the joint use of Moravians, Independents and Baptists. The walls are of coursed rubble with ashlar dressings and the roof is covered with slates. The NW front has plain terminal pilasters, an inscribed platband and a ball finial on the gable; above a small ashlar porch is a window of two round-arched lights. Side windows have round-arched heads and wooden Y-tracery. A vestry wing projects to the right. The interior has a single rear gallery supported by two iron columns. The pulpit and lower seating were renewed in the late 19th century but some original box-pews remain in the gallery.

Inscriptions: on platband of front gable 'O come, let us enter, into the house of our God'; on square tablet above 'Union Chapel 1835 J. Pinnegar Builder'.

England (1886–7) I, 9–10; II, pl. XIII.

(83) PRIMITIVE METHODIST, Silver Street (ST 926771). 'Erected 1814 [?44], rebuilt 1848'; small building of stone with hipped roof covered with open slating. Pointed-arched openings.

PRIMITIVE METHODIST CHAPEL, KINGTON LANGLEY   C.F.S 1974

LACOCK

(84) CONGREGATIONAL, Cantax Hill (ST 915687). The chapel was built in 1808 on land given by Mary Stephens and registered for Independents on 4 June as 'a house lately built by subscriptions'. Coursed rubble with ashlar dressings and a hipped roof covered with small stone slates. Front with segmental pointed-arched doorway, flat stone canopy, and window with stone Y-tracery above. The side and rear walls have each two similar windows. The interior (33 ft by 23 ft) has an original rear gallery but has otherwise been refitted. (URC)

Fittings – *Gates*: at entrance from road, wrought-iron gates, piers and overthrow, early 19th-century. *Monuments*: in chapel (1) Mary Stephens, 1834, recording gift of ground in 1808, modern tablet; in burial-ground (2) Robert Stephens, 1821, and Mary Stephens, 1834.

(85) WESLEYAN (ST 925681). Gabled front with three graduated lancets above porch and plain scrolled band above; opened 1860.

LIMPLEY STOKE

(86) BAPTIST (ST 781607). Three-bay gabled front of ashlar with round-arched openings, dated 1815. (Demolition proposed 1988)

LONGBRIDGE DEVERILL

(87) Former BAPTIST, Crockerton Green (ST 868432). A Particular Baptist church was in existence here by 1669 and houses were registered for Baptist use in 1701 and 1704. A small congregation which met for reading sermons is said to have been presented in 1723 with a folio volume of the works of John Flavel which still remained in the chapel in 1879.

The chapel, which stands on the E side of the main road, was built in the mid 18th century. The walls are of squared stone laid in shallow courses and the roof is tiled. The broad W front of four bays has rusticated stone quoins and a moulded stone cornice below the eaves; the entrances are in the end bays, that at the N end now blocked; the windows have semicircular heads but without structural arches. The rear wall has corresponding windows but with square heads and some traces of alteration to those in the end bays. The N wall is gabled. At the S end is an extension of later 18th-century date in a similar style containing two storeys of rooms.

The interior of the chapel (20¼ ft by 40 ft) was refitted in the mid 19th century and has a single gallery of that period at the S

Former Baptist chapel, Crockerton Green.   (87)

end. The pulpit, re-sited at the N end, was probably originally between the front windows.

Fittings – *Baptistery*: external, between front windows, with steps at N and S ends. *Clock*: 'contemporary long wall clock' reported MHLG lists 1960, unlocated. *Monuments*: in chapel, on N wall (1) John Clark, 57 years pastor, 1803, signed 'Biggs, Bath'; (2) Joseph Thresher, 39 years minister, 1842, erected 1861; in small burial-ground E of chapel, a few 19th-century headstones. *Pulpit*: re-sited, hexagonal with fielded-panelled sides and back-board, mid 18th-century.

(Chapel converted to commercial use since 1970)

Daniell (1879) 238. Oliver (1968) 79–80. VCH *Wiltshire* III (1956) 111–12.

LYNEHAM

(88) PROVIDENCE CHAPEL, Bradenstoke (ST 999794). A congregation was gathered at Clack (now Bradenstoke) by John Cennick about 1742 and a dwelling-house registered in 1743 as a meeting place. Although perhaps regarded for a short period as a Moravian society, the congregation retained a high degree of independency and included Baptists amongst its members. These had grown to sufficient strength by 1843 to re-organize the society, in spite of some opposition, into a Strict Baptist church which it remains.

Providence Chapel, Bradenstoke.   (88)

The chapel, built in 1777, has walls mainly of red brick with stone dressings and traces of diaper work below the front windows; the roof which is covered with stone slates has a half hip to the south and is surmounted by a small square wooden bell-cote. The S front has a stone plinth, rusticated quoins and a moulded stone cornice at the base of the gable; the windows have segmental-arched heads with keystones; the original arched entrance is covered by an ashlar porch of the early 19th century. The N wall of rubble has two windows matching those in the front and two attic windows in the gable. The E and W walls had each one window near the S end, and centrally in the E wall was an original doorway, all now blocked. A contemporary house adjoins to the west.

The interior (27 ft by 18 ft) has a lofty ceiling with moulded cornice and two exposed beams supporting an attic floor. The pulpit is centrally at the N end and there is a small S gallery from which a staircase rises to the upper floor. The attic is divided into three rooms of which that to the N is now approached from the adjoining house. The roof is supported by two trusses with pegged collars.

Fittings – *Bell*: in bell-cote, inscribed 'IOHN : BROOM CASTLE : COOMBE 1779 GOD : SAVE : THE : KING & QUEEN'. *Coffin Stools*: two, late 18th-century. *Monuments*: in chapel (1) Edward Bryant, 1782, Susan his widow, 1791, William their son, 1809, and Mary Bryant, 1838; (2) John Sutton, 1830, and Ann his wife, 1828; (3) James Sutton, 1839, *et al.*; (4) Sarah, wife of Richard Prior, 1791, and Ann, daughter of Richard and Sarah Prior and 'grand-daughter of the above', 1793; also 19th-century monuments in burial-grounds in front of chapel and N of house. *Plate*: includes a cup of ?1833 and contemporary plate, presented to the Baptist church, Marlborough, 1848. *Pulpit*: with paired corner pilasters and dentil cornice, late 18th-century. *Seating*: in gallery, mid 19th-century, lower seating renewed *c*.1928.

England I (1886–7) 7–8. Oliver (1968) 45–6.

(89) PRIMITIVE METHODIST, Bradenstoke (SU 002795). Chapels of 1828 and 1886 stand adjacent; each with a gabled front of three bays, the latter with a circular window above the porch.

MALMESBURY

(90) STRICT BAPTIST, Abbey Row (ST 932874). The chapel,

built for a church formed in the late 17th century, is dated 1802 although only registered as 'lately erected' in January 1816. A gallery was added in 1814 and the building enlarged to the rear in 1816. The walls are of coursed rubble with ashlar dressings. Three-bay gabled front with two pointed-arched windows and central doorway with Tuscan-columned porch.

Communion Cloth: Oliver (1968) refers to a communion cloth inscribed 'For the use of the Ordinance at the Baptist Church, Malmesbury, March 24th 1815'. *Monuments*: in burial-ground, several early 19th-century monuments including a pedestal tomb with draped urn to Giles Canter, 1839, and Mary his wife, 1823.

Bird, J. T., *The History of the Town of Malmesbury* (1876) 192. Oliver (1968) 27–30.

(91) CONGREGATIONAL, Westport (ST 930875). The formerly Presbyterian congregation (now URC) was formed in the late 17th century; the meeting-house rebuilt in 1788 included a range of cellars below. The present chapel, of stone with an octagonal turret and spire at one corner, by W. J. Stent of Warminster, was built in 1867.

Bird, op.cit. 191, 201–2.

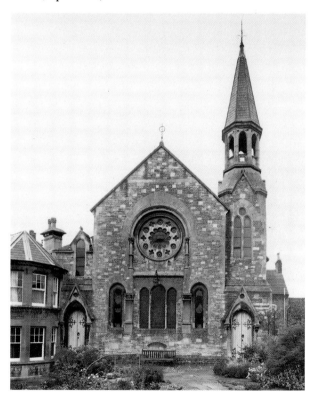

Congregational chapel (URC), Malmesbury. (91)

(92) MORAVIAN, Oxford Street (ST 934873). A society formed in 1742 as a result of John Cennick's preaching joined the Wiltshire congregation of Moravian societies in 1748. A maltster, Mr Lyne, fitted up a malt-house for use as a meeting place which remained in use until 1770. The present chapel, on the site of its predecessor, was opened 4 November 1770 and a gallery was added in 1787. The building was greatly altered in 1859 when it was enlarged to the west.

Strict Baptist chapel, Malmesbury. (90)

The walls are of rubble with ashlar quoins, rendered to the E, and the roof is slate covered. The E front has three round-arched windows with beaded stone surrounds and renewed glazing; below the end window to the N is a doorway with moulded canopy of the late 18th century. The N wall is blank but the outline of the original gable remains visible. An 18th-century house adjoins to the south. The W wall of 1859 has two windows to the chapel and a staircase wing at the N end. The interior (36¼ ft, by about 20 ft enlarged to 32¼ ft) has a pulpit at the S end with a gallery opposite.

Fittings – *Monuments*: in front of chapel to E, several early 19th-century marker-stones; in burial-ground to W, stones of late 18th century and after. *Plate*: two-handled cup given 1840 by James Montgomery, the hymn writer. *Pulpit*: hexagonal with fielded-panelled front on shaped base, staircase with turned balusters, 18th-century, possibly 1752 when a new pulpit was provided.

England I (1886–7) 9–10, pl.10.

MANNINGFORD

(93) STRICT BAPTIST, Manningford Bohune (SU 138577). Chapel dated 1869 replacing a tenement registered for worship 22 November 1826.

Oliver (1968) 22. Paul VI (1969) 241–50.

MARKET LAVINGTON

(94) Former FRIENDS (SU 017544). The meeting-house, at the E end of the town NW of the Congregational chapel, was built in 1716; it was sold at the beginning of the 19th century to a newly formed Congregational church. The new owners enlarged the meeting-house to twice its original size and after building a new chapel in 1891 retained it for the purposes of a Sunday-school; it now serves as an artist's studio.

The walls are of rubble and brickwork and the roof is hipped and tiled. The original structure (said to have measured 33 ft by 22 ft) is probably represented by the S end of the building (now enlarged to 33 ft by 41¾ ft externally). The S wall facing the road is of rubble and has one segmental-arched window with ashlar surround. The E front rebuilt or refaced in the early 19th century is of five bays with two tiers of windows and entrances in the penultimate bays. The roof is of irregular shape and is supported internally by a central post on the line of extension. There is an early 19th-century gallery along the E side. Former stables to the N have been converted to a cottage. In the burial-ground to E and N are some early 19th-century tombstones.

Atley, H., *A Topographical Account of Market Lavington, Wilts. . . .* (1855).

MARLBOROUGH

(95) Former CONGREGATIONAL, The Parade (SU 190691). An Independent congregation was formed by William Hughes, ejected vicar of St Mary's, Marlborough, who was licensed as a dissenting minister in 1672. A meeting-house built in 1706 appears to have been abandoned by *c.*1755, possibly as a result of divisions within the society. About 1725 two separate congregations of Presbyterians and Independents existed. The congregation revived about 1770 when a new meeting-house was built but at the beginning of the 19th century possession of that

building also was lost. The present chapel was built on a new site in 1817.

The chapel, of brick with a hipped tiled roof, has a front of three bays with a central pediment and two tiers of round-arched windows. A porch was built in 1873. The interior, which has a rear gallery, was also refitted at that date. (Converted to commercial use *c.*1985)

Gale, J.W., *Marlborough Congregational Church* (1957). Steadman, A.R., *Marlborough and the Upper Kennet Country* (1960) 201–9, 360.

(96) Former WESLEYAN, Oxford Street (SU 190692). Brick and slate with three-bay front, pedimental gable and circular window above entrance. Built in 1816, polygonal rear bay added 1872. Superseded by adjacent chapel in 1910 and since converted to a Masonic Hall.

Methodist Recorder (Winter Number, Christmas 1896) 46.

Former Wesleyan chapel, Marlborough. (96)

MARSTON

(97) PRIMITIVE METHODIST (ST 966568). Three-bay gabled front of brick, dated 1835.

MELKSHAM WITHIN

(98) BAPTIST, Old Broughton Road, Melksham (ST 902643). Part of the present site was acquired in 1714 by a church originating in the late 17th century and a meeting-house (29 ft by 18 ft) was built and registered in that year. By 1771 a larger building had become necessary and the present chapel was consequently built on an adjacent site in 1776–7. The accommodation was enlarged in 1795 by the erection of a gallery and in 1806 a vestry was built and the chapel extended 'at the pulpit end'. The gallery was enlarged in 1839, and in 1879 the

interior was entirely refitted. A Sunday-school, by W. W. Snailum of Trowbridge, was built in 1908–9. The roof of the chapel was repaired or renewed in 1919.

The chapel has walls of rubble with ashlar dressings and a tall hipped roof covered with patent tiles. The NE front of three bays has round-arched upper windows and a central doorway with pilasters and a pedimented entablature with bolection-moulded frieze. The side walls each have two round-arched upper windows; a blocked window in the NW wall indicates a major refenestration. Two windows in the rear wall formerly flanking the pulpit have been blocked. The interior (40½ ft by 30¼ ft) has a gallery around three sides with open cast-iron balustraded front.

Monuments: in chapel (1) John Ledyard, 1790, and Mary his wife, 1784; (2) Jane Ann, wife of Rev. Joshua Russell, 1840; externally on SE wall (3) Sa...[?son of] Rev. George Wickenden of Trowbridge, 1779, cartouche with baroque ornament; (4) Charles Parker, 1837.

Cooper, F. W., *Broughton Road Baptist Church, Melksham* (1969). Oliver (1968) 49–50.

(99) STRICT BAPTIST, Union Street, Melksham (ST 905641). 'Ebenezer Chapel' was built 1835 for seceders from the foregoing who had separated in 1821. Coursed stone with ashlar dressings and slate roof. Low gabled front with three plain sash windows and central doorway. An external baptistery behind the chapel was in use until 1926 or later.

Oliver (1968) 50–1. Paul VI (1969) 221–7.

(100) Former CONGREGATIONAL, Market Place, Melksham (ST 905636). The chapel, built *c*.1776, was said to have been 'already licensed, but recently enlarged' when it was re-registered in August 1837. The walls are of rubble with an ashlar front and the roof is slated. The gabled W front, partly obscured by a porch of *c*.1925–30 incorporating the original pedimented doorcase, has

three tall round-arched upper windows with stone Y-tracery. The side walls have two tiers of windows, those at gallery level having pointed-arched heads. The interior (60½ ft by 27½ ft) was refitted and the roof rebuilt in the late 19th century. There is a continuous gallery with an open cast-iron front.

Fittings – *Monuments*: in chapel (1) Ann, wife of James Wilshere, 1784, and Ann their daughter, 1782; (2) Rev. Jacob Jones, six years pastor, 'who perished in the wreck of the "Catherine Adamson" off Sydney Heads, October 24th, 1857'; (3) Rev. John Honywill, first pastor, 1836. *Painting*: in vestry, portrait in oils of Rev. John Honywill, pastor 1778–1836.

(Church, now URC, united with Methodists and chapel sold *c*.1981)

EM (December 1837) 594.

(101) Former FRIENDS, King Street, Melksham (ST 904635). A meeting-house in converted premises was in use by 1695. The present building, now occupied by the Melksham Spiritualist Church, was erected in 1776. A women's meeting-house built against the W side in the later 18th century was extended to the S some years later.

The meeting-house has stone walls with ashlar facing to the earliest part and a hipped stone-slated roof at the front. The E front has a moulded cornice and parapet which continue along the side walls; there were originally three segmental-arched windows at the front, of which that in the centre has been removed; the N and S walls have each two windows of a matching design and this is repeated in the W windows of the rear extensions. The original entrance may have been in the W wall but is now at the S side.

The principal meeting-room (24¼ ft by 30 ft) has a long stand against the E wall with plain panelled front and stairs with rectangular balusters and turned newels. The original W wall has

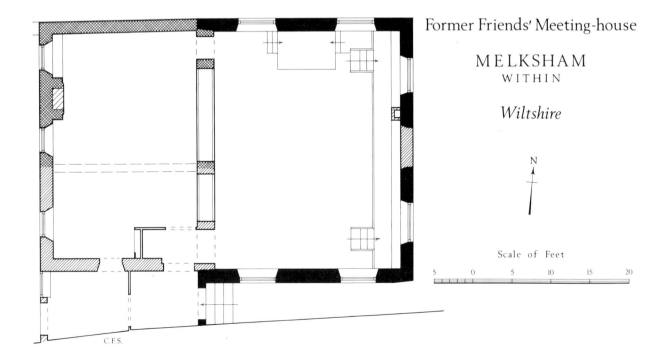

Former Friends' Meeting-house

MELKSHAM
WITHIN

Wiltshire

N

Scale of Feet

5   0   5   10   15   20

C.F.S.

Former Friends' meeting-house, Melksham.   (101)

been replaced by double shuttered partitions and doorways at each end. In the NW room is a fireplace with late 18th-century stone surround.

Monuments: in burial-ground to W, uniform headstones including John Moxham, 1787, and Esther Moxham, 1798. (A small enclosed burial-ground immediately S with 19th-century monuments belongs to another denomination.)

(102) WESLEYAN, High Street, Melksham (ST 905637). Built 1871–2; pedimented front with four giant Corinthian columns and short end-bays with urns on balustraded parapets. 'Wesleyan Sunday School' to N dated 1860.

Wesleyan chapel, Melksham.   (102)

MERE

(103) CONGREGATIONAL (ST 814323). A chapel built in 1795 by Robert Butt, a successful grocer, was superseded in 1852 by a new chapel designed by W. J. Stent of Warminster. The present chapel, standing alongside its predecessor, was built in 1868 by the silk manufacturer, Charles Jupe.

Congregational chapel (URC), Mere.   (103)

The former chapel, of stone with a slate roof, was refronted and converted to a British School in 1868; the side wall has five bays with lancet windows and single-stage buttresses. The present chapel (now URC) of stone and tile is an elaborate Gothic building comprising a polygonal chancel, transepts, nave of four bays and entrance bay to west. The nave arcades are carried by cast-iron columns, which also support a gallery around three sides. The roof has arched braces and enriched tie-beams and king-struts.

Fittings – *Chair*: in vestry, domestic chair with label recording that it was one of six 'being the first distraint in Mere, Wilts., for refusal to pay that portion of rate applied to sectarian education – sold in the market place 23.9.1903' in opposition to the Education Act of 1903. *Painting*: watercolour sketch of first chapel made from memory by the minister, E. P. Erlebach, 1852, after demolition.

Williams, D. E., *History of the Congregational Church, in Mere, Wilts, from... 1795 to... 1895* (1919).

(104) FRIENDS (ST 814324). On S side of main road, built 1863 with former Temperance Hall behind; small meeting-house added *c*.1927. Lintel of front windows inscribed 'Lecture Hall'.

(105) PRIMITIVE METHODIST, North Street (ST 814325). Three-bay front of stone with clasping buttresses and two tiers of narrow round-arched windows, dated 1846.

MINETY

(106) STRICT BAPTIST, Sawyers Hill (SU 024908). Rubble front with brick sides in rat-trap bond; tablet in gable inscribed 'Peculiar Baptist Chapel rebuilt in 1862'.

Oliver (1968) 31.

'PECULIAR BAPTIST CHAPEL', SAWYERS HILL.   C.F.S.1971

NETHERAVON

(107) PRIMITIVE METHODIST (SU 148490). In lane off E side of High Street; altered three-bay front of banded brick and flint, built 1847.

A burial-ground to NE, with brick gate piers and ball finials, remains from a Strict Baptist chapel of 1820 burnt down 1946.

Oliver (1968) 20–1.

NETTLETON

(108) BAPTIST (ST 821779). Coursed rubble with rendered gabled front, pointed-arched windows. Opened 1823, schoolroom built *c*.1843, interior refitted and windows altered 1889.

Cruse, C. J., *Castle Combe, Wiltshire* (1965) 66–7.

NEW SARUM (SALISBURY)

(109) Former PRESBYTERIAN, Salt Lane (SU 14603015). The meeting-house was built *c*.1702 at the expense of Thomas Harrison, ironmonger, for a congregation which was formed in the late 17th century; a house was erected on part of the forecourt *c*.1720. The congregation, which survived until 1813, appears to have had a heterodox ministry by the late 18th century and in its later years to have attracted very little support. The building had been lent on various occasions to the Methodists, and on the

failure of the original society the trustees placed the property in the hands of the Wesleyans who used it as a schoolroom in connection with their chapel in St Edmund's Church Street. It was sold to the Salvation Army in 1882.

The meeting-house stands on the S side of the lane. The walls are of brickwork with a later cement rendering and the roof is covered with slates. The side and rear walls of the original building remain but the N wall has been demolished and a small extension built at that end. The former minister's house was rebuilt in 1899.

The front wall had a central entrance with a window to the right and a small room projecting to the left built *c*.1737 by the minister, Samuel Fancourt, as a 'library' or vestry; all this has now been removed. The S wall, now covered by later buildings, has a serrated brick cornice; two former windows have been blocked. Two original windows remain in the E and W walls; the windows in the E wall have early 18th-century oak frames of two lights under segmental-arched heads; those in the W wall have similar frames but with renewed mullions and with arched heads probably added in the early 19th century.

The interior (39½ ft by 45 ft) has been entirely refitted and re-roofed. A photograph of *c*.1880 shows that the building then had a double roof with central valley supported by two tall wooden posts with chamfered corners and a cross-beam near the S end with two similar supports and a wide gallery across that end. The gallery was probably added in 1737 when it is described as new; the staircase was in the SE corner. The original site of the pulpit is uncertain but may have been against one of the side walls.

Deeds and minute books with the Methodist church. RCHM *City of Salisbury* I (1980) 138–9.

(110) BAPTIST, Brown Street (SU 14652985). The Particular Baptist congregation separated from the Porton church (81) in 1690. A meeting-house erected in Brown Street by 1719 was rebuilt in 1794–5, and superseded by a larger chapel in 1829 in a 'debased classical style' by William Henry Roe of Southampton. The chapel, rebuilt or drastically reconstructed in 1881–2 by W. J. Stent of Warminster, has a front of red brick with a large circular window above the entrance. *Monuments*: in chapel (1) Thomas Marsh, 1830, and Elizabeth Marsh, 1823, signed 'Osmond'; (2) Rev. John Saffery, 35 years pastor, 1825.

Ivimey IV (1830) 306–10. [Moore, G. A.] *The Story of Brown Street Baptist Church, Salisbury, 1655-1955* (1955).

(111) CONGREGATIONAL, Fisherton Street (SU 142300). A meeting-house, built on the S side of Scots Lane in 1767 for a church formed ten years before, was enlarged in 1791. In 1806 some members seceded to establish a new congregation for which a chapel was built on the W side of Endless Street in 1810. The congregations reunited at the latter place in 1860, which was then refronted by W. J. Stent of Warminster; the Scots Lane premises were retained for school purposes until 1890. The church (now URC) removed to the present building in 1879. The former chapels have been demolished.

The chapel is a large building of stone with a slate roof, in the Gothic style, by Tarring and Wilkinson. It comprises a nave and aisles, N chancel, and SE tower and spire. *Organ*: from St Mary's Church, Bathwick, early 19th-century.

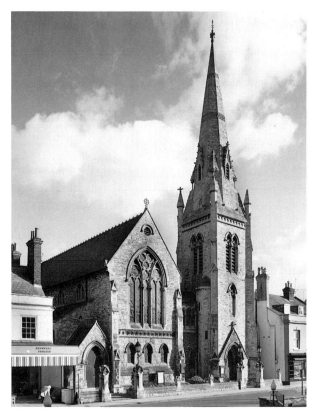

Congregational chapel (URC), Fisherton Street, Salisbury. (111)

(112) Site of FRIENDS, Gigant Street (SU 14682985). A meeting-house built in 1712 on the W side of the street was used in the early 19th century as an Infant School and later as a Temperance Hall and reading room. It survived in reconstructed form until recent years at the S end of Gigant Street Brewery but no traces now remain.

Short, H., *City of Salisbury* (1957) 122.

(113) WESLEYAN, St Edmund's Church Street (SU 14703013). The first preaching-house on this site, built in 1759, was praised by John Wesley, who had offered his advice in its design, as 'the most complete in England'. It was superseded by the present chapel in 1810–11 which was enlarged to the front in 1835, altered internally and the front rendered in 1870 and further additions and embellishments made to the W front in the early 20th century. A Sunday-school was built to the E in 1882.

The walls are of brick and the roof is slated. The W front is partly covered by a later porch. The side walls have two tiers of windows and there are traces of two round-arched windows remaining in the E wall.

The interior, refitted in 1870, has a continuous gallery with an open cast-iron front by Walter MacFarlane & Co. of Glasgow.

Monuments: in room below E gallery (1) Richard Earlsman, 1831, with details of charitable bequests, signed 'Cave'; (2) Joseph Sanger, 1846. *Pulpit*: rostrum incorporating front panel with reeded pilasters and moulded cornice of early 19th-century pulpit.

RCHM *City of Salisbury I* (1980) 46.

(114) Former PRIMITIVE METHODIST, Fisherton Street (SU 14033003). On S side of road behind other buildings; now a Conservative Club. Built 1826, enlarged to rear *c*.1850 and superseded 1869 by new chapel opposite, now a theatre. Rendered brick walls with round-arched windows.

RCHM op.cit. 158.

NORTH BRADLEY

(115) Site of BAPTIST (ST 859554). The chapel, built in 1779–80, was demolished about 1961 and a new chapel was built on a nearby site. The former chapel was extended by 10 ft to the rear in 1803 and enlarged to one side in 1831. The walls were of brickwork with ashlar quoins; the front of three bays with a platband below a pedimental gable had two tiers of pointed-arched windows. The interior, which had been reseated in the late 19th century, had a gallery next to the entrance added in 1796 and further galleries in each of the extensions.

The site is marked by the former entrance gates with stone piers and iron overthrow with seating for a lamp. The date-tablets from the front of the chapel are reset in the wall of an outbuilding. Several table-tombs and other monuments of the late 18th century and after remain in the burial-ground.

Doel (1890) 186–91.

NORTH WRAXALL

(116) Former CONGREGATIONAL, Ford (ST 838750). High above road on N side, rubble with hipped stone-slate roof and segmental-arched windows. Built 1820 for a church which earlier met in a cottage.

Cruse, C.J., *Castle Combe, Wiltshire* (1965) 66.

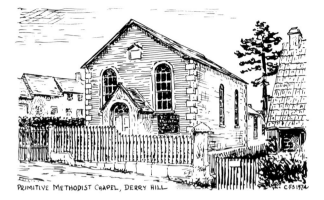

PRIMITIVE METHODIST CHAPEL, DERRY HILL

PEWSHAM

(117) PRIMITIVE METHODIST, Derry Hill (ST 952709). Brick with stone quoins, three-bay gabled front, pedimented date-tablet 1857.

RAMSBURY

(118) CONGREGATIONAL (SU 273715). 'Ebenezer Chapel' dated 1839, rendered front set back between houses, simple Venetian window below gable. (URC)

(119) PRIMITIVE METHODIST, Oxford Street (SU 276717). Red brick and stone, triple-arched front with two tiers of windows, dated 1876.

(120) Former CHAPEL, Chapel Lane (SU 277718). Banded flint and brick, mid 19th-century. Perhaps Primitive Methodist.

ROWDE

(121) WESLEYAN, Marsh Lane (ST 979626). Brick with three-bay gabled front and round-arched windows, dated 1838.

RUSHALL

(122) GENERAL BAPTIST (SU 125562). A church said to have been formed in 1706, which was certainly in existence here by 1743, was greatly reduced in numbers by the early 19th century. Although for most of its existence the congregation derived its support from the old General Baptist Assembly, a brief revival in its fortunes from c.1840 was marked by membership of the New

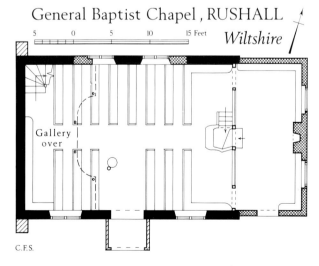

General Baptist Chapel, RUSHALL

Wiltshire

5   0   5   10   15 Feet

Gallery over

C.F.S.

General Baptist chapel, Rushall. (122)

Connexion. Divided or uncertain loyalties appear to have been a feature of its later years.

The chapel was built c.1743 following a bequest by Anne Tyler of property to provide a residence for a minister and to finance the building of a meeting-house. A vestry was built at the E end and the chapel refitted in 1839. A porch was added to the S and the window-frames renewed in 1919.

The walls are of brickwork, covered, except on the N, by later rendering. The main roof is hipped and tiled, the vestry roof is slated. The walls have a brick plinth and a dentil brick cornice below the eaves. The S front of three bays has two segmental-arched windows and a small gabled porch. Before 1919 the entrance had a semicircular fanlight above a pair of panelled doors and two columns supporting a flat canopy. The N wall has two windows, altered in 1839 or later, replacing wider windows which probably flanked the pulpit.

The interior ($18\frac{1}{4}$ ft by 27 ft) was entirely altered and re-aligned in 1839. The ceiling has a segmental-arched plaster vault. The E wall next to the vestry has been replaced by a screen with two doorways, sliding shutters and a former direct entrance to the pulpit which was re-sited in front. A W gallery, also of the date of the refitting, has a panelled front with recessed centre supported by turned wooden columns.

Fittings – Pulpit: hexagonal with two tiers of fielded panels, mid 18th-century with cornice of 1839 and stairs to N added 1919. Seating: benches in gallery and box-pews below with doors removed, 1839. (Chapel closed 1972, demolished 1982; modern monument remains in triangular enclosure at front of site)
    VCH Wiltshire III (1956) 136. Wood (1847) 230.

SALISBURY (See NEW SARUM)

SEEND

(123) METHODIST (ST 941609). John Wesley preached 'in the new house at Seend' on 4 March 1775. The chapel, which has the dates 1774 and 1775 on later inscriptions, stands close to one end of a contemporary terrace of three-storeyed cottages formerly 'Factory Row'. The walls are of brick with ashlar quoins and dressings and the roof is hipped and slated. The walls were heightened and the windows renewed in stone with pointed-arched heads c.1830. The N front has a central doorway with pedimented hood supported by stone brackets and a two-light gallery window above. In the S wall are two windows of two

Methodist chapel, Seend.   (123)

lights and in the W wall two windows of three lights. In the E wall a single window at gallery level with a wooden frame of two lights has been blocked.

The interior (30 ft by 19¾ ft) has an early 19th-century N gallery supported by cast-iron columns. The rostrum pulpit and seating are also of the 19th century.

Dolbey (1964) 75–6.

(124) PRIMITIVE METHODIST, Seend Cleeve (ST 931610). The chapel, opened September 1841, is of brick with stone quoins and dressings and has a hipped slated roof. The front is of three bays with round-arched windows.

Petty (1880) 449.

SEMLEY

(125) BAPTIST (ST 890267). 'Bethesda Chapel' dated 1823 has walls of coursed stone and a slate roof. Galleries were added shortly after 1841 and the building extended to the N with a vestry and upper schoolroom at that period. The S front is gabled; the windows have round-arched heads of the mid 19th century but traces of earlier fenestration are visible in the W wall. The interior has a gallery next to the entrance and narrow side galleries supported by cast-iron columns.

B.Hbk (1886) 124. Bowles, C., Modern Wilts., Hundred of Chalke (1830) 86.

BAPTIST CHAPEL, SEMLEY

SHERSTON

(126) Former BAPTIST, Grove Road (ST 85378575). Rubble with rendered front and half-hipped slate roof. Round-arched window of three lights with wooden tracery above segmental-arched doorway in end wall. Early 19th-century.

(127) CONGREGATIONAL, Cliff Road (ST 85238585). Rendered rubble walls and half-hipped roof covered with stone slates. Three round-arched windows with intersecting wooden tracery on W side face the road, with oval tablet dated 1825 above middle window. End entrance with window above. The interior has a gallery at the S end and pulpit opposite of 1825. Seating renewed in late 19th century.

Monuments: in chapel (1) Thomas William Deverell, 1831, and Sarah his daughter, 1831; Thomas Deverell, 1844, and Mary his wife, 1834.

CONGREGATIONAL CHAPEL, SHERSTON   C.F.S. 1971

(128) PRIMITIVE METHODIST, Grove Road (ST 85458582). Rubble and slate with two round-arched windows facing the road; dated 1851.

SHREWTON

(129) BAPTIST (SU 069436). 'Zion Chapel rebuilt 1846', brick with stone dressings and pedimented doorway.

SOUTHWICK

(130) Former GENERAL BAPTIST (unlocated). A congregation which formed part of a joint church with Conigre Meeting, Trowbridge (see (142)), was in existence by 1714. A meeting-house in Goose Street was closed and demolished c.1800. The clock was later purchased by Samuel Martin, minister at Conigre Chapel, where it remained until c.1974 when it was transferred to the General Baptist Chapel, Ditchling, Sussex (TQ 327153). Octagonal dial with short pendulum case inscribed 'Lo! Here I stand full in thy sight to tell the hour of day and night therefore example take by me and serve thy God as I serve thee'. A paper pasted on the back records the provenance.

Ivimey II (1814) 586–7. Murch (1835) 70–1, 76.

(131) PARTICULAR BAPTIST (ST 841550). The church claims to have originated in the mid 17th century when meetings were being held at North Bradley. The present site was acquired in 1709 and is described as 'in a certain close called Wyndsom's Bridge Close, within the parish of North Bradley'. The first

OLD BAPTIST CHAPEL, SOUTHWICK

meeting-house was a building 30 ft by 16 ft with low walls 9 ft high, a thatched roof and a very low gallery at the entrance.

The present 'Old Baptist Chapel' was built in 1815 on a site adjacent to the former which was then demolished. In 1846 the pulpit was removed from the SW side to an adjacent wall and the gallery altered. The interior was substantially refitted in 1872–3. The walls are of brickwork and the roof is hipped and slated. The NW front of three bays has two tiers of segmental-arched windows with stone dressings, and diaper-patterned brickwork below continuous upper cills. The side walls have similar fenestration; the SE wall has two round-arched windows, presumably of 1846. The interior has a gallery around three sides.

Baptistery: 150 yards NW of chapel, close to river, square enclosure bounded by rubble walls, reconstructed 1937.

Doel (1890) 1–90. Oliver (1968) 60–1.

(132) STRICT BAPTIST (ST 838553). 'Providence Chapel' built 1861 for seceders from the foregoing has a gabled stone front of three bays with two tiers of round-arched windows.

Oliver (1968) 61–2.

STAVERTON

(133) WESLEYAN (ST 856608). Stone walls and hipped slate roof; three-bay front with pointed-arched openings, dated 1824.

STEEPLE ASHTON

(134) PRIMITIVE METHODIST (ST 905571). Brick with ashlar dressings, 1851.

STRATTON ST MARGARET

(135) BAPTIST, Swindon Road, Stratton Green (SU 172867). Chapel rebuilt 1934 on site of earlier building for church formed 1750–1. *Inscription*: tablet reset in annexe, 'T:S 1801'. *Monuments*: in burial-ground, many late 18th-century headstones including (1) William Lawrence, 1759, and Ann his wife, 1753; (2) Ann, wife of John Parsons, 1760; (3) William Wiggins, 1768; also (4) Robert Jordan, 1833, and Mary his widow, 1834, table-tomb.

(136) Former PRIMITIVE METHODIST, Swindon Road (SU 174869). Chapel built 1830, enlarged 1842, superseded by a new chapel in Ermin Street (SU 175872) in 1883, used for Sunday-school 1883–91 and then converted to a pair of cottages. Three-bay front of brick, now rendered, with stone quoins; formerly with two tall round-arched windows, now subdivided, and central entrance. Lunette-shaped tablet dated 1830.

Fuller, F., *Stratton in Camera* (1984).

SUTTON BENGER

(137) PRIMITIVE METHODIST, Upper Seagry (ST 946807). Brick with three-bay gabled front, dated 1825.

SWINDON

(138) BAPTIST TABERNACLE, Regent Circus (SU 152845). Built 1886 to designs by W. H. Read of Swindon, superseding a chapel of 1848. Brick with stone front and dressings and a slate roof. The front of five bays has a pedimented Tuscan portico in front of two tiers of windows. The side wall facing Temple Street is of ten bays. The interior has a continuous gallery with open cast-iron front supported by iron columns which rise to arcades of semicircular arches. (Closed 1977 following the amalgamation of several congregations, demolished 1977–8)

B.Hbk (1886) 341–2.

(139) WESLEYAN, Bath Road (SU 154838). The first Methodist chapel in Swindon built c.1813–16 was an octagonal building 'behind the Corn Exchange'; it was rebuilt in 1862 and subsequently sold on being superseded in 1880 by the present chapel designed by Bromilow and Cheers. This is of stone with a gabled front between octagonal turrets and flanking staircase wings with continuous ranges of clerestory windows.

Wesleyan chapel, Bath Road, Swindon.   (139)

TISBURY

(140) Former PRESBYTERIAN, High Street (ST 944296). The meeting-house was registered in April 1726 as a 'newly erected building on William Furnall's close in Tisbury'. The society, which may have been a continuation of that meeting in 1669 at Samuel Combes' house, suffered in the late 18th century from the establishment of a separate congregation of Independents who built a new chapel in 1782. In 1797, following the death of the Presbyterian minister, the two societies united at the older meeting-house where they remained until the erection of a new chapel in 1842 (*see* (141)). The 1726 building was then used for a day-school and a Sunday-school.

Baptist Tabernacle, Swindon.   (138)

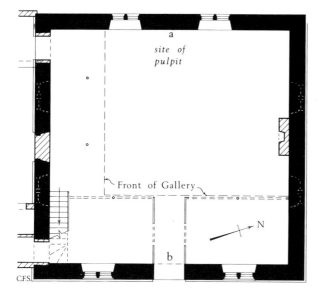

site of
pulpit

Front of Gallery

N

a

b

C.F.S.

Former Presbyterian Meeting-house
TISBURY   *Wiltshire*

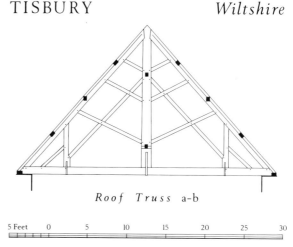

Roof Truss a–b

5 Feet 0 5 10 15 20 25 30

Former Presbyterian chapel, Tisbury.   (140)

The meeting-house has stone walls and a pyramidal roof covered with tiles. The E front of ashlar has a stone plinth and a coved plaster cornice below the eaves which continues around the building. The central entrance has a round-arched head with keystone and is flanked by two windows of two lights, similarly arched, with mullions and transoms. Two windows with square heads in the rear wall mark the site of the pulpit. The side walls have each two upper windows of two lights; an original doorway on the S side has been blocked.

The interior (29½ ft by 31 ft) has a gallery along the S and E sides of 18th-century date with a fielded-panelled front and moulded cornice which rises at the ends. The roof is supported by a central king-post and scissor braces.

Monuments: in meeting-house, on W wall (1) Rev. John Morgan, 32 years pastor, 1796, 'interred at the foot of the pulpit stairs'; (2) Rev. William Moore, 1798, 'late pastor of the United Churches meeting in this place and at Bird-Bush', interred 'near the door in south passage'; (3) Rev. John Rogers, 1815, and

Elizabeth his wife, 1812. *Plate*: includes a mug of 1717. *Weathervane*: dated 1726.

Miles, E., *Tisbury, Past and Present* (1920) 36–9.

(141) CONGREGATIONAL, Zion Hill (ST 947297). The chapel 'in the pointed style' built for the congregation from the old meeting-house was opened 1 June 1842. Stone walls and slate roof; front of three bays with stepped gable, corner pilaster buttresses and octagonal finials. Rear gallery with original seating. (URC/Methodist)

EM (September 1842) 447.

TROWBRIDGE

(142) CONIGRE CHAPEL (ST 854582). A General Baptist church meeting in Trowbridge and Southwick was in existence by 1714. Its earlier history and doctrinal attachment are unclear although meetings were being held in 1669, perhaps by a section of the Particular Baptist church of North Bradley. By 1736 a gradual change in the accepted beliefs of the church led to a secession of members to form a separate Particular Baptist society (*see* (143)). Although the congregation tended to support the Unitarian position by the early 19th century, distinctive Baptist practices continued to be observed into the following century.

The first meeting-house, superseded 1856–7, was built at the beginning of the 18th century on a scale suited to the means of a substantial and wealthy congregation. It had a broad front of three bays with two doorways and two tiers of windows with mullions and transoms which were repeated in the side walls. Two round-arched windows at the rear flanking the pulpit were of three lights with traceried heads, perhaps of later date. The double roof was hipped and had a central valley at collar level, supported internally by two tall columns carrying impost blocks from which sprang a ribbed and vaulted plaster ceiling. The gallery was carried around three sides.

The present chapel of stone in the Gothic style by William Smith is dated 1856; it comprises a nave and aisles of four bays with minor buildings to the side and rear. The front is gabled and

Congregational chapel (URC), Tisbury.

(141)

Conigre Chapel, Trowbridge.

Former Conigre Chapel, Trowbridge.   (142)

has stepped buttresses and octagonal pinnacles; the central entrance has a gabled surround and a five-light traceried window above; there is a corresponding window at the opposite end behind the pulpit. The interior has galleries around three sides.

Fittings – Brasses: (1) over pulpit, recording opening of chapel 1 October 1857; (2) loose, to Samuel Martyn, gent., 1643, with Latin inscription, origin unknown. Chairs: in vestry, three, two with arms, 17th-century. Clocks: see Southwick (130) and Warminster (152). Coffin Stool: one, with turned legs, 18th-century. Glass: in window behind pulpit non-representational pattern of coloured glass in tracery, with coloured borders to lower lights. Monuments: in chapel (1) Samuel Martin, 50 years pastor, 1877, Maria Sims his first wife, 1846, Irene his second wife, 1885; (2) John Grant, gent., 1755; (3) Rev. Daniel Jones, 10 years pastor, 1810, and Eleanor his daughter (nd); (4) Rev. William Waldron, 50 years pastor, 1794, et al.; (5) John Waldron, 1827, et al.; in vestibule (6) Rev. Richard Wright, 1836, and Isabella his wife, 1828; (7) Lieut Thomas Linthorne R.N., 1833, et al.; (8) Hannah Besser, 1826. Plate: includes four cups, 1822, and brass alms dish. (Chapel demolished 1988)

Doel (1890) 100–10. Evans (1897) 244–5. Murch (1835) 70–83.

(143) PARTICULAR BAPTIST, Church Street (ST 857581). Seceders from Conigre Chapel in 1736 built a meeting-house in Back Street (now Church Street) in 1754–5 which was enlarged in 1784 and virtually rebuilt c.1810; it was further altered in 1846 and later. 'Back Street' or 'Emmanuel' chapel has walls of stone with an ashlar front. The front wall of four bays with a cornice and pedimental gable has upper windows of c.1810 and a wide projecting vestibule of c.1846. The interior has a gallery around three sides with an open cast-iron front of the late 19th century. Sunday-schools behind are dated 1884, by 'W. Smith, architect and builder'.

Doel (1890) 111–22. Oliver (1968) 63–5.

(144) STRICT BAPTIST, Union Street (ST 858582). 'Zion Chapel' was built in 1816 for seceders from the foregoing. A baptistery was constructed in the chapel in 1825, opposition to which led to a secession to 'Little Bethel' which lasted until 1863. The interior was refitted in 1870. The chapel is of rubble with an ashlar front of three bays with two tiers of round-arched windows.

Doel (1890) 123–30. Oliver (1968) 65–6. Paul VI (1969) 37–85.

'Zion' Strict Baptist chapel, Trowbridge.   (144)

(145) Former PARTICULAR BAPTIST, Court Street (ST 855579). 'Bethesda Chapel' was built in 1823 for seceders from 'Back Street Chapel' (143) who removed in 1931 to Gloucester Road. The building suffered damage by fire shortly after being vacated; it is now in commercial use. The front is of ashlar in three bays with a pedimented centre, rusticated lower stage and round-arched windows. The central doorway has two attached columns and a Doric entablature. The interior formerly had two tiers of galleries around three sides.

Doel (1890) 131–41. Goodrich, P.J., Trowbridge and its Times (1932) 162–3. Oliver (1968) 66–7.

(146) THE TABERNACLE, Church Street (ST 855582). An Independent church was formed in 1767 by a society which had been gathered a few years earlier. A chapel was built in 1771 and named 'The Tabernacle' in accordance with Calvinistic Methodist custom. This building, originally 30 ft by 40 ft, was extended in length to 60 ft in 1794; it had two wide pointed-arched windows flanking the pulpit. The chapel was rebuilt in 1882 by Paull and Bonella. A schoolroom of 1842 with tall paired lancets remains at the rear. (Now URC/Methodist)

Fittings – *Clock*: octagonal dial, inscribed 'The Gift of Peter Swift 1705', from the former Presbyterian chapel (150). *Monuments*: in chapel (1) Rev. John Clark, 1809, and Catherine his widow, 1826; (2) Thomas Turner, 1833, and Joanna (Cook) his wife, 1784, 'foundress of this Tabernacle'; (3) William Lawrence, 1794, John Heritage, 1810, and Lydia his widow, 1820; externally, on wall of Sunday-school (4) Ann, daughter of James and Maria Cadby, 1845 [?9] *et al.*; (5) [ ] Cadby, mid 19th-century. *Paintings*: in vestry, oil portraits of Mrs Joanna Turner and John Clark, first pastor. *Plate*: includes a baptismal bowl, gift of Thomas Jefferies, 1767.

Huxam, A. (ed), *The Tabernacle, Trowbridge, 1767–1967* (1967).

(147) Former METHODIST, Stallard Street (ST 853580). A preaching-house in Waldron's Square, Frog Lane, opened in 1754 was superseded in 1790 by a new chapel W of the Town Bridge. A gallery was added in 1814 in an attempt to alleviate difficulties caused by flooding and the building was enlarged in 1821. The congregation removed to a new chapel in Manvers Street in 1836 and the former chapel was eventually incorporated into the Innox Mills. It was demolished *c*.1980. The walls were of stone with ashlar quoins and dressings. On the E side at gallery level facing Stallard Street were three pointed-arched windows with Y-tracery. An upper storey with three gables on this side was added *c*.1870.

Proceedings of the Wesley Historical Society VI (1907–8) 115, pl. fcg 101.

(148) Former WESLEYAN, Manvers Street (ST 855581). The chapel, standing on an elevated site on the E side of the street, was designed by John Dyer, an 'engineer', who was also one of the trustees. The walls are of stone with an ashlar front and the roof is covered with slates. The foundation stone was laid on 9 June 1835 and the building opened 4 May 1836. The design and internal dimensions closely follow those of Coppice Hill Chapel, Bradford-on-Avon (21), of 1818, but with greater elaboration of ornament. The W front is of five bays with two tiers of round-arched windows with altered frames. The three middle bays have a raised pediment. The lower stage is rusticated and has a central doorway with paired Doric columns; the upper stage is divided by Corinthian pilasters carrying an entablature with the inscription over the centre bay 'SACRED TO GOD'. The side walls are of four bays with two tiers of round-arched windows

Wesleyan chapel, Manvers Street, Trowbridge (148)

above a basement storey. A rear projection originally forming a communion recess with 'orchestra' or singers' gallery above was altered in the late 19th century to form an organ chamber.

The interior (56½ ft by 43 ft), largely refitted in the late 19th century, has galleries around three sides supported by cast-iron columns. At the E end is a wide rostrum pulpit with organ and choir recess behind. The basement is divided into two rooms; eight iron columns with Corinthian capitals support the floor above.

Fittings – *Glass*: reset in N wall of NE staircase, circular communion window with border of sunburst on red ground: a printed 'Memento of the opening' records 'Mr. W. Wickham presented two very elegant Stained Glass Windows for the Orchestra and Communion Recess; in the centre of the latter is a beautiful representation of the Saviour blessing the bread, after the celebrated picture by Carlo Dolci.' (Mutilated *c*.1972, in compliance with current advice to trustees.) *Monuments*: in chapel (1) Susannah Elizabeth Martin, 1847; (2) Samuel Marvin, trustee, 1857, Elizabeth his wife, 1836, and their daughters Dorcas, 1840, and Elizabeth, 1836, signed 'Chapman, Frome'; (3) Abraham Bowyer, 'one of the promoters of the erection of this chapel', 1873, *et al.*; (4) John Dyer, 'of this town; Engineer, *(The Architect of this Chapel)*', 1856, Sarah his wife, 1851, *et al.*, large monument with standing female weeper, signed 'Chapman, Frome'. (Congregation united with Tabernacle 1968, chapel demolished since 1973)

Goodrich, P.J., *Trowbridge and its Times* (1932) 167–9.

(149) WESLEYAN, Wesley Road (ST 853575). By W.J. Stent, 1871.

(150) Former PRESBYTERIAN, Silver Street (ST 857580). A small society in existence by the early 18th century registered a 'newly erected' meeting-house in 1723. The church became Congregational in the 19th century but had ceased to meet by 1932 when the building was in use as a Conservative Club. It was demolished *c*.1960. The meeting-house had rendered walls of rubble and a hipped roof covered with pantiles. The front had a simple round-arched entrance to the left of centre, perhaps one of a pair, three upper windows of two lights with transoms and one or probably two similar windows below. *Clock*: dated 1705, now in The Tabernacle (146).

CHST II (1905–6) 207–18. Goodrich, op.cit. 160–1. MHLG listed building description (1948). VCH *Wiltshire* VII (1953) pl. fcg 162.

UPAVON

(151) STRICT BAPTIST (SU 133550). Rendered walls and half-hipped slate roof. Original doorway, now blocked, between two round-arched windows in side wall; tablet above inscribed 'Cave of Adullam Baptist Chapel A.D. 1838'. New end entrance made in late 19th century. *Chandelier*: brass, five-branch, early 19th-century.

Oliver (1968) 22. Paul VI (1969) 228–41.

WARMINSTER

(152) THE OLD MEETING-HOUSE, North Row (ST 87464518). Presbyterian meetings were being held in 1669, with the assistance of several of the ejected ministers, at William Buckler's

house and at 'St Laurence Chapel'. By 1687 a regular society had been organized and the barn of Edward Middlecott in Beastleaze Meadow was fitted up as a meeting-house. When the present site was placed in trust, in April 1704, it was already occupied by a 'barn or meeting-house', which the trustees were empowered 'to pull down and set up a new Meeting House for use of Presbyterians'. This was done and the new building opened 8 October 1704. The doctrinal orthodoxy of the ministry was shortly afterwards called into question and about 1719 some members left to form a separate society; the original society thereafter supported increasingly heterodox preaching until 1866 when the last minister retired. The building was sold in 1870 after which it became a British School; it is now used for further education.

The Old Meeting-house, Warminster.   (152)

The meeting-house stands on the E side of North Row, formerly Meeting-house Lane. The walls are of brickwork with ashlar dressings and the roof, which is hipped and has a central valley, is covered with tiles. The W front of five bays has stone quoins, a rubble plinth and a two-course brick platband between two tiers of two-light mullioned windows; a gabled porch inscribed 'Girls British School' was added c.1870. The rear wall has two windows of two lights with transoms flanking the site of the pulpit. The side walls have each two upper and two lower windows matching those in the front wall, some of which are now blocked.

The interior (37 ft by 45 ft) has two substantial oak posts, of octagonal section with moulded capitals but no bases, supporting the valley-beam of the roof. The galleries have been removed but notchings for the fronts of N and S galleries remain on the posts and offsets in the end walls; the fenestration also allows for a cross gallery.

Fittings – *Clock*: latterly in Conigre Chapel, Trowbridge (142), Parliament clock with shaped dial, case decorated with an eagle, signed 'Hugh Shore, Warminster', 18th-century. *Plate*: set of flagon, two tankards and two plates with shield-of-arms of Langley, 1789.

Daniell, J.J., *The History of Warminster* (1879). Evans (1897) 248–50. Murch (1835) 86–94.

(153) COMMON CLOSE CHAPEL, The Close (ST 87324521). The 'New' or 'Lower Meeting' was formed about 1719 by secession from (152) and the first meeting-house was built on the present site in that year. The building was much enlarged in 1798 and replaced by the existing Congregational Chapel (now URC/Methodist) in 1840. The chapel was refitted and a separate school building erected in 1862.

The walls are of rubble with an ashlar front. The front is in three bays with a projecting centre, two gabled porches and grouped lancet windows. Tall pinnacles which originally surmounted the corner buttresses were removed c.1960–70.

Daniell (1879) 236–7.

(154) BAPTIST, North Row (ST 87424521). 'Ebenezer Chapel', on the W side of the street, was built in 1810 for a newly gathered congregation. It has brick walls and a hipped tiled roof. In the front wall are two large round-arched windows with a lunette between, all with tracery inserted in the late 19th century, and a central doorway with keystone. The side walls are of three bays with two tiers of windows. An organ chamber was built at the W end in the late 19th century. The interior is square and has an E gallery with open cast-iron front of the late 19th century (refitted 1981). *Organ*: case with five bays of pipes, early 19th-century.

Daniell (1879) 238, 240. Oliver (1968) 80.

WESTBURY

(155) BAPTIST, Westbury Leigh (ST 860498). A branch of the Particular Baptist church at Southwick was formed here in 1662. In 1714 a barn belonging to Stephen Self was converted for use as a meeting-house by the addition of seating and galleries. The present chapel, of brick with stone dressings and a slate roof, was built in 1796–7. The NW front has a pedimental gable with a lunette and two tiers of round-arched windows in three bays, all with renewed glazing and with moulded stone kneelers added to the gable in the late 19th century. The central doorway has a pedimented stone head supported by scrolled brackets. The side walls, of three bays, have windows matching those at the front. A schoolroom was added to the rear c.1900.

The interior (50¼ ft by 40¼ ft) has a continuous gallery with panelled front supported by iron columns. The schoolroom has a large arched opening into the chapel at gallery level, closed with shutters.

Fittings – *Benefaction Boards*: (1) painted wood, shield-of-arms of Wilkin with inscription around frame to John Wilkins, 1730, recording various bequests; (2) painted board with arched head, recording 1729 deed of gift by John Wilkins, formerly of Dilton, clothier, of £20 per annum from his estate at Honey Bridge to trustees for the minister and poor; (3) painted board, repeating the former bequests of which one moiety is set aside 'to the use of the Poor of the said Congregation called Baptists to be laid out in Cloth and made up in Coats' and recording the substitution of a percentage of revenue for the fixed sum by order in Chancery 1834; (4) brass tablet 1892 repeating the same. *Chair*: in vestry, comb-back Windsor chair formerly belonging to John Marshman, father of Joshua Marshman D.D., Baptist

Baptist chapel, Westbury Leigh.   (155)

Missionary. *Monuments*: in chapel (1) Thomas Gough, pastor, 1842; (2) Robert Marshman, pastor over 43 years, 1806. *Pulpit*: polygonal with panelled front supported by two Roman Doric columns, twin staircases, mid 19th-century but perhaps incorporating earlier material. *Seating*: in gallery, late 19th-century; some earlier box-pews remain below.

Doel (1890) 91–9. Ivimey II (1814) 587–8; IV (1830) 314.

(156) THE OLD MEETING-HOUSE (ST 872508). A society formed in the late 17th century to which Philip Hunton, ejected vicar of Westbury, ministered in 1672, was long regarded as Presbyterian; it had become Congregational by the early 19th century (now URC). The meeting-house, rebuilt in 1821, was refronted in a mixed style in 1876. The original side walls, of brick, in three bays have two tiers of segmental-arched windows. There are galleries around three sides. *Plate*: two cups dated 1806.

CHST II (1905–6) 445. *Reform* December 1989. [Ruddock, J. B.] *History of the Old Congregational Church, Westbury, Wilts.* (1875).

(157) THE UPPER MEETING-HOUSE (ST 870507). The Congregational church formerly meeting here claimed to have been formed in 1762; it united with the Old Meeting *c*.1940–50; the building, now in commercial use, was erected *c*.1790. The walls are of brickwork and the roof is covered with stone slates

THE UPPER MEETING-HOUSE, WESTBURY   CFS 1970

and tiles. The gabled front of three bays with a large lunette and two tiers of round-arched windows resembles that of the Baptist chapel (155); the doorway has a stone canopy supported by shaped brackets. The side walls have four bays of round-arched windows at gallery level only.

The interior ($52\frac{1}{4}$ ft by $30\frac{1}{4}$ ft) has a gallery around three sides with cast-iron columns replacing earlier supports; the fronts have moulded cornices of the late 18th century and a wide pediment to the back gallery. The gallery staircases have columnar balusters and balustrades at gallery level.

Inscriptions and *Scratchings*: on top of gallery front in rear gallery 'T. WHITE. June 1797'; on front of side gallery 'W W 1797'. *Railings*: at entrance with gate, standards and overthrow, on MHLG listing description 1947, have been removed.

WILCOT

(158) WESLEYAN, Oare (SU 158631). Brick with hipped slate roof, opened 1841.

WILTON

(159) CONGREGATIONAL, Crow Lane (SU 096313). The church formed *c*.1700 as a Presbyterian society had become known as Independent by 1791 in which year the former meeting-house was rebuilt. Joseph Adams, Baptist minister in Salisbury, recorded in his diary '7 March 1791 Wilton Meeting was begun to be taken down' followed on 11 March by a note of the laying of the foundation stone of the new building by the minister James Edwards. The chapel was enlarged to the rear *c*.1810 and extensively altered and repaired in 1872. Further repairs were carried out in 1885.

The chapel, on the NW side of the lane, has brick walls and a hipped tiled roof. The front wall of three bays with a central entrance and two tiers of round-arched windows was embellished in the late 19th century by the addition of a stone plinth, a platband of white brick, and the insertion of stone surrounds of two-arched lights into the windows. The side walls, originally of three bays with one bay added, have been similarly altered; the front bay on the NE side is covered by a Sunday-school wing 'rebuilt 1853'. An organ chamber was built against the NW wall of the chapel *c*.1872 or later.

The interior (originally $41\frac{1}{2}$ ft enlarged to $54\frac{1}{2}$ ft, by $33\frac{1}{4}$ ft) has been extensively refitted. Galleries around three sides are supported by cast-iron columns of quatrefoil section and have open iron fronts of the late 19th century. The NW wall is pierced by a three-centred arch to the organ chamber.

Fittings – Monuments: in Sunday-school (1) William Gardner, 1797, *et al.*; externally on NE wall (2) Rev. William Gardner, 1782, *et al.*; also other monuments, on outer walls and loose in burial-ground, 19th-century. *Plate*: includes a pair of two-handled cups, 1791. *Seating*: fielded panelling from former box-pews reused in gallery. (URC/Methodist)

Haynes (1956) 5–6, 32.

(160) Former PRIMITIVE METHODIST, Kingsbury Square (SU 097312), was built in 1875; the society united with the foregoing after 1960 and the chapel is now used by Roman Catholics. Brick and stucco with palatial front of five bays; entrance between minor rooms with chapel above.

Former Primitive Methodist chapel, Wilton. (160)

WINTERBOURNE

(161) Former INDEPENDENT, Winterbourne Dauntsey (SU 176347). The Methodist chapel, on the SE side of the main road, was built in 1799 as an Independent meeting-house by the Blatch family. It passed into the possession of the Methodist New Connexion c.1844. The walls are built of cob with flints on brick footings and the roof is half-hipped and covered with thatch. The end entrance, facing the street, is covered by a later porch; the lintel of the inner doorway has a keystone carved with a garlanded head. Above the porch is a small upper window. The side walls have each three windows, the centre window being the widest. There is one upper window in the rear wall. All the window-frames were renewed in the mid 19th century. The interior (29 ft by 19¼ ft) was refitted in the late 19th century. (Front wall entirely altered c.1976)

Bray, C. H., *The History of Winterbourne* [c.1950] part II, chapter 4 (two pamphlets, Salisbury Museum Library).

WOODBOROUGH

(162) WESLEYAN (SU 112600). Brick with hipped slate roof, round-arched doorway with circular gallery window over, two round-arched windows in each side wall. Gallery at entrance now closed by partition. Opened 1850.

WOOTTON BASSETT

(163) PRIMITIVE METHODIST, High Street (SU 065824). Built 1838, rubble with dressings of brick later rendered, three-bay gabled front with ornamental finials and round-arched windows. Interior altered 1975.

WORTON

(164) WESLEYAN (ST 971575). Brick with stone dressings, three-bay gabled front with round-arched windows and later porch. Dated 1848.

WESLEYAN CHAPEL, WORTON C.F.5.1971

Former Independent chapel, Winterbourne: before 1976 (left); after 1976 (right). (161)

ABBREVIATIONS

DRO	Devon Record Office
MHLG	Ministry of Housing and Local Government
NMR	National Monuments Record
RCHME	Royal Commission on the Historical Monuments of England
URC	United Reformed Church

BIBLIOGRAPHICAL SOURCES
other than those fully titled in the text

Allen, N. V. 1974	*Churches and Chapels of Exmoor*. Exmoor Press, Dulverton, Somerset.
Arnold, H. G. 1960	'Early Meeting Houses', *Transactions of the Ancient Monuments Society*, NS VIII (1960), 89–139.
1976	*Victorian Architecture in Reading*.
Ball, R. 1955	*Congregationalism in Cornwall: A Brief Survey*.
B.Hbk	*The Baptist Hand-book* (Baptist Union of GB & Ireland, from 1861).
BHST	*Transactions of the Baptist Historical Society* (7 vols, 1908–21).
Bolitho, P. 1967	*The Story of Methodism in the Liskeard Circuit, 1751–1967*.
Bourne, F. W. 1877	*The King's Son; or, a Memoir of Billy Bray* (15th edn).
1905	*The Bible Christians: Their Origin and History (1815–1900)*.
BM	*The Baptist Magazine* (from 1809).
BQ	*The Baptist Quarterly* (from 1922). Incorporating *Transactions of the Baptist Historical Society*.
Brockett, A. 1962a	*Nonconformity in Exeter 1650–1875*.
1962b	*Witnesses: A History of the Six Members of the Exeter Council of Congregational Churches and their Forerunners*.
Chambers, R. F. 1952	*The Chapels of Surrey and Hampshire*: vol. I of *The Strict Baptist Chapels of England* (5 vols, 1952–68).
Chick, E. 1907	*A History of Methodism in Exeter and the Neighbourhood from the Year 1739 until 1907*.
CHST	*Transactions of the Congregational Historical Society* (21 vols, 1901–72).
CMHAJ	*Journal of the Cornish Methodist Historical Association*.
Crosby, T. 1738–40	*The History of the English Baptists* (4 vols).
CYB	*The Congregational Yearbook* (Congregational Union of England and Wales, 1846–1972).
Daniell, J. J. 1879	*The History of Warminster*.
Davies, M. F. 1909	*Life in an English Village. An Economic and Historical Survey of the Parish of Corsley in Wiltshire*.
Densham, W. and Ogle, J. 1899	*The Story of the Congregational Churches of Dorset, from their Foundation to the Present Time*.
DNB	*Dictionary of National Biography*.
Doel, W. 1890	*Twenty Golden Candlesticks! Or A History of Baptist Nonconformity in Western Wiltshire*.
Dolbey, G. W. 1964	*The Architectural Expression of Methodism: The First Hundred Years*.
Dymond, F. W. 1899	*Trust Property within the County of Devon*.
EM	*The Evangelical Magazine* (1793–1904).
England, J. 1886–7	*The Western Group of Moravian Chapels… The West of England and South Wales*. In 2 parts.
Evans, G. E. 1897	*Vestiges of Protestant Dissent*.
FHSJ	*Journal of the Friends Historical Society* (from 1903).
Hague, G. R. and Hague, J. 1986	*The Unitarian Heritage: An Architectural Survey of Chapels and Churches in the Unitarian Tradition in the British Isles*. The Unitarian Heritage.
Hayman, J. G. 1885	*A History of the Methodist Revival of the Last Century and its Relations to North Devon from the First Visit of the Wesleys to the Centenary Year in 1839* (2nd edn).

Haynes, J. J. 1956 — *The First Eleven Years (1945-1956) of the Wilton, Broadchalke and Ebbesbourne Group of Congregational Churches.*

Hindmarsh, R. 1861 — *Rise and Progress of the New Jerusalem Church in England, America and Other Parts.*

Hutchins, J. 1861–74 — *The History and Antiquities of the County of Dorset* (3rd edn, 4 vols).

Ivimey, J. 1811–30 — *A History of the English Baptists* (4 vols).

Jones, W. H. 1907 — *Bradford on Avon.*

Lidbetter, H. 1961 — *The Friends Meeting House.*

Marsh, A. E. W. 1903 — *A History of the Borough and Town of Calne.*

Murch, J. 1835 — *A History of the Presbyterian and General Baptist Churches in the West of England; with Memoirs of Some of Their Pastors.*

Oliver, R. W. 1968 — *The Chapels of Wiltshire and the West*: vol. V of *The Strict Baptist Chapels of England* (5 vols, 1952–68).

Palmer, S. 1802 — Revision of Edmund Calamy's *The Nonconformist's Memorial...* (2nd edn, 3 vols).

Parsons, R. K. 1972 — *Souls for your Hire. A History of the Northlew Circuit of the Methodist Church from 1811–1932.*

Paul, S. F. 1951–69 — *Further History of the Gospel Standard Baptists* (6 vols). Gospel Standard Baptist Trust.

Payne, E. A. 1951 — *The Baptists of Berkshire through Three Centuries.*

Penney, N. (ed) 1907 — *'The First Publishers of Truth' being Early Records... of the Introduction of Quakerism into the Counties of England and Wales.*

              (ed) 1928 — *Record of the Sufferings of Quakers in Cornwall 1655–1686.*

Petty, J. 1880 — *The History of the Primitive Methodist Connexion.*

PHSJ — Journal of the Presbyterian Historical Society of England (14 vols, 1914–72).

Probert, J. C. 1966 — *The Architecture of Cornish Methodism.*

RCHM 1952–75 — *An Inventory of the Historical Monuments in the County of Dorset*: I, West, 1952; II, South-East, 1970; III, Central, 1970; IV, North, 1972; V, East, 1975.

          1980 — *Ancient and Historical Monuments in the City of Salisbury*, Vol. I.

Rowdon, H. H. 1967 — *The Origins of the Brethren, 1825–1850.*

Southall, K. H. 1974 — *Our Quaker Heritage: Early Meeting Houses Built prior to 1720 and in Use Today.*

[Seymour, A. C. H.] 1839 — *The Life and Times of Selina, Countess of Huntingdon* (2 vols).

Shaw, T. 1967 — *A History of Cornish Methodism.*

Short, B. C. 1927 — *Early Days of Nonconformity in Poole.*

Stanley, J. *c*.1935 — *The Church in the Hop Garden.*

Stribling, S. B. 1897 — *History of the Wilts & East Somerset Congregational Union... 1797–1897.*

Summers, W. H. 1905 — *History of the Congregational Churches in the Berks, South Oxon and South Bucks Association.*

Taylor, A. 1818 — *The History of the English General Baptists* (2 vols).

Temple, J. H. 1974 — *The Mighty Oak, The Story of the Devon and Dorset Mission.*

Thomas, J. L. 1896 — *'Historical Sketches of the Churches', in Annual Report of the Somerset Congregational Union*, pp. 39–76.

Thompson, D. (ed) 1885 — *'A Book of Remembrance' or A Short History of the Baptist Churches in North Devon.*

Thompson, T. R. (ed) 1961 — *Materials for a History of Cricklade.*

UHST — *Transactions of the Unitarian Historical Society* (from 1917).

VCH — The Victoria History of the Counties of England.

    1953 — *A History of the County of Wiltshire*, vol. VII.

    1956 — *A History of the County of Wiltshire*, vol. III.

    1980 — *A History of the County of Wiltshire*, vol. XI.

WAM — *Wiltshire Archaeological and Natural History Magazine.*

Waylen, J. 1859 — *A History, Military and Municipal, of the Ancient Borough of The Devizes.*

White, B. R. 1971–4 — *Association Records of the Particular Baptists of England, Wales and Ireland to 1660* (3 vols). Baptist Historical Society.

Wood, J. H. 1847 — *A Condensed History of the General Baptists of the New Connexion.*

Woolcock, J. 1897 — *A History of the Bible Christian Churches on the Isle of Wight.*

INDEX

NOTES: Personal names are indexed under the heading 'surnames' and also under headings such as 'artists and engravers', 'benefactors', 'ministers, preachers, etc.'. The index reflects the coverage of the book in emphasising buildings and fittings dating from before 1800.

Coad's Green, Cornwall, 38a.
Codford, Wilts., 217b.
Coffin Stools: 18th-cent., 76a, 91b, 122b,
178b, 179b, 198a, 206b, 226a, 230a,
243a.
Coldharbour, Cornwall, 53a.
Collingbourne Kingston, Wilts., 218a.
Colwell, Hants, I. of Wight, 155a.
Colyford, Devon, 68b.
Colyton, Devon, 67b–68b; clockmakers of,
76b.
Combwich, Som., 186b–187a.
Come-to-Good, Cornwall, xiii, 21a, 21b,
32b–34b.
Communion Cloths, 19th-cent., 92a, 230b.
Communion Cups, see Cups; Plate.
Communion Rails, 19th-cent., 189b, 191b,
210b.
Communion Sets, see Plate.
Communion Tables: 18th-cent., 2a, 67a,
72b, 166b; 19th-cent., 10b, 40b, 41a;
undated, 220a.
Compton Martin, Som., 172a.
Congregational Chapels, dating from before
1800, see Chapels and Meeting-
houses.
Connon, Cornwall, 52a.
Cookbury, Devon, 68b.
Cookham, Berks., 6b.
Copperhouse, Cornwall, 30b.
Copplestone, Devon, 68b.
Copythorne, Hants, 138b.
Corfe Castle, Dorset, 103b, 112b–113b.
Corsham, Wilts., xiv, 204a, 206b, 205b,
218a–220b.
Corsley, Wilts., 220b–221a.
Coryates, Dorset, 104a, 125b.
Cote, Oxon., 6a.
Countess of Huntingdon's Connexion,
chapels, dating from before 1800, see
Chapels and Meeting-houses.
Cowes, Hants, I. of Wight, 135b, 154b–155a.
Cranborne, Dorset, 113a.
Crediton, Devon, xvii, 58a, 58b, 68b–71b,
89b.
Crewkerne, Som., 159a, 172a–b.
Crickham, Som., 198b.
Cricklade, Wilts., 221a.
Cripplestyle, Dorset, xvii, 104a–106a.
Crockerton Green, Wilts., 204a, 229a–b.
Crockery, see Cups.
Crofthandy, Cornwall, 30a.
Crondall, Hants, 138b.
Croscombe, Som., 159a, 172b–173b, 186a,
199b.
Croucheston, Wilts., 208a–b.
Crowan, Cornwall, 27b–28a.
Crowlas, Cornwall, 36a.
Cruwys Morchard, Devon, 72a.
Cubert, Cornwall, 21a, 28a.
Cullompton, Devon, 72a–b, 86a.
Culmstock, Devon, 72b–76a, see also Prescott;

Spiceland.
Cups, ceramic: communion lustreware, 37b,
42a; cups and saucers, commemorative,
184b; love-feast, 24a, 48a. Metal, see
plate.
Curry Rivel, Som., 173b–174a.
Cury, Cornwall, 28b.

Dalwood, Devon see Loughwood.
Dartmouth, Devon, 77a–78a.
Dauntsey, Wilts., 221a.
Davidstow, Cornwall, 28b.
Dawlish, Devon, 78a.
Derry Hill, Wilts., 236a see also Studley.
Deveral, Cornwall, 30a.
Devizes, Wilts., 204a, 204b, 221a–223a.
Devonport, Devon, 58b, 94a–b.
Dilton, Wilts., 245b.
Dilton Marsh, Wilts., see Penknap.
Dinnington, Som., 174a.
Ditchling, Sussex, 237b.
Dobwalls, Cornwall, 36a.
Dodbrooke, Devon, 86b–87a.
Donhead St Andrew, Wilts., 146b–147a.
Dorchester, Dorset, 103a, 104b, 113–116a.
Downgate, Cornwall, 52b.
Downside, Som., 188b.
Downton, Wilts., 123a, 204b, 223a–b.
Draycott Moor, Berks., 6b.
Drayton, Berks., 7a.
Duloe, Cornwall, 28b.
Dulverton, Som., 174a.
Dunheved otherwise Launceston,
Cornwall, 21a, 28b–29a.
Dunkerton, Som., 174a.
Dunkeswell, Devon, 78a.
Dunsford, Devon, 58a.
Dunster, Som., 174a.
Dunstone, Devon, 101b.
Duntish, Dorset, 112a.
Dutson, Cornwall, 28b.

East Buckfastleigh, Devon, 78a.
East Budleigh, Devon, xiii, 58a, 78a–b.
East Coker, Som., 160b, 174a.
East Garston, Berks., 3b.
East Orchard, Dorset, 116a.
East Prawle, Devon, 65a.
East Tytherton, Wilts., xiv, 204b,
213b–214b, 228b.
East Worlington, Devon, 78b.
Eastleigh, Devon, 101b.
Easton, Dorset, 126a.
Ebberly Lodge, Devon, 58b, 94b.
Ebbesborne Wake, Wilts., 223b–224a.
Edington, Wilts., 224a.
Edmondsham, Dorset, 116a.
Egloskerry, Cornwall, 29a.
Elm, Som., 174a, 174b.
Elmore, Devon, 99a.
Engravers, see Artists and Engravers.
Erlestoke, Wilts., 212a.

Exbourne, Devon, 78b.
Exeter, Devon, xiii, xvii, 58a, 58b, 79a–83b,
102a, 194a; architects, surveyors and
builders of, 72a; clockmakers of, 95a;
organ builders of, 197b.
Exford, Som., 174a.
Exmouth, Devon, 83a–84a, see also Point-in-
View.

Fair Oak, Hants, 139a.
Falmouth, Cornwall, 29a–b, 91b.
Fareham, Hants, 135a, 139a–b.
Faringdon, Berks., see Great Faringdon.
Farleigh Hungerford, Som., 186b.
Faulkland, Som., 179a.
Feniton, Devon, 84a.
Fenny Bridges, Devon, 84a.
Feock, Cornwall, 29b, 32b.
Fernham, Berks., 7a.
Filleigh, Devon, 84a.
Finchampstead, Berks., 7a.
Fittings, see Almsboxes; Baptismal Basins;
Bells; Benefaction Boards and
Tablets; Books and Libraries;
Bootscrapers; Candle Sconces;
Chairs; Chandeliers; Chests;
Clocks; Coffin Stools; Communion
Cloths; Communion Rails;
Communion Tables; Cups;
Fontlets; Fonts; Glass; Hatchments;
Hat Rails and Pegs; Lamp
Brackets; Lecterns; Light Fittings;
Musical Instruments; Noticeboards;
Organs; Paintings; Plate; Pulpits;
Radiators; Railings and Gates;
Rainwater-heads; Reredoses; Royal
Arms; Sculpture; Speaking Tubes;
Sundials; Tables; Tables of Lord's
Prayer, Creed and Decalogue;
Texts, painted; Weathervanes.
Flushing, Cornwall, 37b–38a.
Flutes, 98a.
Folly Gate, Devon, 86a.
Fontlets: 19th-cent., 10b, 137a; see also
Baptismal Basins.
Fontmell Magna, Dorset, 116a–b.
Fonts: 17th-cent., 127a; 19th-cent., 52b, 96a,
152b; see also Fontlets.
Ford, Devon, 64b–65a.
Ford, Wilts., 235b.
Fordingbridge, Hants, 139b 223a.
Forest, Cornwall, 25b.
Forrabury, Cornwall, 29b.
Fortuneswell, Dorset, 126a.
Four Forks, Som., see Spaxton.
Fovant, Wilts., 224a.
Fowey, Cornwall, 30a.
Foxham, Wilts., 214b.
Fremington, Devon, 84a.
Freshford, Som., 174a–b.
Freshwater, Hants, I. of Wight, 155a.
Friends, Society of, meeting-houses, dating